Who Killed the T

Who Killed the Twins?
Religion. Terrorism. Globalization

V. Ratis

ISBN : 1-59457-826-5

To order additional copies, please contact us.
BookSurge, LLC
www.booksurge.com
1-866-308-6235
orders@booksurge.com

Who Killed the Twins?

CONTENTS

FOREWORD

One of the main characteristics of mythological consciousness we will discuss in this book is its ability to neutralize binary oppositions, opposed concepts and phenomena which are divided in ordinary human's consciousness and occupy strictly defined positions in it. In mythological consciousness, the boundaries which separate those oppositions are vague or absent altogether. The distinctions between good and evil, life and death, illusion and reality, truth and lie, and cause and consequence are eliminated in mythological consciousness, like it was in the case of the Twins' murder, which was committed in New York on September11th, 2001.

On that tragic day, an explosion thundered in the North Tower of the Twins. The explosion was unexpected by the American people and the whole world community. The gap formed in the result of the explosion was so large that an airplane, which appeared in the New York City sky as if with a wave of a magic wand, could easily fly into it. It blew up later in the spacious "womb" of the Twin, which could be seen on news programs that were on air, right at that moment, and by means of video cameras that were set in advance on the spot from which that horrible crime of all times and nations was being broadcast.

Further course of events is well-known to everybody. In the sky, as if with a wave of a magic wand, appears another airplane. The second plane rams the South Tower of the Twins into its right corner. Then the explosion follows; the flame of conflagration violently devours bearing constructions of the building and in a while, slanting to the left (although, thinking logically, we would assume that the top of the tower would have slanted to the side where the blow happened and where the bearing constructions had been weakened), the head of the South Tower collapsed down carrying away thousands of people who were peacefully working in the World Trade Center into the gloomy hell. Later, the headless and breathless body of the North Tower falls down, burying more thousands people under its debris.

The facts following these events are astonishing. It seems that everything was prepared in advance and long before the event took place. Decorations (The Twins) were built in advance, video cameras were prepared and put on the spot in advance, pyrotechnics for creating immense trick effects were professionally brought and set up in advance, everything was elaborately designed and thoroughly prepared for a terrific show, the greatest one the world has ever seen.

As if some evil genius has prepared the scenario of a horrible play having lumped together reason and consequence, illusion and reality, lie and truth. Things, which cannot be imagined by a normal human mind, were turned into reality by primitively developed mythological consciousness, which is still inherent to some humanlike troglodytes-superanimals (whom we will also speak about in this book), striving to dominate the world and to establish the New World Order. But "any action naturally evokes counteraction, and extremism of power arouses harsh protest of lower classes. The conflict between "the rulers" and "the masses" assumes tragic forms nowadays, for stalwarts of Satanism believe it is time they reign the world, so they lost pity to "the paltry of the world," which was the base of European humanism. The elite, having robbed the whole world, put it on heavy trials and, by their hard-heartedness, is just heating the brazier, on which they will have to writhe, melting into tears...The midnight has passed, the carnival is over. Replete and drunk, having lost the feeling of danger, they threw off their masks and veils and showed their souls, naked and unadorned, and this hell turned out to be disgusting."[1]

In this book, we have attempted to look into that hell. We tried to investigate the entire way of development of destructive info-energy matrixes, beginning with the times immemorial, when the man had only learned how to kill those of his kind in order not to die of hunger, and ending with shocking events of nowadays when the man kills his brothers and sisters just to amuse himself or sacrifice thousands and millions of them to the "golden calf" hoping that it will fulfill his insatiable wishes and make him "the Lord of the world."

In the book, we tried to clarify the following questions:

1. Why did the Twins Towers collapse without any logical reason while the air attack could not be the cause of their destruction? (Even Osama ben Laden was astonished at the effect produced by the air attacks, for reasoning logically he thought that "ignition of fuel of the plane may fuse steel constructions of a building in the impact area, and result in collapsing of **only the top floors**."[2])

2. Why did the building of WTC 7 collapse in the same way the Twins did without any logical reason (It was not hit by an airplane, there was no fire in it, and it happened about six hours after the Twins collapsed)?
3. Why was it necessary to deceive the whole world by representing the explosion in the Pentagon as an air attack (If one possesses even a bit of intelligence, one will guess that there must be big fragments of an aircraft such as wings, fuselage and engines left on the spot of the crash. Look at the pictures taken just after the "air attack," watch the documentary CNN film *America Remembers* just to be convinced that there is not even the slightest trace of any presence of an airplane. Ask president Bush, ask the FBI or CIA where the airplane was which supposedly hit the Pentagon, and what happened to its crew and passengers!)?
4. What happened to the airplane, the crew and the passengers of UA Flight 93 that crashed over Pennsylvania? (The pictures taken on the spot show only very small fragments of the aircraft and a fuming crater which is very unusual for a crash site. Most likely, the plane was shot by a missile, and another missile was fired to the ground to create the semblance of an airplane crash).
5. Why was the investigation of the terrorist acts of September 11, 2001 sealed as "secret" right after the event?
6. Why did Congress not start to investigate the causes of that tragedy immediately after the attacks?
7. Why do we, talking about love and mercy, keep on killing each other?
8. Why do we, believing in a loving and merciful God, engage ourselves more and more into the vortex of hostility and violence, in which the uncountable multitude of humans' sons and daughters have found their death?

Based on tremendous factual materials, we try to give answers to those questions, explaining in a popular way the essence of main religious and quasi-religious teachings, which, acting as a matrix, program peoples' behavior, making them commit dreadful atrocities, witnesses of which we become once too often nowadays. The book contains sensational materials that disclose lies and hypocrisy the myths we believe in are encircled with.

However, superficial investigation of problems humankind faces nowadays reveals apparent strangeness of the link between religious myths, the latest events, and the urgent desire of the world elite to build the New World Order. But, what seems to be strange to the man of the XXI century was quite obvious for the father of psychoanalyses, Sigmund Freud, who, as far as at the beginning of the last century said: "There was not another page of the religious history that opened itself to us with such a clarity as the establishing of monotheism with Hebrews and its continuation in Christianity even if we put aside the development from an animal totem to a humanlike God with one or another animal companion (each of the four Christian evangelists still has his favorite animal), which is quite clear and understandable too.

If, as a first approximation, one considers the pharaoh's world domination as a ground for the origin of monotheistic religion, one can see as this monotheistic idea, having torn off from its basis, passes to the other nation, takes possession of it after a long period of latency, is protected by this nation as a precious treasure and, in turn, saves nation's life and gives it the proud of choosiness. Here is the religion of the forefather, the hope for reward, for oneness and, ultimately, **for the world dominion**."[3]

INTRODUCTION

> Behold how good and pleasant is for brethren to dwell together in unity.
>
> Psalms. CXXXIII.

Man, where do you go along the road of life? What will you and your children face in the future? What will the world be in fifty or in a hundred years? Will it be light and peaceful or will it be evil, cruel and merciless? Will people be able to overcome hostility and hatred or will they continue to hate and to kill each other? Perhaps every man asks such questions and tries to answer them. Perhaps every man is aware of the necessity of a new understanding of historic and cultural way of mankind.

The necessity of such a new understanding reached its crisis point long ago, but only now we have made ourselves certain of it. Now, when almost every day explosions thunder in Israel and Palestine, in Iraq, in India and Pakistan, in Chechnya, in Dagestan and in Russia; now, when religious fanatics kill themselves by their own will, killing thousands of innocent people, we see our task as to find an explanation of why a human being can kill other people so cynically and cruelly even in spite of morality regulations and holy scriptures which forbid such murders.

In our book, producing sensational materials which were kept secret, forbidden and concealed, we intend to show the causes which make people commit monstrous crimes against humans and humanity. We intend to disclose the ways of myth production and to show the reality; opening the veil which hides the great mystery of the building of the New World Order which has now entered the last phase.

Each intelligent person is able to see that we live in a strange, incomprehensible world. From times immemorial we tried to change it, make it better, kinder, more fair and more perfect. But with each day, with each instant of our life, we notice that our efforts are spent all for nothing.

During the entire history of mankind we tried to eradicate lie and hypocrisy, but looking around, we see that these defects of human hearts and souls still exist in our world and are not going to disappear. We tried to eradicate hatred and cruelty, we have invented ethical and moral laws, but, speaking about love and compassion, we still continue to hate and to kill each other. We tried to create a certain uniform and monolithic community of nations, unity of world culture institutions united by uniform and universal idea, but, looking around we see that the world still remains broken into pieces which are at enmity one with another in fruitless attempts to divide among themselves the One God who is indivisible, the One who belongs to everybody.

The problem of dialogue between cultures, the aspiration of world community to reach the cultural unity of the world and unification of cultural standards were always the main tendency in a cultural-historical development of mankind. By the end of the XX century, intensive peace and reforming processes broke borders both between the states and between hearts and souls of human beings. The local cultures came in closer interactions among themselves and we began to speak about a "new era" of cultural and public relations, which, as we hoped, had to be finished with cultural unity of mankind.

Such a unity, which is beginning to emerge for the first time in history, "essentially changes mechanisms that determined the destiny of separate cultures and civilizations before. We can consider M. Cagan's idea of coming of a new era, in which the many-dimensional dialog of cultures comes out on the proscenium of the world history, to be fair. The participation in this dialogue becomes a major condition of development of any culture."[4]

But sharp and unexpected breaking of borders, especially of those that divide local cultures, and also the closer interaction of people, as it turned out, can cause such negative consequences, that it would be better not to touch those borders at all. Then, in 1997, when A. S. Carmin wrote the book, nobody knew that. At that time people built iridescent hopes for the unity of world cultures, which "will create the ground for the coordination and unification of various forms, in which the cultural standards, norms, values and ideals common to all mankind are shown and expressed in different cultures."[5]

Those hopes collapsed suddenly, when on September 11, 2001 mankind became the witness of impertinent, unprecedented and monstrous terrorist acts which have shaken all the world and have taken the lives of several thousand American citizens. That day America became the world epicenter of pain and horror. The myth about a perfect, powerful and firm country, "the crystal palace on a hill," was smashed into smithereens within a few hours. Within a few hours, the myth about our invulnerability was shattered. We have understood, that our world is too small for the games we play to satisfy our insatiable desires. We have understood that a death has no borders and, having passed any distances and overcame any barriers, it can reach us at any place where we don't expect it, and take the lives of those whom we love most of all.

We have understood, that the peace dialogue of cultures and their unification is even out of the question. That terrible September day the world was divided into two hostile camps, and there began a great opposition of cultures; an obvious and open opposition of barbarity against even more brutal barbarity which hid itself under the mask of civilization and democracy since time immemorial. That opposition existed always, and always it was restrained by borders between the states and cultures. Now, when borders have fallen, two implacable enemies stood up against each other for internecine battle.

It seems to us, the picture of the world has been changed. But it is only an apparent change because there happened only rearrangement of picture elements, while the picture itself always remains the same. And, if in the process of cultural-historical development of the world the elements of a picture remain the same, the cultural picture of the world will hardly undergo serious changes and rearrangement of its elements. It is just as in a kaleidoscope. You turn it, look at a peephole and see another picture. But the colored bits of glass which move between the mirrors remain the same, and regardless of how many times one turns that wonderful toy, one will see glimpses of the same pictures.

The world is arranged similarly to a kaleidoscope. Pictures change each other creating illusion of novelty and progress, but the one who knows a history sees that events repeat themselves from time to time giving us an opportunity to remember the lessons of history; but we don't remember them for some reason, and as soon as something extraordinary happens to us, we think that the world has changed.

If we consider cultural space of the world as a kaleidoscope, we can liken the local cultures to the colored bits of glass which are inside of it. Great and Almighty God rotates that wonderful toy, and in order to see a cultural picture of the world, it is necessary to ask his permission to glance into the peephole. But it is still not enough—we must be a good hand when glancing inside of every "bit of glass" to see each local culture as though from within, and only then we will be able to see a true picture of the world.

But what is a "local culture" and what determines its face? We have already mentioned the concept "cultural space of the world," and we should explain that this space is more spiritual rather than physical. It is the space where ideas, concepts and doctrines, which determine world outlook of local cultures (which also have more spiritual nature, rather than material), are formed and developed. And as we shall consider a myth a basis of the world outlook of one or another group of people, we shall also consider local cultures not as territorial formations, but as communities of people incorporated by a certain cultural-ideological doctrine constructed on a certain mythical concept. In a context of this definition we can speak, for example, about Christianity as we can speak about local culture, which border passes not on territory of any certain state, but in hearts and souls of people who can live in any place of the world. Now we can allocate eight local cultures (Christianity, Islam, Judaism, Hinduism, Buddhism, Sintoism, Confutsioism, Daoism), which, as a rule, are divided on subcultures which very frequently are in enmity among themselves, and aspire to world domination (especially western cultures).

The face of a local culture is determined by the world outlook of people, which are inside of its space. And, if we manage to trace the genesis of that world outlook, we shall see true cultural condition of the group of people who adhere to it; we shall see the condition of a local culture and that artificial environment which that group of people creates around itself. We shall see the way of its interaction with other cultures. If this cultural environment is human and peaceful, the relations of the given local culture with other local cultures will also be human and peaceful. If this artificial environment is aggressive and mixed with aspiration to expansion, such a culture will aspire to take root into other cultures, and, by destroying their originality, absorb and dissolve them in its space.

It is necessary to note here, that people and culture are not the same. In a context of our work, we speak about people, as an ethnic formation occupying a certain territory. While the borders of culture pass, we already have determined in hearts and souls of humans. At the initial stage of evolutionary development, an ethnic group has no culture yet. It begins to develop later, when the man creates the artificial world of artifacts around him. At that stage, his consciousness is collective and mythological, he lives in a natural environment in which he is in a harmonic state, and is still indissoluble, or, it is even possible to say, in intimate unity. That was the childhood of mankind, when it did not separate itself from the outer world, from Mother Nature, and did not know any division inside of human communities.

At first, man began to surround himself with material things. Those were the artificial dwellings, work tools and primitive works of art. For example, rock paintings; then, with the origin of abstract thinking and writing, man began to simulate the internal world, representing the internal conditions and feelings at first as mythical epos. Then abstract ideas and theories developed, which, in the final analysis, formed the face of local cultures.

Thus, **our task: by investigating genesis of the main local cultures, or, which is more correct, of their world outlook concepts, we will show the modern picture of cultural space of the world and reveal the reasons which have brought it to such a terrible condition**.

In a context of the present research we shall proceed from the fact that all the dominant world outlook concepts of local cultures have a religious nature and represent, by themselves, informational-energy matrixes, which, being the basis of cultural-historical development of a society, determine its behavior both in the whole and that of separate individuals of which it consists.

But, to continue our research successfully, it is necessary to explain the term "matrix". The English historian H. G. Wells was probably the first to apply the term "matrix" to the description of a cultural phenomenon. As a matrix he named the Christian Church, which tried to supervise all displays of life in Europe in the Middle Ages: "**The Church** had sheltered and formed a new Europe throughout the long ages of European darkness and chaos; it **had been the matrix in which the new civilization had been cast**. But this new-formed civilization was impelled to grow by its own inherent vitality, and the church lacked sufficient power for growth and accommodation. The time was fast approaching when this matrix was to be broken."[6] It means, that matrix, in a literal sense, is a form in which any subject is cast. In metaphorical sense, this term designates a certain informational-energy system, which is a basis for the construction of social-ideological doctrine, which forms and determines the cultural space of the man and the world.

Then, we should take into account that any text representing the set of signs in which the social information is "ciphered" (that is content, meaning, or the sense enclosed in it by the man), can become the matrix capable to render quite certain influences on the consciousness of the man, even if it is perceived at an unconscious level. A word, like a seed thrown in soil, will slowly and inevitably ripen in the heart of man in order to give sprouts and to bear a fruit, which, however, is not always sweet. Moreover, the text, perceived at an unconscious level, can snap into action in a completely unexpected mode and force the man to perform an act described in a matrix. To prove this thesis, we shall give some examples taken from a real life.

Some years ago, a brutal, severe and monstrous murder was committed in England. Two teenagers (9 and 11 years old), seized the opportunity of a carelessness of a young mother who was doing shopping in a supermarket together with her four-year old son, stole the boy. They tortured him cruelly until he died. Then the teenagers smeared the boy with paint and put him under a train. Policemen, psychologists, criminalists, as well as all the English people, were shocked with that terrible murder. Trying to find an explanation to such a severe crime of the teenagers, they decided to examine the television programs which were broadcast on the eve of the murder. To everyone's great surprise, a movie was found in which the same murder had been shown. The teenagers repeated what they had seen on a TV screen; thus proving that we must consider such things quite seriously.

The previous case is not a unique one. "There was revealed the rule: **unusually "famous" by their cruelty teenagers' crimes (the arson of the teacher in Boston, stoning of the Norwegian girl etc.) were provoked with similar plots "for imitation" shown by TV on the eve**."[7] But we, as always, have not taken any lesson from these terrible events. And, when the Twins of the World Trade Center in New York crashed down, we clasped our hands and uttered a scream: "Ah, we have already seen it in Hollywood movies!" And it is quite true because there was such a movie. "Tom Clancy has brought the plane down on the Capitol building in 1994 in the novel *The Debt of Honor*. The pilot of the Boeing—747 was a Japanese pilot-kamikaze who took revenge on Americans for the bombardment of Hiroshima and Nagasaki in 1945, and for his parents, who committed a suicide in order not to be taken prisoners by American soldiers. The pilot's dream has come true: Congress was in session in the Capitol, and the President held a speech. By the way, one of the versions of tragedy says that the terrorist act was committed by the semi-mythical Japanese Red Army just out of revenge for the nuclear bombardments."[8]

And now, when we hear about "holy jihad" and about the desire of Moslem fundamentalists to destroy America we clasp our hands again and utter a scream: "Ah, we have already heard it somewhere!" Of course we have. This is in the Koran that Allah says: "You shall kill infidel!" Those words act as a matrix, making a terrorist to go and to kill those who do not worship Allah.

The matrix works like that. It works in such a way that the huge charge of hatred and cruelty contained in the matrix, which is the basis of our world outlook, is transferred from one century to another and from one generation to another. The main concepts of the matrix, being repeated a countless number of times, become with the course of time so-called archetypes—conceptions and ideas (common for the large groups of people) contained in the structure of collective unconscious. "There are as many archetypes as typical life situations,"—wrote —. G. Jung.—The endless repetition has engraved that experience on our mental constitution—not in the form of filled with content images, but, first of all, as forms without contents representing only an opportunity of a certain type of both perception and action.

When the situation appropriate to the given archetype comes about, the archetype becomes active, a compulsion appears, which, like an instinctive inclination, paves its way contrary to any reason and will or produces pathological effect."[9]

The matrix works this way. It works at an unconscious level, at a level of archetypes, which are "the forms without content;" forms which we are not aware of (because they are without content, but, nevertheless, contain the opportunity of action), but under the certain circumstances, "when the situation appropriate to the given archetype comes about" (for example, those teenagers, who watched the movie about murder, kept the memory of it in their unconscious like an archetype; when they saw the unattended boy, "the archetype" was activated and induced them to commit a murder), this archetype is made active and "paves its way contrary to any reason and will." This example shows us, that even short-term influence of an informational-energy matrix can result in formation of the "archetype," which will inevitably be made active under certain circumstances. What must we say about those matrixes which determine the world outlook of whole nations during centuries and millenniums then?

And, as the Christian Church, according to H. G. Wells, during more then thousand years was the only matrix in which "a new civilization had been cast," it is rightful to assume that thanks exactly to it and to its teaching we have the present condition of the cultural space of the world. And, as the Bible is the basis of the Christian Church teaching, we shall consider this book to be the informational-energy matrix which determines the world outlook of people who use it as "the textbook of life."

We can confirm this idea by words of William Lyon Phelps, a former Yale professor who said: "Our civilization is founded upon the Bible. More of our ideas, our wisdom, our philosophy, our literature, our art, our ideals come from the Bible than from all other books combined."[10]

This citation is taken from the book of D. James Kennedy and Jerry Newcome *What if the Bible Had Never Been Written?* The authors declare in it: "The impact on our culture, on our nation, on world history has been enormous. The purpose of this book is to show that the overall impact of the Bible on civilization has been overwhelmingly positive."[11]

The purpose of our book is to show that the overall impact of the Bible on civilization has been overwhelmingly negative. Moreover, we intend to prove that the Bible is the very matrix of destruction that has been specially designed to destroy the world of "infidels" and to establish the New World Order on Earth. Certainly, such attempts were undertaken before by different authors, But at first, nobody approached the analysis of religion as a cultural phenomenon in the way we did; secondly, never before was there such an urgent need for such analysis as nowadays when the forces, which have brought the world to such a terrible condition, came into movement, resulting in the situation when further peaceful coexistence of the nations and cultures becomes absolutely impossible; when we came close to the matrix's final program realization stage which anticipates the total destruction of all the existing civilizations in the "fierce anger of Sovereign God." Do you remember Tchechov, the Russian play writer? His plays are written in such a way that, if in the first act there hangs a gun on a wall, it will inevitably shoot in the last act. The matrix of destruction works in the same way. If one of its program items is "the Last Judgment" or "the Final Destruction," it will inevitably be done. And it does not matter whether God exists or not; it does not matter whether he or we ourselves shall destroy the world; important is the fact that this item of the matrix program must inevitably be realized...

Now we are standing at the edge of abyss, at its very edge. Behind our back is a huge arsenal of every possible kind of weapon. Behind our back is a huge charge of human hatred and cruelty we have accumulated during the entire history of our civilization's development. Behind our back is the cruel and heartless matrix which slowly and inevitably is coming near to us in order to push us off into that abyss, into impenetrable gloom of chaos and non-existence that we will hardly be able to escape.

ABOUT THE METHOD OF RESEARCH

"We shall consider a myth as if it were an orchestral score rewritten by an ignorant amateur line after line as a continuous melodic sequence; we do try to restore its initial arrangement."

Claude Levi-Stros

First of all, we should declare that the present work is not merely an academic scientific work in which scientific hypotheses are put forward, scientific experiments are done and scientific results are got. Our work can be related to a scientific-journalistic genre in which an urgency of considered problems and its topicality are more important rather than its scientific character. Accordingly, the results we aspire to receive will be not so much in the field of science as in the field of human world outlook; for the sphere of its realization lies not so much in the field of reason as in the field of feelings.

During our work on the book we used the actual material taken from sources of different authors which, in one way or another, concerns the subjects considered by us. Therefore, we can hardly apply for absolute originality. **We have only taken the trouble to generalize what had been told by the other authors, and to submit this material in such a way that it could not only interest a curious reader, but, having penetrated into their hearts and souls, wake them from indifference and inactivity and make them think about why our world is so cruel and unfriendly towards a little, defenseless person, and what we should do to make this world lighter, more kindly and more humanly**.

To continue our research, it is necessary to clear our position in relation to the main philosophical question: what was the first—consciousness or matter? We proceed from the fact that consciousness was the first. That is to say, we confirm that any action is preceded with an idea of that action, or, in the other words, conscious or unconscious intention to do something. Homo Sapiens was created by God so that he thinks at first and then acts. Certainly, among representatives of the kind of mammals, there are those who at first act and then think. The result of such actions turns out to be a little bit different from that which we expected. We hope that our readers are such as they were created by God; therefore we shall continue our further narration as if we deal with decent, civilized people who think at first and then act. And as the idea precedes an action it is natural to assume that certain ideas organized in a certain single whole, representing a text, can render a certain influence on a person and induce him or her to do certain actions. Especially, if that person perceives those ideas as stated by a certain authority. Repeating themselves during centuries and millennia, those another's ideas penetrate into consciousness of whole generations of people so strongly that they become archetypes and begin to be perceived as their own. Those archetypes operate as a matrix, which form our world outlook and determine our behaviour.

Therefore, we should be very cautious with info-energy matrixes that we come across during our life; otherwise, we can face even more serious accidents than the atrocities of September 11, 2001. Trying to understand the causes of a serious threat to the very existence of the life on the Earth, we have started to build different guesses and created various theories to explain what occurs to us. But, like a bad doctor who, having not found the cause of illness, treats only its symptoms; so we try to solve a problem, having removed only visible symptoms of illness. The real cause escapes from us. We cannot see it, for we have not got used to see far, because we do not learn lessons of history, because we have not got used to trouble ourselves with long and hard searches for the truth.

In some days after the atrocities of September 11, 2001, the causes of that tragedy were discussed in Vladimir Posner's talk show on Russian TV. One of Posner's opponents argued with him and said: "Look, those unprecedented terrorist acts were performed by twenty kamikaze who cruelly and professionally directed the high-jacked airplanes to the targets which had to be destroyed. It was not individual, but a collective act. Those people got appropriate training, they were brought up in an appropriate way. There must be a certain ideology encouraging and justifying similar acts behind their actions...." But Posner did not pay due attention to that remark. He sharply interrupted his opponent and directed conversation to a completely other direction.

By what reason can we explain such a behavior? Shall we explain it by misunderstanding of a problem, or by Posner's unwillingness to pay attention of the audience to the true causes of the events? Of course we cannot know what was in his mind. But this example shows us the way our resistance works when we express our persevering desire to learn the truth.

We have gotten used, or, to be more exact, have been inured to live in a world of lies and hypocrisy, hatred and cruelty, rage and division. Therefore, all of our attempts to find out the truth always are stopped, and will be stopped until we live in the world of double standards, in the world of double morals.

And so, if Vladimir Posner had allowed the opponent to finish his speech, we would have recognized that by performing the atrocity, the murderers-kamikaze were guided by a certain ideology which was generated due to a certain myth, namely to an Islamic myth.

So, what is a myth? Whether its influence on a culture and human behaviour is so great that a person can neglect even a threat to his own death and the death of thousands of innocent people for the achievement of entirely doubtful purposes which that myth puts before him? Yes, we have to state that the influence of myth on a person who believes in it and builds his life according to it is enormous. Otherwise, there would be no murderers-kamikaze who, committing the monstrous crimes, fanatically believe that right after an explosion they will get to heaven, to Allah, who will provide them with a paradise and the finest women for their harem.

The one who does not believe in myth will say that myths are fairy tales; therefore, they cannot have an influence both on the man and on the culture of all mankind. Who is right here, and what point of view should we accept in order to restore the initial arrangement of a myth? It is quite clear: neither of them. Both a blind belief and a full denying of something cannot be our instruments in studying such an intricate and many-sided cultural phenomenon as a myth is; which, during the further development, finds continuation in the religious outlook of people.

It is also impossible to understand a myth as the whole being; blindly believing in it and implicitly following its doctrine, for being inside the whole, one cannot comprehend that whole as the whole. For this purpose, it is necessary to leave its limits and look at it from the outside. Only in such a way will we be able to have full imagination about that whole. A myth cannot also be comprehended being considered as just deceit or a fairy tale without taking into account its influence on a culture and actions of certain groups of people. In addition, to have an unbiased objective, and impartial sight at a thing, we, by no means, can rely on faith.

In fact, what is faith? A faith is an acceptance of anything we can neither prove nor deny as the absolute truth. For example, we believe in God. If one asks a priest whether God exists or not, the priest will answer in the affirmative. However, if one asks him to prove it, the priest will never be able to do it. He will tell you that firstly, the very fact of raising such a question is a mortal sin. Secondly, one can learn about God from the Holy Scriptures (which he himself has given to people). And thirdly, we are not bestowed the knowledge of it. It means that the one who tries to prove what cannot be proved is simply a deceiver and a charlatan. We, while answering similar questions, say: "We do not know." Thus, we open ourselves for the knowledge of truth, whether it is pleasant to us or not.

In our enterprise, we shall choose a position of a detached onlooker, who objectively and impartially looks at the world as though from the outside and produces judgments about everything which take place in it. However, if everyone looks objectively at the world and produces his judgments, we shall have as many judgments as we have observers. Quite clearly, we will not be able to know the truth. In order to do it, we should choose a certain universal criterion by means of which we shall estimate everything we see. Then, comparing what we see with that uniform universal criterion, each of us will come to the same conclusion and thus together we shall know the truth.

The basic subject of the humanities is a human being and a culture as a certain artificial environment created by man in which they live and improve themselves. That artificial environment is not always friendly to humans; on the contrary, it is frequently hostile and even unacceptable for normal existence of the man.

Here we closely approach a concept of value or a valuable sense of objects and phenomena, which take place in the world. These phenomena or objects have a certain value for us if we consider them as means of satisfaction of our needs and desires. If these phenomena or objects do not satisfy our needs and desires or even prevent their satisfaction, they either have no value, or have a negative value—"antivalue." We try to bring values near to our life in every possible way, and to exclude "antivalues" from it.

During the history of humankind, man has created certain values; so-called cultural universal criterions that, on the one hand, distinguish them from an animal, and on the other hand, satisfy the most intimate and the most essential needs that are typical for a Homo Sapiens. The most important value is love, but not as a bargain, rather as a desire and aspiration to pure, unconditional self-sacrifice for the sake of happiness and well-being of another person without dependence on a skin color, nationality or creed. Concomitant to love or derivatives from it are such values as compassion (compassion in general, without dependence on a skin color, nationality and creed), forgiveness and aspiration to live in peace and harmony.

As an examples of such common cultural criterions can be the list of the ethical standards which express the laws of morals which were produced at different times in different cultures:

1. **The Law of the Common Benefit:**
   a) "Do not speak words which could be harmful to a person." (India)
   b) "Never do to others what you would not want them do to you." (Ancient China, Jesus Christ).
   c) "People have been created to do kindness towards each other." (Rome).
2. **Duties In Relation to Parents, to Elders and to Ancestors**
   a) "He hates the father or the mother?" (Babylon)
   b) "The duty of everyone is to take care of parents." (Greece)
3. **Duties In Relation to Children and Posterity**
   a) "The Nature gives special love to its posterity." (Rome)
   b) "The Teacher has told: "respect young." (ancient China)
4. **The Law of Mercy**
   a) "I have given bread to those who are hungry, water to those who are thirsty, clothes to nude, a boat to those who does not have it." (ancient Egypt).
   b) "It is not allowed to anybody to beat a woman even with a flower." (India).
   c) "So, Torahs, you will be dishonoured, if you strike a woman." (Scandinavia)
   d) "You will see, that they take care of widows, orphans and the aged, never reproaching them." (Red-Skinned Indians)
5. **The Law of Magnanimity**
   a) "There are two kinds of injustice: we find the first in those who makes the violence, the second—in those who does not want to protect weak, if he is able to do it." (Rome)
   b) "Not to pay attention to a rough attack means to strengthen a

heart of the enemy. Strength is valour, but the cowardice is meanness." (Ancient Egypt).

c) "The Nature and Reason induce us not to think and not to do anything unattractive, anything thoughtless, anything lewd." (Rome)

Accordingly, lies, hypocrisy, hatred, cruelty, rage and division should be considered as "antivalues." Any sort of mockery at the man and at their dignity, violence, murder, and especially infanticide should be considered in the view of the values set forth above as reprehensible and completely inadmissible in relations between people.

Hardly anyone will challenge this statement. In this case, we have the right to assume that we succeeded in finding the universal criterion which we shall name "humanity," and the analysis in which we shall use our criterion, we shall name "the humanistic analysis," i.e. the analysis on humanity. From now on, analyzing any cultural phenomenon we shall subject it to check on humanity. If the result will be positive, i.e. if the cultural phenomenon will appear to be capable to satisfy a person's need for truth, friendship, love, compassion and justice, then we shall include that phenomenon in our life and use it for our development and for the establishing of relations with other people. If the result of the analysis will be negative, i.e. if we shall find out that the given cultural phenomenon is "antivalue," then we shall have to exclude it from our life.

It is quite strange, but we must admit that hardly anyone used "the humanistic analysis" while interpreting any texts (especially holy scriptures) or cultural phenomena. We have examined many books devoted to both Bible studying and other scriptures, but we could not find even something similar to our "humanistic analysis." Thus, we were convinced that neither the academic science, nor other institutes applied "the humanistic analysis" to Bible studying, i.e. they did not investigate it from the point of view of humanity. It happened partly from servility before authority, partly from fear before "almighty" God. Both of these factors compel the person to consider the text "sent" by "authority" as indisputable truth, irrespective of the fact of how it corresponds to the cultural universal criteria.

Now let us imagine a completely impossible picture. A certain president writes a book in which he expresses his love for a certain country and its people and orders to kill all the inhabitants of other countries. Should we accept such a book as the "value" from the point of view of humanity? Certainly not. We must recognize it only as the "antivalue," and any normal and decent person will hardly argue with us. But there can be such humans who will approve such a book, and, having armed with its misanthropic ideology, will go to kill all those who will get to them in the heat of the moment.

In the Bible, the Jewish God Jehovah himself kills everybody and orders his chosen people to do the same. But those who are not the chosen people also consider the book to be sacred. They use it as a textbook of life and, having learned about all the details of the organization of massacres, go to destroy Jews, Moslems and everyone who will get to them in the heat of the moment.

The matrix works in such a way. In such a way laws of double morals, the best textbook of which is the Bible, work. So, we have to look at this book as on a certain whole; we need to track the entire way of its coming into being from the very beginning up to the end in order to understand the mechanisms of its influence on human hearts and souls.

At the analysis of any text we shall hold to an idea that **if a text contains scenes of violence, mockeries at animals and people, direct or indirect order to kill or approval of such actions towards human beings, we shall have to recognize that such a text should be declared as "antivalue" and withdrawn from the use both as an example for imitation and as "the textbook of life," which is obligatory for studying both by children and adults**.

In order to make our analysis more evident we have worked out a scale of positive and negative universal cultural criteria. Now, having such a scale, we can analyze any text or any matrix with the object to humanity, and, having unwrapped this analysis on an axis of time, we can construct the diagram of evolution of these universal cultural criteria within the limits of a text or a matrix. Then, by a simple calculation of the sum of figures we can determine a positive or negative charge of a matrix. As the unit of a positive charge, we shall use "1 hum." (abbr. from "humanity"), as the unit of a negative charge—"1 antihum." Having analyzed some texts in such a way, we can reveal their comparative value, and having looked at a diagram, we shall see a difference between them. Thus, "the humanistic analysis" opens a way to statistical estimation of cultural phenomena in connection with a degree of their value for both a human being and the world.

The scale of universal cultural criteria can look as follows:

9. Self-sacrifice
8. Universal love

7. Human love
6. Mercy
5. Compassion
4. Forgiveness
3. Magnanimity
2. Kindness
1. Honesty
0.
- 1. Lie
- 2. Hypocrisy
- 3. Jealousy
- 4. Discrimination
- 5. Anger
- 6. Meanness
- 7. Murder
- 8. Mass murder
- 9. Infanticide

Despite apparent strangeness and even absurdness of such a calculation, it can give a rather exact picture of any cultural phenomenon. With the help of such analysis, it is possible even to define, for example, a total info-energy charge of a historical way of mankind. Having arranged all basic historical events on an axis of time and having noted numerical values on an axis of universal cultural criteria, we shall see the dynamics of development of humanity, and, having counted a total numerical value, we shall define info-energy charge, which we have accumulated for the entire history of existence of the human being. If the result appears to be positive, that will mean we have nothing to worry about; if the result appears to be negative, it will be necessary for us to think of our future life and of our future actions.

Certainly, we can be reproached that we try to reduce great spiritual value of "holy scriptures" as well as of other "less holy" texts to a soulless material level of dry statistics, destroying, thus, the entire spiritual experience which has been accumulated by mankind during the whole history of its existence.

The matter is that we are compelled to enter all this statistics for those who are not capable of distinguishing a lie from truth and illusion from reality, who does not see true faces of gods which remind those of humans in the most obscene moments of their life, behind beautiful and effective pictures, which a church and holy scriptures paint before our astonished eyes. We have to invent all of these statistics in order to show to the man a digital equivalent of all the nasty things they have done, hoping that they, having seen their meanness, will be terrified and will understand that it is brutally and unfair to kill other humans simply because they do not agree with us, because they are a bit different from us, because they do not profess the religion we profess and do not serve the God whom we serve.

A reasonable person does not need all of these statistics because such a person understands without any statistics that the statements like: "Now go and smite Amalek, and utterly destroy all that they have, and spare them not; but **slay both man and woman, infant and suckling**, ox and sheep, camel and ass."[12] or: "Verily, I am with you; make ye firm then those who believe; **I will cast dread into the hearts of those who misbelieve,- strike off their necks then, and strike off from them every finger tip**." That is, because they went into opposition against God and His Apostle; for he who goes into opposition against God and His Apostle—verily, **God is keen to punish**,"[13] can be only "antivalue" and it is impossible and very dangerous to build the life, being guided by such a text, because it is brutal and inhuman.

This Book Is Dedicated
To The Victims Of Terrorist Acts Of September 11th, 2001.

"Humankind must be ashamed of its "heroic" past, like one is ashamed of one's yesterday's crazy scuffle resulted in fratricide and infanticide. It is necessary to take history off the pedestal of Science, and study it thoroughly and wisely, like one studies a case history."

Didenco B. A.

CHAPTER 1.

MYTH AND RELIGIOUS IDEAS OF ANCIENT MAN

"I keep to the same view on religion, as Lucretius did. I consider it as an illness caused by fear, and the source of incalculable sufferings for mankind."

Bertran Russel[14]

1. 1. Myth, as a Cultural Phenomenon

There is a concept known as a collective unconscious in a modern psychology. Carefully ciphered knowledge of a historical way of mankind, it had walked through during the entire history of its existence, is kept in it in some incomprehensive and unimaginable way. Psychologist K. G. Jung considers it both as the result of a previous phylogenetic experience and as a set of collective thoughts, ideas and images of mankind, as well as mythological concepts which were widespread in this or that epoch of human history.

In the Oxford classical dictionary, Herbert J. Rose defines myth as a "prescientific and speculative attempt to give an explanation to some real and imagined phenomena which raise curiosity of the composer of myth, and probably, if to be exacter, as an attempt to achieve the feeling of satisfaction instead of painful confusion caused by this phenomenon."[15]

By means of myth, man tried to express predominant ideas about the structure of the world; in myth, he built cosmological theories in which gods and goddesses lived like human beings and defined the destinies of people and nations. Myth was also used for justification of social-political relations which were developed in a society. On the one hand, myth was the reflection of terrestrial life, depicting it in fantastical, symbolical form; on the other hand, myth was that matrix on which the culture of people, who produced the myth, was built. The will of gods, as well as the will of kings, endowed with a divine origin and divine powers, was considered sacred and indisputable, and its infringement or even disagreement with meant the exile from a community outside of which the ancient man couldn't imagine his existence, or even death. Therefore, myth had a great influence on development of the ancient world, and it was always used by the mighty of this world to subordinate people and nations.

Myth, among other things, is also the reflection of internal world of the people who created it. It is a history of its forming and development as independent social—ethnic formation endowed with its own will and self-consciousness. It is also a case history in which the vicious and perverted nature of human mentality is described.

Myth making was also a certain psychotherapeutic process which relieved society of certain fears and tensions which aroused during its forming and development. Later, psychologists discovered that to get rid of fear, for example, one must go through a situation in which this fear had been arisen once again. Experiencing his fear and realizing it, the man gets rid of it.

In antiquity people did not know about the achievements of psychology we know nowadays, but they intuitively felt them and created myths in which human defects and sufferings were represented quite clearly and frankly. The dramatic art which arose from myth and began to develop as its evident continuation enabled people not only to hear, but also to see the gloomy depths of the human soul. It also enabled them, together with heroes of a drama, to experience and to go through passions and sufferings of which they were exposed in their life in order to take off that intolerable burden from a soul and to achieve "catharsis"—the blissful feeling of spiritual purification and deliverance both from fear and from suffering.

But it was the final stage of myth development, when it became the story unwrapped along the axis of time. For the ancient man time did not exist yet. The human consciousness was syncretic. That means that the man, in his consciousness, did not separate himself from the outer world. It was the very stage when the myth began to form.

1. 2. The Structure of Myth

The Dictionary of the Culture of the XX Century says that "the most important thing characteristic for the structure of myth is a phenomenon, which is called participation. In myth, each object, each action is co-participant to other objects and actions. The image of man is not simply an image; it is a part of the man whom it represents, one of his forms. Therefore, it is enough to create any manipulations with the image, and something will happen with the represented man. For example, if one pierces the image with a pin, the man will die (contagious magic). Because the part is the same thing as the whole is one of its manifestations.

The characteristic feature of a myth is its general werewolfness. It means that in a myth everything is connected to everything and is reflected in everything. A special language and special consciousness is necessary for this purpose. For example, when someone says: "I came out of the house,"—he simply describes his action. Such a language cannot be mythological. An object, a subject and a predicate are distinguishable too clearly in it. But myth did not distinguish either subject or object or predicate; myth did not know either words or syntax in a modern sense. There existed neither parts of a sentence, nor parts of a speech then.

In mythological consciousness the most primitive syntactic or incorporative order is dominating. A sentence and a word is the same. The whole meanings string themselves one upon another like beads. The ancient man did not say: 'I came out of the house,'—he said something like: 'Me—house—outside—coming.' Certainly, in such a whole language and consciousness, there can not be either differentiation between truth and lie (it arises as the articulate speech function); or distinction between illusion and reality (it arises when there are subjects and words); or differentiation between life and death (it arises when there is a beginning and the end of a sentence and, in general, the beginning and the end—that is linear time)."[16]

Therefore, the idea that myth is a certain ancient legend or a story is simply incorrect, for at a stage of mythological thinking, what is spoken is not separated from what is spoken about. Mythological consciousness did not know fundamental opposition between reality and fiction and between truth and lie, yet these very oppositions are necessary to create the story unwrapped in time.

According to *The Dictionary of the Culture of the XX Century*: "There is different time and space in mythological consciousness. Time is cyclic in it. One of the basic myths of mankind is the myth about eternal returning. The space of myth is the space of agrarian ritual, in which everything is interconnected. Each phenomenon, including natural one, is interpreted in the terms of space-time connected to crop, maturing and harvesting of a crop.

When a historical consciousness and the idea of future, which will not repeat the past, appears, myth begins to break and demythologize itself. From here appears the idea of myth as a story written in the spirit of Legends and Myths of Ancient Greece. These are the odds and ends of myth extended in a line and artificially provided with features of narrativeness."[17]

Therefore, we should attribute all those historical-artistic narrations and scriptures in which the heroes and gods act to the products of postmythological culture. And if we, nevertheless, call them myths, it is only because the mythological thinking, in which there is neither time, nor space, in which there is no border between truth and lie, between illusion and reality, between life and death, is a basic component of their influence on a human being and on the culture as a whole. And it is a mythological thinking that becomes one of the major cultural categories in XX and XXI centuries. Such a type of thinking becomes a neutralizer between all fundamental cultural binary oppositions. First of all, between life and death, between truth and lie, between illusion and reality. That is why in the times of totalitarian consciousness, for example, in the times of Stalin's mass repressions, myth works without failure. And now we are more and more persistently made to return to the level of mythological consciousness. In order we could not distinguish lie from truth, illusion from reality; in order we, being slaves, could consider ourselves to be the owners of our country and of the world; in order we, being poor and hungry, could be pleased with the fact that we live in an independent country and glorify the Almighty Lord for his having granted us such a liberty.

It means that we should assume that the influence of mythological concepts, produced by mankind during the entire history of its existence, always had decisive importance in the formation of world outlook of the large masses of people, and that it was not always positive. Even on the contrary, those mythological concepts submitted very often in perverted interpretation and being a basis of religious ideological systems were an obstacle in cultural progress of mankind. Moreover, it was the power which led to enmity, bloodshed and destruction of millions of innocent people. That is why the knowledge about myth is so important nowadays. And in order to get that knowledge, it is necessary to do the analysis of the basic myths which mankind has produced during the entire history of its existence. But first we should understand why myth has been turned into epos, why human consciousness has made such a sharp turn from polytheism to monotheism, which, strange as it may seem, turned out to be a source of many our troubles and problems.

1. 3. Totemism and Religion

There are various forms of religions. Names of gods and goddesses are so numerous that they cannot even be counted and catalogued. Rituals which man use for protection or blessing make up a variegated scale, which at one moment falls down to the lowest notes of fear and animal horror, and soars up to unattainable heights of mercy and to the subtlest movements of human spirit at another one. The description of religious customs can make tens of thousands of volumes, and even it is not capable to contain all the variety of internal world of the human being and his culture.

The whole arsenal of humanitarian sciences is involved into its exploration, and with the course of time, there appeared newer and newer discoveries concerning the life of our ancient ancestors. Although they are different, they prove the only fact that the man was religious during the entire history of its existence.

Wherever man goes, whatever he does, all days of his life he carries an unquenchable faith in some supreme, supernatural power, in spirits, demons, in gods or in one universal god in his heart and soul. Religious faith determines his world outlook; it elevates him up to the greatest heights of human mercy, and then plunges him into infernal glooms of monstrous and cruel crimes and atrocities. That faith unites all its followers in monolithic indestructible unity, and, at the same time, separates them from that part of the world which does not profess that faith. Then, those who do not profess it are announced to be pagans, sinners, scoundrels and heretics; their names are deleted from "the book of life," and they become subject to ruthless physical destruction and eternal tortures in the blazing inferno.

The ancient man was entirely religious. Belief in spirits, angels, gods and idols was an integral part of his consciousness. A question to trust or not to trust in supernatural forces never arose in the consciousness of ancient man. It was something self-evident for him. In the nature and in the depth of his inner-self, the man saw mysterious work of some powerful and uncontrollable forces. When a child was born, man thanked a spirit or a god for his having sent him such happiness. When an illness or misfortune came, the man thought that it was a god or an evil spirit who had punished him for his sins.

That belief has certainly arisen through the humanizing of nature. Primarily, the forces of nature were alien to man. He was afraid of them and consequently he allocated them with human qualities in order to struggle with them by the means he used for arranging relations with the species of his kind. Thus, his reasoning was probably as follows: "Why not to use against superhuman aggressors, i. e. against the forces of external nature, the same means, that we use in a human society; why not to try to bewitch, to propitiate or to bribe them, depriving them by such influence of some part of their power?"[18]

Such approach to the decision of a problem gave not only an instant relief, it also specified the way of mastering the situation; for such a situation was not new at all. Earlier in his childhood, being a helpless child, man was in a similar situation, and his memory has kept traces of these early experiences of children's fear and feebleness, both before the terrible forces of nature and before the strict father on whom he could rely in the case of danger. Therefore, "...the man turns the forces of nature not simply into humanlike creatures he can equally communicate with, but gives them the father's character and transforms them into gods, going thus not only after infantile, but also after philogenetic prototype (the image of forefather, who was killed and eaten by the sons of primeval tribe chieftain, which is inherent to entire human kin)."[19]

In order to make our further investigation clear to an unsophisticated reader, it is necessary to explain what that mysterious philogenetic prototype is. This term has appeared in the work *Totem and Taboo* by Sigmund Freud, published in 1912. The hypothesis standing behind this term is so unusual and so interesting that it is necessary to give its short explanation here.

The events took place in ancient times when a strong male was unlimited in his authority. He carried out through cruelty and violence, and he was master and father to the entire horde. All the female species were his property. Very often, the sons suffered a lot from the vagaries of their cruel and imperious poppa. When they raised his jealousy, he either killed, castrated, or expelled them out of the herd. Younger sons had certain privileges, as they were closer to their mothers and had a chance to replace the father after his death. In legends and fairy tales we can hear both about exile of the grown-ups and about preference of younger ones.

The expelled sons rallied among themselves, overcame the father and, according to the custom of those times, devoured him. It is interesting to note that that primitive cannibalism is spread to the later times and its traces can be present even nowadays. Freud attributes the same emotional installations to these primitive people that he ascertained due to his analytical research at primitive people of the present, namely at our children. And he seems to be right. Above we mentioned the examples of severe children and teenagers' behaviour which we can use as proof of Freud's conclusions.

Cannibalistic act becomes quite clear as an attempt of the sons to provide the themselves with identification with the father through entering of his pieces in their own bodies. It sounds ridiculous, but such severe customs were considered as quite a normal phenomenon in ancient times. And even later, at first centuries of the Christian era, they practiced human sacrifices during which the body of a victim was devoured. The vestiges of that barbarous custom remain until present days as the sacrament of Eucharist, during which the piece of symbolical "Christ's body" is eaten and "his blood" is drunk.

That barbarous custom shows us the way a matrix works. It shows the way the archetype acquired by mankind at an early stage of its development works. In addition, this fact proves once again that we remain barbarians-cannibals who eat our God again and again, and all of us are more and more convinced in the programming influence of a matrix on the consciousness of large masses of people. What a brutal and monstrous "salvation" should be if it is received at the expense of murder and "devouring" of other man? Nevertheless, many modern, civilized people have another opinion on this account, and, coming to a "sacred" Eucharist, they crucify the one who has given his life on a cross for them again and again, "...in order that whoever believes in him was not perished, but had eternal life."

The elimination of the father has resulted in rallying of a collective and in occurrence of some kind of a social compact.

In such a way the first form of social organization with refusal from impetuous impulses, with recognition of the mutual obligations, with establishment of special institutes, announced to be inviolable (sacred), i. e. with the first principles of morals and right, appeared. Each separate individual refused from his ideal—from taking father's place, from possession of the mother and sisters. Thus, the taboo on incest (sexual relations with the mother), the commandment of exogamy, becomes firmly established. The considerable part of imperious functions, liberated after elimination of the father, has passed to women and there came the times of matriarchy.

Some strong and terrible animal, which was considered as a totem, became a substitute of the father. Totem was, on the one hand, a bodily forefather and a spirit- defender of a clan and, on the other hand, the holiday was established, in which it was sacrificed and eaten.

Thus, the humanization of the forces of nature and their personification results from the need to put the end to a human ignorance and powerlessness before frightening forces to establish relations with them and, ultimately, to affect them. That necessity springs from man's natural predisposition to project his inner self on the world and to see actions of beings which are similar to him in all observable phenomena because he cannot understand things in another way.

"But where is a religion here?"—one can ask. It is right here in totemism with its reverence of the father substitute, with ambivalence which manifests itself in totemic meal, with introduction of memorable holidays and interdictions which infringement inflicts death penalty. Here in totemism all the religious ideas of mankind take the beginning. Freud says: "We have the right to assume that **in totemism wee can see the first form of religion manifestation and to ascertain initially existing connection of religion with social formations and moral obligations.**"[20]

Then totem is humanized. The place of animals is taken by humanlike gods, the origination from totem is obvious. God is depicted now in a shape of an animal; totem becomes God's main companion, or the legend makes God to kill the very animal that was a former totem. Then comes the time when great maternal deities appear on a stage, but with the restoration of patriarchal right, the images of male deities take their place and those antroph-amorphous deities of polytheism reflect the circumstances of patriarchal epoch.

Gods carry out a triple task: they neutralize a horror before a nature, reconcile the man with redoubtable fate that appears in an image of death, and reward for sufferings and deprivations which the man are experienced living in a cultural community. The most interesting fact here is: "In religious doctrines and rituals, we shall see double sided sort of elements: on the one hand, the fixity on an old patrimonial legend and its vestiges, on the other—renewal of the past, returning of the forgotten after long intervals of time.

It is necessary to lay a proper emphasis on the fact of unusual power with which each fragment of the past comes back from oblivion making unexpectedly strong influences on human masses and declaring its irresistible claim on the verity so that the protests of logic can do nothing against it (according to a principle: 'credo quia absurdum' (I believe, because it is absurdly)).

This surprising feature can be understood only as a sample of crazy mania of psychotonics. We already have understood a long time ago, that a crazy idea hides in itself a fragment of the forgotten truth which is inevitably perverted and not properly understood at its returning to consciousness. That obtrusive persuasiveness the crazy idea is encircled with, proceeds from this grain of truth that is distributed upon accumulated mistakes. We should recognize such a truth, which can be named historical, as inherent in concepts of the religious faith. Although those concepts contain in themselves the features of psychotic symptoms, they are not subject to a damnation of isolation.

There was not another page of the religious history that opened itself to us with such a clarity as the establishing of monotheism with Hebrews and its continuation in Christianity, even if we put aside the development from an animal totem to a humanlike God with one or another animal companion (each of the four Christian evangelists still has his favourite animal), which is quite clear and understandable too.

If, as a first approximation, one considers the pharaoh's world domination as a ground for the origin of monotheistic religion, one can see as this monotheistic idea, having torn off from its basis, passes to the other nation, takes possession of it after a long period of latency, is protected by this nation as a precious treasure and, in turn, save nation's life and gives it the proud of choosiness. **Here is the religion of the forefather, the hope for reward, for oneness and, ultimately, for the world dominion.**"[21]

Thus, thanks to the father of psychoanalyses we could see the sources of the religious world outlook of ancient people and convince ourselves that the heartless and cruel matrix we are talking about in this book began to form itself at distant prehistoric times and even at that time it already got that great charge of human anger and cruelty which determines human behaviour till nowadays, making them commit impudent and bloody crimes against humans and humanity.

1. 4. Sacrifices and Religion

Above, we have shown that religious ideas evolved firstly from humanization of nature, and secondly, from the transfer of man's inner world outside and perceiving it as some illusory, invisible one inhabited with gods and spirits. The development of religious customs and rituals we deduced from a totemism, which sprang up on the basis of feelings connected with the murder of the father, who was the owner of all the female species of the herd and the usurper towards his sons.

Thus we see that religion, especially its ritual side, began with a murder and the memory of that murder has been fixed in a collective unconscious in some incomprehensible way. Coming up from the dark depths from time to time, that memory makes the man do certain actions, i. e. works as a matrix. Otherwise, we could hardly be able to explain the man's passion for sacrifices, as well as the interpretation of Jesus Christ's death as the final sacrifice which had been made in order to cleanse our sins with his blood. Otherwise, we could hardly be able to explain the monstrous ritual of Eucharist when people devour symbolical "Christ's body" and drink his symbolical "blood."

Thus springs up quite a reasonable question: "Could there be good and light continuation at such a dark, loathsome beginning?" In other words, the question is whether some light and spiritual religion can be originated from such a monstrous, barbarian ritual as totemism is, or did the religions of nowadays come from some other source? Of course, the vast majority of representatives of Homo sapiens believe that the western religions have nothing to do either with totemism, or with animism, or with sacrifices, and attribute all those abominations to pagan religions. **We do intend to prove the opposite. In order to do that we have to prove that the biblical God Jehovah, who became our Russian God after Christening of Russia, is the same pagan God as all ancient gods, it being known that he not only received human sacrifices but also actively demanded them.**

If we manage to do it, we will understand quite clearly the obvious fact that a good, light and spiritual religion cannot be based on the belief in vicious, cruel and bloodthirsty pagan monster which demands human sacrifices. Only unlimited tyranny, which needs thousands and millions of human lives to satisfy its bloody appetite, can be built on such a basis. Since all the modern western religions (Judaism, Christianity, Islam) are based on the Bible (in which the same dreadful and bloodthirsty God Jehovah is starring), it is quite natural that the world, which believes in such a God and builds its life according to his commandments, will be more like a slaughterhouse rather than "God's kingdom."

World outlook based on the Bible places peace and beatitude in the future, on a new heaven and a new earth that will appear after the extermination of the old ones, and so far all the necessary victims are justified if they are made to move near that long awaited time of happiness and felicity.

The idea of sacrifice, as we stated above, appeared after the murder of the archaic forefather. Some very intelligent barbarians came suddenly to the idea that it is possible to join to father's power having killed him or his animal substitute and eaten a piece of his flesh. Since that time that abominable practice has became usual in the ancient world, and modern people still use it to join to God Son's glory. Later, when people learned to cultivate soil and gather crops, they began to associate the idea of sacrifice with that of growth and dying of a seed planted into soil. Wels, H. G. in his *Short History of the World* says: "It was an entanglement, we must remember, in the childish, dreaming myth-making primitive mind; no reasoned process will explain it. But in the world of a few thousand years ago, it would seem that whenever seed-time came round to the Neolithic peoples there was a human sacrifice. And it was not the sacrifice of any mean or outcast person; it was the sacrifice usually of a chosen youth or maiden, a youth more often who was treated with profound deference and even worship up to the moment of his immolation. He was a sort of sacrificial god-king, and all the details of his killing had become a ritual directed by the old, knowing men and sanctioned by the accumulated usage of ages."[22]

Thus, it is obvious that the ritual of sacrifice went a long way from ritual killing of the forefather through totemism; sacrifice associated with the agriculture cycle to the final sacrifice of "the lamb" as a symbol of dying and resurrecting God. It is true. There were crusades, religious wars and fires of inquisition, in the flames of which millions of sacrifices were made to a cruel and bloodthirsty God Jehovah in the name of God, his Only Son and Holy Spirit. Never in the history of pre-Christian world had been so many sacrifices made as in the Christian era. Then, other wars and revolutions added more millions of human sacrifices. Then, there were terrorist acts both in Russia and in America, which carried away thousands lives in the name of "utmost justice" and "salvation" of "oppressed" nations from the dreadful phantom of globalization, which rambles about the world and threatens to turn it into the unilateral one which we discuss later.

And now, it seems that human consciousness moves inside the exclusive circle trying from time to time to get outside, but being unable to overcome the gravity of a heavy, invisible center comes back again and again, repeating the same behavioral stereotypes, imposed by the center. The matrix works this way: it programs human behavior and, in the guise of good intentions, makes them commit the same atrocities again and again.

1. 5. Human Sacrifices to the Biblical God Jehovah

As we mentioned above, we need to establish the fact of human sacrifices to the Biblical God Jehovah. If we establish it, if we establish that his face is the same as that of any of pagan god, we shall prove that God Jehovah is the same pagan god as all the other ones that people are invented in their perverted, morbid imagination.

Sacrifices, including human ones to the Semitic gods were usual phenomenon. Human sacrifices were made to the goddess Astarta, to Moloch and Baal. They were also made to the Jewish God Jehovah. Jehovah's instructions concerning animal sacrifices were as follows: "And thou shalt kill the bullock before the Lord, by the door of the tabernacle of the congregation. And thou shalt take of the blood of the bullock, and put it upon the horns of the altar with thy finger, and pour all the blood beside the bottom of the altar. And thou shalt take all the fat that covereth the inwards, and the caul that is above the liver, and the two kidneys, and the fat that is upon them, and burn them upon the altar. But the flesh of the bullock, and his skin, and his dung, shalt thou burn with fire without the camp: it is a sin offering. Thou shalt also take one ram; and Aaron and his sons shall put their hands upon the head of the ram. And thou shalt slay the ram, and thou shalt take his blood, and sprinkle it round about upon the altar. And thou shalt cut the ram in pieces, and wash the inwards of him, and his legs, and put them unto his pieces, and unto his head. And thou shalt burn the whole ram upon the altar: it is a burnt offering unto the Lord: it is a sweet savour, an offering made by fire unto the Lord."[23]

Following Jehovah's instructions are about human sacrifices: "**Sanctify unto me all the firstborn**, whatsoever openeth the womb among the children of Israel, **both of man and of beast: it is mine**."[24] Then he gives more detailed instructions: "Thou shalt not delay to offer the first of thy ripe fruits, and of thy liquors: **the firstborn of thy sons shalt thou give unto me**. Likewise shalt thou do with thine oxen, and with thy sheep: seven days it shall be with his dam; on the eighth day thou shalt give it me."[25]

Thus, we have direct evidence of crime. However, many human beings will say that it is an allegory, that it means we must sacrifice our sins to God, not our children. And one very reasonable man said that it was the tribe of Levy that didn't work, but just worshiped God that was meant as the sacrifice of firstborns. Of course, the Holy Scripture is the whole allegory for such men and they will not believe us even if the world falls down on their heads.

But we are reasonable beings and we know that ancient Jews accepted those instructions word for word. That is why they literally made human sacrifices, and that is why they literally killed "...both man and woman, infant and suckling, ox and sheep, camel and ass..." carrying out all God's commandments word for word. We are honest and civilized human beings and that is why we understand that if human firstborns are mentioned together with animals, so they must be sacrificed together with animals. "Kind and merciful" God does not discriminate between humans and animals. Both humans and animals are under his power and equally use his "mercy." That is why everybody must pay for that "mercy."

If you think that it was the only mentioning about human sacrifices in the Bible, if you think that "kind and merciful" God made a slip in speaking, then let us open the Leviticus 27: 28-29, where we shall read: "Notwithstanding no devoted thing, that a man shall devote unto the Lord of all that he hath, **both of man and beast**, and of the field of his possession, shall be sold or redeemed: every devoted thing is most holy unto the Lord. **None devoted, which shall be devoted of men, shall be redeemed; but shall surely be put to death**." Here a man is also mentioned together with an animal and it serves as a proof that Jewish God Jehovah likes both animals and human firstborns, especially if they are dismembered and grilled upon a fire.

When Jews took inhabitants of the land "flowing with milk and honey" as prisoners, Jehovah ordered: "And levy a tribute unto the Lord of the men of war which went out to battle: one soul of five hundred, both of the persons, and of the beeves, and of the asses, and of the sheep: Take it of their half, and give it unto Eleazar the priest, for an heave offering of the Lord."[26]

Then we read the following instructions from God: "And the half, which was the portion of them that went out to war, was in number three hundred thousand and seven and thirty thousand and five hundred sheep. And the Lord's tribute of the sheep was six hundred and threescore and fifteen. And the beeves were thirty and six thousand; of which the Lord's tribute was threescore and twelve. And the asses were thirty thousand and five hundred; of which the Lord's tribute was threescore and one. And the persons were sixteen thousand; of which the Lord's tribute was thirty and two persons. And Moses gave the tribute, which was the Lord's heave offering, unto Eleazar the priest, as the Lord commanded Moses."[27]

This and other similar places in the Bible can serve as a proof of the fact that ancient Jews made human sacrifices to Jehovah. Here, we can see that thirty and two persons together with animals were sacrificed to "kind and merciful" God Jehovah. And Jephthah sacrificed even his own daughter to Jehovah.[28]

Blavatscaya in *Isis unveiled* reported: "In 169 B. C. Antioch Epiphany discovered a man who was kept in the Jewish temple for a sacrifice."[29] This is one more example that proves Jehovah's monstrous crimes. Wee see that God Jehovah not only received human sacrifices, but he also categorically ordered to make them. Will anyone who represents a genus of Homo sapiens contend that it is an allegory after all those examples of God's bloody deeds. Well, those mammals that are of another genus can express their disbelief, and they have a reason not to believe us. They have full rights to think that all those stories are just allegory and wait with joy and happiness for the Last Judgment when "kind and merciful" God Jehovah grills some more billions of victims in the fierce fire of his rage.

It is interesting to note that both prayers and sacrifices made by Jewish priests are magic actions which the Orthodox church rejects, but, nevertheless use while practice its cults and rituals. As an example, we can take the textbook of *Ancient Highest Magic* and compare its instructions with those of Jewish rabbis: "There are propitiatory and purifying sacrifices. In the first case, a ram or a calf is sacrificed, in the second—a goat. To make a sacrifice fire is set on the altar. A magician who slaughters a sacrifice animal blesses the fire. At first, intestines and fat are burned; then the rest of meat is cut into pieces."[30]

The formula of spell or initiation sounds like this: "Oh, Adonai, Iehve, Zebaot, oh, the most high God, the creator of the sky and the earth, of the four elements and the highest spirits, I conjure you to consecrate this..... (the thing is named) for the sake of your power and mercy..."[31]

It can be noticed quite obviously that a magician, applying to God (or probably to a Devil), use the names of Adonai, Iehve, Zebaot that are the names of the well-known God Jehovah. Adonai (or Shechina) is the name of one of the members of dyad Malcut-Shechina, the tenth sephirot of Cabbala—Jewish magic book. Later the name Adonai was replaced by the tetragrammaton [YHVH]—Jehovah. In Hebrew, we have letters YHVH for God's name. The word Adonai has been changed by this name. In English, we sometimes give him the name Jehovah. Iehve is the short name of Jehovah, Zebaot, as you probably guess, is the well-known Sovereign God.

In the rituals of black magic, sacrifices of infants were made, and although those rituals were a bit different from those of human sacrifices to God Jehovah, they are identical in essence. Moreover, modern worshippers of bloody magic rituals call for an evil spirit that, as we will show later, comes out from Jewish tribal God Jehovah. Such a ritual is called "the black mess" and is carried out as following: "Magicians and adepts of Black Magic wishing to get aid and favor of Evil spirit resorted to so-called "black mess". The black mess was a parody of liturgy and was carried out at medieval times. Usually it was performed by a priest-apostate. As an altar, they used the belly of a naked woman. The chalice with Eucharist was placed between her breasts or legs. During the black mess, an infant was brought to altar, killed by a priest, and his blood was poured out to the chalice. Both the priest and the woman-altar drank from it and then they copulated."[32]

When devoted Christians read about such rituals, they are unspeakably shocked and they threaten those apostates with the lake burning with fire and sulfur. But, reading about human sacrifices to the Biblical God Jehovah, they, for some reason, are not shocked, and even prove such his actions, rejoicing about the fact that Jewish priests very often gave their God such an unspeakable and exquisite pleasure to regale himself with delicate children's meat, to taste soft children's brains and to smell aromatic fragrance of burning human flesh.

1. 6. Mythical Epos: from Polytheism to Monotheism

Now we have to trace the further development of myth in order to notice the moment of transformation of its polytheistic form into monotheistic one, otherwise we shall not be able to understand why the latter has replaced all the other myths and, having become a matrix, gained such a tremendous power over human hearts and souls.

As we stated above, myth had a great influence on a human conscience; moreover, human thinking was mythological at ancient times. Then, with the course of time, myth became a story unwrapped on the axis of time and as a mythical epos. It gained great development in ancient Greece and Rome.

The influence of myth over human conscience decreased, giving place to poetry, drama, science and fine arts, especially after the appearance of philosophical schools in Greece. Myth remained mainly as a source of artistic images, and, though Greek and Roman religions were a continuation of mythical epos, they did not have such an influence as they have in ancient Greece before Gomer. The whole galaxy of great poets and philosophers who gave the beginning to the new era in literature and art, appeared in V century B. C. Having been liberated from bondages of religion of myth, human genius soared to unprecedented heights and gave the world unsurpassed creations of Plato, Aristotle, Eschil, Sophokl, Euripi, Goracius and other great Greek and Roman poets and philosophers.

Almost at the same time, in V-VI centuries B. C., several remarkable persons, known as prophets, appeared in Judea. It was the time of great suffering of the Jewish people, especially after disintegration on two kingdoms—Israel and Judea. Prophets carried "the word of God" which he himself gave to the people. These were the words of rage and indignation because the people of Israel became corrupted, fell into deadly sin of idolatry and turned away from God. That is why God punishes his people sending Persians and Assyrians in order to destroy Jerusalem and capture Jews.

The activity of prophets was aimed to bring the Jewish people to reason and return them to the Biblical teaching of monotheism. "Foremost of these Jewish ideas was this: that their God was invisible and remote. An invisible God in a temple not made with hands, a Lord of Righteousness throughout the earth. All other people had national gods embodied in images that lived in temples. If the image was smashed and the temple raised, then that present god died out. But this was a new idea, this God of the Jews in the Heavens, high above priests and sacrifices. And this God of Abraham, the Jews believed, had chosen them to be his peculiar people, to restore Jerusalem and make it the capital of Righteousness in the world."[33]

It was the messianic idea, which was turned then into the idea of "salvation." It was the very idea that, having been embodied in Christianity, has ruined the genius of the ancient world and plunged Europe into the bloody whirl of religious obscurantism which devoured thousands of millions human lives in its dark depths.

But it seems quite strange that wild, barbarous tribes could have an idea of monotheism, for they lived in a company of tribes and nations, the myths of which were inhabited with many gods and goddesses. And the Jewish people themselves worshiped Mesopotamic gods and goddesses and made sacrifices to them up to the very Babylon captivity. Of course, among the Jews, there were those who worshiped God Jehovah, but it was rather an exception than a rule.

This interesting fact is impossible to understand if we take into account only Mesopotamic influence. But we must remember that there was Egypt, where circa XIV-XIII centuries B. C. Moses, the Jewish citizen, served at the pharaoh's court. It was that very Moses who, having talked to God Jehovah on the mount of Sinai, said: "Hear, the people of Israel! God is One!" From where did Moses take that progressive for that time idea? Freud, S answers this question: "It turned out, contrary to everything, to be possible that **the religion, taught by Moses to the Jewish people, was, nevertheless, his own religion; one of Egyptian believes, though not all-Egyptian.**"[34]

The fact is that in 1375 B. C. a young and very active pharaoh ascended to the Egyptian throne. He called himself Amenhotep (IV).

By that time thanks to the gains of Thotmes III, Egypt had become an empire. New international position was inevitably reflected on the pharaohs' world outlook. Freud, S. says: "This imperialism has been reflected in religion as universalism and monotheism. As the tutelage of a pharaoh covered in edition to Egypt Nubian and Syria, the deity had also to reject its national limitations and, like a pharaoh was the unlimited ruler of the known world, the new Egyptian deity had to get universal features."[35]

The origin of Egyptian monotheism can be found in the teaching of priests of the solar temple in Ohn (Heliopolis). From ancient times, priests developed the idea of one universal God. The worship of one God has already gained a new scope during the reign of Amenhotep III, the father and predecessor of Amenhotep IV. The old name of Aton or Atum has been evoked from oblivion and, in that belief, the young pharaoh has found the very religious movement that he had to restore and make it a state religion.

This ruler has intended to impose to Egyptians a new religion which contradicted to all their traditions and habits. As Freud, S says: **It was a strict monotheism, the first experience of this sort in the world history, and together with belief in one universal God there sprang up the religious intolerance, which was alien both to the entire previous history and to the big segment of subsequent antiquity**."[36]

The new world outlook needed a thorough change of the entire traditional religious system of Egypt and the new pharaoh began, brutally and without ceremony, to break the old ideology. Temples were closed, public worships were banned, and temple belongings were confiscated. Pharaoh's eagerness was so great that he ordered to examine all the monuments and erased the word "god" if it was written in the plural. He also changed his mane, the part of which was now rejected name of Amon. Instead of Amenhotep, he began to call himself Echnaton.

Any religious rites and mystical and magic actions were forbidden, and a death penalty was imposed for infringement of the interdiction. It is natural that all the ideas connected to Osiris, the god of dead and the extraterrestrial world, of which continuation nobody cared so carefully as Egyptians, were etched with exasperation from national memory.

It is necessary to note a very important fact that the old Jewish religion has also completely disowned the idea of immortality and of the other world. One cannot find even a mentioning of an opportunity of continuation of existence after death. "All go unto one place; all are of the dust, and all turn to dust again."[37] That is why this wise man advised: "Whatsoever thy hand findeth to do, do it with thy might; for there is no work, nor device, nor knowledge, nor wisdom, in the grave, whither thou goest."[38]

Judaism is the religion of the law, and this law is relentless and works only during human life. Accordingly, only during one's life one receives either reward for his good deeds or punishment for sins. Christianity, having cancelled the primacy of the law and recognized the primacy of faith. Thus, on the one hand, it has roughly broken God Jehovah's commandments. On the other hand, it promoted, by this infringement, the expansion of Christianity, for the very idea of "salvation"was regarded as the necessary precondition for achievement of eternal life. It has become that "opium for people" which has ensured pathological dependence of them on a church.

This fact of renunciation of Jewish religion from the idea of immortality is interesting because the later experience has shown a successful combination of faith in the extraterrestrial world and monotheism in religion which is absolutely impossible in the space both of the Old Testament and of orthodox Judaism in its Sadduces variant.

Unexplainable in the light of Mesopotamic influence, which did not provide such an attitude to a question on immortality, the fact of its denying in Judaism becomes clear in the light of influence of the Egyptian religious ideology of the solar god Aton, the world outlook of which Moses has acquired, being the manager at the court of the pharaoh-reformer.

Echnaton's reign was short. It lasted only 17 years. Soon after his death, the new religion was abolished, and the memory about the heretic ruler was etched from the consciousness of people. With Echnaton's death, the entire system of power in Egypt has been changed. Moses as the manager of the pharaoh-heretic did not fit to the new system any more, and, being removed from the court, was even persecuted and had to escape from Egypt. Having understood that it is impossible to live like that, Moses concluded that he had to become a "savior" of the Israeli people who were severely oppressed by the authorities of a new pharaoh and craved for such a "savior."

Moses decided to become their leader and, having given them the religion of the solar God Aton, established an empire in which he could become king and a chief priest. But the Jews, who had been brought up in a spirit of polytheism and idolatry, rejected a new religion and killed Moses. The idea of monotheism was kept only due to oral tradition, which, having saved it in a national memory, has managed to convey it to the time of prophets and reformers of Judaic religion.

The prophets have included it in the historical epos of the Jewish people and united it with the myth about Jewish tribal God Jehovah (Iahve). A Russian philosopher Vladimir Solov'jov says: "From this side, the example of the Jewish prophets, the greatest patriots and, at the same time, the greatest representatives of universalism, is in a maximum degree instructive for us, for it specifies that if true patriotism is necessary free from national exclusiveness and egoism, so together with this and by this the true, common to all mankind ideas, true universalism in order to be something to have the real power and positive contents, should be necessary either an expansion or universalisation of a positive national idea, instead of empty and indifferent cosmopolitism. Thus, in a prophetical consciousness, a subjective, personal element of Old Testament Jahve (existing) has been united for the first time with the objective idea of universal divine personality."[39]

The problem is that this universal divine personality has totally lost its universality just after it was squeezed in narrow frameworks of religions, each of them has declared the universal right on possession of the God's glory and of a rank "God's people."

Thus, we see that the faith in one uniform universal God is strictly a confessional one nowadays. According to the essence of the idea of a uniform and universal God, he should be God of all mankind and everyone should be equal before him. But in reality, each religion formally recognizes this fact, nevertheless considers that only it has both the exclusive right to be "the God's people" and to preach the doctrine about God in the interpretation of only this confession. If the eschatological Christian myth asserts that before the Last Judgment the Gospel should be taught to all peoples of the world and only after that a long awaited end of all things will come, each Christian church or a sect believes that it should be taught only in interpretation of this church or a sect. And, the acceptance of this interpretation as absolutely correct is necessary, but still not a sufficient condition of "salvation." For the total sufficiency, the faith in Jesus Christ is necessary, but in a strictly confessional interpretation. Any of these churches or sects considers all the other interpretations to be wrong and consequently unacceptable for "salvation." Jehovah Witnesses, for example, assert that **"all the opponents of God's Kingdom, and also those who is a part of this malicious system of Satan, will be destroyed**. Only those who are utterly devoted to Jehovah will stay alive."[40] And as only Jehovah's witnesses are utterly devoted to him, so only they will stay alive. In reality, only Jews who observe the law given to them by their God are devoted to him. All other churches and sects which are only camp followers of the Jewish God roughly break the law, and consequently do not have the right both to call themselves "the God's people" and even to live because Jehovah said about such camp followers: "that soul shall be cut off from his people." If you ask an orthodox priest about a nation that is worthy to be "the God's people," he will tell you that such honor can be received only by the orthodox Christians, and he will name Jews, Jehovah Witnesses and all the others as the opponents of God's kingdom.

But all of them forget for some reason that Jesus Christ has told the following: "Wherever two men get together in my name, I will be with them there." And it was all the same for him in what interpretation his name would be mentioned. If only they got together, if only they remembered that the "savior" has given his life on a cross not just in order we to divide his "body" and his "blood" among themselves. Jesus wanted us get together in his name and pray to God who is one for everybody and who are not interested either in our interpretations, or in our enmity and religious intolerance. The most important is our love to Him as well as to other person, who is a God's spark and, therefore, is worthy of love and respect.

But such a love turns out to be very much like unidirectional. It turns out that Jehovah loves only those who are utterly devoted to him, and only them he will save on the day of the Last Judgment. All the others should be destroyed by him. Where does such a crazy idea come from? What fevered imagination could give birth to such a "pearl" of human wisdom? It is hardly possible that Jehovah Witnesses were able to rise up to such unachievable heights of a cultural progress. Certainly, they could not. They have found such a "pearl" in the Bible. And this fact of religious intolerance existing in Christianity is one of its most surprising features.

Bertran Russel says: "I think this intolerance spang up from the Jewish belief in God's righteousness and exclusiveness. I do not know why did the Jews need those strange believes. Probably, they have appeared during captivity, as a reaction to attempt to assimilate the Jews in the structure of outlandish population. But anyway, the Jews, and in particular prophets, were the first to emphasize the importance of personal righteousness and stated the idea that it was vice to show tolerance to any religion, except for their own. **Both these ideas have rendered extremely pernicious influence on the history of the East.**"[41]

This is in the Bible that God Jehovah says: "He that sacrificeth unto any god, save unto the Lord only, he shall be utterly destroyed."[42] That is to say, in order to have the right to live in the space of the Bible, one would be a Jew, or he would be exterminated, the third is not given, for the man "shalt worship no other god: for the Lord, whose name is Jealous, is a jealous God."[43]

Among other things, Jews were forbidden even to communicate with foreigners. "Take heed to thyself,—the Lord says,—lest thou make a covenant with the inhabitants of the land whither thou goest, lest it be for a snare in the midst of thee."[44]

And, as the inhabitants of the land of Canaan did not want to accept Jewish religion, they were ruthlessly killed by Jews who carried out word for word all the commandments of "kind and merciful" God Jehovah. In the Bible, the very picturesque stories are given which, in full detail, show as "the God's people" out of the great love for his neighbor, severely killed both men, and women, youths and infants, and even camels and donkeys, in order that they not become a snare for them.

The Jews did not have another way out. Either they had to destroy infidels, or they had to be destroyed by Jehovah; for they have broken his commandment of "love and mercy" which says: "Now go and smite Amalek, and utterly destroy all that they have, and spare them not; but **slay both man and woman, infant and suckling, ox and sheep, camel and ass**."[45]. It is the formula of genocide of the purest water. And, having armed with this formula, fathers of church, crusaders, inquisition founders, tyrants of black, brown and red stripes, have begun mass destruction of infidels, heretics and race defective elements. But they, of course, are out of blame. They have put it on the evil one, on a serpent, on the Devil or on whoever they invented to hide their bloody crimes.

That is why, due to the extremely "progressive and human" idea of monotheism which has totally changed human consciousness by turning it upside down, we have now "the ideal and human world," "an ideal and human society." This society, in its fierce struggle with the "enemy" for the sake of "salvation" of humbled and offended God's children, severe and brutally destroys billions of innocent people and with pleasure and hope expects the Last Judgment in order to destroy still as much.

And now, let us recollect our scale of cultural universal criteria and try to estimate by its means the monotheism with its religious intolerance and genocide. It is quite clear that its info-energy charge will be extremely destructive. If one manages to drum this "progressive and human" concept into another one's head by promising him a paradise life on Heavens at once after destruction of one or another thousand of "infidels," one will tie grenades round oneself and rush into a crowd of those "infidels." One can even high-jack an airplane and ram a skyscraper with thousands of peaceful people who do not know that they have been ordered to be killed more than two thousand years ago when Biblical God Jehovah uttered unforgettable advises of how to treat the one, who, for one or another reason, does not want to be a Jew. These commandments were picked up by grateful progeny, who began to call themselves as Christians and Moslems. They hate all God's enemies with fierce hatred, and destroy thousands and millions of them, thus promoting the approaching of the kingdom of "utmost justice."

And here we must take into account and remember very well that in the pre-Christian era there was neither religious intolerance nor genocide of those kinds which we now have. Pre-Christian, "barbarous" world was friendly to people practicing different religions. If we compare, as an example, the attitude of pagan Indian king Ashoca (III century B. C.) to this question, and that of Christian Saint Augustine, who carried out the commandments of "love and mercy" in III century A. D., we shall see surprising things.

The ancient Hindu king Ashoca says, for example: "Pijadasi, the king beloved by gods wishes that ascetics **of all creeds** could live everywhere. All these ascetics equally preach commandments, which people would apply to their life, and use for cleanliness of their souls. But people have different opinions and different propensities."[46]

And here we have what the Saint Augustine said after his baptizing when the God's spirit blessed him by its sacred whiff and put words worthy of a real Christian in his lips: "The depth of your words are amazing! Their appearance! Look! They are before us, they invite the little ones! And, nevertheless, there is amazing depth in them, oh, my Lord, amazing depth! **You—contemptible beasts, you—pagans and sinners, you—God's enemies! Oh! How much I hate you! Oh Lord, If you only kill all of them with your double-edged sword just not to let them be His foes; for I want so much all of them to be killed**."[47]

Are they not surprising words? How much "kindness." how much "human warmth" and "mercy" are in them? If we estimate these statements on our scale of cultural universal criteria, we shall see that the statement of the barbarous pagan king Ashoca is on its uppermost mark, expressing by itself an example of universal love and acceptance of the man as they actually are, regardless of both their skin colour and their creed. The statement of the Christian Saint Augustine will fall down to the lowermost mark since it expresses by itself an extreme degree of religious intolerance burdened with a very powerful genocidal impulse which tells about the author's sadistic inclinations and of his considering himself to be capable to determine the destinies of the world.

Thus, we have shown that the concept of monotheism as it was accepted in the western world had been developed from the ideas of Jews about uniform tribal God Jehovah who chose them to be "the God's people" and doomed other people to destruction if they did not want to accept Jewish religion. To adopt such destructive ideas was in reality totally absurd and an inhuman mistake. Thanks to these very ideas, the religious intolerance, genocide, wars, revolutions and terrorism were spread all over the world and this bloody expansion resulted in the death of millions of human sons and daughters.

Humankind, as it turned out, was not ready to apprehend the concept of monotheism in its absolute, philosophical meaning, namely, as the concept of **uniform God for the uniform people of the planet Earth**. Instead, mankind, being divided into countries and nations because of its heterogeneity and social-cultural distinctions, has began to use the idea of uniform God in its narrow, confessional meaning which actually brought the world to the state of enmity and division.

At last, we have traced a long development of religious ideas beginning from a ritual murder of the forefather of primitive herd, through polytheism and monotheism, up to ritual murders of thousands and millions of innocent people represented as the result of struggle with an omnipresent enemy. The final result of that struggle is "salvation" of human souls or the triumph of "utmost justice."

In the next chapter, we shall start to investigate the very religious myths in order to convince ourselves once again that everything told by us above is not a fruit of our bad imagination, but the pure truth which does not need to be proved because it expresses itself not in empty, pointless phrase-mongering or in "universalization of positive national idea," but in the precise and relentless language of facts which speak for themselves.

CHAPTER 2.

JUDAIC MYTH

"The Bible is the eternal constellation of stars shining in the sky above us, while we move in a worldly life, contemplating them all in invariability but also in a new position to us."

S. Bulgacov

2. 1. The Bible As It Is

While discussing the Jewish myth we need first of all to notice that the Jewish people, in spite of its paucity and insignificance, have rendered such a great influence on the development of mankind that no other great nation had ever done. Created by The Bible, it was the very nutrient medium that gave birth to the huge tree of Christianity that spread its roots all over the world and blessed with its crown many people in each corner of our planet.

However, "According to the law of great works, the creator, having given existence to something else, breathes as though his last. Having grafted his life in its total integrity to the one who will continue it, the initiator is changed into a dry twig, a powerless creature. However, very seldom this verdict of the nature is executed immediately. The plant, which produced a flower, does not agree to die because of that. The world is full of such walking skeletons that have survived the sentence uttered over them. The Judaism is among them. **In a history, there is no more striking sight as this existence of the whole nation, which during almost thousand years has lost the feeling of fact, has not written even one page, suitable for reading, has not impart any information that would be acceptable**. No wander that, having lived like that during centuries beyond free atmosphere of mankind, in a basement, I even dare to say, in the state of a partial madness, it comes out, pale, amazed, dazzled with light."[48]

But what flower has produced the Jewish people? What constellation of stars has already been illuminating our life for almost three thousand years? And at last, why did the Jewish people not write even a page suitable for reading during those three thousand years? The matter is that they borrowed many things from neighboring nations. As Cosidovski, S asserts: "It is quite enough to note here as an example that the **ten commandments and the Moses' laws were developed under the influence of Mesopotamic legislation. That the story about genesis, as well as the story about flood and some other events, has been borrowed from the Babylon mythology. That even the entire eschatology of prophets (for example, the pictures of the Last Judgment, of the other world, of the heavens and hell, of angels and Satan) has been borrowed from the alien sources**. That is to say, all the Christians religious concepts are several centuries older than the Bible itself."[49]

It appears that the Bible, which during many centuries was considered as original creation of ancient Jews who have written it down from God's words, ascends by its roots to Mesopotamic tradition. Many details and even whole legends are borrowed from a rich treasury of Sumeric myths and legends, and the concept of monotheism as we already have shown above is an Egyptian idea about the solar god Aton, which was imposed to the Jews by Moses. It appears that Moses did not write Thora—the first five books of the Bible—other people wrote it much later. It appears that we—Christians—use pagan myths and consider their authors to be atheists, who are not worthy of eternal life.

Having adopted their pagan myths, we ourselves became pagans and condemned them to eternal torment in a lake burning with fire and sulfur. Is it good or bad if we estimate it from a point of view of humanity? It is probably very bad. But it is not the worst, for we did not know that the entire Bible consists of pagan myths.

And the most terrible thing is that the Biblical God Jehovah, in whom we trust, is the pagan God too. He is not any better than Baal or Moloch who was worshipped by pagans. They made sacrifices to their gods, and we made sacrifice to our Biblical God; moreover, human sacrifices. The statement is, certainly, and completely blasphemous, but quite true as we have proven it in the previous chapter. Here it is necessary to note that monotheism, originally practiced by Jews, most likely had completely other forms. But then it was distorted and substituted with a cult of malicious and cruel tribal God Jahve (Jehovah), whom we perceive as "kind and merciful universal solar God, who has "come" to Jews together with Moses from Egypt.

And we find the conformation of our deductions in the book of Douglas Reed, who has written the most impressing and shocking description of Jewish history. He tells: "We have already spoken about the origin of idea of uniform God, though it is quite possible that Egyptians had adopted it from other peoples. Both the figure of Moses and his Law were borrowed from an already existing material. A story about Moses, who had been found in reeds, is an obvious retelling of a much more ancient legend about a Babylonian king Sargon the Older who lived one or two thousand years before Moses. Moses' commandments are very similar to ancient codes of laws of Egyptians, Babylonians and Assyrians. Ancient Israelites followed to ideas of the time and were obviously close to acceptance of universal religion when they were absorbed by history.

To that time, Levites have turned this process back similarly to display of film in the opposite direction, from the end to the beginning. Dominating in Judea and creating their law, Levites also used the legends of other peoples, **but they have given them the form, suitable to their purpose**. Having begun with the uniform fair God for all people, they have transformed him in a tribal, bargaining Jehovah, promising land, riches, blood and power in exchange for sacrificial ritual, which should be made in a place, ostensibly specified by him, in a certain country.

Thus, by identifying Judaism with the doctrine of self-separation, racial hatred and bloodshed under a religious flag and revenge, Levites have generated a constant contrast to all universal religions.

Studying the Old Testament, one can trace the moment of the distortion of its contents. In the beginning Moses is the bearer of moral laws and good-neighborhood, but **in the end he is the murderer and racist. Moral commandments turned into exact antithesis between the Book of Exodus and the Book of Numbers. The character of God changes too. He starts with the orders "you shall not kill" and "do not wish either the wife of your neighbor, or his belongings" and finishes with the order to exterminate the neighboring people, leaving alive only virgins.**

Thus, nomadic priests who ruled for a long time over the Jewish tribe could, by restoring a cult of bloodthirsty tribal deity and racial exclusiveness, avert the small captured people from

the incipient of faith in the uniform God in order to send those who have accepted this faith in future centuries, having entrusted them with the mission of destruction."[50]

In this chapter, we shall discuss Judaism—the religion of the Jewish people which appeared almost three thousand years ago and became a life basis of all the Jews. But the analysis of Judaism is impossible without the analysis of the Bible; in particular, of its Old Testament, which is a holy scripture both of Jewish and Christian world.

The well-known Catholic author Daniel-Rops says about the Bible: "It is the unique book, absolute inexhaustible book of God and man."[51] And if we dare to make its historical analyses, "...we should not forget: first of all, this is God's work."[52] So let us see if it is true.

The first five books of the Old Testament make up the so-called Moses' Pentateuch. The church-synagoguical tradition attributes it to a mythical Moses, to whom God has supposedly opened the "Law" on the mount of Sinai.

Nevertheless, a Russian scientist Crivelev, I. A. asserts that "most likely, at the time to which the "historical" books of the Old Testament and the most part of the prophetical books are attributed, the Pentateuch did not exist yet, and, therefore its origin dates from the later times. It should be dated the whole millennium later than it was determined both by church and by synagogue. Moses, as the author of the Pentateuch, as well as Joshua the son of Nun as the author of the book named after his name, cannot be considered as the authors of the Torah. For example, the Pentateuch tells us a story of Moses' death and of difficulties in finding of his burial place (Deuteronomy, 34). Moses definitely could not tell such things about himself! If so, then this chapter was probably written by Joshua, the son of Nun. But how can we explain the fact that Moses is spoken about all the time in the third person and given the laudatoriest characteristics (like "he was as meek as a lamb") in the text? And, of course, it is possible to find the answer even to this question: to speak about oneself in the third person was a common thing in those days... And, nevertheless, earlier or later it is necessary to concede to evidence. Nowadays, fewer and fewer theologians assert that Moses was the author of the Pentateuch."[53]

The Dictionary of Biblical Theology also rejects a hypothesis about Moses' authorship of the Pentateuch. It asserts that they "could be developed only in a rather late epoch, already after an establishment of David's monarchy. All the early epochs—the times of patriarchs, of Moses, of Canaan conquest, of Judges and of Saul's reign—date from the period of the oral tradition."[54]

The Dutch Catechism is quite categorical on this account: "These five works (which together are called "the Law" or the "Pentateuch"), according to the tradition are attributed to Moses. It certainly does not mean that he actually has written them, and testifies only the fact that he was an outstanding figure in the basis of our legislation."[55] Thus, the Catechism does not deny the historicity of a Moses figure, but completely rejects his authorship of the Pentateuch.

Remarkable is the opinion of the Jewish theologian Cohon, S.: **"The critical research, — he says, — has destroyed the belief that the Pentateuch had been told to Moses in a supernatural way on the mount of Sinai... and also has shown it as the longstanding product of the Israeli national folk art**... The portrayal of Moses that we find in the Pentateuch is rather a portrayal of ideal interpretation, than that of a historical figure... In the light of historical and comparative research of religion, the Moses' uniqueness and Supreme dignity have lost their dogmatic meaning."[56]

Except for the Pentateuch, there are more than thirty other books that have been included in the Canonic Bible. Usually they are divided by theologians into two groups: historical books and scriptures. In Judaism, this division has found its expression in the fact that all the Old Testament is called the Thanach. Three consonants in this word mean Thora (the Pentateuch), Nebim (prophets) and Chsubim (scriptures). In the Christian literature the books of prophets are included in a heading "historical."

If we approach more precisely to classification of the Old Testament books, we should separate "historical" books from "prophetical" ones; for in the Old Testament there are a number of books which have much greater historiographic importance than the others. They are the book of Judges, two books of Samuel, two books of Chronicles, the book of Ezra and the book of Nehemiah. As to the prophets, they are divided ccording to a tradition on large and small ones. To the first ones belong Isaiah, Jeremiah, Ezekiel and Daniel; to the second ones belong Hosea, Joel, Amos, Obadiah etc.

As a whole, the Bible represents by itself the assembly of different fragments, texts and books. Nevertheless, Christian and Jewish ideologists upload the idea of unity of the Bible as being the one integral work saturated by common ideas.

On this occasion the Catholic Dictionary of Biblical theology says: "Though the Bible consists of many separate books, the Biblical message has a certain deep unity."[57] This unity is announced at the same time to be one of a specification of faith. However, how is it possible to prove the statement of Bible unity while it is a completely shapeless conglomerate of very different elements? The authors of the dictionary recognize that it is impossible. They assert that "the unity of the Bible gained a foothold with a complete reliability only by faith, and only faith determines its borders... The criterion is determined here only by faith."[58]

But faith, as we have stated above, can not be a criterion of truth since it is the tool of the ideological system which it uses to make people believe in everything the system imposes to them to achieve complete control over their minds. Thus, the faith in a divine origin and the infallibility of the Bible, being inculcated in a human consciousness by religious ideological system, becomes a matrix which programs the behaviour of people who practice this religion.

In this connection it is worthwhile to recollect the conclusion of the Ecumenical working group of evangelists (Lutheran) and Catholic theologians which were in session in April, 1979, in Germany.

The basic point of issue was a question of the church unity. The Gospel as a part of the Bible as well as the whole Bible was recognized as the base of such a unity. The document testifies: "The church unity can be only the unity in the Gospel. The Bible, as a whole, is norma normans non normata. The given Latin formula means that the Bible is the norm which set norms, but can not be normed. **It means, that the Bible is the last and final instance of truth which is not dependent on the decision of any social institute, and neither reason nor science can norm it; nevertheless, the rest that happen both in life and in human spirit, as well as in theology can be called normans normata, that means: norming and normed. Normed by whom? By the Bible, as being the Supreme authority, of course.**"[59] Thus, the above-stated group of theologians has recognized the Bible as a matrix, i. e. the norm which set norms, but can not be normed.

So, what the Bible actually is and who wrote it? To begin with, let us have a brief look at its contents. The book of Genesis, chapter 1, tells us the story of creation of the Earth within six days by *gods*, it being known that humans (man and woman) were created on the sixth day. Having opened the second chapter, we find out with a great surprise that it tells again about creation of the world, but here this significant act is performed by only one person, whose name is the Lord God. It being known that at first he created a man. Then, having narcotized him, the Lord God performed a small operation and took out man's rib; from which he created a woman.

Having opened the second chapter of the book of Exodus, we read an exciting story about the birth and further adventures of Moses. But, having reached chapter 6, we come in a great confusion because we read the same story again in it. It looks as if the author has completely forgotten that in the second chapter he had already spoken about it in a completely different way. How is it possible that the omniscient and almighty Lord God could forget something? If the Lord God is really omniscient and almighty, we have to admit that there were those who compiled the books of the Old Testament, and, having copied a pair of pages, totally forgot, what they had written several pages before.

Crivelev, I. A. says on this occasion: "When one reads the Old Testament in Russian synodal translation, one pays attention to the fact that in one case it is spoken about God, in the other—about Lord, in the third, these names are connected together in the formula the Lord God. In other language translations it looks like that: in German—Gott and Herr Gott; in English—God and Lord; in French—Dieu and L'eternel (Eternal); in Spanish—Dios and Senor. But in Hebrew (the original language of the Old Testament) we find something different. There, in the first chapter of the book of Genesis, it tells about Elohim. Beginning from the fourth verse of the second chapter, there appears a name Jahve, then, almost through all the Old Testament, sometimes the first name is mentioned, sometimes the second, sometimes both at the same time. The conclusion made from this fact is that there are two different sources connected in one: the author of one of them was the admirer of the gods Elochim, the author of another one was the worshiper of one of those Elohim whose name was Jahve.

In the Old Testament, the special narration, independent from the others but mixed with it in the text, is connected with one or another name of God. If we divide the texts connected with Jahve and Elohim, we will have two separate narrations, each of them being consecutive and whole.

Obviously, in the beginning there had been parallel texts that were then connected; in some cases it was made intelligently and coherently, and in others—unreasonably and mechanically, which resulted in the contradictions in the contents. It is noticeable there where the parallel texts are connected not by separate verses and their fragments, but by whole chapters."[60]

Most likely the real story was as follows: When the Solomon's empire was broken up, there began the struggle between two Jewish states. It was very important for Judea to illuminate Jewish history in the spirit which would glorify the tribe of Judah, for it played the main role in a southern empire. To realize this political-ideological need, the document, illuminating a history of the world and a role of the elected people with a stress on the special importance of the tribe of Judah and its kings in it, has been written down by temple writers under the management of priests or even under their dictation.

The god of the tribe had his own name, Jahve, and the document has received in bibliography the name Jahvist. It is designated with a literary symbol J, the initial letter of a name Jahve. In some decades in a counterbalance to this document, another Jewish state, Israel, has created its own religious and historical document. As the matter concerns the deeds of Elohim, but not Jahve in it, it is called Elohist in historiography of the Bible and is designated by a symbol E, the initial letter of a word Elohim.

In the middle of XIX century, German biblicist Gupfeld, G. divided this source into two: the first was left with the former dating, the second (Elohist) was dated to much later time, namely to the period of the Babylon captivity and even after it (VI-V b. c.). In bibliography it is called the Code of Priests, or P (from a German word Priestercodex).

The comparison of Jahvist with Elohist shows not only difference in names of gods, but also in a general orientation of both texts. Jahve was considered as tribal God of Judah; therefore, in documents expressing ideology of the tribe of Judah, they avoided to name God with this name and instead they use the ancient name Elohim, meaning not one God, but gods (plural). And even by its contents Elohist differs from Jahvist: an especially important role was played by Josef. He was considered to be an ancestor of North-Israeli tribe of Ephraim and Manassas, and the basic events occur at Betel, Sihem and other cities located in the north.

In the Babylon captivity the priests of the Jerusalem temple tried to fix the basis of religion of tribal God Jahve and, in particular, the schedule and the rules of a temple cult and all its rituals. Obviously, the record of this new document began during captivity; it is possible that it was completed after captivity. Such is the history of the Code of Priests, designated by a symbol P. Circa 444 b. c. The new manuscript was delivered in Jerusalem by the priest Ezra and proclaimed there before the large crowd of people.

The text of the Priest code can now be found in different books: almost all of the book of Leviticus, a large part of the book of Numbers, and significant parts of the books of Genesis and Exodus are the elements of the Priest code.

It is interesting to note one detail concerning the figure of God in the Priest code. He is called Elohim in it, but thus the author or the authors do not put in this term the meaning "gods" and consider it, probably, as a name in singular.

During separate existence of Judea and Israel there appeared also some other documents which were included in the text of the Old Testament. One of them is the book of Amos which appeared in the middle of VIII b. c. It became the first prophetical book of that time. The second prophetical book of Hosea appeared circa 735 b. c.

The content of those books is identical in general. They are saturated with the feeling of extreme anxiety and excitement concerning circumstances experienced by Israel. To the time of their appearance, the threatening danger connected with aggressive aspirations of Assyria had already been designated. On the other hand, class contradictions inside the Israeli people, abuse of power, oppression of deprived and defenseless, and corruptibility of the system of justice became evident more and more.

In such a situation it was necessary to give a mining to a doubtful Jahve's attitude towards his chosen people, as well to the fact that it was the very God who led his people along the ways of history. The concept, according to which all the troubles of Israel were presented as the punishment imposed by Jahve on his chosen people, was worked out. The concept assumed further and heavier punishments, the result of which would be the loss of independence of Israel and another captivity. At the end, however, Jahve will show mercy towards his people, forgive them all their sins and reward with a former privileged position.

This concept is the base of all the subsequent books of prophets. It is crowned with the doctrine of God's messenger-messiah ("anointed sovereign") who will come in a certain time to execute the task assigned to him. He will head the people of Israel and lead it to a final victory above all its oppressors.

Only in such a way have Jews imagined their messiah. And it was the very Israeli people (not Russian, not German, not American), who could expect the advent of messiah. Christianity has borrowed this idea from Jews and adjusted it to the doctrine about Jesus Christ as God's "anointed sovereign" or a "sacrificial lamb." They believed that one day he will come in order to wash all our sins with his blood.

In the meantime the real historical events went on under the scenario, depicted by prophets; not because of their awareness of Jahve's intentions, but due to the sober analyses of international political situation and probable prospects of its development.

2. 2. How God Created the World and Then Nearly Destroyed It

First of all, we should note that the Judaic myth, as well as the Greek one, is material, at least, at an initial stage of its development. It begins with the creation of the world performed by God and his Spirit which "moved upon the face of the waters." But further we find out that God was not alone there, that the creation was a collective act: "And God said, **Let us make man in our image, after our likeness**: and let them have dominion over the fish of the sea, and over the fowl of the air, and over the cattle, and over all the earth, and over every creeping thing that creepeth upon the earth."[61]

That is what they have made: "And the Lord God formed man of the dust of the ground, and breathed into his nostrils the breath of life; and man became a living soul."[62] Then Elohim made a small operation on the first man, removed one of his ribs, and created a woman.

As we know, the names of the first human beings were Adam and Eva. They lived not somewhere on the heavens, but in Eden, the beautiful garden which was situated somewhere in the east and was quite material. The trees in that garden were also quite material; only the tree of the knowledge of good and evil was a forbidden one. God did not permit eating fruits off that tree, for he was afraid that the first people would know good and evil and would become as powerful as gods. Moreover, God said that exactly in the day when they eat those fruits, they would die. It turned out that God deceived the first humans. They did not die, but "the eyes of them both were opened, and they knew that they were naked; and they sewed fig leaves together, and made themselves aprons."[63]

And it was a serpent that opened the eyes of the first people. Later it would be called Satan, an enemy, the Devil, and he would be accused of all the troubles of the world. Certainly, the Eden serpent had nothing to do either with Satan or with the Devil, not to mention an enemy. It was just a serpent, a snake—one of the animals that had been created by God: "The serpent was more subtil than any beast of the field which the Lord God had made."[64] Satan, as it will be then found out from the book of Job, was one of the God's sons: "Now there was a day when the sons of God came to present themselves before the Lord, **and Satan came also among them**."[65] As for the Devil, nobody knows where he came from, for in the list of beings created by God, he is not mentioned at all. And the enemy (the evil one, the evil spirit) is, strange as it may seem, one of God's spirits: "And it came to pass on the morrow, that **the evil spirit from God** came upon Saul, and he prophesied ("raved" in the Russian translation) in the midst of the house."[66] It is strange, but in the Gospel, Jesus Christ drives out evil spirits from the possessed, and those evil spirits came from Devil. Hence, the question arises: isn't it possible that God Jehovah and the Devil are the same personality? You see, from God's evil spirit, Saul raved precisely the same way as those possessed whom Jesus had healed. It means that a church has presented God in a pared-down shape. Hence, "everything a synagogue and a church teaches us about is a product of creative work of both Jewish rabbis and Christian writers of the first centuries."[67] It is not a God's revelation, as we can see.

Both the serpent and human beings have been punished for their deadly sin. The serpent was sentenced to "go upon its belly and eat dust all the days of its life." Adam and Eva were expelled from Eden.

Their children were not distinguished with special virtues, and the end was tragic. Cain killed □bel. And it is not surprising, for with mother's milk the murderer has absorbed the knowledge of good and evil which she had received from God by tasting his forbidden fruit.

The following events are much more awful. God's sons began to enter human daughters, and they gave birth to giants. Just notice, quite material God's sons enter to quite material human daughters and give birth to quite material giants. The end of this story was also tragic. Humankind became extremely corruptive, and God had to bring down the waters of flood on the earth and to drown all his sons together with human daughters and their children, thus to acknowledge the fact that the experiment on creation of intelligent life on the earth had failed. "And it repented the Lord that he had made man on the earth, and it grieved him at his heart."[68]

But, strange as it may seem, there was a righteous man on the earth, who "went before God." His name was Noah and he was the very man whose life God decided to spare; hoping that now, when there is a righteous man and his righteous family, everything will be different. But also this time almighty and omniscient God made a mistake. The man falls into a sin again: a mortal sin of buggery (homosexuality), which had to be severely suppressed and done away with in flows of burning sulfur.

"But where did the sin come from?"—one may ask. Curiously enough, there remained only righteous people on earth because they were Noah's descendants, who himself was righteous. How could they fall into such a sin? What does it mean? It means that almighty and omniscient God can not control the situation. The only thing he can do is to destroy everybody—men, women, old men and even infants—in the same way as it was done by the Olympic gods of Greek myth. Is it humane? Is it merciful? By no means. Then, put another negative mark to the Judaic myth.

Further narration is the story about Abraham, Isaac and Jacob. God concludes a covenant, i. e. some kind of a contract with Abraham and promises to give him uncountable posterity from his sterile wife Sarah. In return God demands the Jews to become his "chosen people," to worship only him, to serve only him and to execute the commandments given to them only by him.

2. 3. How Did the Jews Get to Egypt?

There was a time when God cared for the poor Jews and decided to make them his own "chosen people." And then God appeared before Abraham and told him: "And I will make thee exceeding fruitful, and I will make nations of thee, and kings shall come out of thee. And I will establish my covenant between me and thee and thy seed after thee in their generations for an everlasting covenant, to be a God unto thee, and to thy seed after thee. And I will give unto thee, and to thy seed after thee, the land wherein thou art a stranger, all the land of Canaan, for an everlasting possession; and I will be their God."[69] And Abraham fell down before God, and the Lord said onto him: "Thou shalt keep my covenant therefore, thou, and thy seed after thee in their generations. This is my covenant, which ye shall keep, between me and you and thy seed after thee; **Every man child among you shall be circumcised. And ye shall circumcise the flesh of your foreskin; and it shall be a token of the covenant betwixt me and you**. And he that is eight days old shall be circumcised among you, every man child in your generations, he that is born in the house, or bought with money of any stranger, which is not of thy seed. He that is born in thy house, and he that is bought with thy money, must needs be circumcised: and my covenant shall be in your flesh for an everlasting covenant. And **the uncircumcised man child whose flesh of his foreskin is not circumcised, that soul shall be cut off from his people**; he hath broken my covenant."[70]

The chosen people turned out to be strong and cruel and rather worthy of God's choice. Some of its sons could even fight against God, and not without success. Once, when Jacob was left alone, Jehovah struggled with him until the breaking of the day, and, as the Bible says: "When he saw that he prevailed not against him, he touched the hollow of his thigh; and the hollow of Jacob's thigh was out of joint, as he wrestled with him. And he said, Let me go, for the day breaketh. And he said, I will not let thee go, except thou bless me. And he said unto him, What is thy name? And he said, Jacob. And he said, Thy name shall be called no more Jacob, but Israel: for as a prince hast thou power with God and with men, and hast prevailed... And he (Jehovah) said, Let me go, for the day breaketh."[71]

Here we see a very interesting detail about Jehovah's figure. It turns out that he, like any of the evil forces, is afraid of the daylight and tries to escape to his world of darkness with the first beams of the sun.

And Jacob lived in the land where his father was a stranger, in the land of Canaan. He had a son, Josef. Jacob loved Josef more than all his children because he was the son of his old age: and he made him a coat of many colours. When his brothers saw that their father loved him more, they hated him, and could not speak peaceably to him. And Josef dreamed a dream in which he saw himself and his brothers were binding sheaves in the field, and Josef's sheave arose, and also stood upright, and the brothers' sheaves stood around and made obeisance to Josef's sheave. The brothers understood from that dream that Josef would reign over them in the future and they hated him yet more.

And his brothers went to feed their father's flock in Shechem. Josef went after his brothers and found them in Dothan. And when they saw him afar off, they conspired against him to slay him. But on seeing a company of Midianites merchantmen heading to Egypt, they decided to sell Josef to them. Then they took Josef's coat, killed a kid of the goats, and dipped the coat in the blood and brought it to their father. And Jacob took his clothes, and put sackcloth upon his loins, and mourned for his son for many days. And the Midianites sold Josef into Egypt to Potiphar, an officer of Pharaoh's, and captain of the guard.

And the Lord was with Josef, and he was a prosperous man; and he lived in the house of his master the Egyptian. Josef was made an overseer over the master's house, and everything he had was put into Josef's hands. But on malicious intention of the master's wife, who wanted Josef to lie with her, he was thrown in a prison.

After having interpreted Pharaoh's dreams about seven fat and seven skinny cows (that meant seven years of great plenty and seven years of famine), Josef was set over all the land of Egypt. And he gathered up all the food of the seven years, which were in the land of Egypt, and laid up the food in the cities. When the seven years of plenteousness that were in the land of Egypt ended, all countries came into Egypt to Josef to buy corn; because the famine was so sore in all lands.

When Jacob saw that there was corn in Egypt, he sent his sons to buy it. And Josef saw his brothers and he knew them, but they did not know him. In the end of this story Josef opened up to his brothers and ordered them to bring his father to Egypt. And Josef dwelt it Egypt, he and his father's house, and died being a hundred and ten years old: and they embalmed him, and he was put in a coffin in Egypt.[72]

2. 4. Exodus From Egypt

And the children of Israel were fruitful, and increased abundantly, and multiplied, and the land was filled with them. And there arose up a new king over Egypt, which did not know Josef. And he said to his people: "Behold, the people of the children of Israel are more and mightier than we. Come on, let us deal wisely with them; lest they multiply, and it come to pass, that, when there falleth out any war, they join also unto our enemies, and fight against us, and so get them up out of the land. Therefore they did set over them taskmasters to afflict them with their burdens. And they built for Pharaoh treasure cities, Pithom and Raamses. But the more they afflicted them, the more they multiplied and grew. And they were grieved because of the children of Israel."[73]

And here we come to the birth of Moses, the prophet and the teacher of the law, who had taken the Jews out from Egypt. The details of his birth are so interesting that we should examine them more elaborately to be convinced once again that the book recognized as "the textbook of life" all over the world is mendacious from the very beginning to the very end.

In the first chapter of the book of Exodus we read as the Egyptian king ordered Hebrew midwives to watch the delivery of Jewish women and to kill each newborn boy. But midwives were afraid of God and did not obey to king's order. "And Pharaoh charged all his people, saying, Every son that is born ye shall cast into the river, and every daughter ye shall save alive."[74]

From the second chapter we find out that a man of the house of Levi took a daughter of Levi as his wife. The woman conceived and gave birth to a son: and when she saw him that he was a goodly child, she hid him for three months. When she could no longer hide him, she took an ark of bulrushes, daubed it with slime and with pitch and put the child therein; and she laid it in the flags by the river's brink. And the daughter of Pharaoh came down to wash herself at the river; and when she saw the ark among the flags, she sent her maid to fetch it. And when she had opened it, she saw the child; and she had compassion on him, and said: "This is one of the Hebrews children." And the child grew, and was brought unto Pharaoh's daughter, and he became her son. And she called his name Moses: and she said, "Because I drew him out of the water."

Further narration gives us amazing pictures of Moses' activity on "salvation" of the Jewish people from pharaoh's oppression, but in the sixth chapter the narration unexpectedly begins to unwrap itself as though Moses had not been born yet. In verse 20, we read: "And Amram took him Jochebed his father's sister to wife; and she bare him Aaron and Moses: and the years of the life of Amram were an hundred and thirty and seven years."

And in order we do not have doubts whether this is the same Moses, in a verse 26 is specified: "These are that Aaron and Moses, to whom the Lord said, Bring out the children of Israel from the land of Egypt according to their armies."

Strange, as it may seem, but here we do not see even a word about both the wonderful rescue of Moses from water by the daughter of the Egyptian pharaoh or about his service at pharaoh, as though old Jehovah (who is considered by church as to be the author of the Bible) has lost his memory to such a degree that he has absolutely forgotten what he had written on the previous pages. Moreover, Jehovah forgets even what he has written several lines earlier. At the end of the second chapter the name of Moses' father in law is Reuel,[75] but in the beginning of the third chapter his name is already Jethro.[76] But, and it is quite obvious, God can not run into such a forgetfulness, because he is the Lord God. It means that only Jewish rabbis (who have written the Bible) could fall into such forgetfulness, and this fact proves once again the human, terrestrial origin of the Bible.

After the death of Amenhotep IV, the power in Egypt was seized by a pharaoh who returned to the old religion and began to persecute those who worshiped the God of the sun. Moses ran away from him in a desert and found a shelter with his father in law.

Once he led the flock far in the desert and came to the mountain of God, even to Horeb. And the angel of the Lord appeared unto him in a flame of a fire out of the midst of a bush: and he looked, and, behold, the bush burned with fire, and the bush was not consumed.

And when the Lord saw that he turned aside to see, God called unto him out of the midst of the bush, and said, "Moses, Moses". And he said, "Here am I". And the Lord said, "Draw not nigh hither: put off thy shoes from off thy feet, for the place whereon thou standest is holy ground". Moreover he said, "I am the God of thy father, the God of Abraham, the God of Isaac, and the God of Jacob". And Moses hid his face; for he was afraid to look upon God. And the Lord said, "I have surely seen the affliction of my people which are in Egypt, and have heard their cry by reason of their taskmasters; for I know their sorrows; and I am come down to deliver them out of the hand of the Egyptians, and to bring them up out of that land unto a good land and a large, unto a land flowing with milk and honey; unto the place of the Canaanites, and the Hittites, and the Amorites, and the Perizzites, and the Hivites, and the Jebusites".

But Moses said unto the Lord, "Behold, when I come unto the children of Israel, and shall say unto them, 'The God of your fathers hath sent me unto you; and they shall say to me, what is his name? What shall I say unto them?'" And God said unto Moses, "I AM THAT I AM (Jehovah)".

And God said moreover unto Moses: "Thus shalt thou say unto the children of Israel, The Lord God of your fathers, the God of Abraham, the God of Isaac, and the God of Jacob, hath sent me unto you: this is my name for ever, and this is my memorial unto all generations. Go, and gather the elders of Israel together, and say unto them, 'The Lord God of your fathers, the God of Abraham, of Isaac, and of Jacob, appeared unto me, saying, I have surely visited you, and seen that which is done to you in Egypt'."

"But I know, 'said the Lord God, 'that the king of Egypt would not let you go, no, not by a mighty hand. And I will stretch out my hand, and smite Egypt with all my wonders which I will do in the midst thereof: and after that he will let you go.'"

And Jehovah has given a great force to Moses in order he could make terrible and bloody signs. Also he said, "When thou goest to return into Egypt, see that thou do all those wonders before Pharaoh, which I have put in thine hand: but **I will harden his heart, that he shall not let the people go**."[77]

Of course, the pharaoh did not let the Jews go, for Jehovah hardened his heart. That is why Moses had to perform another bloody miracle which resulted in sufferings and deaths of many Egyptians. And again the pharaoh did not let the Jews go. Neither the plague of frogs, nor the plague of lice, nor any other plagues could make the pharaoh not let the Jews go, for again and again God hardened the heart of the pharaoh.

Finally, the Lord God said, "I will pass through the land of Egypt this night, and **will smite all the firstborn in the land of Egypt,**

both man and beast; and against all the gods of Egypt I will execute judgment: I am the Lord."[78]

Don't you think, it sounds familiar? Of course, it is a politic of double standards, a provocation of the first water. In the Bible, we see an interesting picture. Moses made cruel and bloody miracles before the pharaoh to intimidate him. The pharaoh almost agrees, but here, quite unexpectedly, God Jehovah interfered in the process and by a quite unexplainable reason, hardens the pharaoh's heart. It would be quite right to soften his heart, and the pharaoh would have let the crowd of those unfortunate Jews go, lest Egyptian people did not suffer from all kinds of plagues which God incurred on them.

But God does not like to solve a problem peacefully. He thirsts for blood, the blood of infants, the blood of Egyptian firstborns. If we assume that Jehovah is almighty God, we shall admit that he could have softened pharaoh's heart: and then it would be not necessary to kill infants. But he did not do it, instead he hardened pharaoh's heart in order to enjoy blood and suffering of innocent infants.

Do you remember our scale of the cultural universal criteria? Infanticide occupies the lowest position and has the charge of 9 antihum. Of course, you can think of infanticide as a very kind and merciful deed if it is performed by God. Moreover Egyptian infants are the children of infidels and, therefore, are infidels themselves. And, as you may think, the fate of all infidels is in the lake burning with fire and sulfur. But we call everything by its own name and, therefore, estimate the infanticide as the most inhuman action. **We must also acknowledge that the religion, which picture such abominable deed as a virtue has to be regarded as both inhuman and dangerous for humankind. From the point of view of our humanistic analyses, such a deed has to be regarded as the most cruel and unprecedented provocation**.

And after that we call our God "kind, loving and merciful." John says: "He that loveth not knoweth not God; for **God is love**."[79] Is it not possible that John spoke about the other God? And, as we shall see, this question is not groundless. Take your intelligence and your feeling of reality and try to think whether the one who loves, moreover, the one who is love, is able to kill thousands of innocent people and even children. **Only a madman can admit that God, who commits mass infanticide, is love**. And if it is so, put one more negative mark to the Jewish myth.

2. 5. How Did Moses Execute the Commandment "You Shall Not Kill"?

Now, knowing the true qualities of our "kind and merciful" God, we shall not be surprised any more about the deeds he has done. After God Jehovah had mercilessly killed all the Egyptian firstborns, the pharaoh decided to let the Jews go. Jahve could not do anything against it. The pharaoh could hardly decide to detain the Jews even another moment, being afraid of more plagues. With God's help, Moses takes out the Jewish people from Egypt and leads them to the land "flowing with milk and honey." On their way they stop at the bottom of the mountain Sinai, and God invites Moses to climb on the mountain where he [God] hands over to Moses the stone tablets with the text of the Law, which later becomes the manual of life for each Jew.

So, Moses has climbed the mountain and Jehovah has uttered his ten commandments that are well known to everybody. "You shall not kill" was one of them. Besides, God gave to Moses instructions concerning rituals and sacrifices. As for the worshiping and sacrificing to other gods, Jehovah was quite categorical: "He that sacrificeth unto any god, save unto the Lord only, he shall be utterly destroyed."[80]

What sacrifices demanded the Biblical God Jehovah? As you remember, he demanded to sacrifice the firstborns to him: "Thou shalt not delay to offer the first of thy ripe fruits, and of thy liquors: **the firstborn of thy sons shalt thou give unto me**. Likewise shalt thou do with thine oxen, and with thy sheep: seven days it shall be with his dam; on the eighth day thou shalt give it me."[81]

What do we see? Our "kind and merciful" God, whom we worship and serve, demands human sacrifices, just as the pagan gods did! But it cannot be so! It is an allegory! It is a parable! No! It is not an allegory, it is not a parable, it is the most genuine reality! Let us be honest and decent people and call everything by its own name. It is quite obvious that if human firstborns are mentioned together with animals which were definitely sacrificed to God Jehovah, so they were sacrificed to him together with animals. As we have shown in the last chapter, the Jews really made human sacrifices to God Jehovah. As you remember, they sacrificed captives to please God and ask for another victory; as you remember, they held men in the Jewish temple in order to sacrifice them to God; and Jephthah sacrificed to Jehovah even his own daughter after coming back with a victory from a battlefield.[82]

In order to see all those abominations, it is not necessary to be very clever; it is necessary just to read the text attentively and to subject it to a humanistic analysis. And a sacrifice (both of human and of animals) is absolutely immoral and an inhuman thing. And if the text pictures such abominable, immoral and inhuman things, it means that such a text itself is immoral and inhuman. And if the text, which is God's revelation, is immoral and inhuman, it means that God, who has given it to people, is also immoral and inhuman. On the contrary, he is distinguished by his unprecedented cruelty and hatred towards mankind. Otherwise, he would have not ordered Moses to kill and exterminate thousands of people so cruelly and unmercifully: "But of the cities of these people, which the Lord thy God doth give thee for an inheritance, **thou shalt save alive nothing that breatheth**: But thou shalt utterly destroy them; namely, the Hittites, and the Amorites, the Canaanites, and the Perizzites, the Hivites, and the Jebusites; as the Lord thy God hath commanded thee...[83] **And spare them not; but slay both man and woman, infant and suckling, ox and sheep, camel and ass.**"[84]

This is the formula of genocide of the purest water, and, as we have already stated above, genocide always has a religious nature, for it springs up from the idea of monotheism and god choosiness which recognizes the right on life only for "the God's people." All other people **are obliged** either to accept alien for them religious faith, or, according to God's commandments, to be perished: "that soul shall be surely put to death". The third is not given. **This is where genocide came from. It has a totally religious nature, for only religious wars assume total extermination of "infidels."** An economic war (war which does not have religious motives) never has such a task for its object. Its task is to gain territory, to subordinate people and to impose tribute on them, or to use them as slaves. The task of utter extermination of those who do not wish to accept the religious faith of "the God's people," have as their object only the religions based on the authority of the Biblical God Jehovah, i. e. the religions of "salvation." Such is the essence of monotheism.

Meanwhile, as Moses was receiving God's instructions on the mount of Sinai, the Jews, led by the priest Aaron [the Moses' brother], decided to make a golden calf, an idol, which they could worship and serve to. In the morning of he next day they made sacrifices and peace offerings to the golden calf. And Jehovah said to Moses: "I have seen this people, and, behold, it is a stiffnecked people: now therefore let me alone, that my wrath may wax hot against them, and that I may consume them: and I will make of thee a great nation."[85] But Moses managed to convince Jehovah not to consume the Jewish people. "And the Lord repented of the evil which he thought to do unto his people.

And Moses turned, and went down from the mount, and the two tables of the testimony were in his hand. And the tables were the work of God, and the writing was the writing of God, graven upon the tables...

And it came to pass, as soon as he came nigh unto the camp, that he saw the calf, and the dancing: and Moses' anger waxed hot, and he cast the tables out of his hands, and brake them beneath the mount. And he took the calf which they had made, and burnt it in the fire, and ground it to powder, and strawed it upon the water, and made the children of Israel drink of it...

Then Moses stood in the gate of the camp, and said: "Who is on the Lord"s side? Let him come unto me. And all the sons of Levi gathered themselves together unto him. And he said unto them, Thus saith the Lord God of Israel, **put every man his sword by his side, and go in and out from gate to gate throughout the camp, and slay every man his brother, and every man his companion, and every man his neighbour**. And the children of Levi did according to the word of Moses: **and there fell of the people that day about three thousand men.**"[86]

Let the one who has ears to hear listen, for here we face a very interesting moment. Moses went down from the mountain with the tables, where God wrote the words "**You shall not kill**" by his own hand. But what did Moses do? He said: "**Go in and out from gate to gate throughout the camp, and slay every man his brother, and every man his companion, and every man his neighbour**."

In such a way God's commandments are executed in reality. And God does not blame Moses for this cruel act, for it completely conforms to the ideology of the religious system of the Judaic myth. The system, forbidding the murder of a single man, always reserves for itself the right to kill as many people as it is necessary for its bloody purposes. So it was, and it will be so as long as we use this monstrous bloody ideology and build our life according to its cruel laws and commandments.

2. 6. How Did Biblical God Jehovah Manage to Kill Tens of Thousands Men, Sitting in a Wooden Box?

Where on earth dwelt Biblical God Jehovah at that time? So far, he lived amidst smoke and darkness on the mount of Sinai, but after the Jews had built the ark of covenant, he moved into that small gold-clad box. There, on the cover of the arc between two cherubs, God appeared to Moses in order to teach and edify him.

Now after the death of Moses, it came to pass that the Lord spoke unto Joshua the son of Nun, Moses' minister, saying, "Moses my servant is dead; now therefore arise, go over this Jordan, thou, and all this people, unto the land which I do give to them, even to the children of Israel. Every place that the sole of your foot shall tread upon, that have I given unto you, as I said unto Moses."[87]

The ark of covenant was a sacred thing for the Jewish people, for God himself dwelt in it and helped them to gain victories over their enemies. However, the ark was a dangerous thing. Some great and evil power, which killed everybody who neared it, was hidden inside of that magic box. That is why it was recommended not to come closer than at least two thousand cubits.

The ark also made great miracles. When the Jews crossed Jordan, for example, it was by means of the ark that "the waters which came down from above stood and rose up upon a heap very far from the city Adam, that is beside Zaretan: and those that came down toward the sea of the plain, even the salt sea, failed, and were cut off: and the people passed over right against Jericho. And the priests that bare the ark of the covenant of the Lord stood firm on dry ground in the midst of Jordan, and all the Israelites passed over on dry ground, until all the people were passed clean over Jordan."[88]

Now the city of Jericho, which had to be seized, lay on the way of the Jewish people. And again they used the ark to capture the city. "And Joshua the son of Nun called the priests, and said unto them, take up the ark of the covenant, and let seven priests bear seven trumpets of rams' horns before the ark of the Lord. And he said unto the people, Pass on, and compass the city, and let him that is armed pass on before the ark of the Lord...

And Joshua had commanded the people, saying, Ye shall not shout, nor make any noise with your voice, neither shall any word proceed out of your mouth, until the day I bid you shout; then shall ye shout. So the ark of the Lord compassed the city, going about it once: and they came into the camp, and lodged in the camp. And Joshua rose early in the morning, and the priests took up the ark of the Lord...

So the people shouted when the priests blew with the trumpets: and it came to pass, when the people heard the sound of the trumpet, and the people shouted with a great shout, that the wall fell down flat, so that the people went up into the city, every man straight before him, and they took the city. And "**they utterly destroyed all that was in the**

city, both man and woman, young and old, and ox, and sheep, and ass, with the edge of the sword."[89]

The city of Hazor was occupied with the same hatred and cruelty: "And Joshua at that time turned back, and took Hazor, and smote the king thereof with the sword: for Hazor beforetime was the head of all those kingdoms. **And they smote all the souls that were therein with the edge of the sword, utterly destroying them: there was not any left to breathe: and he burnt Hazor with fire**. And all the cities of those kings, and all the kings of them, did Joshua take, and smote them with the edge of the sword, and he utterly destroyed them, as Moses the servant of the Lord commanded."[90]

The war for the "land flowing with mild and honey" was long and bloody. There was not a city that made peace with the children of Israel, exept the Hivites—the inhabitants of Gibeon: all other they took in battle. "For **it was of the Lord to harden their hearts**, that they should come against Israel in battle, that he might destroy them utterly, and that they might have no favour, but that he might destroy them, as the Lord commanded Moses."[91]

And again we see Jehovah's style to solve the problems. Again he hardens human hearts and souls so they do not make peace with the Jews and be utterly exterminated by them.

Thus, Joshua occupied all the land Jehovah had given to the Jews. The people served God during all the days of Joshua and during all the days of elders. But after Joshua's death, the children of Israel did evil in the sight of the Lord: they forsook the Lord, and served Baal and Ashtaroth.

And the anger of the Lord was hot against Israel, and he delivered them into the hands of spoilers that spoiled them, and he sold them into the hands of their enemies round about so that they could no longer stand before their enemies. Nevertheless the Lord raised up judges which delivered them out of the hand of those that spoiled them. However, when the judge was dead, the Jews returned to the evil, and corrupted themselves more than their fathers. They began to follow to alien religions and to serve other gods.

"And the anger of the Lord was hot against Israel; and he said, Because that this people hath transgressed my covenant which I commanded their fathers, and have not hearkened unto my voice; **I also will not henceforth drive out any from before them of the nations which Joshua left when he died: that through them I may prove Israel, whether they will keep the way of the Lord to walk therein, as their fathers did keep it, or not**. Therefore the Lord left those nations, without driving them out hastily; neither delivered he them into the hand of Joshua."[92]

Here we see strange inconsistence of the Lord God. Or did he forget what he had ordered to Moses? As you remember Jehovah said then: "But of the cities of these people, which the Lord thy God doth give thee for an inheritance, **thou shalt save alive nothing that breatheth**: But thou shalt utterly destroy them; namely, the Hittites, and the Amorites, the Canaanites, and the Perizzites, the Hivites, and the Jebusites; as the Lord thy God hath commanded thee... **And spare them not; but slay both man and woman, infant and suckling, ox and sheep, camel and ass**."

Strange, as it may seem, but till now there was not even a mentioning about Satan or the Devil in the Bible. God himself hardens human hearts and souls and put them to temptation; God himself spares his people and he himself kills them. Satan, Devil, enemy, adversary [all are the same] is a cunning invention of Christian priests which enables them to lay Jehovah's blame on the fragile back of the "enemy."

And again, as it was in the case with pharaoh, "loving and merciful" God Jehovah hardens human hearts and souls in order to wage war on the people of Israel. In other words, our "loving and merciful" God drives people to war in order to be perished in that war. But if Jehovah was almighty God, he could have softened human hearts and souls. And there would not have been bloodshed then; there would not have been written such an abominable, such a bloody book as the Bible is.

And the children of Israel dwelt among the Canaanites, Hittites, and Amorites, and Perizzites, and Hivites, and Jebusites. And they took their daughters to be their wives, and gave their daughters to their sons, and served their gods. And the children of Israel did evil in the sight of the Lord, and forgot the Lord their God, and served Baalim and the groves. Therefore the anger of the Lord was hot against Israel, and he sold them into the hand of Philistines: and the children of Israel served Philistines seven years.

At last Israel went out against the Philistines to battle, and pitched beside Ebenezer: and the Philistines pitched in Aphek. And the Philistines put themselves in array against Israel: and when they joined battle, Israel was smitten before the Philistines: and they slew of the army in the field about four thousand men. And when the people came into the camp, the elders of Israel said: "Wherefore has the Lord smitten us today before the Philistines? Let us fetch the ark of the covenant of the Lord out of Shiloh unto us, that, when it comes among us, it may save us out of the hand of our enemies."

So the people sent to Shiloh, that they might bring from there the ark of the covenant of the Lord of hosts, which dwells between the cherubims. And when the ark of the covenant of the Lord came into the camp, all Israel shouted with a great shout, so that the earth rang again. And the Philistines were afraid, for they said, God is come into the camp.

Nevertheless, the Philistines fought, and Israel was smitten, and they fled every man into his tent: and there was a very great slaughter; for there fell of Israel thirty thousand footmen. And the ark of God was taken; and the two sons of Eli, Hophni and Phinehas, were slain.

And the Philistines took the ark of God, and brought it from Ebenezer unto Ashdod. When the Philistines took the ark of God, they brought it into the house of Dagon, and set it by Dagon. And when they of Ashdod arose early on the morrow, behold, Dagon was fallen upon his face to the earth before the ark of the Lord. And they took Dagon, and set him in his place again. And when they arose early on the morrow morning, behold, Dagon was fallen upon his face to the ground before the ark of the Lord; and the head of Dagon and both the palms of his hands were cut off upon the threshold; only the stump of Dagon was left to him.

But **the hand of the Lord was heavy upon them of Ashdod, and he destroyed them, and smote them with emerods**, even Ashdod and the coasts thereof. And when the men of Ashdod saw that it was so, they said: "The ark of the God of Israel shall not abide with us: for his hand is sore upon us, and upon Dagon our god." And they carried the ark of the God of Israel to Gath. And it was so, that, after they had carried it about, the hand of **the Lord was against the city with a very great destruction: and he smote the men of the city, both small and great, and they had emerods in their secret parts**.

Therefore they sent the ark of God to Ekron. And it came to pass, as the ark of God came to Ekron, that the Ekronites cried out, saying, "They have brought about the ark of the God of Israel to us, to slay us and our people." So they sent and gathered together all the lords of the Philistines, and said, Send away the ark of the God of Israel, and let it go again to his own place, that it slay us not, and our people: for there was a deadly destruction throughout all the city; the hand of God was very heavy there. And the men that died not were smitten with the emerods: and the cry of the city went up to heaven. And the ark of the Lord was in the country of the Philistines seven months.

To get rid of such a dangerous thing the Philistines had to make sacrifices to God Jehovah and glorify him. To do that they brought the ark of the covenant to Bethshemesh, the inhabitants of which were very curious. Their curiosity was so great that they dared to look into that dangerous magic box. But you know: black magic is very dangerous. If one has anything to do with it, one has to be very careful: otherwise, one can die. The inhabitants of Bethshemesh did not know about it. That is why Jehovah "smote the men of Bethshemesh, because they had looked into the ark of the Lord, **even he smote of the people fifty thousand and threescore and ten men: and the people lamented, because the Lord had smitten many of the people with a great slaughter**."[93] And the men of Bethshemesh said, "Who is able to stand before this **holy Lord God**? And to whom shall he go up from us?"[94]

Who can say after that that the Bible is not a slaughterhouse? And such bloody slaughters, as one can see, take place throughout the entire Old Testament. Perhaps the ability to kill tens of thousands of people and to smite them with the emerods is the sign of God's holiness. Generally, murder, mass extermination of men, women, old men and even infants is, most likely, the favorite business of God Jehovah—the very Jehovah, who is considered by all the Christians to be Jesus' father whom they worship and glorify hoping to obtain the "salvation" of their souls from the bloody hands of that tyrant and filicide. And it was not in vain that the Jews noticed that if God would stretch out his hand, it would be done only to kill somebody or to destroy something. They also have noticed that it is better not to see Jehovah's face, for one who does it will inevitably die. Certainly, God's hand is very heavy.

How can we consider such bloody deeds from the point of view of our humanistic analyses? We must admit them as to be absolutely inhuman, and such deeds occupy the lowest place of our scale of universal cultural criteria, for, being classified as mass killings, they contain it themselves the most powerful negative info-energy charge, which is very dangerous both for the human being and for humanity.

2. 7. "Good" Deeds of Kings of Israel

There was a time, when the people of Israel did not have a king. And God erected them judges who rescued them from the hands of robbers. But they were not satisfied with judges, they grumbled and required a king. And then God Jehovah sent Samuel to anoint Saul to be a king. And Samuel told to Saul: "The Lord sent me to anoint thee to be king over his people, over Israel: now therefore hearken thou unto the voice of the words of the Lord." The words were as following: "Now go and smite Amalek, and utterly destroy all that they have, and **spare**

them not; but slay both man and woman, infant and suckling, ox and sheep, camel and ass."[95]

And Saul smote the Amalekites from Havilah to Shur, that is over against Egypt. And he took Agag, the king of the Amalekites alive, and utterly destroyed all the people with the edge of the sword. "But Saul and the people spared Agag, and the best of the sheep, and of the oxen, and of the fatlings, and the lambs, and all that was good, and would not utterly destroy them: but **every thing that was vile and refuse, that they destroyed utterly**."[96]

Reasoning logically, we have to admit that vile and refuse things must be inhabitants of occupied lands, for all the rest was good (the best of the sheep, and of the oxen, and of the fatlings, and the lambs, and all that was good). These words show that the life of infidel, pagan, the one who is not a Jew, are not worth even a pin in the space of the Bible. It is referred to a class of things which are "vile and refuse" and, therefore, have to be exterminated according to the word of God. The life of an animal is worth more than that of a pagan. And again we have the possibility to see genocide of the purest water here.

And there was another God's word to Samuel: "I am sorry that I have set up Saul to be king: for he is turned back from following me, and has not performed my commandments."

And Samuel said to Saul: "Why didst thou not obey the voice of the Lord, but didst fly upon the spoil, and didst evil in the sight of the Lord? And the Lord sent thee on a journey, and said, Go and **utterly destroy the sinners the Amalekites, and fight against them until they be consumed**."[97]

And it was because of this disobedience, that God Jehovah was sorry about Saul's anointing to the kingdom. And he told Samuel to fill his horn with oil and to anoint David, the son of Jesse, and the spirit of the Lord came upon David from that day forward.

"But the spirit of the Lord departed from Saul, and **an evil spirit from the Lord troubled him**. And Saul's servants said unto him, Behold now, **an evil spirit from God** troubleth thee."[98]

Isn't it strange that an evil spirit comes from God, but not from the Devil, as the Christian church teaches us? We have already mentioned that the Devil, Satan, a serpent, an animal and an enemy are later invention of the "holy" fathers. Probably, priests developing Christian dogmas have missed the fact that God is not a trinity, but the whole concourse of various spirits, of which an evil spirit and the spirit of lie [II Chronicles 18:22, "Now therefore, behold, **the Lord hath put a lying spirit** in the mouth of these thy prophets, and the Lord hath spoken evil against thee"] are the main ones. Thus, they have presented God to us in an abridged version.

There is not even a mention of the Holy Spirit in the Old Testament. It appears only in the New Testament as the integral attribute of **God who is love**. One could hardly say that about the Biblical God Jehovah. One will not have the heart to say that an abominable creature which dwells in darkness, which is afraid of daylight and kills tens of thousands of innocent people, even children without any reason, is love. It can be hatred, baseness, cruelty, blood-thirstiness, revengefulness, rage; it can be whatever, but not love! **Love cannot kill, love cannot hate, love cannot be cruel, mean and blood-thirsty because it is love**.

And if the western Christian world has accepted this blood-thirsty monster as their heavenly father, and the book, which cannot be called anything other than a slaughterhouse as the textbook of life, then we could hardly expect the world to be kind and friendly towards a little defenseless man. Devoting our love and soul to this God-butcher, we cannot understand why this "loving and merciful" God cannot protect us against the escalation of hatred, cruelty and terrorism that overflows the world more and more, taking away the lives of those who do not deserve such a dreadful death.

Meanwhile, Saul suffered more and more from God's evil spirit. He prophesied and raved in his house and could have nothing to do with such a punishment. Then someone advised him to ask David, who "played with his hand" and could relieve Saul's sufferings to play for him. But, as Saul envied David because of his greater success in a battle, Saul had a temptation to kill David. "And it came to pass on the morrow, that **the evil spirit from God** came upon Saul, and he prophesied in the midst of the house: and David played with his hand, as at other times: and there was a javelin in Saul's hand. And Saul cast the javelin; for he said, I will smite David even to the wall with it. And David avoided out of his presence twice. And Saul was afraid of David, because the Lord was with him, and was departed from Saul."[99]

Here we become witnesses of a very interesting moment which can help us to see the real face of the biblical God Jehovah. Above we have already mentioned that Jesus Christ drove out evil spirits that had come from the evil one (Devil). And, if the same evil spirits come out from God Jehovah, we can make quite a logical conclusion that Jehovah is the very Devil that appears in the New Testament.

The fact is that during Old Testament times there was not even a mention of the Devil. God personified in himself both positive and negative functions, and, most likely, when there appeared the threat of disclosure of Jehovah's "good" deeds, it was necessary to divide those functions having left positive ones for God and negative ones for the Devil [Satan, as you remember, was God's son].

The idea of the Devil appears in Christian era in the book *The Heavenly Hierarchy* by Dionysus Areopagit, and represents by itself entirely lame and reasonless interpretation of chapter 14 of the book of Isaiah. *The God's Law* [the popular textbook of orthodox dogmatic Christianity] says: "Once, the highest and mightiest angel, whose name was Dennitsa [Lucifer in the KJV Bible], grew proud with his might and power, refused to love God and serve him, but instead wished to become God. He began to slander against God, began to resist to everything and deny everything, and became a dark, evil spirit—Devil, Satan. [He could not become Satan end evil spirit simultaneously, for Satan and evil spirit are different things. Satan is God's son, and evil spirit is one of God's manifestations]. The word "devil" means "slanderer," and the word "satan" means God's "adversary," the enemy of everything good. This evil spirit has tempted and carried along many other angels that also became evil spirits, which we call demons.

Then archangel Michael, one of the highest God's angels, step forward against Satan and said, 'who is equal to God? No one is!' 'And there was a war on the heaven: Michael and his angels struggled against Satan. But evil forces could not resist to God's angels, and Satan together with all the demons fell like a lightning down to the nether world, to hell. "Hell" or "the nether world" is the place far from God where evil spirits are now. There they suffered in their malice, understanding their weakness before God. All of them, because of their impenitence, strengthened themselves in evil to such a degree, that they cannot become good again. They, by means of their craftiness and ruses, try to tempt us, by suggesting false thoughts and desires, in order to destroy us. Thus *the evil* appeared in God's creation."[100]

Isaiah pictures the situation in another way. He names the king of Babylon as Lucifer: "He who smote the people in wrath with a continual stroke, he that ruled the nations in anger."[101] It was the very Lucifer that said: "I will ascend into heaven, I will exalt my throne above the stars of God: I will sit also upon the mount of the congregation, in the sides of the north."[102]

And it was on the occasion of his defeat that Jews were so exalted: "Hell from beneath is moved for thee to meet thee at thy coming: it stirreth up the dead for thee, even all the chief ones of the earth; it hath raised up from their thrones all the kings of the nations. All they shall speak and say unto thee, Art thou also become weak as we? art thou become like unto us? Thy pomp is brought down to the grave, and the noise of thy viols: the worm is spread under thee, and the worms cover thee. **How art thou fallen from heaven, O Lucifer, son of the morning**! How art thou cut down to the ground, which didst weaken the nations!"[103]

Isaiah does not even mention about angels and demons in his narration. The king of Babylon died and fell down to hell which at once moved to meet his soul at his entering there. In the printed KJV Bible, this part of Isaiah's book has a corresponding heading: "King of Babylon to lose power."[104]

And "holy fathers" dragged in both angels and demons for better convincingness in order a believer to read and to be terrified by such a dreadful Devil with his innumerable demons, which try "to tempt us, by suggesting false thoughts and desires, in order to destroy us."

It was in the same way, that at times of great tyrannies, the image of an enemy was invented. And all the blame for the tyrant's crimes was shifted on it. In order the existence of "enemy" looked real, it was necessary to organize repressions and public trials where those "enemies" publicly confessed the crimes they have never done. Thus, the heavy and bloody fly-wheel of that hellish machine of death was turned faster and faster, demanding for its turning more and more human sacrifices.

To stop that fly-wheel meant tyrant's ruin, for people (having known that there is no enemy, that all the cruel and bloody deeds are done by the one whom they considered to be "the father of nations" or "the heavenly father") would have hardly tolerated such a mockery at the innermost and sacred displays of human life.

Thus, having acknowledged the absence of enemy, having acknowledged that all the dreadful atrocities (that take place in the space of the Bible) have been performed by order and with the connivance of God, we have to admit that God Jehovah in not loving and merciful at all, that he is cruel and bloody tyrant demanding more and more human sacrifices for maintaining the myth about his guiltlessness.

And David, in the meantime, has escaped to the land of Philistine to be rescued from Saul's hand, for Saul searched to kill him. "And David and his men went up, and invaded the Geshurites, and the Gezrites, and the Amalekites: for those nations were of old the inhabitants of the land, as thou goest to Shur, even unto the land of Egypt. And **David smote the land, and left neither man nor woman alive**, and took away the sheep, and the oxen, and the asses, and the camels, and the apparel, and returned, and came to Achish. And Achish said, whither have ye made a road today? And David said, Against the south of Judah, and against the south of the Jerahmeelites, and against the south of the Kenites. **And David saved neither man nor woman alive, to bring tidings to Gath, saying, Lest they should tell on us**, saying, So did David, and so will be his manner all the while he dwelleth in the country of the Philistines. And Achish believed David, saying, He hath made his people Israel utterly to abhor him; therefore he shall be my servant for ever."[105]

It was the very David—robber, racketeer and murderer—whose psalms Christians love so much. And, in general, as you have already noticed, neither God, nor the above-mentioned Biblical characters did not stop at nothing, regardless if it was robbery or murder. And what a cautious man was David! How professionally he worked, eliminating all witnesses, who could inform on him!

Thus, we see that terrorism and massacres were the favourite occupation of "the God's people," camp followers of which we became so successfully, having adopted all its wild customs and the same wild bloody book, which we use as "the textbook of life." If one is quite intelligent person, one probably will guess what we can learn from such a textbook.

The further history of Jewish judges was as follows: "Now the Philistines fought against Israel. And the men of Israel fled from before the Philistines, and fell down slain in mount Gilboa. And the Philistines followed hard upon Saul and upon his sons; and the Philistines slew Jonathan, and Abinadab, and Melchishua, Saul's sons. And the battle went sore against Saul, and the archers hit him; and he was sore wounded of the archers. Then said Saul unto his armour-bearer, Draw thy sword, and thrust me through therewith; lest these uncircumcised come and thrust me through, and abuse me. But his armour-bearer would not; for he was sore afraid. Therefore Saul took a sword, and fell upon it."[106] Such was Saul's death, after which David became the king of Israel.

And the king and his men went to Jerusalem unto the Jebusites, the inhabitants of the land, and they said: "Except thou take away the blind and the lame, thou shalt not come in hither: thinking, David cannot come in hither. Nevertheless David took the strong hold of Zion: the same is the city of David. And David said on that day, **Whosoever getteth up to the gutter, and smiteth the Jebusites, and the lame and the blind**, that are hated of David's soul, he shall be chief and captain. Wherefore they said, **The blind and the lame shall not come into the house** [of God]."[107]

Just look! What a "merciful" great psalmist David was! With what a great "compassion" he ordered "to getteth up to the gutter and smiteth (smite) the lame and the blind," which were completely defenseless before his warriors, for they physically could not resist them! What mercy and compassion we can talk about after that? And, as you see, God Jehovah did not say even a word against such brutal deeds of David, his anointed sovereign. It means that God has approved both the murder of the lame and the blind and their "excommunication" from a temple.

And if we recognize the Bible as to be a God's word and trust in such a "merciful" God, we then should approve such monstrous lawlessness. But someone will object to us and say that again we perceive the Holy Scripture literally instead of reading it just as an allegory. You see, it was just for fun that David killed the lame and the blind, and actually, he loved them to distraction and probably carried them in a temple with his own hands. Someone can think that it was just so, but the trouble is that the Jews executed God's Law word for word and killed not just for fun. And several thousands of American citizens were really exterminated not without the help of Islamic terrorist-kamikazes who, perceiving the Koran allegorically, has committed, nevertheless, quite real, cruel and bloody terrorist acts.

David built a fortress and named it the city of David. He also brought up the ark of God from the house of Obededom into the city of David. "And it was so, that when they that bare the ark of the Lord had gone six paces, he sacrificed oxen and fatlings. And David danced before the Lord with all his might; and David was girded with a linen ephod. So David and all the house of Israel brought up the ark of the Lord with shouting, and with the sound of the trumpet. And as the ark of the Lord came into the city of David, Michal Saul's daughter looked through a window, and saw king David leaping and dancing before the Lord; and she despised him in her heart. And they brought in the ark of the Lord, and set it in his place, in the midst of the tabernacle that David had pitched for it: and David offered burnt offerings and peace offerings before the Lord. And as soon as David had made an end of offering burnt offerings and peace offerings, he blessed the people in the name of the Lord of hosts."[108]

But again, the anger of the Lord was kindled against Israel, and he moved David against them saying: "Go, number Israel and Judah."[109] So, when they had gone through all the land, they came to Jerusalem at the end of nine months and twenty days. And Joab gave up the sum of the number of the people unto the king: and there were in Israel eight hundred thousand valiant men that drew the sword; and the men of Judah were five hundred thousand men.

The Bible says: "And David's heart smote him after that he had numbered the people. And David said unto the Lord, I have sinned greatly in that I have done: and now, I beseech thee, O Lord, take away the iniquity of thy servant; for I have done very foolishly. For when David was up in the morning, the word of the Lord came unto the prophet Gad, David's seer, saying, Go and say unto David, Thus saith the Lord, I offer thee three things; choose thee one of them, that I may do it unto thee. So Gad came to David, and told him, and said unto him, Shall seven years of famine come unto thee in thy land? or wilt thou flee three months before thine enemies, while they pursue thee? or that there be three days' pestilence in thy land? now advise, and see what answer I shall return to him that sent me. And David said unto Gad, I am in a great strait: **let us fall now into the hand of the Lord; for his mercies are great: and let me not fall into the hand of man**.

So the Lord sent a pestilence upon Israel from the morning even to the time appointed: **and there died of the people from Dan even to Beersheba seventy thousand men**. And when the angel stretched out his hand upon Jerusalem to destroy it, the Lord repented him of the evil, and said to the angel that destroyed the people, It is enough: stay now thine hand. And the angel of the Lord was by the threshingplace of Araunah the Jebusite."[110]

We plead you, please, read attentively the previous paragraph once more and think, what a madman could produce such a pearl of poetry of "the God's people?" You see, Jewish people did nothing sinful or reprehensible at that time. But suddenly, by a totally unexplainable reason, "the anger of the Lord was kindled against Israel" and he excited David "to number Israel and Judah." David has executed Jehovah's order and suddenly he was struck with an idea that by this act he (not knowing why) "has sinned greatly in that he has done."

Of course God's anger flared up at once, and he through the prophet offers David to choose the punishment. David, knowing that it is better not to fall into peoples' hands, chooses a pestilence, hoping, that "his [God's] mercies are great." And again David's calculation appeared to be correct, for the "merciful" Lord God spared his servant and colleague David, and subjected the innocent people of Israel to a pestilence, having exterminated 70.000 men.

Here we see as with one movement of a white and fluffy angel without any logical reason were destroyed tens of thousands human lives. And this angel even intended to pass over Jerusalem to devastate it. But the "mercy" of the Lord God was so great that he "had pity" on the defenseless people, and ordered to the angel to lower his hand.

How should we estimate such an act of Biblical God Jehovah from the point of view of humanity? Of course it must be considered as completely evil and cruel. How is it possible to consider such a deed as human if God makes the man do any action and then punishes for its fulfillment? But, strange as it may seem, he did not punish the executor of an action; instead he punished totally innocent people, who, without any secret thought, allowed their king to number them.

This example shows us the total slavery of human spirit, its complete submission to a cruel bloody authority of the heavenly hierarch who in his irrepressible thirst of blood and power demands more and more human sacrifices. Due to this enlightenment in the essence of things, we can see "uncovering of an animal" in our beloved God Jehovah's image, which, being perceived without any critical control of consciousness, conducts inevitably to "uncovering of an animal" in the man who perceives all these beastly and scurvy Jehovah's tricks allegorically and commits, nevertheless, real atrocities. Trubetskoy, E. in his book *The Sense of Life*, says: "Sometimes we have here just the simple fading of spirit; then a person becomes a fat beast: lifeless porcine faces testify of this transformation. But it can be differently. Sometimes we see as a wolf muzzle peeps out obviously through human features. Sometimes a person looks at us with sharp malicious eyes of a predatory bird, and we see with our own eyes a satire's face deformed with inhuman voluptuousness, with oily cheeks and sweet laughing eyes which make us suspect the existence of a tail. At such a site, the soul runs into a tremor, for it perceives sensibly the transition of a bad infinity of a biological circle into a fiery circle of a black magic. We experience such an impression when we face all the unnatural defects: for example, that inhuman cruelty which is expressed both in causation of tortures and in deliberate trampling of everything human as it is."[III]

Is it necessary to have any special outstanding abilities in order to notice "a satire's face, deformed with inhuman voluptuousness, with oily cheeks and sweet laughing eyes which make us suspect the existence of a tail" in the image of "kind and merciful" God Jehovah, whose inhuman cruelty is expressed "both in an aimless causation of tortures and in a deliberate trampling of everything human as it is?"

Recollect an evil spirit which came from Jehovah and made Saul rave precisely in the same way as those raved cured by Jesus Christ.

Recollect Jacob's struggling with God who hastily ran away at the first sight of daylight which he [God] was afraid of as much as any evil force. Recollect all these things and the existence of a tail at Biblical God Jehovah will not seem an impossible thing. Recollect human sacrifices to God Jehovah, recollect sprinkling of Jewish people with blood as a sign of conclusion of the covenant with God (or, probably, with the Devil?). Recollect human sacrifices of "friends and brothers" who dared to worship the golden calf, and your soul will "run into tremor, for it will perceive sensibly the transition of a bad infinity of a biological circle into the fiery circle of black magic."[112] Because it is in the rituals of black magic that human sacrifices are made, and contracts with the Devil are sealed with human blood, preferably with blood of friends and relatives.

Certainly, in the above-stated citation, Russian religious philosopher Trubetskoy did not mean God Jehovah; certainly, he meant another creature, but, for some reason, it is very much similar to our heartily beloved Jewish tribal God Jehovah. And "all unnatural defects," and "inhuman cruelty," and "aimless causation of tortures," and "deliberate trampling of everything human as it is" are equally inherent to both "a satire with a tail and a wolf muzzle" and to biblical God Jehovah who is perceived in Christianity both as "the Heavenly Father" and as the unsurpassed example for imitation.

Certainly, if we had only "God's Law" and the books of Evgeny Trubetscoy as the holy scripture where God is pictured as kind, loving and merciful, and hence, the one who is unable to offend even a fly, we would have no problem or no need to write anything. And, as we deal with a completely different God; as we deal with impudent deceit and monstrous falsification, we should say millions of words in order to make the reader understand what is contained in only one word. And this word is a "humanity."

If someone really knows this word, its meaning and importance, one will not be deceived by a sweet baby's dummy, which, on getting in a mouth, poisons heart and soul with bitter venom of hatred and cruelty. And it is not necessary to say anything to such a man, for he sees by himself what is human and what is inhuman. And, as not everyone has grown to such an understanding, we shall continue our story and have a look at what was going on in the ancient Israel while we picked God Jehovah to pieces.

When king David grew old, he anointed Solomon, his son, to be a king of Israel. At that time, tribes of Judah and Israel lived quietly, and Solomon reigned over all kingdoms from the river unto the land of the

Philistines, and unto the border of Egypt: they brought presents, and served Solomon all the days of his life. And God gave Solomon wisdom and understanding exceeding much, and largeness of heart, even as the sand that is on the sea shore. And Solomon's wisdom excelled the wisdom of all the children of the east country, and all the wisdom of Egypt. And Solomon's wealth excelled that of all the kings of the earth. "Now **the weight of gold that came to Solomon in one year was six hundred threescore and six (666)** talents of gold."[113]

Here is wisdom. Let him that has understanding count the number of the beast; "for it is the number of man; and **his number six hundred threescore and six**." It appears that king Solomon used the number 666 in his business, without being afraid of both the number and the beast, probably because of his being served to that beast. Most likely, no one even thought about the beast and his number at Solomon's time. At that time people did not invent unnecessary things, but held sacred all the commandments of their God.

Solomon was the king who built God's temple. As you remember, up to that time God dwelt in the ark of the covenant. It was a rather small box, and God could hardly feel himself comfortably in it. It was necessary to build a temple where Jehovah could feel more comfortable.

After finishing the temple all the elders of Israel came, and the priests took up the ark. And they brought up the ark of the Lord, and the tabernacle of the congregation, and all the holy vessels that were in the tabernacle. The Bible says: "And it came to pass, when the priests were come out of the holy place, that the cloud filled the house of the Lord. So that the priests could not stand to minister because of the cloud: for the glory of the Lord had filled the house of the Lord. Then spake Solomon, **The Lord said that he would dwell in the thick darkness**."[114]

And Solomon stood before the altar of the Lord in the presence of all the congregation of Israel, and spread forth his hands toward heaven. And he said: "Lord God of Israel, there is no God like thee, in heaven above, or on earth beneath, who keepest covenant and mercy with thy servants that walk before thee with all their heart: who hast kept with thy servant David my father that thou promisedst him: thou spakest also with thy mouth, and hast fulfilled it with thine hand, as it is this day. Therefore now, Lord God of Israel, keep with thy servant David my father that thou promisedst him, saying, There shall not fail thee a man in my sight to sit on the throne of Israel; so that thy children take heed to their way, that they walk before me as thou hast walked before me. And now, O God of Israel, let thy word, I pray thee, be verified, which thou spakest unto thy servant David my father. **But will God indeed dwell on the earth? behold, the heaven and heaven of heavens cannot contain thee; how much less this house that I have builded?**"[115]

And the Lord God answered Solomon: "If thou wilt walk before me, as David thy father walked, in integrity of heart, and in uprightness, to do according to all that I have commanded thee, and wilt keep my statutes and my judgments: then I will establish the throne of thy kingdom upon Israel for ever, as I promised to David thy father, saying, There shall not fail thee a man upon the throne of Israel. But if ye shall at all turn from following me, ye or your children, and will not keep my commandments and my statutes which I have set before you, but go and serve other gods, and worship them: **then will I cut off Israel out of the land which I have given them; and this house, which I have hallowed for my name, will I cast out of my sight; and Israel shall be a proverb and a byword among all people**."[116]

Here we become witnesses of the very remarkable event. On this page of the Bible, God Jehovah left his wooden box and made his home at the temple which was built for him by Solomon, and by means of his prayers God departed to live on heaven, becoming thus the universal God.

We must notice on this occasion that appearance of God was so exciting, that even priests could not stand it because of the cloud in which God "would dwell in the thick darkness." And then they decided to send that demon to heavens, to get out of harm's way. "Will God indeed dwell on the earth?" they said. Such was their decision.

2. 8. God-Butcher of Jewish Prophets

Meanwhile, the Jewish state was divided into two separate parts. The Jews were captured by the king of Babylon, and at last, Israel and Judea got under the authority of a powerful Roman empire. It was the time of great troubles and sufferings of the Jewish people. However, the archaic Jewish consciousness did not want to accept new ideas. It wanted, like it was before, to live with God here on the earth, but not somewhere on the heaven. It even wanted to approach this God's Kingdom; and then somewhere in inexplicable depths of the Jewish people, the idea was born: the great messianic idea.

This intense expectation of Messiah connected with the great cry about the destiny of Israel, the expectation of the Jewish king who will deliver the people of Israel from all troubles and misfortunes, gives rise to an eschatological conception about the last days of this world that will be ended with the Last Judgment. The Last Judgment will do away with all the enemies of Israel.

These ideas were embodied in the works of the Jewish prophets Hosea, Ezekiel, Isaiah, Joel, Amos, Daniel and many others. Reed Douglas says: "Almost all the prophets were Israelis, mainly of the houses of Josef. They were on the way of knowing One Universal God for all the people and wanted to share the destinies of all the humankind. And they were not alone. In India Buddha would soon reject the caste doctrine and idolatry in his Benares sermon with its Five Commandments of Righteousness. The prophets were the true Israelis who protested against the doctrine of Levites, which was identified with Judaism later... They were Protestants of their time, they saw where the racial doctrine led to, and warned people of its inevitable consequences. Their warnings have not lost the importance even until now. Their protest was caused by claims of Leviticus priests, who, referring to so-called "Moses' Law," claimed their rights for firstborns ("the firstborn of thy sons shalt thou give unto me"—Exodus), and demanded bloody sacrifices to Jehovah. As Montefiore testifies, however, this "Moses' Law" was unknown to Israeli critics, and they did not see anything good in altars, filled with blood, in incessant slaughtering of animals and in the smell of sacrificial burnings which, as Levites assured, were so pleasant for God Jehovah. **They also rejected Leviticus doctrine of destruction and enslavement of "pagans."** God, they appealed, demanded people to behave themselves according to ethical laws, to love their neighbors and care about poor, orphans, widows and oppressed, instead of bloody sacrifices and hatred to foreigners. These protests were the first gleams of dawn that would shine eight centuries after. They sound strangely on the background of furious appeals to massacre and murders, which the Old Testament abound in."[117]

That is right. In chapter 66 of the book of Isaiah, this is spoken: "He that killeth an ox is as if he slew a man; he that sacrificeth a lamb, as if he cut off a dog's neck; he that offereth an oblation, as if he offered swine's blood; he that burneth incense, as if he blessed an idol. Yea, they have chosen their own ways, and their soul delighteth in their abominations."[118] God of Isaiah is satiated with animal sacrifices, with burning of incenses and with blood of pigs. So, what does God Jehovah lack? What can he satisfy his bloody appetite with? Certainly, only with human sacrifices.

Douglas Reed is a great connoisseur of Zion secrets and an ardent accuser of Judaism which he considers to be the source of religious intolerance and tension in the world. But even he, as well as Vladimir Soloviev (asserting that "in a prophetical consciousness, a subjective, personal element of Old Testament Jahve (existing) has been united for the first time with the objective idea of universal divine personality"), could not see at the Sovereign God's face, depicted by the prophets, the very familiar face of cruel and bloodthirsty God Jehovah, of whom we have already spoken so much.

It is quite probable that the prophets who, as Douglas Reed asserts, were "Israelis, mainly of the houses of Josef," and, in a contrast to Jews, whose creed was based on the Deuteronomy, tried to get rid of a cruel and bloodthirsty demon Jehovah. They "were on the way of knowing One Universal God for all the people and wanted to share the destinies of all the humankind." They "aspired to knowledge of the Uniform God for all people and wanted to divide of destiny of all mankind," but even they could not get rid of influence of a matrix which name is the Bible. At that time, it was only Old Testament, but it had already been a matrix strictly determining the consciousness and behaviour of people and the humanistic analysis of the text allows us to prove it.

In the first chapter of the book of Isaiah we read: "Zion shall be redeemed with judgment, and her converts with righteousness. And the destruction of the transgressors and of the sinners shall be together, and they that forsake the Lord shall be consumed."[119]

It means that now we see "the chosen God's people" who are called Zion, and their converted sons who will be redeemed. Transgressors and sinners, i. e. people confessing other religions "shall be consumed."

Isaiah says: "And many people shall go and say, Come ye, and let us go up to the mountain of the Lord, to the house of the God of Jacob; and he will teach us of his ways, and we will walk in his paths: **for out of Zion shall go forth the law, and the word of the Lord from Jerusalem**. And he shall judge among the nations, and shall rebuke many people: **and they shall beat their swords into plowshares, and their spears into pruninghooks: nation shall not lift up sword against nation, neither shall they learn war any more**."[120]

From the point of view of humanity these words from Isaiah can occupy the highest position on our scale of cultural universal criteria, but it is still too early to hurry up with the conclusions. Let us read other prophets and have a look at what they speak about. Joel says: "And rend your heart and not your garments, and turn unto the Lord your God: for he is gracious and merciful, slow to anger, and of great kindness, and repenteth him of the evil."[121]

Of course, God described by Joel does not look like cruel and bloodthirsty Jehovah. But further God himself begins to speak: "And I will shew wonders in the heavens and in the earth, blood, and fire, and pillars of smoke. The sun shall be turned into darkness, and the moon into blood, before the great and the terrible day of the Lord come. And it shall come to pass, that whosoever shall call on the name of the Lord shall be delivered: for in mount Zion and in Jerusalem shall be deliverance, as the Lord hath said, and in the remnant whom the Lord shall call."[122]

But just imagine [God forbid!] that we, by mistake, call someone another's name (for example Jesus Christ's, or Allah's, or Krishna's, or Buddha's) rather than that of Jehovah! To fight against such obstinate representatives of humankind Jehova gives the following instructions: "**Beat your plowshares into swords, and your pruninghooks into spears: let the weak say, I am strong**. Assemble yourselves, and come, all ye heathen, and gather yourselves together round about: thither cause thy mighty ones to come down, O Lord. Let the heathen be wakened, and come up to the valley of Jehoshaphat: for there will I sit to judge all the heathen round about. **Put ye in the sickle, for the harvest is ripe: come, get you down; for the press is full, the vats overflow; for their wickedness is great**."[123]

It seems, however, that Isaiah and Joel talk to the different gods. God of Isaiah says that "**they shall beat their swords into plowshares**, and their spears into pruninghooks: nation shall not lift up sword against nation, neither shall they learn war any more"; the God of Joel says something totally different: "**Beat your plowshares into swords, and your pruninghooks into spears... put ye in the sickle, for the harvest is ripe**." The result of such a "harvest" is "the true universalism," which means that "shall Jerusalem be holy, and **there shall no strangers pass through her any more**."[124]

Do you recognize the same handwriting of Jewish rabbis, who now try with all their might by means of prophets' words to prove God-choosiness of the Jewish people and justify the crimes performed by Biblical God Jehovah (or rather by themselves) in relation to "gentiles," i. e. to those who does not belong to the elected "God's people"?

What does it mean? It means that the Biblical text is a very dangerous thing, and one has to work with it very carefully. One cannot analyze the Biblical text expecting from it what one needs. With such an approach to its analysis one will receive everything one wants, for the matrix is informationally superfluous. Its categorical imperatives which influence the consciousness of people are sometimes so screened with unimportant or opposite by their meaning words and phrases that very often it is quite difficult to detect them. That is why the one who does not know about humanistic analysis usually does not notice those imperatives in a text.

But the most interesting fact here is that these imperatives act on all the people equally. The power of their influence and a fear inspired by them are so great that any group of people who uses the Bible as a basis of their creed learns very fast that "salvation" can be received only on a mountain Zion and only from the "hands" of the Jewish God Jehovah who, certainly, is considered by these people as only their God. As for them, they certainly rank themselves to "the God's people." Moreover, having adopted his commandments, they begin to execute those who do not belong to Jehovah's followers.

And, as God Jehovah recognizes only those who worship him and orders to exterminate all the others, those who trust in this God have nothing to do as to approve his actions or even to execute them word for word as it has been written in the Bible. By approving his actions, we put ourselves in the opposition to the entire world. We begin to hate the world and with a great hope and pleasure expect the Last Judgment in the fire of which our "loving and merciful" God will exterminate all our enemies and provide us with a comfortable place in a paradise.

But we, for one reason or another, forget that the Law had been given by God to the Jewish people, and Jehovah always demanded them to execute his Law word for word. And they executed all God's commandments and do it until nowadays. Those who had refused to obey the Law were subjected to destruction. We, having accepted Paul's teaching, rejected the Law and all its instructions, thus having sinned before Jehovah. Therefore, on the one hand, we have accepted a completely alien concept of Judaic belief in the tribal Jewish God Jehovah; on the other hand, we have broken all his commandments, and consequently we are to be subjected to his judgment.

And the judgment will be really terrible. Hardly any one of us will be saved, for "the wrath of the Lord of hosts is the land darkened, and the people shall be as the fuel of the fire: no man shall spare his brother."[125] "For the Lord God of hosts shall make a consumption ["extermination" in a Russian translation] even determined, in the midst of all the land."[126]

The prophet already sees him coming; he sees his terrible face, his blood-stained garment and his blood-stained hands, and somewhere in the depth of his prophetical soul the doubt is born. "Maybe it is not

God; probably it is just a butcher with a bloody axe coming back home from his workplace" Isaiah thinks to himself.

In order to dispel all his doubts, the prophet asks the one approaching: "Who is this that cometh from Edom, with dyed garments from Bozrah this that is glorious in his apparel, travelling in the greatness of his strength?" And the one approaching answers: "I that speak in righteousness, **mighty to save." "Wherefore art thou red in thine apparel**, and thy garments like him that treadeth in the winevat?" asks the prophet. And the Sovereign God answers very blandly, **"I have trodden the winepress alone**; and of the people there was none with me: for **I will tread them in mine anger, and trample them in my fury; and their blood shall be sprinkled upon my garments, and I will stain all my raiment**. For the day of vengeance is in mine heart, and the year of my redeemed is come. And I looked, and there was none to help; and I wondered that there was none to uphold: therefore **mine own arm brought salvation unto me; and my fury, it upheld me. And I will tread down the people in mine anger, and make them drunk in my fury, and I will bring down their strength** ["blood" in the Russian translation] **to the earth**."[127]

As you see, our Biblical God Jehovah has chosen a very nice method of "salvation." If you are attentive and clever enough, you, of course, will understand what a method it is and will estimate it at its true worth. For such a method of "salvation" by means of "**treading down the people in anger" and "bringing down their strength** [blood]" could invent only our favourite God Jehovah, the greatest inventor of instruments for tortures and mockeries at man and humanity. Look, how masterly he uses it, managing without any help, as he has such a strong arm, such a great fury, that he does not need any assistants in the business of "salvation." "Salvation" from what? Nobody knows. Probably from his own evil spirit, for at that time there were neither Devil nor the beast.

In a behaviour of our "kind and merciful" God Jehovah we recognize something very familiar, something that terrifies a soul and makes it shudder with a great horror, for this something opens such "heights" of our cultural and spiritual growth, that it would be better not to look at it.

There is a Russian movie which is called *Dog's Heart*. It tells about a famous doctor who made an operation in order to examine the reaction of a dog to implantation of a human hypophysis. The donor turned out to be a drunkard and a hooligan, therefore all his bad qualities passed to the dog along with the implanted hypophysis. After the operation, the dog changed into a man, was given the name Sharicov, and soon began to show his bad character. At last, with the help of one party organization man, Sharicov got the position of the head of the city department of cleanup ["salvation"] from stray cats. There is a scene in the movie where Sharicov, on his coming back home after a busy day on "salvation" of the city form stray cats, takes off his blood-stained leather jacket and says in ecstasy: "We throttled them, we throttled them, throttled..." ...And their blood sprinkled upon his garments, and he stained all his raiment and brought down their blood...

Can it be that we, looking at blood-stained Jewish God-butcher Jehovah, whom we have accepted to be our "savior," do not see that his psychology and ideology does not differ even a bit from those of mister Sharicov, half a dog-half a man, who has imagined himself to be the "savior" of the world from every kind of scum and has began to throttle it with all his frenzy; not yielding in this respect to the great "savior" Jehovah.

Can it be that we shall never understand that we again and again repeat the nightmare which has been inculcated into us by the matrix, whose name is the Bible? Can it really be that we shall never understand that having had such an abominable beginning and having come from the murder of the forefather (about which we spoke in the beginning of our narration) the religion adopted by the Jewish people calls into being anything except for hatred and cruelty? These hatred and cruelty lead, at the final account, to enmity and division among people and nations.

Only a nation totally distraught with rage and hatred could give rise to such a "child" as the Bible is. We, by adopting its teaching, become as mad as those ancient Jews-barbarians who, being taught by Levites, followed God's commandments word for word and killed "both man and woman, infant and suckling, ox and sheep, camel and ass," carrying out the mission of "salvation."

Certainly, we have accepted Jehovah's son Jesus Christ as our "savior," but as you know, like father like son. Therefore, at the Last Judgment, our beloved God-butcher Jehovah will come together with his son Jesus Christ [or rather with Satan, his other son] in order to crash as many people as it is necessary to fill a river onto the horse bridles deep and 300 kilometers length. ("And the angel thrust in his sickle into the earth, and gathered the vine of the earth, and cast it into the great winepress of the wrath of God. **And the winepress was trodden without the city, and blood came out of the winepress, even unto the horse bridles, by the space of a thousand and six hundred furlongs.**"[128]).

And now try to imagine how many people have to be "saved" in order to squeeze out so much blood. Here we have an opportunity to see again how the matrix, in spite of everything, even in spite of the great moral sermon of Jesus Christ, again and again makes people come back to that nightmare which is incorporated into its basis. For "the winepress of God's anger," invented by the Jewish prophets during the VI century b. c. confirms and fixes forever, for all the future history of mankind, severe and brutal imperatives of the matrix. This "winepress of God's anger" comes back again in John's revelation, binding everyone who trusts it with fear and the thirst of destruction, and make them kill, crash, trample all those who does not trust in God-butcher Jehovah and does not want to worship him.

The "salvation" will be put into effect as follows: "Howl ye; for the day of the Lord is at hand; it shall come as a destruction from the Almighty (italics is ours)... Behold, the day of the Lord cometh, cruel both with wrath and fierce anger, to lay the land desolate: and he shall destroy the sinners thereof out of it (italics is ours). For the stars of heaven and the constellations thereof shall not give their light: the sun shall be darkened in his going forth, and the moon shall not cause her light to shine. And I will punish the world for their evil, and the wicked for their iniquity; and I will cause the arrogancy of the proud to cease, and will lay low the haughtiness of the terrible... Therefore I will shake the heavens, and the earth shall remove out of her place, in the wrath of the Lord of hosts, and in the day of his fierce anger... And it shall be as the chased roe, and as a sheep that no man taketh up: they shall every man turn to his own people, and flee every one into his own land. Every one that is found shall be thrust through; and every one that is joined unto them shall fall by the sword. Their children also shall be dashed to pieces before their eyes; their houses shall be spoiled, and their wives ravished... Their bows also shall dash the young men to pieces; **and they shall have no pity on the fruit of the womb; their eye shall not spare children**,"[129] speaks Isaiah from God's lips, and we recognize the familiar handwriting. We recognize all the same hatred, all the same cruelty and insatiable thirst for blood and vengeance. The truth is that here God does not affect to be kind and merciful. He declares openly and loudly: "Now will I shortly pour out my fury upon thee, and accomplish mine anger upon thee: and I will judge thee according to thy ways, and will recompense thee for all thine abominations. And mine eye shall not spare, neither will I have pity: I will recompense thee according to thy ways and thine abominations that are in the midst of thee; **and ye shall know that I am the Lord that smiteth**."[130]

Who will be punished by this Lord that smiteth? Do you think it will be only sinners? It appears that the Lord that smieteth will punish all the people without any discrimination, for God considers them all to be sinners. He "loves" them all to such a degree that is ready to exterminate both the righteous and the sinners: "And say to the land of Israel, Thus saith the Lord; Behold, I am against thee, and **will draw forth my sword out of his sheath, and will cut off from thee the righteous and the wicked**."[131]

And what does the humanistic analysis say about such deeds? It says that from the point of view of humanity, such deeds are absolutely brutal. One can imagine what will happen if we follow an example of our Lord God and begin to kill all those who do not want to share our creed. As you see, murder, massacres, infanticide are the favorite businesses of our beloved God Jehovah. And he does it with such eagerness that he looks more like a butcher, rather than a decent God.

The end of Isaiah's book sounds as an optimistic apotheosis to the "true universalism" and the triumph of the "objective idea of universal divine personality" which administers justice and punishment, exterminating for the sake of "salvation" both the righteous and the wicked: "For, behold, the Lord will come with fire, and with his chariots like a whirlwind, to render his anger with fury, and his rebuke with flames of fire. For by fire and by his sword will the Lord plead with all flesh: and the slain of the Lord shall be many. **They that sanctify themselves, and purify themselves in the gardens behind one tree in the midst, eating swine's flesh, and the abomination, and the mouse, shall be consumed together, saith the Lord**.

For I know their works and their thoughts: it shall come, that I will gather all nations and tongues; and they shall come, and see my glory. And I will set a sign among them, and I will send those that escape of them unto the nations, to Tarshish, Pul, and Lud, that draw the bow, to Tubal, and Javan, to the isles afar off, that have not heard my fame, neither have seen my glory; and they shall declare my glory among the Gentiles. And they shall bring all your brethren for an offering unto the Lord out of all nations upon horses, and in chariots, and in litters, and upon mules, and upon swift beasts, to my holy mountain Jerusalem, saith the Lord, as the children of Israel bring an offering in a clean vessel into the house of the Lord.

And I will also take of them for priests and for Levites, saith the Lord. For as the new heavens and the new earth, which I will make, shall remain before me, saith the Lord, so shall your seed and your name remain. And it shall come to pass, that from one new moon to another, and from one sabbath to another, shall all flesh come to worship before me, saith the Lord. And they **shall go forth, and look upon the carcases of the men that have transgressed against me: for their worm shall not die, neither shall their fire be quenched; and they shall be an abhorring unto all flesh**."[132]

As we see, the problem of "true universalism" and brotherhood of all the people is solved by Jehovah in a very "merciful" and "democratic" way. The Judaic teaching "shall declare Jehovah's glory among the Gentiles" offering them to renounce voluntarily those creeds and customs, which they profess. Otherwise "the slain of the Lord shall be many." Whom and for what sins will the Lord slay? It appears that he will slay all those who "sanctify themselves and purify themselves in the gardens behind one tree in the midst, eating swine's flesh, and the abomination, and the mouse." "All of them shall be consumed together," saith the "loving" and "merciful" Lord.

We Christians, thank goodness, do not sanctify ourselves in the gardens behind one tree in the midst, but we do it in churches that are full of different images of God and of saints which jealous God Jehovah has strictly forbidden to worship as early as in the times of Moses. That is why Jehovah will hardly forgive us for such an infringement of his commandments, for the prohibition to worship other gods and any images was the first, the most important and obligatory for "the God's people."

As for swine's flesh, we ate it, we eat it nowadays and we shall eat it despite of all interdictions given to us by our beloved God Jehovah, for there was one man whose name was Paul whom Jewish rabbis sent to Christians in order to avert them from Jesus Christ's teaching and bring them back into the bosom of the Biblical matrix. Thus, having adopted pagan Paul's teaching, they were plunged into all mortal sins and changed into carcasses for physical exercises of God-butcher Jehovah. This very Paul has induced Christians to reject the doctrine of justification by Law, replacing it with the doctrine of justification by Faith.

But, in spite of accepting the Bible as a basis of their creed, Christians continue to sin against God Jehovah, attracting his anger, which he will pour out on them at the day of his vengeance.

And it can hardly be otherwise. For if everyone will accept Judaism and will execute all Jehovah's commandments, no one will be left to be crashed and killed, and God-butcher Jehovah will not have his bloody food, and will have to play tricks upon people in order to tempt them, to lead them astray, to plunge them into a sin, and then to crash and kill them for this very sin.

Thank goodness we also do not eat "the abomination and the mouse," but this fact will hardly help us. And those who will come to the Lord God "from one new moon to another, and from one sabbath to another," will see our "corpses" which will be "an abhorring unto all flesh." It is the very God's kingdom: the new earth and the new sky, where the throne of God-butcher Jehovah shines in azure height, where 144 000 immaculate sons of twelve Jewish tribes fall down day and night and glorify his divine justice. And below, in the dark depths of the old world lies the old earth, tormented and covered with blood and corpses of those who have not come to bow before God Jehovah; of those who "sanctify themselves, and purify themselves in the gardens behind one tree in the midst, eating swine's flesh, and the abomination, and the mouse;" of those, who have not wished to betray their gods and their culture, making thus a deadly sin of idolatry.

But the most interesting fact is that people, reading all these cruel and terrible words, do not express any negative emotions. Some of them can even be pleased with God's killing one or another thousand of human sons and daughters. When you ask such "Christians" whether they have a pity towards those unfortunate pagans (men, women, old men and children) who are trampled down, crushed and exterminated in the great God's anger, they answer they have not even a trace of pity towards them. "They are infidels. That serves them right!" is almost a standard answer of those "loving and compassionate" "Christians."

How indifferent we are towards another's pain! We got used to murders and mockeries of other people made by the mighty of this world, but we grieve immensely when the trouble concerns ourselves! And here springs up quite a reasonable question, "Why did the religious imagination, expressed in the Judaic myth, portray the God's personality in such an unattractive form?"

Crivelev, I. A gives the answer: "The answer to this question is easy to find if to proceed from a rule that people create God in the image and likeness of themselves. It is also very important to take into account, that this image is not abstract and timeless, but concretely-historical, caused by certain stages of mankind development. Biblical God is antroph-amorphous and humaniform. The latter means that he is similar to the man not only by external forms and fleshly needs and feelings, but also by mental characteristics, by an intellectual level, by intellectual and moral demands and interests and by his moral aspect. **People who create God in their imagination transfer onto him their own physical, intellectual and moral properties**.

People allocate God with their own, extremely exaggerated

properties: human power turns into omnipotence, knowledge—into omniscience, moral values—into infinite virtue and sanctity. And all these actually remain only in the form of words, for religious imagination cannot keep constantly this boundless exaggeration of God's qualities.

People cannot make God stronger, or cleverer, as well as more moral, than they are themselves. All the magnificent epithets applied to God, are not justified in any degree in the light of what the Bible says about him, as well as the written documents of other religions (italics is ours). Being almighty, he appears to be unable to overcome any obstacle; in particular, he can not do away both with his antagonist Satan and with evil forces, headed by him. Being omniscient, he always gets into trouble and makes unforgiving mistakes. Being good and saint, he incessantly makes improper acts which are perceived by the consciousness of the modern man as just shameful. As for the world outlook of the man of those times, when biblical myths and legends were developed and fixed in books, the portrayed above physical, mental and moral shape of God corresponded to the historically determined consciousness of that man."[133]

And now imagine a completely impossible picture. At the same time, several nations accepted a completely brutal, malicious and severe ideology of Judaic myth in their own interpretation and made it the basis of their life, according to which the people who are not "the God's people" should be exterminated. Now each nation will consider only its interpretation as to be absolutely true, and all others to be false. Now each nation will consider only itself to be "the elected God's people," and all the others to be "infidels" and thus rejected by God.

The words of Reverend Father Rouse[134] can serve as a proof to this assumption. Once people asked him: "The Gospel has been already preached almost to all the peoples. Does it mean that there comes the time of the Last Judgment? "No," answered the Reverend Father, "**the Gospel of Jesus Christ should be preached in all the languages of the world in the orthodox understanding**. Only then the Last Judgment will come."[135]

"Infidels," according to the Judaic teaching, are to accept one or another of its form, or to be exterminated. According to the Father Rouse, the whole world should accept the Christian religious model, but only "in the orthodox understanding." Then it is not clear what is the Last Judgment for, if everyone professes correct teaching. Ah, yes, we have absolutely forgotten that our "kind and merciful" Lord God "will exterminate both righteous and wicked."

But the fact is that people do not want to change the form of their creed even under the threat of death. Then the religious intolerance, enmity and division among peoples and nations spring up; then crusades, inquisition, religious wars, Varfolomey nights and the nights of long knifes begin; then a religion from the force, which is to unite the people and nations, turns into a huge, insurmountable power which divides them.

But it appears that the gloomy picture drawn by us is not so impossible. On the contrary, it is very possible. Doesn't it remind the modern situation in the world when we have, on the one hand, Judaic myth as the Moses' Law, i.e. as so-called Old Testament, and, on the other hand, its various interpretations such as Christian and Moslem Churches and sects? And each creed leaves the right on the truth in the last instance only for itself. Is it possible to have peaceful coexistence of people and nations in the world in the present state of affairs? Certainly, it is not. Therefore, the entire world floats in blood of innocently exterminated human sons and daughters, who cry and groan and ask for help and do not find it ...

Can we, after what we have told about the Judaic myth, consider it to be a positive value for man and humankind? Does it satisfy with those humanistic criteria and ideals which were produced by honor and decent representatives of Homo sapiens? Has the Judaic myth passed the test for humanity? The answers to all these questions can be only negative, for this myth is a product of collective work of the barbarous peoples distinguished with monstrous, unprecedented cruelty and bloodthirstiness. That is why, to use this myth for a spiritual growth and perfection is the same as to build, let us say, a space ship with Paleolithic stone tools.

2. 9. How Many Faces Does the Jewish God Jehovah Have?

The Christian church teaches that God Jehovah has only one face, that he is all-merciful, all-pleased, all-graceful and completely unchangeable at all times and in all circumstances. Seraphim Slobodscoy says in the *God's Law*: "God is the highest being, he is supernatural. It is impossible to know God's essence. It is higher than any knowledge of not only people, but even angels. From the God's revelation, from the clear words of the Holy Scriptures, we can have a concept about God's essence and his basic properties: **God is Spirit** (John 4: 24), **unchangeable** (Jacob. 1: 17, Malachai 3: 6, Psalms 101:28), **omnipresent** (Psalms. 138: 7-12, Acts 17: 27), **omniscient** (I John. 3: 29, Jude. 4: 13),

all-good (Matthew. 19: 17, Psalms 24: 8), **all-pleased** (Acts. 17: 25), **all-blissful** (I Timothy. 6: 15)."[136]

Really, God is a spirit. But what kind of a spirit? As far as we know, God Jehovah has two spirits—the evil one and the lying one, and, though Isaiah mentions the Holy Spirit, it is still inactive. As for God's being unchangeable, we should argue with the *God's Law* because we know very well that Biblical God, like a chameleon, constantly changes his face and his form depending on environmental conditions. God can hardly be omniscient, for he falls into forgetfulness very often and does not know at all what is going on under his nose. As for God's being all-blissful and all-pleased, these qualities were never inherent in God-butcher Jehovah, who cannot live even a day without giving way to rage and killing one or more thousand of innocent people.

Further the *God's Law* says, "God is good (Matthew. 19: 17). The man are not always good. Frequently it happens that one doesn't love somebody. **Only God loves everybody and he does it in a maximum degree unlike anybody of the people**. He gives us everything what we need and takes care of us like a father. God has created everything we see in the sky and on the earth for the benefit of the man ... Therefore God is called all-good or all-merciful (very kind). And we name God our **Heavenly Father**."[137]

Yes, our Heavenly Father is kind and all-merciful. Yes, he loves those who worship him, and out of his great love to the man he kills, crashes, destroys, consumes and exterminates innocent people who worship other gods, who "eat swine's flesh, and the abomination, and the mouse." Isn't it interesting and strange love? If one does not eat swine's flesh, and the abominations and the mouse, if one worships and serves only to God Jehovah, then God loves this man. If this man eat swine's flesh, it is already enough the rage of the Sovereign God (Jehovah) to flare up on this man, and then this "merciful," "all-blissful" and "all-pleased" Lord God-"savior" will "scorn," "crash," "destroy," "consume" or "exterminate" the one who dared to break his instructions.

How can we combine these completely incompatible things about the same God, or we do not understand something? "Yes, you understand everything incorrectly, each faithful man or a priest will tell you. "**We trust with faith which even makes liars to say the truth and can transform even dog's bones in magic relics**."[138] And you subject everything to "humanistic analysis," and thus it never occurred to you that all these things cannot be perceived literally. It is only an allegory and the Biblical text itself is in general the ciphered God's message to people. Therefore, you are not able to understand what you read. It is quite allegorically that God kills innocent infants, it is quite allegorically that he orders to exterminate all the inhabitants of the land of Canaan, and in reality he is kind and merciful."

He probably orders to kill allegorically, but people, for some reason, kill, consume and exterminate not allegorically, they commit real atrocities. And that movie about murder, which English children watched, also was allegorical. Who knows what was on the producer's mind when he made that film? Nevertheless, the murder was real. It was a bloody, brutal murder. And terrorist acts that take away thousands human lives all over the world are real too.

For human consciousness, there is no difference whether it is allegory or not. If it is told: "Go and destroy Amalek," it means it is necessary to go and to destroy that Amalek. If it is told: "Kill infidel," it means it is necessary to go and to kill him. And the Jews went, and destroyed, and killed "both man and woman, infant and suckling, ox and sheep, camel and ass." And they threw stones at fields in order anything not to grow on them. And then crusaders went and exterminated all "infidels", heretics and "God's enemies". Then inquisition in the name of Father, Son and Holy Spirit has burned alive several millions of people, then Moslems by means of sword and fire have converted the half of the world into Islam, then religious wars have began, and they still go on and carry away lives of real people. But at that time the Jews knew only about God-Father, they still did not know about the Son or about the Holy Spirit.

Who was this God-Father? Was it really the original Jewish God, or did they borrow him from someone? Sigmund Freud answers this question: "They have adopted there (in Meriva-Cadesh) the worship of God Jahve—apparently from an Arabian tribe living nearby... Jahve was undoubtedly God of volcanoes... Despite of all reductions, according to E. Meyer, the Biblical version has undergone the initial characteristic image of God which gives way to reconstruction: "**it is dreadful, bloodthirsty demon, wandering at night and avoiding day light**. (Meyer, E. *Die Israiliten und Ihre Nachbarstamme*, 1906. S. 38, 58)."[139] And it is the same God, "**God, possessed with absoluteness as much as no one creation of a religious history, and with cruelty, which anybody has never surpassed after him,**"[140] who stands behind the whole history of Christianity.

In the beginning of the Bible, in the book of Genesis, God is a gray-haired old man who creates the world and the man together with Elohim, his colleagues. Elohim are material beings which create material things, though it is not clear where they came from. One of these Elohim, probably the most important of them, appears in the further narration under the name the Lord God. This God plants a garden eastward in Eden; and he puts Adam and Eva there. There lives a material serpent which tempts the first people. They fall into a mortal sin and God Jehovah expels them from the garden-paradise.

Then material God's sons enter into material human daughters who give birth to material giants. People fall into a great sin, and God destroys with a flood all humankind except for Noah's family. After the flood, God does not venture to have any close relations with man which he had at the dawn of creation. That dawn was slightly darkened with criminal motives of human hearts and souls. Now, he only occasionally appears to his elected peoples and frequently sends his angels if there is a necessity to enter into contact with the man. The angels are also material; one can see them, one can hear them and even touch them.

Where does God live in this period is unclear, for Eden was probably destroyed during the flood. By the time of the exodus of the Jews from Egypt, the material nature of God undergoes a certain metamorphoses which was necessary to find room in the Ark of Covenant because it was not a very spacious structure. Though Moses communicates with him and even sees him "face to face," it is not that gray-haired old man who used to walk in the paradise "in the cool of the day." It is already a certain terrible and awful half-material being, one glance at which could kill a man. It destroys tens of thousands people only for their being dared to look into the Arc of Covenant—the box, in which Jehovah sat and struck people with terrible "emerods in their secret parts." And this being stays every day with the Jewish people during their wandering in the desert, and then it inspires them on fits of arms during their battles with the inhabitants of Canaan.

After the first temple had been built, this strange and obscure being, which is called Jahve or Jehovah, achieved such a level of development that the space of the temple became cramped. It happened because Jahve lost its materiality and moved to live in the heaven, whence days and nights it kept an eye on each step of the man; whence it tempted him and then severely punished for a sin that was made with its connivance.

This resettlement to the heaven takes place approximately in IX century b. c., and later, beginning approximately with VI century b. c., the knowledge of Greek philosophers begins to penetrate to Palestine and radically changes the world outlook of the ancient man. There appears the ideas about the certain ideal spiritual world, in which God lives together with the angels. There develops the concept about a soul as immortal, indestructible substation containing in itself the human self which can exist even after death.

2. 10. For Whom and for What Purpose Was the Jewish Law Written?

If you ask an orthodox priest about whom the Moses' Law was written for, he will certainly answer that it was intended only for the orthodox Christians because the Jews were rejected by God, and, therefore, they cannot be "the God's people." And if orthodox Christians have become "the God's people," so the Moses' Law had been written only for them. However, for some reason, Christians do not trouble themselves with its execution. Certainly, they can say that Jesus Christ has given them the new law, thus, having cancelled the old one. And if the old law, i. e. the Old Testament, is cancelled, what do we need this abominable, bloody book which is called the Bible, for? But, nevertheless, we constantly use it, successfully realizing on practice its cruel and man-hating principles of "salvation."

As a matter of fact, the Jews always remained and remain up to this time the elected "God's people." That is why, among those 144 000 who will ascend to the new earth (to the great regret of orthodox priests and their parishioners), will be only representatives of twelve Jewish tribes. And our fate on that holiday of the Jewish life is to be those carcasses, at which the Jews will look, leaving Jerusalem after their coming weekly for worshiping God-butcher Jehovah because we have broken all his instruction and commandments.

Of course, we shall refer to Jesus Christ and to his New Testament which is a new covenant that God Jehovah concluded, ostensibly, with us, but, as you probably know, the "savior" has told once, "I have come not to break the law, but to execute it." It is also possible to refer to Paul, who, ostensibly, has cancelled the Law. But who was Paul? Was he an insane epileptic who, during one of his epileptic seizures, imagined that Jesus directed him on the right way, or was he an agent of Jewish rabbis who sent him to subordinate pagans to the influence of the "holy book" which name is the Bible?

Anyway, the Bible itself asserts that the Moses' Law was intended exclusively to the people of Israel. Psalm 147: 19-20 says, "**He sheweth his word unto Jacob, his statutes and his judgments unto Israel. He hath not dealt so with any nation**: and as for his judgments, they have not known them."

God has not given the Law to Gentiles. The Bible clearly says that

"Gentiles have not the Law."[141] The Jews, as Paul asserts, were given the advantage before Gentiles "because that onto them [Jews] were committed the oracles of God."[142] He says: "Who are Israelites; to whom pertaineth the adoption, and the glory, and the covenants, and the giving of the law, and the service of God, and the promises. Whose are the fathers, and of whom as concerning the flesh Christ came, who is over all, God blessed for ever. Amen."[143]

None of these laws were given to Gentiles. "**Actually, during the whole history of the world, ancient Israel was the only people elected by God in order it live according to his sacred Law**."[144]

It means that we have no right to attach ourselves to the Jewish God-butcher Jehovah, as well as to his Law given exclusively to the Jewish people. Since the time immemorial, they professed Judaism and do it till now, thus proving every day that it was not in vain that God Jehovah had elected them to be "the God's people."

Now we should find out for what purpose and for whom the Jewish Law was written. The Jewish writer Morris Samuel once told: **"We, Jews, are destroyers and we will remain destroyers for ever... Whatever other peoples do, it will never meet either our needs, or our demands.**"[145]

These words mean that the one who was born a Jew and still is a Jew, receives, according to the matrix [the Bible] influence law, the destructive impulse which he must realize during his life. The fact is that deviating from the Law, a Jew ceases to be a good one in the eyes of his leaders. If one wants or is compelled to be a Jew, one must obey to this Law, for the sense of the Law consists in this obedience: "**This [obedience] explains the fact that the role of the Jewish leaders always was, throughout the entire history, and could not be other than destructive one**."[146]

In the life of our generation of the XX century, its destructive mission has achieved the greatest force that leads to totally unexpected results. And not only the author of this book has such an opinion. **Both Zion scholars and rabbis who betrayed Judaism, even without mention of non-Jewish historians, always agreed among themselves about Jewish mission of destruction**. All the serious researchers have no doubt in it, and, perhaps, this is the only question in the answering of which we can find complete unanimity.

The entire Holy Scripture, the whole history of mankind is presented by the Jews in such account that destruction is the necessary precondition for executing of the Jewish Law and for a final triumph of the Jewry. The history of mankind is imagined by a Jew differently than it is imagined by a Christian. If for the Christian the history means the chronicle of Christianity and little bit earlier to the time of legends and myths; for the Jew the history is written down in □ora-Talmud and in the sermons of rabbis. The beginning if this history goes as back as 3 760 years b. c., ostensibly, exact date of the world creation.

Douglas, R. asserts: "There is no difference between "the Law" and "the history," and there is no other history, except for Jewish one; **the entire narration is developed before the eyes of a Jew as a consecutive line of destructive actions and Jewish vengeance**, regardless it is nowadays or 3. 000 years ago. In such an account, the life of all other peoples and nations loses any interest and importance. It is rather instructive for non-Jews to look both at the present and at the future of the world with the Jewish eyes: **they will see that everything which seemed to them essential, everything they could be proud or ashamed of, will appear simply not existing or will be only a grey background for a colourful history of Zion. As though one looks with one eye at oneself through the back end of a telescope, and with another one at Judea through a magnifying glass.**"[147]

A truthful Jew imagines the world as a plane, and he places Judea as the future owner of this world, in its centre. That is why the urgent aspiration of Jewish leaders to expansion which expressed in imposing of their theories and ideas to the Western world, becomes quite understandable.

The basis of the Law created by Levites is the order "to destroy." "If one throws it [the order "to destroy"] out, there will not be any sense in the Moses' Law, and the whole religion will turn into something absolutely different. **Imperative: "destroy"—is its basic characteristic**, and this very word had been chosen not unintentionally. It was possible to put other words: win, capture, subordinate, and so on, but only "to destroy" had been elected. **The word had been invented by scholars and was put in God's lips**. And it had been this very distortion of the Old Testament, that Jesus Christ exposed, by telling to Jewish scholars, "you... teach to the human laws."[148]

If we recollect the book of Genesis, we shall see a completely different God. That God (even not God at all, but gods) who engage themselves in their own businesses, creating the world, the man and animals are being pleased with their creation, for everything they had created "was good." Elohim lived in a paradise and, as it may seem, was pleased with everything. Only animal sacrifices were made to this God (or gods), and he (or they) has never demanded to sacrifice "the firstborns of human sons." In the book of Genesis we already see a completely different God. This God is a terrible, shady personality, which lives on the mount of Zion in darkness, in fire and in smoke and threatens everyone who dares to come nearer to this mountain with death and demands human sacrifices. In the shape of this monster we recognize Jahve, the God of volcanoes, whom Jewish rabbis successfully used to create the religion of death and destruction.

It was necessary for them to occupy the land "flowing with milk and honey," or in the other and more modern words, for the building of the "brilliant future." Levites, i. e. Jewish priests, pursuing their aggressive purposes, have attributed to the Lord God the terrible words ostensibly told by him before the occupation of the "promised land," "... you will exterminate all the peoples, which your Lord God gives you in possession."

Reed Douglas says: "**Beginning with this {order}, requirement "destroy" passes through the entire Law. It stands on the first place, and only after it the description of historical events follows.**"[149]

And the act of destruction is represented very often as a bargain between God and his elected people. At that, the "destruction" of people that Lord God gives in possession to Jews is the main condition of this bargain. In the book of Exodus, God Jehovah says, "If you... execute everything, I shall tell you, I shall be the enemy of your enemies... and you will destroy all the people, that your Lord God gives you."

When Israel had rejected the Jews, leaving them alone together with Levites, they {Jews} fell under absolute authority of their priests. The meaning of their doctrine consisted in that the main Jehovah's requirement was destruction of everything "foreign", or of "every thing that was vile and refuse," and that they, the Jews, were elected for this purpose by God himself.

Thus, the Jews had been turned into the only people which mission was destruction as it is, and it was the unique case in the history of mankind. Destruction, as the accompanying factor of war, is a well familiar feature of the world's history. **But destruction, as the openly announced purpose, was not known until then; the only source of this idea, known for us, is Tora-Talmud**...

During all the time when the large majority of people scattered among other nations submitted to this cruel law, their energy inevitably should be directed on destruction. In 458-444 years b. c., when Levites managed, with the Persian help, to put the weeping crowds of their people into chains of the Jewish Law, "**the nation was born, which since then plays a role of the catalyst: not being changed itself, it systematically changes the vital conditions and character of the**

neighboring nations. The Jews have become this universal catalyst, and **the changes caused by them were always destructive**. This process has brought much grief and misfortunes to non-Jewish peoples (who themselves, by their complaisance to a ruling sect, incurred these disasters), not having given, however, anything good to the Jews, who have inherited this sad mission."[150]

But the most interesting fact here is that the Law ordered to "the elected God's people" to destroy with special diligence those peoples, among which they were scattered by God Jehovah in punishment for their own sins. In the book of Exodus, this principle is proclaimed for the first time. According to it, "the God's people" should help the enemies of the country which has sheltered them. The history of the fall of Babylon, for example, is stated in the Bible so that to emphasize this very principle. The Jews are portrayed as the assistants of Babylon's enemies who met Persian conquerors with joy. The destruction of Babylon is depicted as Jehovah's revenge for the sake of the Jews. Even the death of the king of Babylon looks as the act of God's vengeance for his being oppressed by the Jews, which he did with the connivance of God Jehovah. It is doubtless that historically, both facts are fiction, but it is important for us as the deliberately composed precedent.

Further Douglas, R. says: "The events, as they are depicted in the Old Testament, end with one more act of vengeance. This time it falls on the heads of Persian liberators. In our twentieth century, western politicians frequently feel themselves flattered, when Zion emissaries compare them to the Persian king Cyrus, the liberator of the Jews. They hardly read the Law attentively, or they did not pay attention to what happened then to Persians, who had to pay for the Jews being lived among them."[151]

Thus, we have traced the process of transformation of Jews into "the only people in the history of mankind which mission is destruction as it is." This "destruction," this "extermination" has been openly announced as the main goal of "the God's people."

And, as the small people scattered throughout the world can not physically realize their goal of destruction of the Gentile world, the only way in the solving of this problem is the stimulation of hatred, enmity and division among people and nations, which will result in their mutual destruction. And how is it possible to do that? It is necessary just to distribute the Biblical doctrine throughout the world. It is necessary to submit it so that it becomes a matrix which could form human consciousness programming it on destruction.

Then the goal put before the Jews by God-butcher Jehovah will be achieved, and the Jews will gain "the God's kingdom," promised by their Jewish rabbis. They will receive so much "boons of the future age," that they will not be able to carry them away. They will live happily on a new earth and look with great pleasure at the old one heaped with carcasses of Gentiles whom they had twisted round a finger so boldly and skillfully.

The first attempt was carried out in the III century b. c., when seventy Jewish translators translated the Tora (Moses' Pentateuch) into the Greek language. All seventy translations coincided to the last letter, having presented to the world the translation of the Bible known as Septuagint. Modern historians assert that this translation was made, ostensibly, for the Jews, who, living in Diaspora in Greece and in Asia, had forgotten their native language. It is hardly so, because, as it is well known, ethnic minorities living in Diaspora always aspire to preserve the native language and all the cultural values. Moreover, after Jews' resettlement, not too much time has passed, that they could possibly have forgetten the native language. It means the Bible has been translated not for the Jews. Certainly, Jewish rabbis tried in such a way to distribute the influence of destructive ideas at least within the limits of the world accessible to them. But neither Greeks, nor Romans, as well as other people of the world, wanted to accept the belief in a completely alien God Jehovah.

The second and more successful attempt was carried out during the reign of John Gircan (60th b. c.), who, waging war with Hellenic Syria, offered to its population to accept Jewry voluntarily. Those who did not want to accept the belief in God Jehovah were cruelly and ruthlessly destroyed on the occasion of which Arnold G. Fruchtenbaum [quoted above] said that it is not necessary to deny the positive value of Judaism as a religion just because of incidental murders perpetrated in the name of Jehovah.

"'It will be completely unfair,' he complains, 'because from the fact of John Gircan's using the name of Moses and killing in the name of Judaism does not follow that Moses or Judaism themselves teach that these murders should be perpetrated."[152] And what shall we do with the fact that the Tora from the beginning to the end is literally staffed with the orders to kill and to destroy all the "infidels," including women, old men, children, camels and even asses? What shall we do with its orders to exterminate all the "vile and refuse" things [infidels], to destroy all the places of service to other gods etc.?

Both Jewish and Christian apologists of the Jewish God Jehovah will answer that all these cruel and bloody things are just allegory, that one does not have to perceive God's words literally, thus approving both allegorical and real murders perpetrated in the name of their God.

Herod, who had built the temple to God Jehovah in Jerusalem, also contributed to conversion of Gentiles into Jewry. Besides, in the "holy city," he erected pagan temples with the statues of Zeus and Rome; he built gymnasiums, palaces, markets, water-pipes and bathhouses. The Jewish people grumbled on Herod for his infringement of traditions of their fathers, but Herod also served very much to the expansion of Judaism, giving the daughters from Herod's dynasty in marriage to Asian princes who had to accept Jewry.

However hard did Jewish rabbis exercise their wits to subordinate Gentiles to the belief in God Jehovah, nobody wished to accept Jewry voluntarily. And if some of them, nevertheless, did it, it was not to become a Jew, but only to gain material benefit.

It was necessary to invent something that would make those Gentiles accept Jewry voluntary and even with a large pleasure. It was necessary to inculcate the belief in cruel and bloodthirsty God-butcher-filicide Jehovah, so that these inverted Gentiles made Tora the basis of their life and continued the business of "destruction" of the world which had been started by their ancestors.

The Christian movement that appeared in Judea after Jesus Christ's crucifixion had given the Jews such a chance. And they skillfully used it in order to transform Jesus' moral teaching into the religion of church and Holy Scripture that became at last the very matrix which was to destroy the gentile world.

2. 11. Does the Hidden Biblical Code Exist?

The Bible, as it is believed, is God's word which he has dictated to Moses on the mount of Sinai. Moses wrote down this message on the stone tablets letter by letter without blanks and punctuation marks. This message is known to a modern reader as the "TORA" or the Moses' Pentateuch, and represents by itself the first five books of the Old Testament. These five books, on opinion of a very meticulous reader, contain the hidden code, by means of which "kind and merciful" God Jehovah has ciphered his own prophecies about the future events and about the Last Judgment.

And it is quite in his character. Therefore, God-butcher-filicide Jehovah could not inform people about the future events openly in order that they could prevent them. But he has given the instructions concerning the methods of changing the world into a slaughterhouse quite openly.

Many men of great intellect tried to find this code in the Bible, but all their attempts were in vain. Even the great English physicist Isaac Newton was sure that the Bible contained the hidden code in which the knowledge of the future had been ciphered. Newton was convinced that not only the Bible, but also the entire Universe is the "cryptographic writing of God," and he tried to solve a riddle of past and future events outlined by a divine craft.

The first hint on a cod mechanism solution was discovered more than fifty years ago in Prague by rabbi Veismandel. He noticed that if one skips fifty letters from the beginning of the book of Genesis, takes one, skips again fifty letters and so on, the word "Tora" will appear. The same phenomenon can be found in the book of Numbers and in the book of Deuteronomy.

Israeli mathematician Eliyahu Rips, who also had began the search for the code, learned by chance about the Veismandel's invention. Rips started with entering of the names of thirty-two Jewish sages into a computer. The computer found that all of them are contained in the hidden Biblical text; moreover, the computer has found the dates of their births and deaths standing next to their names.

Michael Drosnin says: "Rips has handed me a copy of an article with the results of initial experiment. The article was called *Equidistant Alphabetic Sequences in the Book of Genesis*. The annotation said that the probabilistic analysis confirms that the text of the book of Genesis contains in itself hidden information in the form of equidistant (located on identical distance from each other) alphabetic sequences. This result has probability 99, 998 %."[153]

The parallel search in the text of *War and Peace*, as Drosnin asserts, has not given any results. The fact of existence of the hidden Biblical code had, thus, been proven; the article with the description of invention and confirmation of results by the independent experts appeared in a magazine *Statistical Science* (Vol. 9 (1994) p. 429-438), and Israeli journalist Michael Drosnin began to write a book about a hidden Biblical code which he published in 1997. The book became at once the best seller. *Newsweek* and *Time* wrote articles about it; and the book had such a success at the reader that its author has undertaken even a worldwide tour demonstrating the epoch-making invention mainly to Christians and atheists. The Jews would hardly believe him and Moslems would not even listen to him.

Drosnin used the method developed by Eliyahu Rips in his work. As well as Rips, he had arranged all the 304 805 letters of the first five books of the Bible in one line without blanks and punctuation marks and entered them into a computer. He began finding out whether a name Yitzhak Rabin is contained in the hidden Biblical text. To the great joy of the journalist, the computer really has found this name with a step 4 772 marks between the letters.

Further, the method anticipates reorganization of a matrix so that the found letters were arranged in one vertical line. After the matrix reorganization Drosnin has found the prediction of Yitzhak Rabin's murder, which crossed his name like in a crossword puzzle.

I. e. the width of the matrix is determined by a number of letters standing between the letters of a key word. In the case with Yitzhak Rabin, the width of the matrix should be 4 772 letters, its height 64 lines and all the other letters should be situated on the right hand side from the key word (it is possible to construct the matrix in such a manner that the letters of the key word will be located on the left hand side, or diagonally). The left hand side of the matrix will be empty. And, if it is so, then it is impossible to make a crossword puzzle out of such a matrix.

But the matrix received by Drosnin looks like a crossword puzzle. In it, the letters are located on the both sides of the key word, which, according to the laws of logic, is impossible. That is why we doubted both the efficiency of the method and good intentions of the Israeli journalist to warn the people about approaching disasters. Having read attentively the whole book, we have found so many mistakes and absurdities that it became quite evident to us that the hidden Biblical code is, as Adolph Hitler said, "the same old Jewish trickery."

Michael Drosnin asserts that he, ostensibly, has found both a mention about many important events of the past and the prophecies about the future disasters in the hidden Biblical text. **There were many prophecies concerning "the Last Judgment" which should come in 1995-1996**. The code predicted "world war," "nuclear holocaust," "pestilence" and "holocaust of Israel." As the place of the future, "Armageddon," the cod indicated Libya in one case, Israel—in the second case and Japan- in the third. It is interesting that in all these cases there were indications that such a great disaster "was postponed by them," or "postponed by you," or "postponed by the friend," which is in a spirit of all the prophets who prophesied before Michael Drosnin.

Many had came and prophesied about the future, but their prophecies did not come true for some reason. As far back as the Old Testament times, the prophets Isaiah, Ezekiel, Jeremiah, Daniel and many others began to prophesy about the last days of the world and about the Last Judgment, which Jehovah would do to clear the Earth from sinners, pagans and unbelievers and to establish God's kingdom on the earth.

Jesus Christ and his apostles had also promised that many living at that time would not taste death before they saw his Second Advent and the Last Judgment to judge all the unbelievers. But all of them have either died, or have been exterminated during persecutions without having waited till the promised god's kingdom in which God would wipe tears out of their eyes, and there would be no mourning, there would be no death.

In his Revelation, John the Theologian gave the wide picture of the Last Judgment, during which all the unbelievers would be punished and thrown forever into the lake burning with fire and sulfur.

In 339, John the Chrysostome announced about the approaching Last Judgment, but the year 400 came and nothing happened. John, trying to clear himself, shifted his mistake on to God, having announced that God, having seen sinners' repentance, decided to postpone his judgment for an unlimited time.

In 1831, William Miller, the founder of Adventism, having taken his own interpretation of prophet Daniel as the base for his calculations, began to announce that the Second Advent would take place in 1843. But Jesus has never come.

On the eve of the XX century, Sergey Neelus spoke of the advent of antichrist and of the approaching Last Judgment. The whole century had passed, but a thunder did not brake out and a fire did not kindle itself to burn all the unbelievers.

In 1919 Vladimir Lenin, prophesying about the victory of the world revolution, promised that many wouldn't die until they saw the golden age of a communism.

The long-awaited year 2000 also fell short of Christians' expectations of the Second Advent and the Last Judgment. And, at last, the Catholic Church, having carried out a computer processing of Virgin Mary's prophesies, which she gave in Fatima, and those of Nostradamus, came to a conclusion that the year 2001 would be the year of the Second Advent and the Last Judgment.

This prophecy could hardly come true because the Life develops itself under the natural laws given by the Creator, and can not be stopped by the cruel and bloody act of the Last Judgment. The year 2001 has passed, but the Last Judgment, promised by the Catholic Church, has not come. Again, "the friend has postponed."

Michael Drosnin predicts "great earthquakes" in 1994, 1995, 1996, 2000, 2006, 2010 and in 2113, "nuclear holocaust" and "world war" in

2000 or in 2006, as well as "the destruction of the earth by a comet" in 2006, 2012 and in 2126. It is strange that the Biblical code does not say even a word about atrocities of September 11, 2001 (Of course, Michael Drosnin discovered it in the Bible just after the event. He wrote about that in his second book about the Biblical code). Probably because God himself is, as asserts one of the American Christian preachers, the executor of these monstrous terrorist acts.

This preacher says that God did it in order to remind Americans about his existence, about which they have begun to forget lately. He did it once towards his "chosen people." Then, God gave them into the hands of Assyrians. After that, he destroyed Assirians for their destroying Jews in spite of the fact that Assyrians destroyed Jews by God's orders. Why the Americans have to avoid this terrible fate? And with the terrorists, God will do the same as he did with Assyrians. He will punish them, and, certainly, that punishment will be very cruel.

Familiar handwriting, is not it? In such a way the mighty of this world deal with the executors of ordered murders, who, having done it, become the dangerous witnesses subject to physical elimination. The speech of this priest appeared on the Internet some days after the tragedy and caused extremely inconsistent opinions among the American people.

So, none of Drosnin's prophecies has come true, as well as the prophecies of many other predictors of the future. What does it mean? It means that, "the source of the mysterious "Bible code" has been revealed—it's homo sapiens."[154]

Such was the conclusion which all the experts, analyzing the invention of Rips—Witzum—Rosenberg—Drosnin, agreed upon. They also found out that, contrary to the authors' statement, the "ciphered" messages can be found practically in any book. "McKay, for example, has found "prophecies" about the murder of Indira Gandhi, Rene Moavad, Leon Trotsky, Martin Luter King and Robert F. Kennedy in the book *Moby Dick* (look at http: // cs.anu.edu.au / ~ bdm/dilugim/moby.html). But Eliyahu Rips himself totally denies the Michael Drosnin's statement that they had worked on together. 'I do not support the book in that form as it is, and I do not agree with conclusions, which follow out of it' he says.'"[155]

But the most serious counter-evidence against existence of the Biblical code has appeared in that very magazine which had published the article about "ingenious" invention of Rips—Witzum—Rosenberg—Drosnin for the first time. Soon, after a careful check of the invention results, the magazine was compelled to publish a refutation, in which the following was spoken: "We are now happy to announce that, after review by four senior statisticians chosen by the journal, *Statistical Science* has published a thorough rebuttal: Vol. 14 (1999) 150-173. The new paper is Solving the Bible Code Puzzle, by Brendan McKay, Dror Bar-Natan, Maya Bar-Hillel, and Gil Kalai."

Here is the abstract: "A paper of Witztum, Rips and Rosenberg in this journal in 1994 made the extraordinary claim that the Hebrew text of the Book of Genesis encodes events which did not occur until millennia after the text was written. In reply, we argue that **Witztum, Rips and Rosenberg's case is fatally defective, indeed that their result merely reflects on the choices made in designing their experiment and collecting the data for it**. We present extensive evidence in support of that conclusion. **We also report on many new experiments of our own, all of which failed to detect the alleged phenomenon.**"[156]

Soon after Michael Drosnin's book had been published, *Time* magazine also published an article which rebutted the Israeli journalist's statement about the Biblical code made by him in his book: "The rebutting of Michael Drosnin's book, made by Rips enabled to refer rather disputable code theory to the genre of a "millennium current..." **Shlomo Sternberg, a mathematician of the Harvard University, professor and rabbi calls Drosnin's book "absolute nonsense..."** Brendan McKay, professor of information science of Australian National University, asserts that "he has undertaken two versions of the experiment, but, as he says in his statement sent via E-mail, he had not detected the alleged phenomenon. Skilled unmasker McKay took for analyses *The UNO Marine Law Code* and has detected some hidden messages in it, including "Listen to the Marine Law." The probability of this phrase appearance, as McKay asserts, is hardly 95 per cent from one million. But the acknowledgment of its divine origin compel us to admit the existence of a rather playful deity."[157]

Edward Thomas has published the results of the analysis also in the *Skeptical Inquirer*: "I downloaded the chapter excerpt of Michael Drosnin's book, *The Bible Code*, from Simon and Schuster's Web site and began searching away. Even though the chapter was only about 4,000 characters in length, I was able to produce a number of hits. One puzzle held a lunar theme: "space," "lunar," "craft," and several "moon's," all authentic hidden words. I found the ubiquitous "Hitler/Nazi," even though the excerpt did not mention those words directly, talking instead mainly about the Rabin assassination. One puzzle has the hidden message "The code is a silly snake-oil hoax." And I even found "The code is evil" hidden in Drosnin's book."[158]

So, the very work of Michael Drosnin cries out to our judiciousness, asserting that the Biblical code is "a silly snake-oil hoax," which is obvious evil. Perhaps the true God, our Universal Father tries in such a way to warn us that we should be very attentive to various theories, which protect the malicious and heartless matrix that harden our hearts and souls and make us hate and to kill each other.

In this assertive desire of the Israeli scientists to present the Bible as a divine code, we see the agony of the matrix which, having felt its end approaching, tries by any means to protect itself from penetration into its animal-like and man-hating essence which represents by itself a monstrous conglomerate of lie, hypocrisy, hatred and cruelty, as well as the most impressive receptacle of double standards, human nonsense and absurdity.

Our world is arranged, most likely, so that on malicious irony of destiny, real prophets finish their lives on a cross. False prophets live long, travel around the world and attract crowds of people to their lectures about nonexistent Biblical code.

CHAPTER 3.

CHRISTIAN MYTH

"If a clever man had to choose a religion looking at those people, who profess it, Christianity would probably be the last he would have chosen."
Bishop Kider.

3. 1. Can the Idea of "God Choosiness" Become an Apple of Discord?

Before we begin to investigate the Christian myth, let us recollect a very interesting episode of the Greek myth of the Troy cycle. Eris (discord), as she, alone of the gods, was not invited to the marriage of Peleus and Thetis, threw among the guests a golden apple inscribed "For the most beautiful." Hera, Athena, and Aphrodite each claimed it, and Zeus assigned the decision to Paris. Paris awarded the apple to Aphrodite, who then helped him win Helen of Troy. In the war that resulted, Hera and Athena remained implacable enemies of Troy.

To recover Helen, the Greeks launched a great expedition under the overall command of Menelaus' brother, Agamemnon, King of Argos or Mycenae. The Trojans refused to return Helen. Small towns near Troy were sacked by the Greeks, but Troy, assisted by allies from Asia Minor and Thrace, withstood a Greek siege for 10 years.

Now let us imagine that a certain group of people invents a very attractive idea of "God-choosiness" and throws it into the world, intending it only for "the God's people," to which both the "salvation" and all the future boons have already been prepared. Now all the people have a burning desire to become the elected "God's people" in order "to be saved" and to receive those boons. Everyone declares the claims on that tasty, juicy "apple," but the trouble is that only one group of people can eat it. Moreover, the trouble is aggravated by the fact that the "apple" has already been awarded by God to his "elected people" on the condition that all other people must be either subordinated to the faith in this God or be destroyed.

But everybody wants to eat the tasty and juicy "apple," everyone wants "to be saved." I. e. there springs up a situation when theoretically it is possible both to become "the God's people" and "to be saved," but practically it is impossible because God himself has already chosen the people and promised "the salvation" only to them.

The normal human consciousness becomes deadlocked in such a situation, but not a religious one. After long, intense meditation, the religious consciousness concludes that, theoretically, it is impossible both to become "the God's people" and to be "saved," but practically it can be quite possible; for the religious consciousness does not care about theoretical possibilities. It is interested only in practical result—"the salvation," and "the salvation" at any cost, even if it is necessary to destroy the whole world, moreover God has promised to create the new one, in which the elected "God's people" will get so much boons of the next century, that they will not be able to carry them away. All the means are good to achieve such a goal, because the goal justifies all the means.

Nevertheless, the situation remains paradoxical. Then the religious consciousness finds a very witty decision. It announces that the elected "God's people" are not elected at all, but on the contrary, are rejected by God, and therefore are an enemy, which is to be destroyed. It announces itself and those who will join it to be "the God's people," to which both "the salvation" and all the boons of the next century have been prepared.

But, as the original contents of this concept (which is a matrix by itself) requires either to convert the whole world into the believers of God who has chosen them or to destroy it, violent expansion of this doctrine soon begins. The "God's word" is preached worldwide, destroying all those who do not wish to accept it on its way.

Besides, there begin to be formed other groups applying to be called "the God's people" which also begin the expansion of the doctrine into the world. And, as two bears cannot live in one den, the enmity and fratricidal wars between the applicants for "the salvation" begin.

Certainly, one of the "bears" appears to be stronger and begins to oust another one from the den. In such a way, crusades, inquisition trials, religious wars, revolutions and wars with terrorism begin; in such a way, "the apple of discord," which is called "God-choosiness," hardens hearts and souls of people and nations, making them to hate and to kill each other. And, while in the Greek myth the so desired apple has destroyed only one city, in the real life the sweet, juicy "apple of God-choosiness," thrown to us by Jewish rabbis, is able not only theoretically, but also practically to destroy the whole world if we carry out all man-hating commandments of the matrix, the name of which is the Bible.

"And what does that ancient Greek myth have to do with Christianity?" A very impatient reader will ask. The fact is that Christianity is completely based on the very idea of "God-choosiness" that Jewish rabbis "have thrown" to the western world, which has resulted in division and exasperation of people against each other.

Our task, hence, is that, firstly, we have to prove, that only Jewish people can be considered as "the God's people" and all the others only try to "attach themselves" to the Jewish God Jehovah. Secondly, to subject both Christianity and its doctrine to the humanistic analysis in order to determine its true value for the spiritual development of man and humankind. Thirdly, to try to understand which God Jesus taught Jewish people about, and whether it was the very God that Christians worship and believe in.

3. 2. What Is the Messiah and How Was He Imagined By the Jewish Prophets?

Jehovah Witnesses say: "From the times of Abel faithful God's servants have been expecting with great impatience the "Seed" predicted by Jehovah... God has reveled that the "Seed" will carry out the role of Messiah, that is "anointed sovereign." Messiah "will seal sins," and in psalms, the greatness of his Kingdom has been predicted ... This "Seed" or his offspring, as has been predicted, will have in the course of time to eliminate the harm caused by Satan-Devil-Serpent. Moreover, the promised "Seed" will have to destroy both Satan and those who follow him."[159]

Thus, we see, that the first prediction about Messiah had been given to people by God at the time when they silently and peacefully spent their days enjoying a life of paradise. Then Satan, which had appeared in the shape of a snake, led the first people into a temptation, having plunged them in a terrible, mortal, first born sin which could be expiated only by Messiah, promised by Jehovah.

Then Jehovah has told: "And I will put enmity between thee and the woman, and between thy seed and her seed; it shall bruise thy head, and thou shalt bruise his heel."[160]

Of course, as we have shown it above, it was not Satan at all. Satan appears for the first time only in the Book of Job, being, strange as it may seem, one of God's sons who "came to stand before Jehovah." But the religious consciousness has recognized an image of Satan in a serpent and saw the prototype of Messiah in "her seed" (i. e. Eve's) who "shall bruise Serpent's head," having finished, thus, with the global evil which this Serpent symbolizes.

The key moment in this verse are the words, "her seed." These words do not represent anything special by themselves, but in the context of Biblical doctrine, they are very unusual because in all Jewish scriptures man's genealogy is always considered on a man's line and never on a female's. But the future Messiah who "will strike" Satan at a head, receiving only an easy wound at his heel, will originate from a woman, being "her seed." Such an origin is extremely unusual for the Biblical tradition. However, in the quoted verse it is quite clear that the future "savior" will originate from the seed of a woman.

Thus, in the fact of the future Messiah's birth, only the mother is important. The father, for completely unclear reasons, is not taken into account at all, which completely contradicts to all Biblical ideas about genealogy.

The situation looks so serious that the entire Biblical science comes to a dead end even into stupor, from which it is brought out only by the prophet Isaiah, who explains at last why this "savior" is called "her seed" instead of being called "his seed."

"'So, the prophet says, 'the Lord himself shall give you a sign; Behold, a virgin shall conceive, and bear a son, and shall call his name Immanuel.'"[161] The fact that the birth of the one Isaiah speaks about is represented as a "sign," specifies certain unusual circumstances connected to his birth. In other words, in order the birth to be a "sign," it should be entirely unusual or even miraculous. Such was, for example, the origin of the Jewish people, which was the "Isaac seed" born from old sterile Sarah for the special deeds of her husband Abraham, with whom God had concluded the covenant. The Isaac's wonderful birth, thus, had been a "sign," which was necessary to ratify the covenant. The birth of the son (Isaiah 7: 14) also had to be "a sign," moreover, entirely special "sign." That time the wonderful birth of the son was not connected with mother's old age, but with her youth and, which is most important, with her virginity.

And it is the future Messiah mother's virginity that gives us understanding of the mystical verse 3:15 of the books of Genesis. The Messiah will be considered as "her seed," for he will not have a father. Because of his Immaculate Conception, his genealogy will be traced only on the mother's line, but in no way on that of father's. Thus, Isaiah makes clear the meaning of a mystical verse of the book of Genesis and asserts that Messiah will enter into the world through the Immaculate Conception.

Isaiah's contemporary, prophet Micah, has predicted even the Messiah's birthplace: "But thou, Bethlehem Ephratah, though thou be little among the thousands of Judah, yet out of thee shall he come forth unto me that is to be ruler in Israel; whose goings forth have been from of old, from everlasting."[162]

It means that Messiah is the one who should become the King of Israel in order to deliver it from all its enemies and to establish God's Kingdom. But Jesus had not fulfilled the expectations of the Jewish people and, being mocked and spited upon, was subjected to a severe and painful death on a cross.

Thus, by not recognizing him as their "savior," Jews have rejected Jesus Christ. As for us Christians, even such a Messiah will do. What do we need a Jewish king for? We do not need a Jewish king. We need our own, Christian, orthodox "savior" who will "save" us—orthodox Christians, but by no means Jews-pagans. But, as we have already convinced ourselves, Jews were not born yesterday. For such an occasion they have prepared another Messiah, the very one who will have to become "the King of Jews." And this Messiah is the very one whom they have been waiting with pleasure and hope for ages.

The matter of fact is that the Old Testament gives a double picture of the future Messiah. On the one hand, we find various predictions about him that represent him as the one who should undergo humiliation, tortures and, at last, die with a terrible painful death, "For he shall grow up before him as a tender plant, and as a root out of a dry ground: he hath no form nor comeliness; and when we shall see him, there is no beauty that we should desire him. He is despised and rejected of men; a man of sorrows, and acquainted with grief: and we hid as it were our faces from him; he was despised, and we esteemed him not. Surely he hath borne our griefs, and carried our sorrows: yet we did esteem him stricken, smitten of God, and afflicted. But he was wounded for our transgressions, he was bruised for our iniquities: the chastisement of our peace was upon him; and with his stripes we are healed."[163]

This death, as the prophets assert, should become the "redemption" (or substitutive death, as at sacrifice) for sins of the Jewish people. On the other hand, we find that the Jewish prophets say also about the Messiah, who should come as a winning king destroying all the enemies of Israeli people and establishing the messianic kingdom of peace and well-being.

Isaiah says: "And there shall come forth a rod out of the stem of Jesse, and a Branch shall grow out of his roots: and the spirit of the Lord shall rest upon him, the spirit of wisdom and understanding, the spirit of counsel and might, the spirit of knowledge and of the fear of the Lord; and shall make him of quick understanding in the fear of the Lord: and he shall not judge after the sight of his eyes, neither reprove after the hearing of his ears: but with righteousness shall he judge the poor, and reprove with equity for the meek of the earth: and he shall smite the earth with the rod of his mouth, and with the breath of his lips shall he slay the wicked. And righteousness shall be the girdle of his loins, and faithfulness the girdle of his reins."[164]

Therefore Jewish rabbis, who compiled Talmud and studied the scriptures of the prophets very attentively, came to the conclusion that they spoke about two different Messiahs. The Messiah, who should suffer and die was called the son of Josef (Messiah ben Josef). The second one, who should follow the first one and to become "the King of Jews" was called the son of David (Messiah ben David). This second Messiah will return to life the first one and will establish God's Kingdom on the earth.

During many centuries, this concept of two Messiahs was generally accepted in the Orthodox Judaism. However, after writing of Talmud, only Messiah ben David has become to be considered as the true Messiah by Jews; and Messiah ben Josef has become to be ignored. Now only few Jews have heard of him or known about his existence in the Jewish theology of the last centuries. The one whom Jews know as Messiah is the one who wins—Messiah ben David. The one who Christians know is, in reality, two in one: the Messiah who was subjected to death for our sins, and, at the same time, the one who will come back in the last days of the world to judge all those who are not Christians.

3. 3. What Was Jesus Christ Teaching About?

What did Jesus Christ want? What did he try to achieve with his sermon and with the tragic example of his life? Cosidovsky says: "Jesus Christ's motive was, obviously, the same, as that of Buddha—to show much favor to mankind as a whole by carrying out a religious reform, which would give it the pure moral religion, true knowledge of the God and of the nature."[165] Our task, therefore, is to find out, what was the real "favor" shown by Jesus to deadly sinful humankind.

The essence of Jesus Christ's teaching has already been expressed by John the Baptist: "Repent ye: for the kingdom of heaven is at hand."[166] Thus, it was the preaching of "a good message" i. e. "The Gospel of Peace," the message that God's Kingdom has already come nearer at such a distance that the delay can be just deadly like. And in order to avoid the death, it was necessary "to make a worthy fruit of repentance."

Further John says: "And now also the axe is laid unto the root of the trees: therefore every tree which bringeth not forth good fruit is hewn down, and cast into the fire. I indeed baptize you with water unto repentance: but he that cometh after me is mightier than I, whose shoes I am not worthy to bear: he shall baptize you with the Holy Ghost, and with fire: whose fan is in his hand, and he will thoroughly purge his floor, and gather his wheat into the garner; but he will burn up the chaff with unquenchable fire."[167]

Then Jesus came from Galilee to Jordan to John, to be baptized by him. And when Jesus was baptized and went up out of the water, the heavens were opened unto him, and he saw the Spirit of God descending like a dove, and lighting upon him: and a voice from heaven, saying: "This is my beloved Son, in whom I am well pleased."

From that time on Jesus began to preach and he said: "Blessed are the poor in spirit: for theirs is the kingdom of heaven. Blessed are they that mourn: for they shall be comforted. Blessed are the meek: for they shall inherit the earth. Blessed are they which do hunger and thirst after righteousness: for they shall be filled.

Blessed are the merciful: for they shall obtain mercy. Blessed are the pure in heart: for they shall see God. Blessed are the peacemakers: for they shall be called the children of God. Blessed are they which are persecuted for righteousness' sake: for theirs is the kingdom of heaven. Blessed are ye, when men shall revile you, and persecute you, and shall say all manner of evil against you falsely, for my sake...

Ye have heard that it was said by them of old time, Thou shalt not kill; and whosoever shall kill shall be in danger of the judgment: but I say unto you, that whosoever is angry with his brother without a cause shall be in danger of the judgment: and whosoever shall say to his brother, Raca, shall be in danger of the council: but whosoever shall say, Thou fool, shall be in danger of hell fire. Therefore if thou bring thy gift to the altar, and there rememberest that thy brother hath ought against thee; Leave there thy gift before the altar, and go thy way; first be reconciled to thy brother, and then come and offer thy gift.

Agree with thine adversary quickly, whiles thou art in the way with him; lest at any time the adversary deliver thee to the judge, and the judge deliver thee to the officer, and thou be cast into prison. Verily I say unto thee, Thou shalt by no means come out thence, till thou hast paid the uttermost farthing.

Ye have heard that it was said by them of old time, Thou shalt not commit adultery: but I say unto you, that whosoever looketh on a woman to lust after her hath committed adultery with her already in his heart. And if thy right eye offend thee, pluck it out, and cast it from thee: for it is profitable for thee that one of thy members should perish, and not that thy whole body should be cast into hell...

Ye have heard that it hath been said, an eye for an eye, and a tooth for a tooth: but I say unto you, that ye resist not evil: but whosoever shall smite thee on thy right cheek, turn to him the other also. And if any man will sue thee at the law, and take away thy coat, let him have thy cloke also.

Give to him that asketh thee, and from him that would borrow of thee turn not thou away. Ye have heard that it hath been said, Thou shalt love thy neighbour, and hate thine enemy. But I say unto you, **Love your enemies, bless them that curse you, do good to them that hate you, and pray for them which despitefully use you, and persecute you**; that ye may be the children of your Father which is in heaven: for **he maketh his sun to rise on the evil and on the good, and sendeth rain on the just and on the unjust**. For if ye love them which love you, what reward have ye? And if ye salute your brethren only, what do ye more than others? Be ye therefore perfect, even as your Father which is in heaven is perfect."[168]

Then Jesus gives instructions on how to communicate with God. It is strange, but he does not mention either of priests or of a temple, as well as of sacrifices and of Holy Scriptures. He clearly let us understand that such an intimate process as a prayer does not need any mediator between man and God. He says: "**But thou, when thou prayest, enter into thy closet, and when thou hast shut thy door, pray to thy Father which is in secret; and thy Father which seeth in secret shall reward thee openly**. But when ye pray, use not vain repetitions, as the heathen do: for they think that they shall be heard for their much speaking.

Be not ye therefore like unto them: for your Father knoweth what things ye have need of, before ye ask him. After this manner therefore pray ye: Our Father which art in heaven, Hallowed be thy name. Thy kingdom come. Thy will be done in earth, as it is in heaven. Give us this day our daily bread. And forgive us our debts, as we forgive our debtors. And lead us not into temptation, but deliver us from evil: For thine is the kingdom, and the power, and the glory, for ever. Amen. For if ye forgive men their trespasses, your heavenly Father will also forgive you: but if ye forgive not men their trespasses, neither will your Father forgive your trespasses."[169]

Then Jesus says: "Lay not up for yourselves treasures upon earth, where moth and rust doth corrupt, and where thieves break through and steal: but lay up for yourselves treasures in heaven, where neither moth nor rust doth corrupt, and where thieves do not break through nor steal: for where your treasure is, there will your heart be also."[170] But "seek ye first the kingdom of God, and his righteousness; and all these things shall be added unto you."[171]

And who can enter the God's Kingdom? "Not every one that saith unto me, Lord, Lord, shall enter into the kingdom of heaven; but he that doeth the will of my Father which is in heaven."[172]

Moreover, **the one who "doeth the will of the Father" must belong to "the lost sheep of the house of Israel,"** for Jesus, sending his twelve apostles to preach the Gospel, has given them the following instructions: **"Go not into the way of the Gentiles, and into any city of the Samaritans enter ye not: but go rather to the lost sheep of the house of Israel. And as ye go, preach, saying, the kingdom of heaven is at hand.**"[173] And, it is already so close that man's Son will come even before they have time to travel through the cities of Israel.

And in order for them to be unable to relax, he warns them: "Think not that I am come to send peace on earth: **I came not to send peace, but a sword. For I am come to set a man at variance against his father, and the daughter against her mother, and the daughter in law against her mother in law. And a man's foes shall be they of his own household. He that loveth father or mother more than me is not worthy of me: and he that loveth son or daughter more than me is not worthy of me... He that is not with me is against me; and he that gathereth not with me scattereth abroad.**"[174]

The same statements we find in apocryphal Gospels, for example, in the Gospel of Thomas. Jesus said: "People may think that I have come to throw peace in the world, but **they do not know, that I have come to throw division, fire, sward and war on their land**. For the five will be in the house: the three will be against the two and two against the three. The father will be against the son and son will be against the father."[175]

Further, in a verse 60, Thomas says: "Jesus said, '**the one who has not come to hate the father and the mother can not be my disciple, and the one who has not come to hate the brothers and sisters and has not carried the cross, as I has, will not become worthy of me**.'"

Then he says, "**The one who has not come to hate the father and the mother, as I has, can not be my disciple, and the one who has not come to love [of the father and the mother], as I has, can not be my disciple. For my mother...** But she, really, has given me life."[176]

And what do we poor Christians have to do now? Do we have to come to hate the father and the mother as Jesus has, or do we have to come to love the father and the mother, as Jesus has for the only reason that her mother gave him life? Is it possible to love as the other one loves, and to hate as the other one hates? And is it possible to love and to hate at the same time? This is a big riddle and, probably, a great mystery. For all this means that if we love the father and the mother and do not hate them, as the Teacher did, we cannot be his disciples. If we hate our parents and do not love them, as the Teacher did, we also cannot be his disciples. And only in the case we come to love and to hate the father and the mother at the same time, as Jesus did, we can be his disciples. But none of us can love and hate at the same time, and none of us can do it as the other one does, which means that none of us can be Jesus' disciples.

What does it mean? It means that here we have confronted with the greatest absurdity which can appear only in religious consciousness; for only in its space there is nothing impossible, for in religious or mythological consciousness everything is possible, it is possible even to love and to hate at the same time.

But in the space of normal human consciousness, capable of thinking logically, the one who makes the statements like those given above, should be considered as a madman. But what will happen if another madman takes such statements too close to his heart and begins to carry out the commandments of the "Teacher" word for word?

One man, on hearing such instructions, will love the parents more than before, but another one will hate them more than ever. Then even his household will become his enemy, then "the five will be in the house: the three will be against the two and the two will be against the three. The father will be against the son and the son will be against the father."

But, you see, not further as some lines back, the same man called for peace and consent and even for love toward enemies.

Is it possible to imagine that those words have been said by the same man, namely by Jesus Christ? Can a normal man call us for general love, even for love toward enemies and then to induce us come to hate both father and mother, both brother and sister and even life, because one cannot be his disciple without it? And, can such a call be human? Certainly, it cannot. And if we agree that all those words have been said by one man (reasoning logically we must admit that in the space of the New Testament only one man whose name is Jesus Christ acts), namely by Jesus Christ, we then should agree that he is a hypocrite and an impostor. He pretends to be kind and pure, calls for love even toward our enemies and himself, and as it turns out, induces people to hatred and cruelty. But, as Jesus Christ can not be a hypocrite, then any normal man is compelled to recognize the fact that those who wrote the books of both canonic and apocryphal Gospels were hypocrites and impostors. Again, we face a monstrous, brutal deceit.

And if we take the eastern version of the Gospel, which was discovered in Tibet by Roerich, Notovich, Abhedananda and Caspari (of which we will tell in the fifth chapter), we shall find totally different utterances of saint Issa, as Jesus was called by eastern people.

It tells the following about Jesus Christ: "And then Issa said, 'A son should not push aside his mother, taking her place. **Who does not respect his mother, the holiest creature after God, is not worth to be called her son**. Hear what I shall tell you about mother. Respect a woman, for she is the mother of the universe, and the whole truth of God's creation is enclosed in her. She is the base of good and beauty, she is the source of life and death. The entire existence of man is dependent on her, for she is his natural and moral support... **Love and respect also your wives, for tomorrow they will become mothers and later the ancestors of the nation... A wife and a mother are the precious gift given you by God**. They are the best decorations of our existence, and they give birth to all those who inhabit the world...

That is why I tell you that after God all your best thoughts must be given to women and wives, for a woman is the temple for you, in which you will gain your happiness in the best way. Derive your moral strength from this temple. Here you will forget all your sorrows and misfortunes and find your lost power which is necessary to help your neighbor.

Do not expose her to humiliation, for doing this you will humiliate only yourselves and will lose that feeling of love without which nothing can exist here, beneath. Protect your wife in order she to be able to protect you and your whole family. **Everything you will do for your wife, for your mother, for a widow or for other sorrowing woman, you will do for God.**"[177] These are the words of the real Jesus! How much human love and warmth are in them!

But the words of hatred to one's parents and neighbors which were attributed to Jesus by a church, had such an influence that St. Jeronim exclaimed in an impulse of awesome delight: "**If your father lies down on your threshold, if your mother exposes her breast which has reared you, trample the lifeless body of the father and the breast of your mother** and with dry eyes rush to your Lord God, who calls you!!!" Could he exclaim such words after reading the real Gospel of Peace?!...

But the most dangerous thing here is that this severe and brutal doctrine has become an absolute moral guiding line for the whole western Christian world. The matter is that even a positive moral law can turn into its contrast because "the moral law is not a certain separate instinct or any set of instincts. This something (name it virtue or correct behaviour) is what directs our instincts and brings them in conformity with life around us. By the way, it has serious practical importance. **The most dangerous thing which the man is capable to do is to select any natural impulse inherent in him and to follow it all the time, at any cost. Each of our instincts could transform us in devils, if we would follow it as a certain absolute guiding line**.

You can think that the instinct of love to all mankind is always safe. It is not true. **Once one neglects justice and it appears that one breaks the contracts and gives false evidences in a court "in the interests of mankind" which, eventually, results in that one becomes cruel and treacherous.**"[178]

Strange as it may seem, but in the space of Christian world outlook "'justice,' as an orthodox priest Alexandr Borisov asserts, 'turns out to be good very seldom. More often, it turns out to be evil. **The Gospel is against any justice**, It is for mercy."[179]

So why do we need a doctrine which brings "division, fire, sward and war" in the world? There is enough such "good" in the world even without "Jesus' teaching." Why do we need such a doctrine which calls for hatred toward our parents and our neighbors? We cannot get on with each other even without it. Why do we need such a doctrine, after learning of which some of us are ready to "trample the lifeless body of the father and the breast of the mother and with dry eyes rush to Lord God, who calls us" (i. e. to do it so cruelly and coolly that any muscle will not move and any tear will not give away the presence of even the most elementary human feelings)? In the world, there are more than enough murderers and maniacs, who (in the name of their God (or, most likely, Devil?)) are ready not only to "trample the lifeless body of the father and the breast of the mother," but even to destroy thousands and millions of innocent people just to please him.

Why, at last, do we need such a doctrine that excites such instincts in us which can transform us into devils if we follow it as a certain absolute guiding line? And what God is it that summons such fiends? Certainly, it is very familiar to us and hotly beloved by us our favorite God-butcher-filicide Jehovah. But, if before it was necessary to prove the fidelity to Jehovah by means of certain deeds (devoted service, hatred to strangers, observance of all Jewish holidays, food interdictions and commandments contained in the Old Testament), now it was enough to believe in the "savior." But, having hated not only parents and neighbors, but also the whole world at that, which we successfully carry out in practice.

From all we have said above, we must conclude that Christianity has failed to "do a great favor to mankind as a whole by putting in practice a religious reform, which would have given it pure moral religion, the true knowledge of God and the Nature." On the contrary, together with adoption of Christianity, "division, fire, sward and war" which the "benefactor" himself (or, to be more correct, those who have perverted his teaching) has thrown on our land, came in the world. Certainly, it had been done by our "savior" for our own sake, i. e. for destruction of fallen, sinful world, but as for us, i. e. for those who are innocently perished in the name of "salvation," we are none the better for it.

Therefore, from the point of view of humanity, the doctrine which brings "division, sward and war" into the world looks completely brutal, and to use it as a textbook to our life means nothing more than to ignite enmity, hatred and division among the people.

3. 4. How the Religion of Heart and Soul Turned into the Religion of Church and Holy Scriptures

Thus, we have to suppose that, if Jesus Christ is not a hypocrite and deceiver, the Christian church is such. It, having perverted his teaching, founded the religion of church and Holy Scripture, in which, being in the clutches of undisputable laws and dogmas, the original Jesus' teaching decayed and withered.

The fact is that to the great regret of the Mighty of this world, in a pure moral religion, there is no place for church as a social institute, and it means that there is no place for bishops and archbishops, or for patriarchs or popes. A moral religion is a religion of heart and soul; it is a particularly individual act of communication with God from heart to heart, from human soul to live soul of the Almighty, and this intimate act does not need any mediator.

A mediator is needed in a religion of church and Holy Scripture in order to keep the people in fear and obedience by means of intimidation with dreadful and abominable god-manslaughterer and eternal tortures in the lake burning with fire and sulfur. A moral religion, the religion of heart and soul is the religion of reasonable people who can be responsible for their actions and at the same time are capable to open their hearts and souls towards the real God.

The religion of church and Holy Scripture is the religion of people whose essences are at the level of development of a child who considers himself an adult capable to decide the fates of the world and thinking with the categories of mythological consciousness, in which there are no distinctions between truth and lie, love and hatred, illusion and reality. Of course, the mythological consciousness itself is not bad at all. At the dawn of humanity, when the human consciousness just began to acquire the forms familiar to us now, it operated solely with the categories of mythological consciousness. There was nothing insincere, nothing false in it. It was natural as the wind blow, as the sound of falling rain, as the flight of a bird.

It is quite another matter, when a modern man who got used to thinking with other categories is returned in an artificial way to the level of mythological consciousness, in which he becomes a weak helpless child who is ready to perceive any raving of a madman that is imposed on him. That is why such a man is easy to be deceived and terrified; it is easy to inculcate cruel and man-hating commandments that can urge on monstrous crimes against humans and humanity in such a man. It is quite natural that both the mean human nature and the strong desire of the Mighty of this world to hold people in leashes did not allow the religion of heart and soul to win the human consciousness. They created their own religion—the religion of church and Holy Scripture, having turned it into a myth, in which lie is given as truth, illusion as reality, death as life.

The religion of church and Holy Scripture developed as following. After resurrection, ascending to the heaven and Jesus' appearance to his disciples, a new period of Christian myth formation (the formation of teaching and infrastructure) begins. Nobody knows what Jesus said during his activity, but it is well known how it is represented by four canonic Gospels which were written decades after Jesus' death; it being known, not by those authors that Gospels are attributed to. "'It is suffice to say, Cosidovsky asserts, 'that of 27 books of the New Testament, 19 are not recognized by scientists as the books of those authors they are attributed to.'"[180]

Historic Jesus Christ could hardly be such as he is depicted by canonic evangelists. Most likely, he really taught about love and justice. But the church has perverted his teaching and remade it for its purposes in order to create the very myth without which it is impossible to deceive people.

The first Christian sects were not Christian in their essence. Formerly, they had no such name or no such symbol. The emblem of the first Christian organizations was the picture of two fishes. Those were the sects of totalitarian type with the strict hierarchy and hard laws.

People participating in this movement firmly believed in the forthcoming advent of Jesus Christ and in an immediate coming of God's Kingdom, in which they would receive much more material welfare than they lost when gave up all their property for the sake of sect. They sold all they had and gave all the money to their mutual cash desk.

One could not hide the money, for he would be sentenced to death if his fraud is opened. In the Acts we become witnesses of the case when Ananias and his wife Sapphira tried to hide the part of their money from their sect-follows. For such a sin **God killed them both**: "But a certain man named Ananias, with Sapphira his wife, sold a possession, and kept back part of the price, his wife also being privy to it, and brought a certain part, and laid it at the apostles' feet. But Peter said, Ananias, why hath Satan filled thine heart to lie to the Holy Ghost, and to keep back part of the price of the land? Whiles it remained, was it not thine own? and after it was sold, was it not in thine own power? why hast thou conceived this thing in thine heart? thou hast not lied unto men, but unto God. And Ananias hearing these words fell down, and gave up the ghost: and great fear came on all them that heard these things. And the young men arose, wound him up, and carried him out, and buried him. And it was about the space of three hours after, when his wife, not knowing what was done, came in. And Peter answered unto her, Tell me whether ye sold the land for so much? And she said, Yea, for so much. Then Peter said unto her, How is it that ye have agreed together to tempt the Spirit of the Lord? behold, the feet of them which have buried thy husband are at the door, and shall carry thee out. Then fell she down straightway at his feet, and yielded up the ghost: and the young men came in, and found her dead, and, carrying her forth, buried her by her husband."[181]

Here it is the right time to recall one of the Papuan cults, which is very similar to Christian belief in the "savior's" forthcoming advent. Both early Christians and their subsequent representatives believed in the forthcoming Jesus' advent very seriously even in spite of the fact that the prophesies about the Second Advent and the Last Judgment did not prove to be true. The last such prophesy based on the Nostradamus' and Virgin Mary's prophesies computer processing had been given by the leaders of the Catholic Church quite recently. The Catholic Church, as *Times* issued in the beginning of 2001 asserted, has announced that the Second Advent and the Last Judgment were expected during that year, namely between the year 2001 and the year 2002. That fatal year has already passed, but one cannot notice any signs of either the Second Advent or the Last Judgment.

"And what about Papuans?" you will ask. As for Papuans, there is a very interesting story about their beliefs: "When the first European ship sailed to the New Guinea, the aborigines were amazed as much as we would be amazed at the scene of humanoids appearance. These people have never seen a white man before, but they believed their ancestors to be white-skinned. No wonder that they recognized the white men as their ancestors who came to them from the "kingdom of the dead." And when they saw a big ship full with a lot of wonderful things, they decided that it really fell on them right from the sky. Though the aborigines realized soon that white Europeans were not their ancestors, the incredible mystery of their cargo origin was insoluble riddle for Papuans. Their home-bred philosophers came to conclusion that the Europeans had received all their crafty tools and riches from some mysterious and powerful spirits. Such religious believes are called "the Cargo Cult."

The most ardent partisans of this cult asserted that such a valuable cargo could be also sent by spirits to them if they learn to properly observe certain religious rules. At the same time, some elders believed that the cargo was stolen by Europeans from aborigines, to whom it had been delivered by their dead ancestors. **When the aborigines acquainted with the Bible, they began to accuse white men that they pulled out the first pages from all the copies of the Holy Book, which said that God had been Papuan**.

The cult founders asserted that long awaited precious cargo would be just about to arrive. They even began to build something like a runway in order to facilitate its delivery. These elders convinced believers to copy the behavior of white men in order to receive the cargo. And aborigines set aside a room for a "private office" in their cabins and began to pass meaningless pieces of paper. Some of the leaders advised to their tribe fellows to change their habits in order to facilitate the cargo delivery. Sexual relations between a wife and a husband were banned and incest was introduced into practice. **When the next date of the cargo delivery was announced, the aborigines began to kill their cattle and destroy all their property which was unnecessary any longer**. Having became disillusioned with their expectations, prompted by a sharp desire that had not been realized, many of them have adopted Christianity, for they believed that only in such a way they would become the happy owners of the priceless cargo. Of course, their expectations were also failed, they have not received their cargo promised by Christian missionaries, and the aborigines began to accuse the missionaries that they had hidden from them some special prayer, which could ensure the delivery of desired cargo."[182]

Now let us continue our story about Christianity. The new teaching was spread by the first apostles who were Jesus' disciples. The main priest was apostle Peter. Then Saul joined them. It was the very Saul who persecuted the first Christian and then, after he had seen Jesus' appearance on his way to Damascus, turned into their stalwart and apostle known to us under the name Paul. Being an educated man acquainted with different local religious schools and, most likely, with the works of Greek philosophers, Paul developed the base of the new teaching.

Of course, that teaching was not new at all. The idea of Messiah and his purifying sacrifice on a cross, the blood of which was capable to cleanse our deadly sins, was firstly expressed by Jewish prophets several centuries before Christ's birth. That was old leaven on new yeast. The teaching has maintained the succession line with the Old Testament, but has added to it the concept of original sin, of the enemy (Satan, Devil, Serpent, Beast, the Evil one), as well as the concept of "justification by means of faith."

Those three concepts totally disarmed a man and drove him into a corner. The concept of original sin (Adam's and Eva's sin) instilled the feeling of fear and inferiority complex into a man. He was suggested to be sinful from the very birth because his forefathers had once committed the deadly sin of a disobedient to God Jehovah. They committed that crime because they listened to the cunning serpent that was just a snake, but, nevertheless the most vise among all the animals. Later people would identify it with Satan, Devil, Beast and the

Evil one which is still tempting the peoples and nations and which we must be afraid of, otherwise it would lead us astray and then our fate would be in the lake burning with fire and sulfur, or in the winepress of God's fierce anger.

But there is a very good remedy for it—the faith in the Messiah, in Jesus Christ who, by means of his death and blood, cleansed us of our sins and now is hurrying to us to save us from our main enemy, the Evil one, as well as from all the other enemies, i. e. from all our relatives and neighbors who do not have such a faith.

All these bear a strong resemblance to an advertisement trailer, which is also a matrix, for it destined to a potential buyer's (parishioner) consciousness program. That is why a well-developed advertisement trailer is the most typical example of a matrix. It can be divided into three parts. The first one shows the problem, the second one shows all the horrors that arose from that problem, and the third one suggests the most effective means to solve that problem.

If we provide this advertisement trailer with a popular myth, the success of selling of advertising products will be enormous. At that, its influence will be multiplied if this myth represents by itself the monotheistic conception in which almighty and all-seeing God who is perceived by people as the strict and cruel heavenly father, is represented. And since he is the heavenly father, one must be afraid of him, otherwise one will be perished in the lake burning with fire and sulfur, moreover one's heredity is aggravated with the original sin. And the enemy is not sleeping.

But for all the cases of our sinful life we have our own, our extremely effective "savior," believing in whom it is possible to be "saved" from all the problems, and even "save" other people. One can be "saved" from original sin, from all the problems, and one can even get the eternal life. Everything exactly as in an advertisement trailer: "You have dandruff! What a horror! You cannot show up in a company of respectable people! What a misfortune! But you have our shampoo "Hair and Shoulders!" It will save you from dandruff forever! It will save you from all your troubles!"

Any religious system built on the religion of church and Holy Scripture, as well as any revolutionary or fascist movement, functions like an advertising campaign of the universal scale. There are goods or some services ("religious teaching" or "salvation") which are to be sold (preached). For that purpose goods are put in a beautiful package (beautiful slogans and "great humanistic goals," as, for example, the idea of love for one's neighbor or the idea of "utmost justice") and an appropriate infrastructure is created. A lot of shops (churches) are opened throughout the world, the net of traveling salesman (missionaries) is created, free of charge catalogues ("Holy Scriptures") are issued and seminars and conferences (religious service and congregations) are held.

But it turns out that there are a lot of competitive enterprises (churches and sects) which advertise a similar product. In order to stand up to this struggle your advertising company enters into competition (religious animosity and intolerance) using all the accessible means; at that it even does not disdain to use any means including the physical elimination of rivals (inquisition, crusades, religious massacres and wars). The expected result is the attraction of as many customers (parishioners) as possible. The ideal result is changing the whole world into the one and indivisible market (different version of Christianity that consider themselves to be the only true religion, "the universal church" etc.), staffed exceptionally with the product of the advertising company (with the religious teaching or with the idea of "salvation").

Now imagine that this victorious company gains during the competition such a power that it begins to dictate its will even to the ruling clique of the world. Then it begins to push its product to the market, let us say "Hair and Shoulders," asserting that those who will use it will be taken to heavens after their death. Such a perspective is, frankly saying, very doubtful, and at first nobody wants to believe in this wonderful shampoo, moreover, nobody wants to buy it. Everybody uses another, well-tried washing substance, and doesn't want to change it.

Then the unprecedented advertising campaign begins. Traveling agents are sent to all the countries of the world and beautiful advertising catalogues, in which the effectiveness of advertising product is explained both from the scientific and from all the other points of view, are issued. Somebody, after reading them and thinking them over, begins to believe in this raving of a madman, begins to buy shampoo and prepares themselves to a trip to the paradise. The others (the majority of people) not only do not want to buy a product, but organize an antiadvertising campaign and begin to issue their own books in which they overthrow all the cases of the "shampoonists."

Of course, "shampoonists" do not like such a competition, and then they announce oppositionists as the enemies of the people and of all the saints. To fight against "antishampoonists," the tribunal is established, and they try and sentence to death penalty all those who have any connection to opposition. Now, the teaching about the wonderful shampoo is being drummed into peoples' heads from their very birth, and subsequent generations of people do not have any doubts about the real "value" of "wonderful shampoo."

Do you think this picture is unreal? Do you think that it cannot be so? You are mistaken. This picture bears a great resemblance to the development of the Christian Church as a social institute which had unlimited power in the middle ages. And there was such a period when one could buy "salvation" for a certain amount of money. The church sold so-called "pardons"—documents that ensured "salvation."

"Stupid people," you will probably say now. It is now, but in the middle ages people believed in the church and gave their last money to buy "salvation"—the goods which the church sold and sell till nowadays. The "pardons" became the cause of reformation.

It began in Germany in the XVI century. Dominican monk Tezel was in charge of that business. He acted by the order of Mainz archbishop, whom Pope Leo X himself charged with supervising of the money income, for he [the Pope] needed the money for his luxurious court and for the building of churches and temples.

In 1517, when Tezel appeared in Wittenberg, people began to buy "pardons" hastily, giving away their last money. A monk named Martin Luther was indignant with that business and tried to act against it by means of his sermons. But sermons did not help. Then Luther made up his mind to take a very courageous step. He nailed to the church door his "95 Theses," in which he proved both the harm from "pardons" selling and their uselessness for the absolution. Say now that it cannot be so.

Today, when the Christian Church has lost the influence and power it had in the Middle Ages, the visible picture of cultural space of the world is determined by the competition, mainly, between "globalization" in its Christian-American version and Islamic revolutionary idea of the "utmost justice." Other Christian churches and sects that compete both among themselves and with different eastern and Satanist sects are somewhere in the tail of this process. Eastern ideological systems such as Hinduism, Buddhism and Confucianism lead a rather isolated spiritual life not pretending to take a "piece of cake" of the world market of washing means both for hair and brain washing.

Now, knowing the laws of material commercial organizations, to which, without any doubt, the Christian Church belongs, you will be more cautious choosing a "product." Now, if you want to buy a "spiritual product," you have to think about if it is possible to compare the activity of the organization which offers it to the activity of quite commercial material organizations. If it is possible, a "product" will hardly be spiritual. Try to compare, for example, the religion of heart and soul which is a pure moral teaching about love and mercy (it does not need for its functioning either a church or a priest, as well as "Holy Scriptures") to the activity of material commercial organization. And you will fail, for a real spiritual teaching does not fit into the frames of earthly, material institutes.

But look here, Jesus Christ taught us this very religion of heart and soul and even gave very good advice about how to practice it in our everyday life. "But thou, when thou prayest, enter into thy closet, and when thou hast shut thy door, pray to thy Father which is in secret; and thy Father which seeth in secret shall reward thee openly. But when ye pray, use not vain repetitions, as the heathen do: for they think that they shall be heard for their much speaking. Be not ye therefore like unto them: for your Father knoweth what things ye have need of, before ye ask him. After this manner therefore pray ye: Our Father which art in heaven, Hallowed be thy name. Thy kingdom come. Thy will be done in earth, as it is in heaven. Give us this day our daily bread. And forgive us our debts, as we forgive our debtors. And lead us not into temptation, but deliver us from evil: For thine is the kingdom, and the power, and the glory, for ever. Amen."[183]

Of course, we could use the advice of the Great Teacher, but bad habits are more contagious for us than something good and kind and we go to church with our sinful head hanged and attend a service mechanically repeating "God, have mercy upon us" like Gentiles do, and our hearts and souls remain empty and motionless. Then we confess our sins and receive the Lord's Sacraments, and leaving the church we again and again forget of our repentance and, as dogs that leak their own spew, we sin again hoping that pure Jesus' blood shed for the sake of salvation of Jewish sons and daughters will cleanse again and again our dirty, abominable "orthodox" loathsomeness.

With the appearance of the image of "enemy," negative functions of God were detached. The fact is that in the space of the Old Testament, God Jehovah executes both positive and negative functions. He creates and he destroys, he gives us life and he takes it away, he tempts us and then punishes us for it. He holds "The Book of Life" in one hand and the keys from hell and death in the other one. He even has several spirits, the main of which are the Holy Spirit and the Evil one. He has even one more spirit—the Lying Spirit.

To recognize that God is the God of spirits means to recognize that he is the very God that is called by magicians during their ceremonies and rituals. **While discussing the nature of God at ecumenical councils, theologians overlooked this fact and represented God in a somewhat pared-down shape. If we want to be exact, it is necessary to add the Evil spirit and the Lying spirit to the Holy Trinity. And then we will have the fool shape of God with all his attributes: God-Father, God-Son, God-Holy spirit, God-Evil spirit, God-Lying spirit**. The Bible describes very well how God's Evil spirit was used to torment King Saul, "But the spirit of the Lord departed from Saul, and **an evil spirit from the Lord troubled him. And Saul's servants said unto him, Behold now, an evil spirit from God troubleth thee**."[184] The first mentioning of the Holy spirit appears only in Isaiah, but it does not do any real actions so far. The Evil and Lying spirits were the most active tools of God Jehovah.

The concept of "justification by means of faith" freed a person from executing of the Law given to Jewish people by Moses, and physical circumcision was changed with the circumcision of heart, i. e. spiritual circumcision. It enabled Gentiles to participate in the Christian movement. **The fact is that there is no room for Gentiles in the space of the Old Testament. All of them, according to the Jewish Law, must be physically destroyed**. Those who were not circumcised were not allowed to attend Jewish synagogue. Now, the new organization invited everybody to participate in its movement. It was fantastic heresy, and Moses, if he would have seen such a crying infringement of the Law, would have chopped all those Christians into pieces, like he did with those "brothers and friends" who dared to serve to a golden calf.

And, if in the beginning of its existence Christianity was the religion of "humbled and aggrieved" who waited for a forthcoming Jesus' advent and establishing the God's Kingdom, "somewhere in the middle of the second century Christianity began to win disciples from the upper class of the Rome empire and till the end of that century it ceased to be the religion of slaves and artisans."[185]

Of course, this new social structure of Christian organizations had a great influence on the content of religious teaching. The former religion, which was the religion of heart and soul, have been transformed into the religion of church and Holy Scripture. But the church has hidden the fact of this transformation, giving out an entirely new religion to be its original version. Fromm, E. tells: "The most important thing is that eschatological expectations, which constituted the core of the faith and hope of early Christians, gradually vanished. The essence of the former messianic preaching consisted in that "the God's Kingdom is near."

People prepared themselves to take part in that kingdom, they hoped to meet it during their lifetime and worried if they would manage to proclaim the Christian message to all the Gentiles for the shot time left till Messiah's advent. The Paul's faith is still full of eschatological expectations, but the time of the God's Kingdom coming begins to be postponed to the future. For him, the final extermination was guaranteed by the appearance of Messiah, and the final battle, which was to come, was losing its meaning in comparison to what had already happened. However, the subsequent development resulted in gradual vanishing of faith in the immediate establishing of God's Kingdom...

The Christianity underwent fundamental transformation. The religion of oppressed masses changed into the religion of rulers and "God's slaves" manipulated by them. The faith in forthcoming Last Judgment and the new age changed into the faith of already accomplished atonement. The prescription of pure moral life changed into the soothing of human conscience with church means of mercy. Believers' animosity toward a state changed into the cordial agreement with it. All these things are associated with the great changes that are to be investigate by us now. The Christianity that was the religion of a community of equal brothers without hierarchy or bureaucracy became "The Church," the reflection of absolute monarchy of the Rome empire."[186]

In such a way, the religion of heart and soul has been changed into the religion of church and Holy Scripture which, as we have already convinced ourselves, is the cruel and man-hating matrix that programs human consciousness on "destruction"—the very "destruction" that Jewish rabbis accepted to be the main form of communication with the world of Gentiles, i. e. the world of non-Jews, the world of pagans which must be destroyed and exterminated in the name of Jewish God-butcher-filicide Jehovah.

3. 5. Is Their Jewish God Our Orthodox God?

It may seem from the first consideration that God acting in the Christian myth (i. e. in the space of the New Testament) is little bit different from the one Jews believe in, even in spite of the fact that Christians use the same Bible and believe in the same God Jehovah as Jews do. But it may seem only from the first site. In reality, this problem is much more complicated than it may seem.

You see, Christianity is one of the greatest world religions consisting of many churches and sects with hundreds of thousands followers, and each follower considers Christianity to be a quite independent, original and unrepeatable phenomena. But no one asks himself, "What God do we serve to?" Do we serve to a terrible and cruel Old Testament God-butcher-filicide, who walks about the world in bloodstained garments and tramples in his fierce anger both "righteous and sinful," or do we serve to God "who is Love?"

Having carefully studied the space of the New Testament, we find with wonder that their God is not our God, i. e. not the Jewish God. Our God "only hath immortality, dwelling in the light which no man can approach unto; whom no man hath seen, nor can see: to whom be honour and power everlasting;"[187] their God "**said that he would dwell in the thick darkness**"[188], he "**made darkness his secret place; his pavilion round about him were dark waters and thick clouds of the skies**"[189], and one can speak to God "**face to face, as a man speaketh unto his friend**"[190] as Adam and Eve as well as his good servant Moses did.

Our God cannot lie and play the hypocrite, "Wherein God, willing more abundantly to shew unto the heirs of promise the immutability of his counsel, confirmed it by an oath: that by two immutable things, in which it was impossible for God to lie, we might have a strong consolation, who have fled for refuge to lay hold upon the hope set before us"[191], their God either lied himself as he did in the case of Adam and Eve or "**put a lying spirit in the mouth of all these thy prophets, and the Lord hath spoken evil** concerning thee"[192]. Their God "**frames evil against you, and devises a device against you**"[193] **and** "**pour out his fury upon thee, and accomplish his anger upon thee**"[194], our God is "not the author of confusion, but of peace."[195] Their God is "**the Lord that smiteth,**"[196] who "**cut off from thee the righteous and the wicked,**"[197] our God "**is love**"[198]

Moreover, Jesus Christ himself has stated that Jews serve not to the real God, but to the god of lie and manslaughterer: "Jesus saith unto them, **If ye were Abraham's children, ye would do the works of Abraham**. But now ye seek to kill me, a man that hath told you the truth, which I have heard of God: this did not Abraham. **Ye do the deeds of your father**. Then said they to him, we be not born of fornication; we have one Father, even God. Jesus said unto them, **If God were your Father, ye would love me: for I proceeded forth and came from God**; neither came I of myself, but he sent me. Why do ye not understand my speech? even because ye cannot hear my word. **Ye are of your father the devil**, and the lusts of your father ye will do. **He was a murderer from the beginning, and abode not in the**

truth, because there is no truth in him. When he speaketh a lie, he speaketh of his own: for **he is a liar, and the father of it**. And because I tell you the truth, ye believe me not. Which of you convinceth me of sin? And if I say the truth, why do ye not believe me? **He that is of God heareth God's words: ye therefore hear them not, because ye are not of God**."[199]

Paul also knew about it. "**He was well-informed, that this Demiurge, whose Jewish name was Jehovah, was not the God Jesus preached about**."[200] As you see, Paul (or rabbi Saul as he still named by Jews) knew that Jehovah was not the God Jesus preached about, and that is why he did his best to inculcate this name together with the Bible into the consciousness of Christians. But we shall speak later about it. And now we must clarify some details concerning the question of the God in which we believe.

In the Gospel according to John (3: 19) Jesus says: "And this is the condemnation, that **light is come into the world, and men loved darkness rather than light**, because their deeds were evil."[201] What does it mean? It means that Christians associate all their expectations, all their hopes for "the brilliant future" and for "salvation" with the light that comes from God, from the very God that "is love." The fact that their Jewish God is not love at all is already quite obvious for us, for we have agreed that love cannot kill, cannot trample on and crash people. It cannot shed their blood on the ground. But, anyway, maybe he is a light? To answer this question let us address to the Jewish prophets who new the nature of their God very well, for they constantly communicated with him and received his instructions on how to organize "the final extermination."

Isaiah says: "**And I will give thee the treasures of darkness, and hidden riches of secret places**, that thou mayest know that I, the Lord, which call thee by thy name, am the God of Israel."[202] It means that Jewish God Jehovah himself is the master and the owner of "treasures of darkness and hidden riches of secret places", for one can give anything only if one owns something.

But we know that the Devil (Satan, Serpent, Beast, the Evil one) is the master and the owner of "treasures of darkness," and God, as Christians believe, "is love," therefore, the God who "is love" can give people only light, otherwise he is not love. It is quite natural that here the appropriate question arises, "Isn't is possible that this God-butcher-filicide Jehovah who crashes, exterminates and destroys people and sheds their blood is the very Devil, Satan, Serpent, Beast or the Evil one? **And if we recall his passion to filicide, we will have**

no doubts any longer, for the one who kills even one of these little ones cannot be God who is love.

If we return to the Old Testament, we shall see how God-butcher-filicide Jehovah expressed his unlimited "love" for children. At first he slew Er, Judah's firstborn, for he was wicked for one or another reason in the sight of God: "And Er, Judah's firstborn, was wicked in the sight of the Lord; and **the Lord slew him** (Genesis 38: 7)." Then we become witness of quite a crazy episode, where God-butcher-filicide Jehovah wanted to kill Moses' son: "And it came to pass by the way in the inn, that the **Lord met him, and sought to kill him**. Then Zipporah [Moses' wife] took a sharp stone, and cut off the foreskin of her son, and cast it at his feet, and said, Surely a bloody husband art thou to me (Exodus 4: 24-26)."

A Little bit later we read of a real massacre of Egyptian firstborns, whom Jehovah killed just because, thanks to his influence, directed on the hardening of Pharaoh's heart the latter did not let Jews go: "For I will pass through the land of Egypt this night, **and will smite all the firstborn in the land of Egypt, both man and beast**; and against all the gods of Egypt I will execute judgment: I am the Lord (Exodus 12: 12)."

During the war with Canaanites, God Jehovah again express his "great love" for children ordering to kill them: "Now therefore **kill every male among the little ones, and kill every woman** that hath known man by lying with him. But all the women children, that have not known a man by lying with him, keep alive for yourselves. (Numbers 31: 17-18)." Or: "Now go and smite Amalek, and utterly destroy all that they have, and spare them not; **but slay both man and woman, infant and suckling**, ox and sheep, camel and ass. (1st Samuel 15: 3)."

We also have to remember that our beloved God-filicide Jehovah could not live even a day without regaling himself with delicate meat of human firstborns: "Thou shalt not delay to offer the first of thy ripe fruits, and of thy liquors: **the firstborn of thy sons shalt thou give unto me. Likewise shalt thou do with thine oxen, and with thy sheep: seven days it shall be with his dam; on the eighth day thou shalt give it me**. (Exodus 22: 29-30)."

And if we recall that God Jehovah is "the Lord of spirits," the main of which are the Lying spirit and the Evil one; if we recall that this very God demands to sacrifice to him human firstborns and kills tens of thousands of innocent people including women, old men and even infants; if we recall that both white and black magicians call for spirits (whose God is Jehovah) during their rituals and make their incantations in the name of the same Jehovah (Adonai, Iheve, Zebaot—these are Jehovah's different names) and seal their agreements with blood in the same way as Moses did during his negotiations with God-butcher-filicide Jehovah, **we have to suspect this Jehovah of having a tail and little horns. We have to confess that we serve to a real incarnated Devil, but not to the God Jesus Christ taught us about, not to the God who "is love." We bow before and serve to a cruel and bloodthirsty demon that dwells in darkness which was placed stealthily in the world by Jewish Rabbis for people to hate and to kill each other, thus, having cleared the space for the building of the God's Kingdom (destined exceptionally for Jews) which we, Christians or Gentiles, do not fit in.**

3. 6. For Whom and for What Christianity Was Created

If we do not fit in the cruel and man-hating configuration of the Jewish God's Kingdom that will be created after "the final extermination" of Gentiles, which we are in relation to Jews, the quite appropriate questions springs up, "Do we have the right to use Jesus Christ's teaching?"

If Jesus presupposed its universal scale, then we have the right to apply this teaching to our everyday life, but, in any way, without allegation that it was created exceptionally for *our* salvation. If this teaching was created only for Jews, then, of course, we hardly can have the right to use it without being Jews.

Matthew says, "These twelve Jesus sent forth, and commanded them, saying, **Go not into the way of the Gentiles, and into any city of the Samaritans enter ye not: But go rather to the lost sheep of the house of Israel.**"[203] It means that Jesus, sending his disciples to preach the Gospel of Peace, presupposed that it would be destined only for Jews. However, Luke does not specify whom the preaching will be destined for, "Go your ways: behold, I send you forth as lambs among wolves."[204]

Most likely, the interpretation of this question depends on the origin and religious orientation of the author of Gospel. Those who were orthodox Jews and practice Jesus' teaching in its Jewish version believed, of course, that this teaching is destined exceptionally for "the God's people, i. e. Jews," but Christians-Hellenists, whose teaching based mainly on the heritage of Greek philosophers, believed that Jesus' teaching was destined exceptionally for them.

Anyway, in John's Revelation, which can be considered as the oldest among Christian scriptures, it asserts that Christ's teaching is destined exceptionally for Jews. It was noticed even by Friedrich Engels, "But the most characteristic in these messages, as well as in the whole book, is the fact that never and nowhere the author did not happen to call both himself and his brothers in faith differently than Jews. He reproaches sect parishioners in Smyrna and Philadelphia, whom he blames that they "say they are Jews, and are not, but are the synagogue of Satan" and of those who are in Pergamos he says that they "hold the doctrine of Balaam, who taught Balac to cast a stumblingblock before the children of Israel, to eat things sacrificed unto idols, and to commit fornication."[205]

Thus, John also asserts that Jesus' teaching was preached exceptionally for Jews, the rest are just "the Synagogue of Satan." It is quite clear all the more that "the number of them which were sealed was **an hundred and forty and four thousand of all the tribes of the children of Israel**."[206] They are the first to ascend to a "new heaven" and only after them those who came to bow before God-butcher-filicide Jehovah and adopted Jewry will go there.

Orthodox Christianity believes that the Jewish people are the ones rejected by God for the favor of orthodox Christians, of course, but for some reason all the "sealed" are Jews and there are no orthodox Christians among them. It means that initially Christ's teaching was preached not for us [orthodox Christians]. Jehovah's Witnesses, for example, believe that there will certainly be "an hundred and forty and four thousand" of the sons of "witnesses" among those who will be "sealed" by Jehovah. They even made a list of the "sealed" and the "Watch Tower" officially announced that the enlistment of "sealed" had been over.[207] Who would have thought that there were so many Jews among Jehovah's Witnesses?

As for Christianity in general, now we have quite a different teaching than what Jesus Christ had taught us. "'We, therefore, see,' Friedrich Engels says, 'that Christianity of that time (the time of apostle John), which still was not aware of itself, was different from later, dogmatically fixed religion of Nikaea council[208], as the sky differ from the earth.'"[209]

Even Paulinism that appeared a couple of decades after the Revelation had been written, was already different from the teaching of early Christian sects. It is impossible to imagine what motives could induce Paul, the man who fanatically and cruelly persecuted Christians-Hellenists, to change his views in one moment and to turn into the apostle of God's Son.

Initially, Jesus' brother Jacob was in charge of the first group of Christians. They have their own Gospel written in Aramaic language and they, for reasons of dynasty, spread the version of Jesus' origin from the tribe of David. But there were so called Hellenists, i. e. Christians who did not want to accept the Jewish Law and used the heritage of Greek philosophers to base their teaching. They were the very Christians persecuted by Elisha-ben-Abujach (rabbi Saul, apostle Paul). Jews persecuted them because they dared to deny the service to God-butcher-filicide Jehovah and accepted Jesus' pure moral teaching about God who is love.

The teaching of the Great Teacher had such a strong influence on their hearts and souls that they were ready to die for the triumph of love and freedom, and, the more they were exterminated, the more followers replaced those who were persecuted and killed. At last, cunning Jewish rabbis understood that, if it was impossible to subdue their obstinacy with power, it was possible to manage it only by ruse. And then they designed a brilliant plan which ensured the destruction of both Christianity and the outer world with the hands of Christians. Elisha-ben-Abujach (rabbi Saul) became the main figure in this game.

What did this "dark horse," which no one researcher of Christianity could bring out into the open, represent by himself? We can learn from Saul's own words: "I am verily a man which am a Jew, born in Tarsus, a city in Cilicia, yet brought up in this city at the feet of Gamaliel, and taught according to the perfect manner of the law of the fathers, and was zealous toward God, as ye all are this day. And I persecuted this way unto the death, binding and delivering into prisons both men and women. As also the high priest doth bear me witness, and all the estate of the elders: from whom also I received letters unto the brethren, and went to Damascus, to bring them which were there bound unto Jerusalem, for to be punished.

And it came to pass, that, as I made my journey, and was come nigh unto Damascus about noon, suddenly there shone from heaven a great light round about me. And I fell unto the ground, and heard a voice saying unto me, Saul, Saul, why persecutest thou me? And I answered, Who art thou, Lord? And he said unto me, I am Jesus of Nazareth, whom thou persecutest. And they that were with me saw indeed the light, and were afraid; but they heard not the voice of him that spake to me. And I said, What shall I do, Lord? And the Lord said unto me, Arise, and go into Damascus; and there it shall be told thee of all things which are appointed for thee to do. And when I could not see for the glory of that light, being led by the hand of them that were with me, I came into Damascus.

And one Ananias, a devout man according to the law, having a good report of all the Jews which dwelt there, came unto me, and stood, and said unto me, Brother Saul, receive thy sight. And the same hour I looked up upon him. And he said, The God of our fathers hath chosen thee, that thou shouldest know his will, and see that Just One, and shouldest hear the voice of his mouth. For thou shalt be his witness unto all men of what thou hast seen and heard. And now why tarriest thou? arise, and be baptized, and wash away thy sins, calling on the name of the Lord.

And it came to pass, that, when I was come again to Jerusalem, even while I prayed in the temple, I was in a trance; And saw him saying unto me, Make haste, and get thee quickly out of Jerusalem: for they will not receive thy testimony concerning me. And I said, Lord, they know that I imprisoned and beat in every synagogue them that believed on thee: And when the blood of thy martyr Stephen was shed, I also was standing by, and consenting unto his death, and kept the raiment of them that slew him. And he said unto me, Depart: for I will send thee far hence unto the Gentiles."[210]

Thus, speaking in the terms of intelligent services and investigating bodies, the "legend" was created which ensured Saul's inculcation into the Gentiles world to spread the teaching about Jewish God, whose name was Jehovah. In such a way rabbi Saul became an apostle Paul and Christianity entered a new phase of its development. This new phase was characterized, first of all, by the fact that "paulinistic church justified slavery and social discrimination. Supporting both slavery and the authority of the Rome Empire in such a demonstrative way, **Paul, from one hand, eased the historic way of Christianity toward the final victory and changing into state religion; but, from the other hand, he deviated from Jesus' teaching and from everything that was connected with the protest against injustice life in it**. He moved, so to speak, far to the right. The social point of Christianity became blunt."[211]

It was exactly what Jewish leaders needed in order to begin mass extermination of Gentiles. Otherwise, why was it necessary for Paul, whose motherland was under Rome's yoke, to support its power? Why was it necessary for him, 'born in Tarsus, a city in Cilicia, yet brought up in this city at the feet of Gamaliel, and taught according to the perfect manner of the law of the fathers,' to 'ease the historic way of Christianity toward the final victory and changing into state religion?' Why did he, chosen for his mission by Jesus himself to be the witness about him for all the people, had to 'deviate from Jesus' teaching and from everything that was connected with the protest against injustice life in it?'

Thus we got quite logical explanation of mysterious transformation of rabbi Saul into apostle Paul, who changed the great moral teaching, the religion of heart and soul, into the religion of church and Holy scripture which became the monstrous weapon of 'the final extermination.'

The whole history of Christian movement, as well as of the whole world, proves the fact that Elisha-ben-Abujach (Saul, apostle Paul), the Jew born in Tarsus, was the agent of Jewish leaders inculcated into Christian movement to transform it into the religion of church and Holy (Jewish) Scripture, the final goal of which was the misinterpretation of the real Jesus' teaching and inculcating the matrix of destruction, which had to ensure "the final extermination" of the whole non Jewish world in the name of triumph of the Jewish "God's Kingdom, into the Gentiles' consciousness."

After all the aforesaid, all the versions of the mysterious "conversion" of the Jewish rabbi Saul into the Christian apostle Paul will appear utterly unfounded, for they do not give any logic of so striking metamorphose. Senon Cosidovsky explains such a prominent case in the Christian history by Paul's mental illness, the symptoms of which looked like epilepsy. Ernst Renan gives an even more absurd explanation: "As for Paul, who did not know Jesus personally, such a metamorphose was inevitable in a certain sense. While the school, possessing the live Jesus teaching, created Jesus of synoptical Gospels, an exalted man who saw the founder of Christianity only in his dreams changed him into superhuman creature, in same kind of metaphysic being that, most likely, had never existed."[212]

The further realization of the plan was quite easy. Paul, who was a nice sophist (phrase-mongerer), could easily blunt poor Gentiles' heads, so that they willingly accepted not only the belief in God-butcher-filicide Jehovah and in Messiah who has a sharp sword in his mouth by means of which he would destroy the peoples and nations, but also all the ravings of a madman that constitute the content of matrix.

Paul used distratumness (the method of binary oppositions or the method of absurdity modeling) a common and well-proved method for creation of the needed form of religious consciousness. The method was very simple. When the human brain receives two alternative irritants, it loses any ability to think for a short moment. At this moment, anything can be inculcated into human's consciousness.

We have already told you about the absurd represented in the Gospel according to Thomas. Do you remember? "If you do not love you farther and your mother as I do, you can not be my disciples.

And if you do not hate your father and your mother as I do, you can not be my disciples." Any ravings of a madman can be implanted into your consciousness while you think about what it means. This is the very neutralization of binary oppositions we are talking about. The directives to love and to hate, colliding one with another in your brain, neutralize one another and then it is possible to suggest you both directive to love and to hate, for the consciousness squeezed into the frames of absurd accepts both feelings as equal.

The first and probably the main obstacle in the way of implanting a new teaching into the Gentile world was circumcision, which was considered by the Hellenic world as an extremely savage and barbaric custom. Food interdictions were another obstacle, for they seemed to Gentiles no less savage and barbaric than circumcision. The problem with these two obstacles could be solved easily just by telling Gentiles the tail that Jesus himself appeared before Paul in his dream and ordered to cancel both circumcision and food interdictions. But it was much more difficult to introduce God-butcher-filicide Jehovah in the form of a loving and merciful God, who is love. In order to do that, it was necessary to "dress" him with such a "dressing" that Gentiles could not notice what they "swallowed." Besides, it was necessary to distort Jesus' teaching so that they would not notice it. A certain skill and keenness of wit were needed for such a business. Paul had such qualities.

Then he went to Gentiles and began his exercises in phrase-mongering. "To all that be in Rome, beloved of God, called to be saints: Grace to you and peace from God our Father, and the Lord Jesus Christ. First, I thank my God through Jesus Christ for you all, that your faith is spoken of throughout the whole world. For God is my witness, whom I serve with my spirit in the gospel of his Son, that without ceasing I make mention of you always in my prayers; Making request, if by any means now at length I might have a prosperous journey by the will of God to come unto you.

Now I would not have you ignorant, brethren, that oftentimes I purposed to come unto you, (but was let hitherto,) that I might have some fruit among you also, even as among other Gentiles. For I am not ashamed of the gospel of Christ: for it is the power of God unto salvation to every one that believeth; to the Jew first, and also to the Greek. For therein is the righteousness of God revealed from faith to faith: as it is written, **They just shall live by faith**. For the wrath of God is revealed from heaven against all ungodliness and unrighteousness of men, who hold the truth in unrighteousness. **But after thy hardness and impenitent heart treasurest up unto thyself wrath against the**

day of wrath and revelation of the righteous judgment of God; Who will render to every man according to his deeds.

For as many as have sinned without law shall also perish without law: and as many as have sinned in the law shall be judged by the law; (For not the hearers of the law are just before God, **but the doers of the law shall be justified**. For when the Gentiles, which have not the law, do by nature the things contained in the law, these, having not the law, are a law unto themselves. For circumcision verily profiteth, if thou keep the law: **but if thou be a breaker of the law, thy circumcision is made uncircumcision**. Therefore if the uncircumcision keep the righteousness of the law, shall not his uncircumcision be counted for circumcision? And shall not uncircumcision which is by nature, if it fulfil the law, judge thee, who by the letter and circumcision dost transgress the law? **For he is not a Jew, which is one outwardly; neither is that circumcision, which is outward in the flesh: But he is a Jew, which is one inwardly; and circumcision is that of the heart, in the spirit, and not in the letter; whose praise is not of men, but of God. What advantage then hath the Jew? or what profit is there of circumcision? Much every way: chiefly, because that unto them were committed the oracles of God.**

For what if some did not believe? Shall their unbelief make the faith of God without effect? God forbid: yea, let God be true, but every man a liar; as it is written, That thou mightest be justified in thy sayings, and mightest overcome when thou art judged. But if our unrighteousness commend the righteousness of God, what shall we say? Is God unrighteous who taketh vengeance? (I speak as a man). God forbid: for then how shall God judge the world? **For if the truth of God hath more abounded through my lie unto his glory; why yet am I also judged as a sinner? And not rather**, (as we be slanderously reported, and as some affirm that we say,) **Let us do evil, that good may come**? whose damnation is just.

What then? Are we better than they? No, in no wise: for we have before proved both Jews and Gentiles, that they are all under sin; As it is written, There is none righteous, no, not one.

Now we know that what things soever the law saith, it saith to them who are under the law: that every mouth may be stopped, and all the world may become guilty before God. Therefore by the deeds of the law there shall no flesh be justified in his sight: for by the law is the knowledge of sin. But now the righteousness of God without the law is manifested, being witnessed by the law and the prophets; Even the righteousness of God which is by faith of Jesus

Christ unto all and upon all them that believe: for there is no difference, **for all have sinned, and come short of the glory of God**.

Being justified freely by his grace through the redemption that is in Christ Jesus: whom God hath set forth to be a propitiation through faith in his blood, to declare his righteousness for the remission of sins that are past, through the forbearance of God. To declare, I say, at this time his righteousness: that he might be just, and the justifier of him which believeth in Jesus.

Where is boasting then? It is excluded. By what law? of works? Nay: but by the law of faith. **Therefore we conclude that a man is justified by faith without the deeds of the law**. Is he the God of the Jews only? Is he not also of the Gentiles? Yes, of the Gentiles also. Seeing it is one God, which shall justify the circumcision by faith, and uncircumcision through faith. **Do we then make void the law through faith? God forbid: yea, we establish the law**."[213]

Here we have the nicest sample of sophistic, the art of cunning arguing and fabricated proofs or, to be more exact, phrase-mongering. The core of his speech is the postulate of justification by faith, the main doctrinal postulate of Christianity. "The just shall live by faith," Paul says. But some lines later the same Paul says that "God will render to every man according to his deeds." Then we read the following: "Therefore by the deeds of the law there shall no flesh be justified in his sight: for by the law is the knowledge of sin." What does it mean? It means that the law is of no importance now, for "by the deeds of the law there shall no flesh be justified," moreover, the law is a very dangerous thing we must get rid of the sooner the better, for "by the law is the knowledge of sin." What for do we need the law, which is "the knowledge of sin?" We have enough things which give us "the knowledge of sin" even without the Jewish law. That is why we do not need such a law. And let us even forget about its existence. Let us be justified just by faith as our Great Teacher Jesus Christ taught us. Let us make void the law through faith. God forbid! The same Paul who earlier tried to convince us that the law is a rather dangerous thing which we have to get rid of in the favor of faith, now call to establish it! He says: "Do we then make void the law through faith? God forbid: yea, **we establish the law**."

Thus, we see that all these beautiful words, all this phrase-mongering is destined, from one hand, to subdue credulous Gentiles to the power of murderous and destructive Jewish law, from the other hand, to distort Jesus Christ's teaching. Rabbi Saul has coped with his task brilliantly. It is not in vain that Talmud says, "he [Paul] has spoiled the work of that man."[214] "That man" is Jesus Christ according to Talmud.

CHAPTER 4.

ISLAMIC MYTH

"And that is why, I, the last among prophets, had been **sent with a sword**. Let them, who preach my faith, not to resort either to proves or to reasoning, but **kill all those who refuse to obey to my law**. Every one who fights for the truth will receive a great reward regardless he is victorious over infidel or dies on a battlefield."[215]

Prophet Mohammed.

4. 1. Islamic Extremism Seen By the Eyes of Islamic and Non-Islamic Worlds

Quite recently, just a little bit more than two years ago, we had a chance to be convinced that prophet Mohammed did not waste his words. All of them fell on the fertile "soil" and gave abundant sprouts. In that terrible September day, we with our own eyes, saw the real face of Islamic religious extremism at the active participation of which the myth about our power and invulnerability was destroyed within tens of minutes, and fear and panic were sewn into our hearts and souls.

This unprecedented terrorist act agitated the whole world and made people think about the causes of such terrible events that take place more often nowadays. All our attempts to understand the causes of these bloody crimes are constantly run against our resistance, which is very difficult to overcome. As if some terrible irresistible power stops us every time we begin to penetrate into the essence of a problem.

In the foreword we spoke of one of Vladimir Pozner's opponents who tried to ground the causes of terrorist acts of September 11, 2001, by some ideology that hides behind this bloody crime against humans and humanity. As soon as he began to speak about it Pozner interrupted him and led the talk away to a different subject.

Nevertheless, many analysts discovered the influence of Islamic religious ideology in these terrorist acts; thanks to which we have numerous terrorist organizations that use this ideology to justify their criminal activity. Strange as it may seem, this can be told not only about Islam.

Abdul Wahed Niyasov, the deputy of the State legislative assembly and the leader of the "Eurasia" group says: "One can hardly name any religious tradition which would not have used by different religious organizations. Soldiers of "Caha" organization used Judaism, "The tigers of liberation of Tamil Ilama" used Hinduism, and some "Ananda Marga" even used Buddhism which is considered to be the most peaceful religion. Ireland republican army struggled against Protestants for the rights of Catholics."[216] But Islamic terrorism, as Niyasov believes, is "the myth stirred up by those for whom it is profitable."

Alexander Prochanov, the editor-in-chief of *Tomorrow* newspaper, "reading the Koran in Russian translation noticed that it was the book of love and peace, that it is directed against all the forms of violence. Koran is the universe which speaks of harmony, of the necessity of chaos and evil overcoming."[217]

The council of muftis of Russia has almost the same opinion. They assert that "the man is the highest of Allah's creations, and that is why the one who kills another one is considered as the one who killed the whole humankind."[218] This highest council blames both the new crime of terrorists and terrorism itself. It is convinced that "Islam demands us to solve our problems only on the base of peace negotiations."

The council of Russian muftis are especially preoccupied with the fact that terrorism tries "to disguise itself behind religious cloths and use very often Islamic symbolic to cover its antihuman and antireligious goals"[219] But they, for some reason, are not preoccupied at all with the fact that a religious teaching itself can become the cause of terrorism.

Russian analysts seem to be inclined to the thought that Islamic terrorism is not a myth, they believed that it is a reality. Academician Zhores Alferov, for example, "sees very distinctly that we have the mutual enemy—extremism and fundamentalism of Moslem type."[220] It is quite obvious for him that "dividing line goes between civilization and barbarity, between science-technological progress and frenzied religious fanaticism."[221]

Academician Nataly Bechtereva considers this crime as "faceless expansion based on faith." Then she expresses very rebellious, as she believes, thought that "every normal human being is endowed with the sparkle of aggression,"[222] confirming by this our "rebellious" thought that religious teaching that contain cruel and man-hating commandments blow out this sparkle very successfully.

And here is the great danger of all the religious teachings. We assert: **if a religious teaching contains even one citation that calls for hatred, religious intolerance, violence, cruelty or murder, there will always be people who, being endowed with the sparkle of aggression a little bit more than other people, will inevitably use this citation to ground and justify this aggression**. Because, as academician Panchenko has noticed, "we live in the Cainistic society, which I call by the name of Cain, the first fratricide."[223]

The opinions of those who suffered from the terrorists' acts are divided. President Bush, for example, respects both Islam and its representatives, as he stated both in a Moslem mosque and at a congress meeting: "We respect your faith. Its teaching is peaceful and good."[224] John Cooksey obviously hates both this faith and all its representatives, about which he had openly stated in his speech on American radio: "If I see somebody with a napkin on his head, I will throw him out."[225] Later he begged to be excused, but words once spoken, you can never recall.

American people in general, and especially president Bush, consider Moslems almost as their brothers. For they serve to one God, God of Abraham, Isaac and Jacob, i. e. cruel and bloodthirsty God-butcher-filicide Jehovah. And, of course, to have anything against Allah is the same as to have anything against Jehovah. Moreover, Islam becomes "American religion," for there are more than seven million Moslems in the USA and their number increases.

Americans consider Moslems, as well as themselves, to be "the people of the book," which accept the Jewish Bible and the New Testament as Holy Scriptures, but, at the same time, consider the exceptionally elegant and expressive language of the Koran to be God's word which is the inviolable truth. They also think: "The followers of Islamic teaching believe that Moses, John the Baptist and Jesus were the prophets, but, the last messenger was Mohammed to whom archangel Gabriel has dictated the Koran."[226]

Jamal Badawi, professor of theology of the Virgin Mary University in Halifax, says that "**the core of both Christian and Islamic faith, as well as that of Jewish, consists in the observance of moral laws, love for a neighbor, justice and mercy**."[227]

Karen Armstrong, an American writer and a great expert of Islam, holds to the same opinion. In her article "The true, peaceful face of Islam" she says: "There are one milliard and two hundred millions of Moslems, and Islam is the most high growth world religion. If the atrocity of September 11, 2001, would have been a typical act of Moslem faith, **if Islam would really have inspired and justified such a cruelty, then the growth and ever increasing presence of Moslems in Europe and America would be a terrible perspective. Fortunately, it is not so.**"[228]

Of course, she acknowledges that the Koran contains "some episodes that tell about armed conflicts," but she justifies their existence with the fact that "Islam was opened to Mohammed in the context of universal war." The chieftains of warring tribes seemed to be not inclined to spare lives of captives. That is why, as Karen Armstrong believes, there appeared the appropriate Allah's instruction, "slay them wherever you find them!"[229]

Osama-ben-Laden likes to quote such places of Koran, but he does it, as Mrs. Armstrong thinks, extremely selectively. In reality, the Koran is a good and kind book, and calls for peace are more characteristic for this book, "Therefore if they withdraw from your but do not fight you, and (instead) send you (guarantees) of peace, then Allah has opened no way for you (to war against them)."[230] She also states that "Moslems are constantly prescribed to respect Jews and Christians, who believe in the same God."

Then, why does the religious terrorism with its killer-kamikazes, hijacking and murder of innocent people exist? Mrs. Armstrong answers that "Koran never approved such actions, for they always contradicted to its innermost orders. But during XX century, warlike forms of religionism, known as fundamentalism, that became the protest against of rapidly developed world, have appeared. Any fundamentalist movement, which I learned in Judaism, Christianity and Islam, believes that liberal, secularized society aspires to destroy religion. They believe that armed conflicts can justify any ignoring of more merciful principles of their faith. But, exaggerating more aggressive principles contained in all our Holy Scriptures, they break a tradition."[231]

Thus, we see that acknowledging the existence of "more aggressive principles contained in all our Holy Scriptures" which form the imagination that armed conflicts for the sake of faith saving "can justify any ignoring of more merciful principles of their faith," people, nevertheless, always try to justify and rehabilitate "more aggressive principles," and represent them as quite normal and harmless things that just "brake a tradition." But, these experts of Islam, for one or another reason, are not troubled by the fact that these "more aggressive principles" became the cause of death of thousands of their fellow countrymen.

The most interesting moment here is that, according to Christian teaching, those who had no time to repent before their death and died without absolution are not admitted to the "God's Kingdom." Their destiny is in the "lake burning with fire and sulfur." But killer-kamikazes, according to Koran, will certainly go to the paradise because "**Allah has purchased of the Believers their persons and their goods**; for theirs (in return) is the Garden (of Paradise): **they fight in His Cause, and slay and are slain: a promise binding on Him in truth, through the Law, the Gospel, and the Qur'an.**"[232]

These cruel man-hating principles, which dishonor and discredit all our Scriptures, were always the causes of terrible atrocities, and they will remain such as long as we understand that if we do not get rid of them, we shall exterminate each other. And, nevertheless, there are "more merciful principles" in our Scriptures, which, to our great regret, lie now under the Twin's debris together with thousands of Americans who had been cruelly killed in the name of the triumph of Moslem "utmost justice," which kind "Uncle Sam" or, to be exacter, Uncle Bush do not suspect of. But we know about them, and cannot hide the truth.

4. 2. Moslem "God's Kingdom"

In July, 2001, a very interesting article with a very resonant title—"Fiery Islam"—appeared in *Tomorrow* newspaper. The editor-in-chief Alexandr Prochanov discussed the world problems with Geidar Jemal who "has the reputation of connoisseur of Islam and Islamic problems, as well as of how is this teaching projected into the actual world politic."[233]

This connoisseur of Islam asserts: "Such was the sign of the Most High that **Islam had been given not for the purpose to organize full, free and happy life on the Earth, but for the purpose of preparing the situation for catharsis solution of history, in order to justify the presence of the Holy Spirit here, and to raise our life to the level of the utmost justice.**"[234]

Yes, there was such a sign of the Most High that in the VII century the great prophet Mohammed organized a new religious movement which name was Islam. This new religion has acquired the great messianic destiny to make, as Geidar Jemal asserts, the "catharsis solution of history." The final result of this catharsis process must be "making of our way to the level of utmost justice," but not for the purpose "to organize full, free and happy life on the Earth." If not on the Earth, then where? It turns out that "on the new Earth and on the new Heaven which will appear after the end of history, after the resurrection of dead and dividing of the reality into hell and paradise where the righteous will get their rewards."

Of course, there is nothing new in the words of this great connoisseur of Islam. We know quite well that Islam, as well as Christianity, is a typical eschatological myth that grew up from Judaism and absorbed all its principles. In Islamic myth, the act of creation, as well as in the Christian myth, represents by itself the collective work of some mighty beings, which later are personified with mighty and mercy Allah. "**It is We Who created you and gave you shape**; then we bade the angels bow down to Adam, and they bowed down; not so Iblis; he refused to be of those who bow down."[235]

In Islamic myth the act of creation takes place not on earth, but somewhere on the heaven, for Adam and Eve are not just expelled to the other place after their fall; they are thrown down to the earth: "Get you down, all (you people), with enmity between yourselves. On earth will be your dwelling-place and your means of livelihood for a time."[236]

Adam and Eve, as it turns out, are endowed with almost godlike authority, for even angels bowed to Adam. Thus, as wee see, from the very beginning, the Islamic myth, in contrast to the Christian one, claims its right to be a spiritual teaching. The Islamic myth is not burdened with grotesque-exaggerated stories about lives of quite earthly and vicious patriarchs; it offers a straight and short way to the heaven, to Allah. That is why "**those who are ready to die for justice on the way of the Most High are the main in Islam**."[237]

The Islamic myth, as well as the Christian one, is a linear movement from some static condition; from the initial chaos where God creates the world, to another static condition, to a new wonderful reality which is created by means of the Last Judgment accomplished by Allah in order to divide this new reality into hell and paradise, where each of us will get a reward according to "our fruits," and where "the way to the level of utmost justice" will be made. But "the way to the level of utmost justice" is made in Islam, as well as in Christianity, by means of the utmost cruelty and bloodshed. "Verily, I am with you; make ye firm then those who believe; **I will cast dread into the hearts of those who misbelieve,—strike off their necks then, and strike off from them every finger-tip. That is, because they went into opposition against God and His Apostle; for he who goes into opposition against God and His Apostle—verily, God is keen to punish**."[238]

Here we have a chance to convince ourselves once more that

the idea of monotheism carries in itself the enormous, irresistible genocide impulse that makes a "believer" consider an "infidel" as some defective creature, which is necessary either to convert to "believer's" faith or to "strike off their necks then, and strike off from them every finger-tip." But it is better to kill the one who, God forbid, refuses to accept Islam, to kill meanly and cruelly, to kill stabbing in the back, when "they slept for their afternoon rest." "How many towns have We destroyed (for their sins)? **Our punishment took them on a sudden by night or while they slept for their afternoon rest**. When (thus) our punishment took them, no cry did they utter but this: "Indeed we did wrong."[239]

How fast is Allah for anger, punishment and bloodshed! You see, it was needed just to say that they "did wrong" in order for Allah's anger to flare up. For such a sin "believers" "strike off their necks then, and strike off from them every finger-tip," or stab in the back "while they sleep for their afternoon rest." This, the very Moslem "utmost justice" which is not different from that of Christian, and in the image of "merciful" Allah we easily recognize the image of the same "merciful" Jewish God-butcher-filicide Jehovah.

But justice must be universal. If we treat one man justly and another one unjustly (even if this one is quite a good person, though is of other faith), such a justice turns into injustice, which is inhuman. In the space of the Koran, justice exists only for Moslems, as well as in the space of the Bible it exists only for Jews or only for Christians: "There are the rights of orphans, the rights of wives, the rights of widows, the rights of criminals etc. The prophet said that **"a Moslem's back is a forbidden field," which means that it is necessary to have strong evidences of his guilt in order to punish him physically... And if such a guilt is not proved by court, nobody has a right to touch him with a stick.**"[240]

It is a Moslem's back that is a "forbidden field," and the law protects his rights. But neither law, nor court, as well as justice, exists for those who are not Moslems. They can be punished without any court; one can strike off their necks and fingertips; "one can blow up an American destroyer, make disabled more than two hundred American seamen, make unhappy their families,"[241] make unhappy the families of thousands of other people perished under the debris of the World Trade Center in New-York, under the debris of houses in Moscow and other cities of Russia and then call these atrocities "**reviving revolution, the genuine political Islam, the advent of which was prepared by Marks, Engels, Lenin and Che Gevara.**"[242]

Do you feel as the warlike and cruel Biblical atmosphere of violence and destruction is passed from Judaism to Christianity, from Christianity to Islam, from Islam to Marxism, from Marxism to Leninism, from Leninism to Stalinism and to Fascism, and from Fascism back to Islam? Such is the "circulation" of hatred and cruelty in the Nature. And this "circulation" of hatred and cruelty determines the cultural picture of the world during the entire "post-mythological" history of mankind.

And in this picture, some composition center can be seen, towards which all the important cultural-historical processes that have quite peaceful and good goals (from the first sight) are drawn. All the great movements such as Christianity, Islam, Marxism, Leninism, Stalinism and Fascism had before them a great humanistic goal of building a new world or "the brilliant future," in which God will "wipe out every tear, and there will be neither lamenting nor death," but, in practice, all these attempts to build a better life **always** turned into a bloody bacchanalia in which millions of people lost their lives.

And now, we are waiting for the second advent of Jesus Christ and for the Last Judgment, in the fire of which both "impious and righteous" will be cruelly and mercilessly destroyed. As if some great, irresistible power returns any good intention to this huge bloodstained mass of human madness that absorbs like a black hole all our attempts to make the world better.

Strange as it may seem, but "the great book," "the book of all books," "the great manual to our life," "the most readable book in the world," our beloved Bible is this terrible, bloodstained "black hole." It is the very book that is a center around which the entire culture of the western world is built and rotates.

Do you remember, in the beginning of our narration we said that myth is, besides all the rest, "the case history of an illness" of the people that created it? You must know that the Jewish myth about God-butcher-filicide Jehovah is a real history of a serious mental illness of the Jewish people. You see, each book carries the imprint of mentality of its author. If it is a man with a normal well-balanced mind who possesses such human qualities as kindness, justice, mercy, compassion, respect and love towards humans and the world, his books will also be kind and good. On the contrary, a mentally deceased man, who is vicious and cruel, will hardly write good and kind books. Carrying the imprint of his mentality, they will glorify mean and vicious human deeds and propensities.

A man or people possessed by megalomania, persecution mania

and the acute form of sadism cannot be good and kind. Their mental decease will inevitably be reflected in their books. To use them as a manual to our life is the same as to use real case history of mental decease taken from any madhouse. And then everything will go on as Jesus said: "If one blind man leads another one, they both will fall into a pit."

Other authors also noticed some "strange" peculiarities of the Jewish people. Ernst Renan says: "A Jew is always cruel as a master. Being a Carthaginians brother, he has shown his real nature during his last days. This people always had splendid by their qualities minority, **but never any group of people had such a rage, such a heat in mutual extermination. Being brought to a certain limit of desperation, a Jew can do anything, even against his own religion. In the Jewish history, we see people who embittered one against another to the degree of extreme madness. One can tell all the best and all the worst about this race without acting against the truth; for a good Jew is a nicest creature, but an evil Jew is the most abominable one.**"[243]

In Islam, as well as in Christianity, there exists the image of enemy, which, as you have already noticed, is passed from one myth to another. The fact is that neither "the religions of salvation" nor revolutionary, as well as fascist-terrorist organizations cannot exist without this notorious image, for if there is no enemy, there is nothing to be saved from and then all these religions and revolutions lose their meaning. But if a real enemy does not exist, it is necessary to invent it. Both "the religions of salvation" and different revolutionary-extremist organizations are occupied with this very profitable business.

And, if in Christianity this enemy is a mysterious being which is called the Devil (Satan, Serpent, Beast, the Evil one), in the modern Islam there appeared like a duce from a snuffbox quite a real, evil, merciless, mortal enemy, which name is "globalization" (the New World Order, "iron heel," "system"). This enemy, as well as the Christian Devil, threatens the whole world and personifies the utmost evil.

But what is this utmost evil? Geidar Jemal, the connoisseur of Islam and Islamic problems asserts that it is an "electronic mass of money which is inaccessible and invisible to everyone, but in which something like dynamics of human kin is formalized. This is globalization."[244]

Isn't it a duce from a snuffbox? Why then is this mortal enemy so terrible? Geidar Jemal asserts that "Islam considers the existing world order to be an enemy, for it regards this order, this system, which has established control over all kinds of human activity nowadays, as evil, as usurpation."[245]

By the way, Russian populists, anarchists and other revolutionary groups, which terrorized and kept in fear the whole Russia at the end of the XIX and at the beginning of the XX centuries, tried to solve the same problems of struggling against the enemy who, as they believed, represented by itself "the universal usurpation."

Characteristic is the fact that none of them asked if this struggle was necessary for common working people who knew nothing about that enemy. But propaganda does its work, people get up for fighting, overthrow the "usurper" and get in return another usurper who turns out to be much more cruel and merciless than kind and merciful Tsar was.

And now we have the examples of metamorphoses underwent by "kind and merciful" Islamic myth, which is changed very rapidly into direct similarity to a bandit organization for which any moral laws do not exist. This fact became quite obvious even to A. Prochanov, who noticed: **"If one organize the deliverance or purifying of Russia from liberal control or from American hegemony by means of hexogen or expansion of liberators from the enclaves of Middle Asia and Hinducush, we will again have disintegration of territories and catastrophe for all that is alive, including dogs, cats and even butterflies that live here. You see, the recent history demonstrates the examples of Islam changing into a ruling politic... Let us take Chechnya of Mashadov. This is, in its essence, a sovereign state with a shariat court, with victorious Islamic ideology, which should demonstrate prosperity, spirituality, people should become like angels and move by means of wings, but not by means of armored troop-carriers. What happened? There happened such events that in Ichkeriya, victorious Islamic republic: the kidnapping is prospered, weak and fallen are humiliated, orphans do not receive any help — nothing but awful discredit of Islam.**"[246]

It is nothing of the kind, Mr. Prochanov! This is not an awful discredit of Islam, but the triumphant establishing of its main principles of "universal love" and "utmost justice" which is expressed in the Koran quite clearly. And, since any "Holy Scripture," any religious myth is not only the history of mental illness of the people which created it, but also a matrix that determines world outlook and peoples' actions, it is quite natural that the world we live in is developed in accordance with the matrix structure.

Since Islam considers the existing world order as evil, as usurpation, it is quite logical to set off "the utmost justice," which is embodied in Islam more than in any other religion against this "utmost evil." And

"today Islam is the last military-political resource of humankind in its struggle against terrible and merciless system."[247]

And "the utmost justice" is its main instrument in this struggle, which is an "about-face swing of Jordan, which is reconstruction of that order that precedes to this vale of life into which we are plunged in the course of our fatal descending. Such a justice is the last mystical link in a long chain that must be ended with the resurrection of the dead. But before Mahdi (Liberator) must come... **Justice belongs to faith and jihad. Faith and jihad—these are the core of Islam.**"[248]

But the main power of Islam are people who are ready to die for this very "justice," having grabbed hundreds or even thousands of people (whose backs "merciful" Allah did not make a "forbidden field") together with them to the heaven. In other words, Islam is changing slowly to the same "system," against which it is fighting. Even Mr. Prochanov has noticed this fact. He said: "**Today, in all the zones where Islam is reviving, where Islam is the part of life, instead of library or museum, cannons are rumbling, buildings are crashed and blood is shed. Tajikistan has proved to the world what is the Islamic revolution which filled the streets of Dushanbe with mutilated corpses of Tajiks, Russians and Uzbeks. Taliban movement has finally turned Afghanistan into ruins, and talibs carry not an olive twig of peace, but a fiery sward, which continues to disembowel people and cut their throats. Chechnya, shechen wachabism, its passionarity mean explosions and endless slaughter.**"[249]

And an image of "the man of our time" (or "the Moslem of our time" or "the Bolshevik of our time") is crystallized persistently and inevitably. He is the one "who actively, with his whole soul and with all his power wants to realize in himself and through himself the vocation of his faith, in this struggle for the triumph of "the utmost justice." Today he is a Bolshevik of our time. **This is a new, real, religious Bolshevism—not national-bolshevism, but religious international-bolshevism.**"[250]

Thus, a new revolution of unprecedented scale, which is going to stop "the immoral and corrupted transnational system that is rolling over all the nations," is prepared in the depths of the Moslem world and in the bright minds of its great ideologists. It will be consisted of "**only unions, military alliances of men, groups, communities and structures that are connected one with another by the dictate of one's heart in order to lead the others just because there is no other way out: either to be dissolved in this universal intestine or to die upright. These alliances must not know the national division.**"[251]

Russia is also included into the vanguard of this "religious revolution." The great theoretic of Islam even determined its status in relation to Islam. Russia for him is "the country charged with a super idea," and it has intimate ties with the Moslem space." The problems of Russia, as Geidar Jemal believes, consist in "political superstructure of westernized Masonic liberal elites which want to use Russia and its human resources for realization of their global goals."

And this very "globalization" attacks Islam. "As the result, Islam turns out to be the ally of all those forces that are losers against globalization. In other words, some universal human factor of confrontation to tyranny is hammered out."[252]

Then Geidar Jemal begins to prophesy: "We can forecast like this. **The XXI century is, of course, the century of wars. This is the century of religious wars. This is the century of guerilla wars. This is the century of religious-guerilla war against electronically-rocket world system that you [A. Prochanov] call "technotronic fascism**." Mr. Prochanov accepts this prophesy with great enthusiasm, "I accept this thesis, for only paradise can be higher than revolution."

Mr. Prochanov seems to have a wish to get there, for he knows that if Russia is liberated from American hegemony "by means of hexogen or expansion of liberators from the enclaves of Middle Asia and Hinducush," we will have "catastrophe for all that is alive, including dogs, cats and even butterflies," and it is the shortest way to Allah.

On the example of this remarkable article we can clearly see the way the matrix works. In the beginning of the article, Mr. Prochanov asserts that while reading the Koran he "saw that it is the book of love and peace, that it is directed against any forms of violence. The Koran is universum which speak of harmony, of necessity of chaos and evil overcoming." Either the journalist did not read the Koran at all, or he read it inattentively. Or there must be one more factor which prevented him from understanding what he had read. Otherwise, he would have noticed that this "holy" book calls for hatred and cruelty quite obviously and openly.

Earlier we quoted the extracts of the Koran in which Allah either orders to beat and to kill innocent people or justifies such murders. Someone can argue with us, saying that one cannot judge the text just by one or some citations torn from the whole context. **But we assert that if a text contains even one citation which calls openly for hatred, cruelty, religious intolerance and murder or justifies such a murder, such a text must be announced to be "antivalue" and excluded from using by normal and honest people, moreover, by**

dishonorable people who will certainly include this citation into arsenal of their means of struggle for the triumph of "the utmost justice."

But how can it happen that the same God speaks of his great love towards people and at the same time orders to kill and even kills himself? The fact is that he expressed his love only for those who bows to him and who serves him. He says about "unbelievers": "**But if any deny the signs of Allah, Allah is swift in calling to account**."[253] "**Allah does not love those who reject Faith**"[254] and orders to "strike off their necks, and strike off from them every finger-tip," or to kill "on a sudden by night or while they slept for their afternoon rest."

Such a love turns out to be some kind of "unilateral love." Such a love does not have anything mutual with a normal human love. The normal human love is unconditional. It demands nothing. It just gives. God just demands. He gives only those who worship and serve him, i. e. those who cringe before him out of the fear of eternal tortures in the lake burning with fire and sulfur. This is love-bargaining, and it cannot be considered as a value from the point of view of humanity: "**Allah has purchased of the Believers their persons and their goods**."[255] Love-bargaining, religion-bargaining can hardly be corresponded to the criteria of humanity. **It is the Devil who purchases souls (persons), but not God**. That is why we have to acknowledge that Islam, as well as Christianity and Judaism, is "antivalue," regardless if we like it or not.

But why, you will ask, reading "Holy Scriptures" we do not notice it? Firstly, in order to do that you must be very attentive and have acute feelings of love and compassion, as well as ability to feel another one's pain. If you are able to feel the pain of a man who is "burned in the hell fire," "put on a chain, the length of which is seventy cubits," if you are able to imagine how it feels to be the one on the head of whom "spill boiling water," "strike off one's neck, and strike off every finger-tip" or kill meanly "by night or while one sleep for the afternoon rest" just because one is not a Moslem, then you will be able to understand the real "value" of such a world outlook for the development of humans and humankind.

Secondly, each Holy Scripture is a matrix, as you know. It programs human consciousness on the subconscious level. You also know about the twenty-fifth frame. This frame is not perceived by consciousness. But subconsciousness fixes the information which is contained in this frame. With the course of time this information is activated and makes the man to do one or another action, very often even not characteristic for him or for her. A matrix works in the same way. The man reading a text, especially if it is a long one, is unable to perceive all the information consciously. But he reads everything, every word. And every word that gets in his memory will be stored in his subconsciousness until the end of his life. Among those words and sentences which he did not remember consciously are sentences-orders like "go and destroy Amalek. And slay both men and women, old men and infants, camels and donkeys" or "strike off their necks then, and strike off from them every finger-tip." Such sentences-orders very often cannon be perceived consciously, for the negative impulse contained in them exceeds the human consciousness perception threshold. For example, the one who blindly believes in God considers him as the creature endowed with absolute positive qualities.

That is why, reading about cruel and bloody deeds of such a God, one cannot perceive this information consciously. But his subconsciousness will inevitably fix it. Sooner or later this information will do its work. And then "kind and merciful" Christians go to crush Jews and brutally kill Jewish women; disemboweling them and sewing up dead cats in their wombs, and the same "kind and merciful" Moslem announces "holy jihad" to the entire "unilateral world" and in the struggle for "utmost justice" kill cruelly and mercilessly, thousands of innocent people.

This the way a matrix works. And as long as we read texts of our "Holy Scriptures," division and enmity among people and nations, religious intolerance and genocide will continue to exist in our world and we will continue to hate and to kill each other. And this will last until we realize all the programs contained in the matrixes on which we build our life, having finished the long way of mankind to its "brilliant future," to apocalypses, to its end, to total destruction of humans and humanity in the struggle for the triumph of the "utmost justice."

4. 3. Does Islam Really Have A True and Peaceful Face?

We have to answer this and similar questions every time we proceed to the study of some teaching based on a certain ideology and on the authority of a supreme hierarchy who exercises total control over his subordinates. At that, these subordinates always regard their "God" as the most kind and merciful creature that incessantly cares for the well-being of his people and prepares for them "the boons of the future age" in which there will be "Gardens in nearness to their Lord, with rivers flowing beneath; therein is their eternal homes; with Companions pure (and holy); and the good pleasure if Allah."[256]

But as soon as this ideology gets its real embodiment in a system which is endowed with power and authority, slaughter and bloodshed begin, inquisition trials and the courts of revolutionary tribunal are established, piles and gas chambers of concentration camps are burned, "cannons are rumbling, buildings are crashed and blood is shed..., streets are filled with mutilated corpses of Tajiks, Russians and Uzbeks. The Taliban movement has finally turned Afghanistan into ruins, and Talibs carry not an olive twig of peace, but a fiery sword, which continues to disembowel people and cut their throats..., Albanian Moslems remind Europe of war, Balkans are smoked with depleted uranium, Christians' monasteries are exploded in Cosovo," and Serbian Christians kill thousands of Moslems and beat Allah's people just because they tried to rebuild their destroyed mosque.

And all these people commit their crimes in the name of their "kind and merciful" gods that have "true and peaceful face." **We are far from thinking that all the believers are such. We are far from thinking that they themselves could come to the idea of world arrangement "by means of Hexogen or expansion of liberators from the enclaves of Middle Asia and Hinducush**." We believe that the majority of people will remain kind and merciful even at the threat of death, but we are sure that there will be always such scoundrels who, having armed with the destructive idea of "utmost justice" that has "true and peaceful face," will declare "the holy jihad" to the whole "unilateral" world and will wage war until "disintegration of territories and catastrophe for all that is alive, including dogs, cats and even butterflies that live here" will happen.

Now let us remember that any religious, revolutionary or fascist-national ideology was born in the condition of war or for war. Jews, having left Egypt, began to wage war against Canaan, that is why they needed the God of battle, God-butcher-filicide Jehovah. Having lost their motherland and their temple, Jews declared war to the whole Gentile world, putting off on it the cruel and bloodthirsty matrix, which Christians began to use to exterminate heretics and "God's enemies." Lenin, Stalin and Hitler used "great" ideas of Jewish rabbis for the building of their "brilliant future," and Arabs adjusted it to wage war at first in the name of the unification of Islam world, and then in the name of the triumph of the "utmost justice." Does such a religion have "true and peaceful face?" Let us look.

The fact that Islam was created under the influence of Christianity and Judaism shows that the new religion which was destined first of all for war, had to adopt all the cruel and man-hating commandments of

God-butcher-filicide Jehovah. There were all the conditions for it in Medina. Among Arabs-ansars, who lived in this town, there were many Christians and Jews including Jewish scholars who argued with Arabs about the question of faith.

In Medina, as we can judge from few sources, separate sides of dogmas, as well as customs and rituals of later Islam, began to assume more or less clear form. From Christianity Arabs borrowed the ideas of the last days of the world, of the Last Judgment, of punishment for sins and reward for good deeds, which facilitated the development of beliefs in fate and the teaching about predestination of all existed things. Its significance in Islam is so great that K. Marx once said: "The core of Islam is fatalism."

Is Islam, as well as in Christianity, the idea of "God choosiness," which is to ensure the "salvation" to each Moslem, became clear very sharply, for the Koran says: "Our Lord, you are He that will gather mankind together against a Day about which there is no doubt; for Allah never fails in his promise. **Those who reject faith,—neither their possessions nor their (numerous) progeny will avail them anything against Allah: they a themselves but fuel for the fire.**"[257]

Why then did such a terrible fate await for the people who did not wish to adopt Islam? You see, our Christian priests and their Moslem imams teach that everybody is equal before God and he loves everybody. It turns out that only those who have adopted Islam are worthy of God's love. But as for unbelievers, "**Allah dos not love those who reject faith.**"[258] It means that those who for one or another reason did not want to adopt Islam will be "gathered together to Hell,—and evil bed indeed (to lie on)!"[259]

What has "kind and merciful" Allah who has "true and peaceful face" prepared for unbelievers in this Hell? The Koran says: "Verily the day of Sorting Out is the time appointed for all of them,—the day when no protector can avail his client in anything, and no help can they receive, except such as receive Allah's mercy: for **He is Exalted in Might, Most Merciful. Verily the tree of Zaqqum will be the food of the sinful,—like molten brass it will boil in their insides, like the boiling of scolding water. (A voice will cry:) "You seize him and drag him into the midst of the blazing Fire! Then pour over his head the penalty of boiling water**"[260]

In another surah "all merciful" Allah orders: "You seize him, and you bind him, and you burn him in a Blazing Fire. Further let him march in a chain, whereof the length is seventy cubits. This was he who that would not believe in Allah Most High, and would not encourage the feeding of the indigent! So no friend he has here this Day. Nor has he any food except the corruption from the washing of wounds, which none do eat but those in sin."[261]

Thus, reading of "good" deeds of "kind and merciful" Allah, we begin to understand that his face is not so "true and peaceful." Rather, it is "true and peaceful" only towards Moslems. But as for all the rest of the representatives of the human race who are infidels, Allah, as it turns out, does not love, and the only thing they can hope for in the last days is an evil bed in Hell, which is very hard to lie on. At first, infidel will be burned in "the Blazing Fire," then he will "march in a chain, whereof the length is seventy cubits," then he will be fed with "the tree of Zaqqum" that will boil like molten brass in his insides," and at last he will be "poured over his head the penalty of boiling water."

As we see, the Moslem Hell is almost identical to that of Christian Hell with the only difference: in the Moslem Hell Allah uses an "evil bed," invented most likely by Allah himself, which is no less a monstrous tool of torture and murder as the Christian "vineyard of God's fierce anger."

Thus, the American president, who regards Islamic teaching as "good and peaceful," as well as the connoisseur of Islam Karen Armstrong who are sure that "Islam has true and peaceful face" could hardly hope for Allah's leniency, for "**the Religion before Allah is Islam (submission to his Will): nor did the prophet of the Book dissent therefrom except through envy of each other, after knowledge had come to them. But if any deny the Signs of Allah, Allah is swift in calling to account.**"[262]

And, as president Bush and most Americans do not believe in the "Signs of Allah" and most likely are not going to do that, they must be conquered and gathered to Hell together with all the rest of "unbelievers" even in spite of the fact that we have the same God—the God of Abraham, Isaac and Jacob.

But Allah doesn't care a damn about anything, for he says: "**But when the sacred months are passed away, kill the idolaters wherever ye may find them; and take them, and besiege them, and lie in wait for them in every place of observation... Fight those who believe not in God and in the last day, and who forbid not what God and His Apostle have forbidden, and who do not practice the religion of truth from amongst those to whom the Book has been brought, until they pay the tribute by their hands and be as little ones.**

The Jews is the son of God; and the Christians say that the Messiah is the son of God; that is what they say with their mouths, imitating the sayings of those who misbelieved before.—**God fight them! how they lie!**.

They take their doctors and their monks for lords rather than God, and the Messiah the son of Mary; but they are bidden to worship but one God, there is no god but He; celebrated be His praise, from what they join with Him!

They desire to put out the light of God with their mouths, but God will not have it but that we should perfect His light, averse although the misbelievers be! He it is who sent His Apostle with guidance and the religion of truth, **to make it prevail over every other religion**, averse although idolaters may be!

O ye who believe! Verily, many of the doctors and the monks devour the wealth of men openly, and turn folk from God's way; but those who store up gold and silver and expend it not in God's way,—give them glad tidings of grievous woe! On the day when it shall be heated in the fire of hell, and their brows shall be branded therewith, and their sides and their backs!—'This is what ye stored up for yourselves, taste then what ye stored up!'

Verily, the number of months with God is twelve months in God's Book, on the day when He created the heavens and the earth; of these are four that are sacred; that is the subsisting religion. **Then do not wrong yourselves therein, but fight the idolaters one and all, as they fight you one and all, and know that God is with those who fear**."[263]

The Koran clearly states what Allah will do with "the people of the Book," i. e. with those whose religion is based on the Bible: " He it was who drove those of the people of the Book who misbelieved forth from their houses, at the first emigration; ye did not think that they would go forth, and they thought that their fortresses would defend them against God; but God came upon them from whence they did not reckon, and cast dread into their hearts! **They ruined their houses with their own hands and the hands of the believers**; wherefore take example, O ye who are endowed with sight!

Had it not been that God had prescribed for them banishment, He would have tormented them in this world; but for them in the next shall be the torment of the Fire! That is because they opposed God and His Apostle: and whoso opposes God, verily, God is keen to punish!"[264]

O, ye who are endowed with sight! Verily I tell you, please pay attention to the words above, for they are prophetic. When you read the chapter "Who killed the Twins?" please recall the words of Koran: **"They ruined their houses with their own hands and the hands of**

the believers" in order to see the terrible truth, in order to understand that we "ruin our houses with our own hands," thus realizing the destructive program of the matrix, which the Mighty of this world use to destroy our world.

And finally, in order that we do not have any doubts of our infidelity towards Allah, who has "true and peaceful face," the Koran says: "In the name of the merciful and compassionate God. Say, "O ye misbelievers! I do not serve what ye serve; nor will ye serve what I serve; nor will I serve what ye serve; nor will ye serve what I serve;—**ye have your religion, and I have my religion!**."

Such God can hardly have "true and peaceful face," and in the image of Allah we recognize so familiar to us, so beloved by us, our own, but, nevertheless, Jewish God-butcher-filicide Jehovah, the God of the Book who had been put stealthily by omnipresent Jewish rabbis to Arabs in order to destroy the Roman empire with their own hands and to subordinate the whole Arab world to the power of the destructive matrix.

4. 4. Victorious Procession of Religion Which Has "True and Peaceful Face"

Of course, with the exception of Christianity and Judaism, a certain influence on Islam exerted other religions prevalent in Arabia including Zoroastrism. "Although none of these sources did not determine the things that appeared in Islam, especially those that was related to its propagandistic character. In this sense, the religion closely related to Islam was Christianity, the followers of which, as we know, lived in Arabia long before the origin of Moslem ideology."[265]

F. Engels determined this new and the most essential side of Islam very clearly, having underlined the direct Islam origin dependence (as well as of other world religions) from those changes that took place in the history of people among those they were originated and developed. He wrote: "Great historical changes were accompanied by the changing of religion since we are speaking about three world religions: Buddhism, Christianity and Islam. Old, naturally originated tribal and national religions did not have propagandistic character and lost any power of resistance as soon as the independence of these tribes and nations had been broken... Only in relation to these, more or less artificially created world religions (especially in relation to Christianity and Islam) we can say that the similar historical movements assume religious coloration."[266]

Islam, as well as Christianity, represents by itself a strictly monotheistic religion based on the faith in almighty Godfather, but, in contrast to Christianity, free of difficult theological constructions. Another distinguishing feature of Islam is its keeping aloof from sacrifices and a temple. This is entirely prophetic religion, which makes impossible the relapse to the rituals of bloody sacrifices. The only ritual ceremony of Islam is a pilgrimage to Mecca.

The cult of Mohammed was impossible, for he himself banished any attempts of idolization of his personality. The third and the most attractive feature of Islam is his teaching about inviolable brotherhood and equality of all the Moslems before Allah regardless of their skin color, originality and social position: "The conditions of adopting Islam were rather easy in Mohammed's times. One had to acknowledge and utter in the presence of witnesses the main formula of faith confession [shahad]: "There is no God but Allah, and Mohammed is his messenger." This act was considered as the act of conclusion of agreement with Allah, on account of which any apostasy was impossible. If it, nevertheless, was happened, it was punished with a death penalty in tmost of the cases,"[267] which is quite characteristic for the religion which has "true and peaceful face."

Besides, Moslems are obliged to pray five times a day, turning their faces to Mecca, to attend Friday worships, to give alms, to fast in the month of Ramadan, and if one has such a possibility, to make a pilgrimage [hadzh] to Mecca. These simple rules and obligations are the "five pillars" of Islam. In addition to these prescriptions, the Koran anticipates certain moral and legal duties. It prohibits eating pork, gambling and usury. Although the Koran does not say anything about circumcision, this all-Semitic habit is practiced by Moslems. The Koran, as well as the Old Testament, prohibits of making of any images of both Allah and his prophet Mohammed.

The most Moslems resemble Protestants because they do not need a mediator between a believer and God, though Shiite minority (10%) almost deifies their imams. Moslems, as well as Christians, carry on an active messianic activity hoping to convert all the humankind in their faith. And they are quite successful in this business. In the USA seven millions people are Moslems and their number increases. In Russia, the number of people converted into Islam also increases, and, according to Niyazow whom we cited above, "every third Russian will be a Moslem in ten years."[268]

As the result of Islamic expansion, the huge empire, the real founder of which was not Mohammed himself but his friend and companion-in-arms Abu Bekr, has been established. If Mohammed with his unsteady character was the mind and inspirer of primitive Islam, Abu Bekr was its consciousness and will. Every time Mohammed was hesitating in the questions of faith, his true friend always supported him. After Mohammed's death, Abu Bekr became caliph, and, having armed himself with the faith that could move mountains, began to subjugate the world to Allah, for the Koran says: **"And fight them on until there is no more tumult or oppression, and there prevail justice and faith in Allah altogether and everywhere.**"[269] Isn't is the same that God-butcher-filicide Jehovah said while instructing king Saul? **"Go and utterly destroy the sinners the Amalekites, and fight against them until they be consumed.**"[270]

In such a way, having the firm belief in Allah and in Islam which has "true and peaceful face," the Arab world began to subjugate other people and nations. That expansion was so impetuous that one could hardly find similar examples of such a fast and victorious procession of Allah's people.

The population of Byzantine and Iran, especially in adjacent to Arabia places, did not resist to Arabs, for, suffering from ever-increasing taxes and the tyranny of their rulers, they did not want to defend them. The army which consisted of hirelings was also unreliable. During battles many of them were chained together "in order to suppress any attempts of retreat." In Iranian infantry, soldiers were also chained together in groups of five or six for the same purpose.

Religious intolerance of Byzantine emperors towards infidels set subjugated populations against them. Emperor Irakly aggravated this situation when in the 30th of the VII century, he issued a decree that forced Jews who lived on the territory of empire to baptize. In the result, as Syrian historiographer Michael Syrian (1126—1199) wrote: "The part of Jews who denied to adopt Christianity run away from Rome empire; they came to Edessa at first, but, having endured new hardships there, they escaped to Persia."[271] This persecuted people, as Armenian writer Gevond noticed in the VIII century, and could incite Arabs to the further actions against Byzantine. "'Rebel with us,' they said, having arrived to the Arab camp, 'and free us from the power of Greek king, and we shall reign together.'"[272]

Thus, persecuted Jews, as well as Arabs from the former tribe unions of Gassanids and Lachmids which suffered a lot from the cruelty of Byzantine and Iranian rulers, began to serve to Caliphate. In his *Book of Conquering*, Arabian historian al-Balazury (820—892) says that one of Caliphate commanders Abu Ubeida ibn al-Jarrach made peace with Palestine and Urdu Samaritans who served for Moslems as spies and guides. Sebeos, describing the battle at Jabiya asserts that "there gathered and joined them [Arabs] all the rest of sons of Israel; together with them they made a great army"[273]

The same situation was also in Egypt that was under the authority of Byzantine. When caliphate army invaded Egypt (639—641), Christians-Copts "met Arabs as their liberators from religious, economical and political yoke of Byzantine."[274]

All these events resulted in the defeat of the Byzantine army at Jarmuk in 1634. Syria, Damascus, Palmira, Antioch and Jerusalem surrendered to Moslems almost without any resistance and adopted the religion with "true and peaceful face." Then the warriors of Islam went through West Turkestan, turned to the East and reached China.

Egypt fell also without any significant resistance, and conquerors, fanatically believing that Koran is the only "Holy Book," destroyed everything that had been left from the Alexandria library. The wave of Moslem conquest swept across the North African coast, reached Gibraltar and Spain, which was occupied in 710. In 732, Arabs reached the center of France, but, having been faced with bitter resistance, had to retreat back to the Pyrenees. Having conquered Egypt, Moslems captured its fleet, by means of which they tried to besiege Constantinople, but the great city repulsed all the attacks, remaining the citadel of Christianity on the Mediterranean sea up to 1154, when it surrendered to Seljuk Turks.

In the religious politic during the first period of conquest, caliphate rulers used most of all the commandments, which were proclaimed as Allah's "revelations" received by him in Medina. Their essence was: "There is no compulsion in religion." They were reflected in some Koran verses, which some researchers attribute to those written in Mecca, but then received new understanding. Here are two such verses: "Call unto the way of thy Lord with wisdom and goodly warning; and wrangle with them in the kindest way; verily, thy Lord He knows best who has erred from His way, for He knows best the guided ones.

But if ye punish, punish (only) as ye were punished; but if ye are patient, it is best for those who are patient.

Be thou patient with then; but thy patience is only in God's hands. Do not grieve about them; and be not in a strait at their craftiness;—verily, God is with those who fear Him, and with those who do well."[275] It was even allowed by Koran to spend some part of alms for the needs of those who joined Islam and surrendered to the will of Allah.

Here we see a very peculiar feature which is characteristic both for individuals and for large groups of people who press towards expansion. In the initial period of development of their teaching, as long as a man or a group of people do not have enough power and authority, expansion is carried out in an exceptionally peaceful way by means of "wisdom and goodly warning." But, together with the system growth and development when it unites many people under the banners of "fiery Islam," the system decides that it is the right time to throw out all the "wisdom and goodly warnings" and begin to use the methods of "mighty onslaught" and "exacting of Retribution."[276]

Keeping to such a moderate politic, "indulgent" rulers, even without creating the State machinery for regular tax collecting, got an excellent possibility to keep comparatively small detachments in their rear, throwing the main troops to conquer more and more countries. Great means that were needed for new campaigns they received mainly as the spoils of war. The latter seems to determine the name of the eighth surah of Koran "The spoils of War." "Eagerness and diligence in struggle with infidels—"jihad"—was understood as "the way of Allah," and loot was considered to be good."[277]

The war against infidels, if it was ended with the victory of Moslems, envisaged burdensome taxes that were imposed upon people in new caliphate lands, for the Koran orders: "**Fight those who believe not in God** and in the last day, and who forbid not what God and His Apostle have forbidden, and who do not practice the religion of truth from amongst those to whom the Book has been brought, **until they pay the tribute by their hands and be as little ones**."[278]

Moslems considered Jews and Christians to be "people of the Book." "There were other commandments which demanded to adopt Islam under the threat of death, and they were used towards the people of other religions."[279]

The conquerors' slogan was the following statement, attributed to "saint" caliph Omar I: "Verily, **Moslems will be fed at the expense of unbelievers who will pay tribute** until we [Moslems] are alive; and when we die and they die, **our sons will be fed at the expense of their sons eternally, and they will be the slaves of Islam followers as long as Islam remains prevalent**."[280]

Thus, the hopes of the population of suburban regions of Byzantine and Iran to be liberated from oppression and devastation by Arabs failed very soon. Arab rulers suppressed peasants and craftspeople with heavy taxes, enslaved and mocked them, recruited to the Arab army, and sometimes were made to wage war against their own brothers. The Jews in Syria and Palestine understood very quickly that with Arab conquest the end came to their messianic expectations. "If the incipient star of Islam gave hope to Jews, they had to be bitterly disappointed in it very soon."[281]

After having read what had been said above, one will hardly dare to call Islam the religion with "true and peaceful face." It is unlikely that religion (the main goal of which is the enslaving of "unbelievers" who have to be slaves "as long as Islam remains prevalent") can be true and peaceful.

Nevertheless, in spite of fanaticism and cruelty of the new religion, Arab influence upon the cultural development of mankind was impressive. Curiosity and thirst for knowledge that were inherent in Arabs became the power which could resist to Christianity with its fierce attempts to exterminate any rays of knowledge if it contradicted to stark principles of Christian dogmatic.

The fact is that wherever Arabs go they came into contact with the cultural heritage of conquered peoples. In Persia Arabs encountered not only with Manichean, Zoroastrian and Christian teaching, but also with works of Greek philosophers, many of which had already been translated into Syrian language. In Egypt Arabs also met with Greek learning. In Central Asia they got acquainted with Buddhism and material achievements of China's civilization, from which Arabs learned how to make paper, and in India they discovered mathematics and philosophy.

Wells, H. G. says: "Uncompromising self-sufficiency of early Islam that considered the Koran as the one possible book went into the past very quickly. Thirst for knowledge and sciences development came to the conquered countries together with Arab conquerors. By the eighth century, educational institutions have appeared on all the territories of huge Moslem empire. In ninth century, educated people of Cordova (Spain) corresponded with scientists of Cairo, Baghdad, Buchara and Samarcand. Jewish scholarship were willingly assimilated by Moslems, and during a certain period of time two Semitic people cooperated one with another, communicating one with another in Arabic language. And this intellectual company of Arab-speaking world remained even after political disintegration of Arab world and continued to give considerable results up to the XIII century."[282]

This unprecedented revival of the Semitic world made possible the systematic knowledge accumulation renewal, which was began by Greeks as far back as in the ancient world. The works of Aristotle and the contents of Alexandria's museum which remained intact and ignored till that time were revived and brought good fruits. Great achievements were made by Arabs in mathematics, medicine and physics. Inconvenient systems of Rome digitals have been changed with that of Arabic, which we use nowadays.

Moreover, Arabs introduced "zero" in mathematical accounts, which considerably facilitated mathematic development. Astronomy and chemistry began to develop rapidly, and Arab philosophical science gave a new life to both ancient and the Middle Age philosophies of French, Italy and the entire Christian world. But, unfortunately, the laws of matrix functioning are implacable.

And, since the Koran is also a matrix derivative from that of Jewish, its destructive influence would inevitably be displayed in the consciousness of people who use this matrix as the base of their life. Of course, **we are far from the thought that the entire Moslem world is guilty in terrorism and religious extremism. Among Moslems, as well as among the representatives of other religions, there are enough clever and honest people who will never lower themselves to such a meanness as a murder of "unbelievers"** "by night or while they sleep for their afternoon rest" or "striking off their necks, and striking off from them every finger-tip." Such actions are handworks of those who organize terrorist acts, in which not the "globalization politic" initiators (against whom Moslem terrorists struggle) are killed, but innocent people who, most likely, even do not know what "globalization" is.

Nevertheless, there will always be those who will use cruel and man- hating commandments of the matrix to justify their criminal goals, which are very far from a true religion. We ourselves, justifying cruel commandments of our gods and regarding the religions based on the matrix, the name of which is the Bible, as the religions with "true and peaceful face," facilitate the origin and development of religious extremism, which is rapidly activated with the course of time, taking away lives of thousands of human sons and daughters.

4. 5. Islamic Extremism: Myth or Reality?

Allah who has "true and peaceful face" gives Mohammed the following instructions: "**O, Messenger, rouse the Believers to the fight**. If there are twenty amongst you, patient and persevering, they will vanquish two hundred: if a hundred they will vanquish a thousand of Unbelievers: for those are a people without understanding."[283]

Thus, the murder of "Unbelievers" was considered as an extremely

God-pleasing deed, and it was always encouraged both by Allah and his messenger Mohammed. "Merciful" and "attentive" Allah provided everything in advance for a warrier who would fall dead on a battlefield. According to the Koran, the one who is killed will not have to wait either for the resurrection of the dead or the Last Judgment: one will go to the paradise immediately. This imagination was used very often; it appears not only in the Koran but also in subsequent Moslem literature.

The Koran says: "**Do not think of those who are slain in Allah's way as dead. Nay, they live, finding their sustenance in the Presence of their Lord; They rejoice in the Bounty provided by Allah**: and with regard to those left behind, who have not yet joined them (in their bliss), the (Martyrs) glory in the fact that on them is no fear, nor have they (cause to) grieve. They glory in the grace and the Bounty from Allah, and in the fact that Allah does not suffer the reward of the Faithful to be lost."[284]

Ibn Itshack-Ibn Hisham, the author of *The Book About Life of Allah's Messenge*r, tells how such an instruction was used by Moslem leaders. From this book, we learn that during the battle at Bedra, after inspirational Messenger's words: "I swear that **today everyone who will fight against the enemy and, out of love for Allah, will be killed in the battle, will get straight to the Paradise**," Omeir ibn Alhuman, one of the warriors who ate dates at that time, exclaimed, "That's the way! So, is it the only death from the hand of these people, that stands between the Paradise and me?" He finished eating dates, grasped his sward and fought until he was killed."[285]

Thus, the institute of terrorist-kamikazes, as you see, appeared long time ago when Islam was just arising. We see that the Koran itself is the source and inspirer of such an ideology. Subsequent generations have just developed and improved the method of war against "unbelievers." It was in the Moslem east that physical elimination of disagreeable statesmen were placed on the "industrial base" for the first time.

It happened in Iran in the XII century, when a certain Hasan ibn Sabbach became the leader of local Islamiilits (Shiite sect). For the first time, he was spoken about when eight high ranked officials including three Baghdad caliphs were killed by his "spiritual children." Due to the fact that an executor of a terrorist act was kamikaze, the effectiveness of "assassins," as these killers were called later, was almost total-lot. But what has to be done in order a killer to accept his own death as his own wedding party? Hasan ibn Sabbach found a genially simple decision: instead of telling stories about delights of the Moslem Paradise which he would inevitably get to after a successful terrorist act, they organized "one day trip to the Paradise."

Earthly affiliate of the Paradise was situated in the fortress of Alamut on the south coast of the Caspian Sea. After a future terrorist, preliminarily intoxicated with hashish, fell asleep, he was brought into the inner yard. He woke up in "the Paradise,"—a nicely cultivated garden with fountains. Angel-like "guries" [beautiful girls specially selected among local prostitutes] surrounded him at once he opened his eyes. After their "explanations" the assassin boldly went to his death: there was nothing to fear any more, for "a ticket to the Paradise" was already in his pocket.

Hasan ibn Sabbach's monkey business would have remained a historical joke if the world would not know recently about "a summer school" organized by the terrorist organization "Islamic Jihad." At this school, boys of 12—15 years old are taught to blow up themselves in the streets and squares of Jerusalem.

The newspaper *In the New World* tells about this school the following: "The group "Islamic Jihad" has organized a summer school for boys. The boys are taught there that they will bring a great public benefit for their country, if they become terrorists-kamikaze. The pupils of the school are Palestine boys of 12—15 years old. In the school, they are taught that murder is a good deed, but it is better to sacrifice themselves in the name of Allah. Experienced instructors tell the boys that terrorist acts in which terrorists blow up themselves in crowded places, are the most effective means to fight against Israel....

14 years old Mohammed is drawing intently. In the picture, he depicted himself with explosive hanging around his body. He is ready to give up his life if he is able to kill as many Jews as possible at that. "'I want to liberate Palestine,' the boy says, 'I want to take part in the revolution.'"

Boys are shown the photos of those who have already realized the same dream. **All of them, as the instructor assures, will go to the Paradise at the gate of which they will be met by seventy girls-guries. Venomous words poison the consciousness, and poisoned consciousness gives rise to violence, terror and murder**. But "Islamic Jihad" is not going to close its school."[286]

Similar ideas were used, for example, in Iran by Shiite imams for encouraging soldiers mobilized in the devastating Iraq-Iran war. The same images are used by modern Moslem extremists to substantiate their "liberating struggle" by means of "hexogen or expansion of liberators from enclaves of the Middle Asia and Hinducush," and, of course, this destructive ideology was used during the preparation of an organized group of Arab terrorist-kamikazes, at the active participation of which, the murder of the Twins of the World Trade Center in New-York became possible.

Looking at all these crimes, we recognize the same "handwriting," the same cruel and man-hating imperatives of the matrix, which, having penetrated into the Arab world, subjugated it to its destructive influence and continues to induce people to hate and to kill each other. If we have a look at the Moslem methods of waging war against "unbelievers," we shall see their full likeness to those of the Bible.

Thus, in 712 in Debal and in Sind, Arabs, having grasped enormous riches, killed all the men older then 17, just because they refused to adopt Islam. But even spreading their faith, the Arab conquerors carried about their enrichment. Indian historians write that "in India Arabs were attracted by fantastic reaches rather than by their desire to propagate Islam."[287] The same testimonies give the most objective middle age Arab historians such as Ibn Haldun (1332—1406), for example, who compared the second wave of Arabs which poured to the North Africa in the IX century with a "cloud of locusts."

In Russia, some Moslem authors also expressed their thoughts on the question that differed from official opinions of Islamic theologians. Thus, Ismail Gasprinsky (1851—1914), publicist and pedagogue, editor-in-chief of the first Turkic language newspaper *Terjiman* (*Translator*), wrote: "Everyone says and writes that Arabs began conquering war to propagate Islam and the Koran. I cannot think like that, for I see very well that Arabs... rushed to gain reach and profitable lands of Syria, Iraq and Egypt..."[288]

Arab commanders acting in the Transcaucasia resorted to the proclaiming of takbir "Allah akbar!" or the other formulas like, "The victory, oh, the Lord of Caaba! Oh, people! **Go up for the holy war and for the spoil! Allah blesses you! And do not hope that I will give somebody or something except for a hard helmet, intact chain armor and smashing sward to help you!**."[289]

Or such proclaiming as: "Go forward, oh, people of Allah! Go forward to the eternal life!" The last motive is close to those that were used by muchadjirs of Medina in the war with kureishits of Mecca. Before the battle, al'- Djarrach ibn Abdalach, the Arab commander, exclaimed: "Oh, people! **There is no shelter where you can hide yourselves, but Allah! I must inform you that those who will be killed in a battle will go immediately to the Paradise, and those who win will attain the spoil and glory!**"[290]

While reading the book of Ibn A'sam al'-Cufi, one automatically recalls an old Azerbaijan saying "Biz gilindzh musul'manlariyik" which means "We, Moslems are from a sward." The same picture is characteristic also for the times of aggressive wars that waged caliphate against Armenia. Here one could hardly find any signs of religious tolerance, about which modern ideologists of Islam like to speak so much. On the contrary, if religious beliefs of conquered nations were used; they were used only to ruin the conquered.

Here is the fact that related to the actions of Arab commander Mohammed ibn-Marvana, who was appointed to be the ruler of al' Jazira, Azerbaijan and Armenia. When this commander and ruler "came with his army to the middle of the Armenia, the great multitude of Byzantine and Armenian troops were set out against him... But Allah made the pagans (al' mushrikin) to run away and strengthened Moslems with his concern. Moslems killed many of them, took many captives, looted their country and all their belongings..."

After that Mohammed ibn Marvan sent for their noble people, promising them his kindness and democratic elections. He admonished them in such a way until they began to trust him and relied on his guarantees. Then they got together at the commander's place and he made a peace agreement with them.

After that he said: "I can not be fully confident in you, that is why you must go into your churches and to swear that you will not break your obligations. Then you will give me hostages and go to your homes!"

Further, he says: "... They agreed and came into their churches in order to swear. And when he [Mohammed ibn Marvan] knew that all of them were gathered in churches, he ordered to close the doors of the churches. They were closed, hammered in, poured over with petroleum and set on the fire. These churches still are called "parched" (al'-muchtarika)."[291]

This terrible, inhuman act of perjury and of burning live people is proven to be true by other historians, both Arab and Armenian. But the most dreadful thing here is that such atrocities are justified by the "holy book." The Koran contains such an appeal to those who believe in Allah: "**And when ye meet those who misbelieve-then striking off heads until ye have massacred them, and bind fast the bonds!** Then either a free grant (of liberty) or a ransom until the war shall have laid down its burdens. That!-but if God please He would conquer them-but (it is) that He may try some of you by the others. **And those who are slain in God's cause, their works shall not go wrong; He will guide them and set right their mind; and will make them enter into Paradise which He has told them of.**

O ye who believe! If ye help God, He will help you, and will make firm your footsteps. But as for those who misbelieve-confound them! And He will make their works go wrong. That is because they were averse from what God has revealed; but their works shall be void!"[292]

And, if such the actions are justified by "the holy book," there will always be those who, after reading this book and perceiving "kind and merciful" Allah's orders literally, will begin to "strike off unbelievers' heads" and "massacre" all those "who misbelieve" without worrying about their [Moslems'] life, for, according to the Koran, Allah "will make them enter into Paradise which He has told them of."

Is it possible that such a cruel and man-hating religion has "the true and peaceful face?" Can the book which orders such cruel and bloody deeds be the book of "love and peace directed against all the forms of violence?" Our humanistic analysis categorically asserts that it cannot be.

And, if one thinks that there will be not many of such fanatics who will, without any reasoning, give up their lives in the name of the triumph of Islamic "utmost justice," then let us have a look at the list of organizations which use "the book of love and peace" in their struggle of the triumph of the Moslem "God's Kingdom."

According to the State Department of the USA the following Islamic terrorist-extremist organizations existed in the year 2001.

1. Al'-Gama'a Al'-Islamia

The number of participants: Unknown; in the past there were several thousands people in the main body of the organization.

Location: Cairo, Sudan, Yemen, Afghanistan, Austria, Great Britain.

The description of organization: The biggest Egyptian terrorist group, organized in the 1970th . The main task was overthrowing of Egypt government. In the past, the group had connections with Osama-ben-Laden. In 1988, the mutual agreement which called for terrorist acts against American civilians was signed.

Goals: Egyptian authorities and Christian-Copts.

Terrorist acts: June of 1955. Assassination attempt at the president Hosni Mubarak in Addis Abeba.

November of 1997. Luxor, Egypt. Terrorist act resulted in killing of 58 foreign tourists.

Organizations-satellites: Abu Nidal, Abu Sajaf Group, Armed Islamists Group, Supreme Truth Aum, Basque Organization Fatherland and Freedom.

2. Al Queda

The number of participants: Several thousands.

Location: The main training camps are situated in Afghanistan. The affiliates can be found in many countries of the world.

The description of organization: The head of the organization is Osama-ben-Laden. The activity of the organization consisted in preparing and coordination of the actions of Islamic extremists, directed to overthrowing of all the non-Moslem governments and expulsion of all "unbelievers" from all the Moslem countries. In 1988, the group of ideologists announced that the duty of each Moslem is to kill Americans and their allies wherever they find them.

Goals: Civilians and military men in Israel and the USA.

Terrorist acts: American government blames the organization in organization and performing of the terrorist acts of September 11, 2001; in the explosion of the building of American embassy in Africa in 1988; in shooting down the American helicopter in Somali in 1993; in attack on American troops in Yemen in 1992.

Organizations-satellites: Revolutionary Armed Forces of Columbia, Revolutionary Organization of the 17th of November, Revolutionary Proletariat Liberation Front, Revolutionary Movement of Tupak Amaru.

3. Hamas

The number of participants: The number of participants of the organization main body is unknown. There are tens of thousands of sympathizing organizations.

Location: The Gaza Strip and the West Bank of Jordan.

The description of organization: The organization is the Palestine affiliate of the Moslem Brotherhood. Established in 1987. The organization activity includes both political and terrorist means directed to overthrowing of Israel and building Palestine state on its territory. The organization has close and friendly relations with Iran.

Goals: Israeli civilians and military troops.

Terrorist acts: The organization has announced its connection to explosion of Discotheque in Tel-Aviv on the 1st of June, 2001. The explosion resulted in the death of 21 people. Another explosion in Jerusalem restaurant on the 9th of August, 2001, resulted in the death of 18 people.

Organizations-satellites: Haracat-ul'-Mudjacheddin, Hesbollah.

4. Hesbollah

The number of participants: The main body of the group consists of several hundreds of terrorists, and there can be several thousands of sympathizers.

Location: Beirut, South Libya. Cells can be found in Africa, Asia, Europe and the USA.

The description of organization: The radical group that strives for political influence in Libya and peace talks on the Middle East problems breakdown. The organization activity is also directed against Israel and western countries. The organization has connections with Iraq and Syria, from which it receives both financial and military support.

Goals: Israeli and American interests.

Terrorist acts: Car explosion at the buildings of American embassy and US navy quarters in Beirut in 1983. Bomb explosion in the building of the Argentine embassy in Israel in 1992.

Organizations-satellites: Islamic Movement of Uzbekistan. Japanese Red Army.

5. Al'-Jihad

The number of participants: The main body of the organization is several thousands of terrorists.

Location: Cairo. The criminal network of the organization embraces Yemen, Afghanistan, Pakistan, Sudan and Libya.

The description of organization: The group began its activity in 1970th . The organization has close ties with Usama ben Laden.

Goals: Official establishment of Egypt and the objects situated in Egypt and the USA.

Terrorist acts: Assassination of Anvar Sadat in 1981. Bomb explosion in the building of Egypt embassy in Islamabad in 1995. Abortive attempt of bomb explosion in the building of American embassy in Albania in 1998.

Organizations-satellites: Cach and Cachane Chai. Kurdistan Working Party. The Tiger of Liberation Tamil Ilama. Palestine Islamic Jihad. Palestine Liberation Front.

The last decade of the XX century can be called "the decade of terrorism," and the first years of the new millennium are characterized by even more significant outbursts of terrorist activity. The history on mankind did not know before such an escalation of terror and violence directed on mass destruction of civilians. If we take into account that all those atrocities were performed mainly by religious fanatics, we will have to confess that this escalation of terrorism means nothing else as the final stage of matrix program realization called "the Last Judgment." Let us have a look at the results of this destructive program realization. Here is an incomplete list of the latest terrorist acts, performed by terrorist-kamikazes.

1. **Buenos-Aires (Argentine). March 17, 1992.**
   The building of Israeli embassy destroyed with a car bomb explosion. Twenty people killed, two hundred and forty two injured.
2. **Algeria. August 26, 1992.**
   Bomb explosion in the International Airport. Twelve killed, at least one hundred twenty eight injured.
3. **New-York (USA). February 26, 1992.**
   Religious fanatics put a bomb under the World Trade Center. Six killed, about one thousand injured.
4. **Matsumoto (Japan). June 27, 1994.**
   Sect members of "Aum Senrique" organization organized "sarin attack" in a residential area. Seven killed, two hundred and seventy injured.
5. **Tokyo (Japan). March 20, 1995.**
   Another "sarin attack" of "Aum Senrique" members in a train of the Tokyo subway. Twelve killed, over five thousand injured.
6. **Oklahoma City (USA). May 19, 1995.**
   In the result of explosion, an administrative building was destroyed. One hundred and sixty eight killed, more than five hundred injured.
7. **Colombo (Sri Lanka). January 31, 1996.**
   Car explosion in the bank building. Ninety killed, more than one thousand injured.
8. **London (Great Britain). February 9, 1996.**
   Ireland terrorists blew up a bomb at a car parking. Two killed, more than one hundred injured.
9. **Jerusalem (Israel). February 25, 1996.**
   Bus explosion. Twenty six killed, eighty injured.
10. **Dhahran (Saudi Arabia). June 25, 1996.**
    Car explosion at the US navy quarters. Nineteen killed, five hundred and fifteen injured.

11. **Pnompenh (Cambodia). March 30, 1997.**
Four grenades were thrown at a demonstration procession. Sixteen killed, more than one hundred injured.
12. **Coimbatur (India). February 14, 1997.**
Religious extremists performed several terrorist acts that resulted in the death of forty three people and more than two hundred injured.
13. **Nairobi (Kenya) and Dar-es-Salaam (Tanzania). August 7, 1998.**
Bomb explosions in the US embassies. Two hundred and fifty killed, more than five thousand and five hundred injured.
14. **Colombia. October 18 and November 3, 1998.**
Two terrorists acts resulted in the death of two hundred and nine people and more than one hundred and thirty injured.
15. **Moscow (Russia). September 3 and 13, 1999.**
Bomb explosion inside two blocks of flats. Two hundred and twelve killed, more than three hundred injured.
16. **New-York and Washington (USA). September 11, 2001.**
The destruction of Twins of the World Trade Center in the result of an air attack and controlled demolition. Bomb explosion in the building of the Pentagon. About four thousand killed and many of injured. The terrorist acts were performed with the active participation of Arab terrorist-kamikazes.
17. **Russia. August—September, 2004.** The terrorist war against Russia. Airplains explosion resulted in the death of eighty nine people. Terrorist act at the Moscow metro station: ten people were kileed. Hostage taking (Beslan. North Ossetia): three hundred and thirty are dead and two hundred and sixty are missed.

The majority of these terrible atrocities were performed by Islamic terrorist-kamikazes. Unprecedented by its boldness and cruelty, the terrorist acts of September 11, 2001, were also performed with the active participation of Moslem terrorists. What does it mean? It means that cruel and man-hating matrix imperatives are successfully realized by us, but we do not want to notice it and consider religious extremism as "the myth which is inflamed by those who want to have profit from it."

Being the witnesses of atrocities performed by religious fanatics at direct orders of their "Holy Scriptures," we, nevertheless, assert that "the core of Islam, as well as of Christianity and Judaism consists in the observance of the moral law, love for neighbors, justice and compassion" and rejoice over the fact that, as it seems to us, "growth and ever increasing presence of Moslems in Europe and America" is not "a terrifying perspective."

We still cannot believe that the Bible, as well as the Koran, "inspire and justify such a cruelty." We still cannot believe that the bloody massacre the witnesses of which we became at the 11th of September, 2001, is undoubtedly "a typical act of Moslem faith," and America will have chances to be convinced in that fact and to think about who and what stands behind those typical religious acts, about who and what enables the matrix to kill our own sons and daughters and destroy our own cities with our own hands in order for the prophesy·"They ruined their houses with their own hands and the hands of the believers" to come true.

4. 6. The Building of "Brilliant Islamic Future" in Afghanistan

Some days after the terrorist acts of September 11, 2001, we received e-mail from our American colleagues. There we found a letter of Afghan writer Tamim Ansari who lived in the USA at that time. The letter was full of pain for his motherland, which was under the authority of a gang of daredevils, who hid themselves behind beautiful slogans of struggle for the victory of the Islamic "utmost justice."

"'I was born in Afghanistan,' Tamim says, 'and, even in spite of the fact that I have already been living here (in America) for thirty five years, I have not lost the feeling of participation in the events taking place there (in Afghanistan). That is why I want to tell everybody who is ready to hear me about how it looks from here where I am.

I speak as one of those who hate Taliban and Osama-ben-Laden. I do not have even a trace of doubt that these people are involved in the atrocities in New York. I am also sure that these monsters must be punished. But Taliban and ben Laden is not Afghanistan, nor they are its government. Taliban is a cult of arrogant psychotonics who seized power in Afghanistan in 1997. Ben Laden is a political criminal pregnant with certain plans. Taliban is the same as Nazism. Osama-ben-Laden is the same as Hitler. And Afghanistan people are the same as "Jews in a concentration camp." And it is not because the Afghan people have nothing to do with this slaughter. The Afghan people have become the first victim of these criminals. Afghanistan would have rejoiced, if there would be anybody who would go to Afghanistan and clear up the rat nest of international daredevils who entrenched themselves in our country.

Some one can ask why do the Afghan people not rebel and throw

Talibs out of their country. They cannot do it because they die of starvation, because they are devastated, wounded. Some years ago UNO made the analyze of the situation in Afghanistan, and, as it turned out, there are half a million of orphans-invalids who die of starvation in the country, the economic life is absent at all, the country is in short supply of food products. There are several millions of widows, whom Talibs bury alive in common graves. The land is staffed with mines, and the agriculture has been destroyed by Soviet troops. These are the reasons that keep Afghan people from driving Talibs out of their country.'" [The end of the letter]

This is a real "true and peaceful face" of the victorious ideology of Islam, which became the government in Afghanistan. Thanks to Talibs, the country was changed into the "hornet's nest" of terrorists and "the warriors of jihad" who learned there the nuts and bolts of "liberating" war against "unbelievers," against "unilateral" world, against "globalization," and against those people whose backs "kind and merciful" Allah did not make the "forbidden field."

The literal interpretation of Koran enabled Taliban ideologists to invent the theory of "pure Islam," which attracted terrorists of all the stripes who wanted to join to the "great victory" of revolutionary Taliban forces in their struggle for the triumph of "the utmost justice."

It is not a secret that many of them were attracted not by Osama-ben-Laden himself and by his gang, but by the idea of talibanization of entire Moslem world. According to the CIA sources, only 3000 fighters out of tens of thousands prepared in Afghan training camps are under the direct command of Osama-ben-Laden. But, in spite of this, mutual ideological and financial interests connect "the terrorist No. 1" with Mulla Mohammed Omar, Al' Queda cells and Taliban movement. This ties are so strong and the network of terrorist organizations and groups is so extensive that destruction of one or even some cells will not be able to finish with terrorism.

Afghanistan became the best example demonstrated the law of unpredicted consequences. This sad story began as far back as in 1979, when the Soviet Union brought its troops to the country to support the puppet communist regime. In this occupation, the USA saw a nice chance to fight with its rival on the land of foreign country. For this purpose, they armed and began to finance the army capable to resist to the interests of the Soviet Union in Afghanistan.

The gang of mudjacheddins or "the warriors of Islam" consisted not only of representatives of separate and ethnically heterogeneous tribes, but also of professional staff of Moslems-volunteers under the command of Osama-ben-Laden. They considered armed struggle against Soviet troops as the protection of Islam and "Holy Land" from "unbelievers" prescribed by Allah. And they won, making utterly demoralized group of Soviet troops to withdraw from Afghanistan in 1989.

As this victory was considered by the USA as the decisive stage in the cold war against the USSR, America lost its interest toward Afghanistan and left country in the state of utter disorder and devastation. Endemic animosity between dominant Pushtu tribes and national minorities, which prevented the successful struggle against Soviet troops, now turned into the power that destroyed what was left from Afghanistan.

The country was plunged in a bloody vortex of lawlessness and violence, political leaders began to form armed gangs, fiercely fighting against each other, looting and cruelly killing local people. And, since all the towns were turned into ruins, agriculture was utterly destroyed, five million people ran away from the country, the only source of income was a drug traffic.

Impoverished people began to accuse America in a great treachery, for Afghanistan, nevertheless, was the front line of American confrontation to the Soviet influence in the region. And now America left devastated and ruined country the people of which had to die of hunger. The fact is that, having switched to their more urgent interests connected with the collapse of the Soviet Union, both the USA and the other western countries forgot about Afghanistan and left it to the mercy of fate. And the ideologists of "pure Islam" immediately made use of it.

In the middle of 1994, thirty-five year old Omar, while preaching Islam in the mosque of Singeshar, a village situated not far from the religious center of Candaghar, put "the holy book" to use. Like all the saints and tyrants of the past, Omar declared that he had received the revelation from Allah himself, who called him [Omar] to liberate Afhganistan from tribal gangs that were at enmity one with another. In the person of Omar Allah has found his faithful Islam warrior, for being a youth, Omar took part in the struggle against Soviet invasion and even lost one eye at that.

Now, being guided by the Koran, he summoned thirty fanatics in order to avenge two women who had been kidnapped and raped. Thus, this murder became the beginning of Taliban movement. Omar himself characterized it as "a common unity of devoted young people **who are**

able to sacrifice everything they have and even their own lives to achievement of their main goal: the establishing of Allah's laws all over the world."

Small group that called itself "Taliban," which means "the students of Islam," began its activity with taking of law observance in the town under their control. Its program envisaged the establishing of peace, legality, order and "purity of Islam" in Afghanistan. Using cruel and man-hating principles, taken by Omar from Koran, Taliban chose for their activity an extremist model, based on exceptionally uncompromising interpretation of Moslem law and on inflexible belief in ever lasting jihad.

Its fundamentalist platform was an obvious continuation of radical branch of Beobandy (which belonged to Islamic sects of Sunni direction) called after the name of Indian town that sheltered influential madrasah, or religious academy, which taught that "according to all the biological, religious and prophetical evidences, a woman is inferior being in comparison to a man."

Taliban movement burdened its faith with hard habits of Pushtu tradition, according to which "**unbelievers must be punished with the most severe punishment, approved by a Shariat court, including amputation of parts of the body, beating up with stones and public execution.**"

Tired with war, Afghan people, attracted by beautiful slogans of newly-made "students of Islam," ran rapidly under the banners of "fiery Islam." Afghan young people began to left refugee camps in Pakistan and, having cross the border, found themselves in Islamic schools of Taliban movement, where Pushtu speaking instructors hammered the Allah's instructions, who blessed ever lasting jihad against "unbelievers," in their young heads.

In 1994, Benasir Bhutto, the head of Pakistan government, asked Taliban leader to organize the convoy of trade routes to the Central Asia. Omar agreed, of course, for this deal opened the way to Pakistan money and weapon. Now Taliban could afford to organize more serious training camps. Pakistani support enabled Taliban grew stronger, so that the whole Candaghar surrendered to the power of "the students of Islam" even without any shot.

After Omar had demonstrated the raincoat, which once belonged to Allah, the militant heat of "students" increased to such an extent that they, having placed Koran against their foreheads, fearlessly came in Kabul and successfully captured it in 1996. By that time even the USA silently encouraged Pakistan to support Talibs, who, as they hoped, will be able to take heroin traffic under their control, as well as to help Americans to get open access to the gas deposits of Shiit Iran.

Of course, not all the Afghan people welcomed such rapid success of Taliban movement. Ethnical minorities were always against Talibs, and the North Alliance actively struggled against Taliban, trying to win back lost towns, the capital and north territories. If it were not bombing of American air forces and land operation of US mariners that scattered and cleansed "the hornet's nest of international daredevils" which the USA once made for the achievement of their "human" goals, this military opposition would hardly be finished with the victory of the North Alliance.

Taliban movement was till lately one of the most mysterious regimes which was financed by not less mysterious "spiritual" leaders. Omar who called himself Amir-ul'-Mominin or "the leader of Believers," was the most influential among them. He led very secluded way of life did not allow photographing himself and showed up very seldom. Omar preferred to give orders from his bunker in Candaghar, while his furious Mercy Development and Evil Preventing ministers embodied Islamic law on the spots by means of religious police.

Wearing black turbans on their heads and having whips in their hands, they beat unmercifully recalcitrant fellow countrymen and forbade women to come up to windows of their houses. The life gripped in a vice of endless prescriptions of the Moslem law created, according to the opinion of Moslem scientists, such a form of Islam, which was unknown in the history of Moslem religion.

We can tell that Moslem scientists forgot, most likely, the history of their own religion, which knew even more impressive examples of practical realization of "kind and merciful" principles of religion with "true and peaceful face." Nevertheless, many Moslem scientists assert that the Islam version represented by Taliban gives absolutely erroneous interpretation of Koran. We state that Talibs acted in strict accordance with cruel and man hating imperatives of the matrix, which orders: **"Therefore, when you meet the Unbelievers smite at their necks; at length when you have thoroughly subdued them, bind a bond firmly (on them)... And fight them on until there is no more tumult or oppression, and there prevail justice and faith in Allah altogether and everywhere." The same instructions, as you know, gave God Jehovah to Saul, "and fight against them until all of them are exterminated."**

Jewish and Christian theologians, by the way, believe that Jews also interpreted the orders of "kind and merciful" God-butcher-filicide

Jehovah to kill "both men and women, old men and infants, camels and donkeys" too literally and wrongly. They could spare the lives of at least camels and donkeys. But in that case they would brake Jehovah's order, and that was a deadly sin. Thus, Jews did not have any other way out as to kill everything alive, for their God ordered to do that. The same with Moslems, "**there is no other way out: either to be dissolved in a world intestine or to die standing.**"

Of course, nobody wants "to be dissolved in a world intestine." Another alternative is "to die standing". But one must fight in order to die standing. So, why don't we use the instructions of Allah, who has "true and peaceful face" and teaches Moslems to "**smite above their necks and smite all the finger-tips off them.**" And, in order this "smiting" to be more successful and safety for Moslems, Allah recommends to execute "their punishment **on a sudden by night or while they sleep for their afternoon rest.**"

And it is quite right. It is much easier to kill those who sleep than those who are awake, because those who are awake can resist to these scoundrels, they can protect their lives or even kill Allah's people, which is not safety for those who wants "to die standing."

The US government, reasoning from their political interests, deny to take into account the peculiarities of such a true Moslem ideology, which "in its attitude towards the outer world is based upon two thesis. Thesis "Din Mohammed bil' sef" (Mohammed's faith rules a sward) and "Dar es salam, dar el'-harb" (world dividing into two camps, "the world of Islam" and "the world of war," which must be conquered and Islamised) remain to be the core of Islam ideology. Islam is the religion of aggression and violence."[293]

It means that from the point of view of humanistic analyzes the religion of aggression and violence cannot be called "good and kind," moreover "the religion with true and peaceful face." **Humanistic analyzes cannot acknowledge the religious teaching which prescribes for its followers to "punish Unbelievers with the most strict and cruel means, approved by the Shariat court, including body parts amputation, beating up with stones and public execution," to "smite above their necks and smite all the finger-tips off them" and to "fight them on until there is no more tumult or oppression, and there prevail justice and faith in Allah altogether and everywhere" to be "the religion with true and peaceful face."**

CHAPTER 5.

VEDIC-ARIAN MYTH

"In another world, in a spiritual one, in Russia, which has managed to save its Vedic culture, my name is Boos Kresen.' This Russia does not exist on a map, and, nevertheless, it is as real as our souls, thoughts and feelings. Every one of us has his own true name, but it is not easy to recall it. We are flesh from flash of our ancestors; we see and feel this world in the same way they did. We are guests, who came from the past to the modern world.

Alexadr Asov.

5. 1. Vedic Past of Russia

Yes, everyone of us has his own true name, everyone of us has true cultural and historical roots, which we, to our great regret, do not remember; for they were taken away from us, etched from our memory and changed with absolutely alien to us names and cultural-historical values, which we, willy-nilly, got used to and absorbed into our hearts and souls as something native, something Russian, as something that was inherent to us from time immemorial, as some integral part of our life and history.

For an average statistical Russian citizen, the history of Russia begins from the year 862, when Varangian prince Rürick, according to the official version, gained a foothold in Novgorod. That year is traditionally considered as the beginning of the Russian state system, and usually, the consciousness of average-statistical Russians even do not try to penetrate beyond this date. Neither secondary school nor Russian universities and academies teach how to do it. Russian students learn, for example, the history and literature of the ancient world, of the middle ages and of Renaissance, but none of the textbooks even mentions that Slavic people, as well as the peoples of ancient Greek and Rome, had their own literature which existed as mythical epos, legends, fairy tales, songs that were passed from one generation to another partly by means of verbal tradition, partly by means of original system of so called "knot literature," the most remarkable of which is "The Songs of Gamayun Bird" dated from III—II A. D.

There are also the other sources which tell that Slavic ethnos inhabited the territory of the north part of modern Russia can be called "the foremother of the world culture."[294] On the Russian North, in the region of the mountain range of Lavoserskaya tundra and sacred Laplander lake Seidosero, the amazing monuments of Slavic culture which can be well compared with those of Shumer and Egypt, have been discovered.

Valery Demin, the head of the expedition Giperborea 97, tells the following about that: "Here, in the mountain region which is difficult of access, on the height of approximately half a kilometer from the lake level, the huge megalithic complex of cult and defensive constructions, geometrically correct slabs with mysterious signs and the traces of man-caused processing, have been discovered. And, at last, the remains of observatory, the fifteen meters long gutter with viewfinders, built in a rock massive that looks like the sextant of famous Ulugbek's observatory at Samarcand. Although, looking at discovered ruins, one recalls the Apollo temple in Giperborea, depicted by Diodor Sicilian which was used not only for religious purposes, but also as astronomical instrument. From it, as the ancient historian says, "the Moon was visible as though it was close to the Earth, and an eye discerned the same heights as on Earth.""[295]

All these facts enable us to state that on the north of Russia, there existed a high developed culture in ancient times, which was genetically connected with other ancient cultures. It means that already written history of Russia and of all the nations, inhabiting it, must be corrected. It means that the lower limit of our motherland chronology must be lowered even more.

The significance of discoveries made in the central regions of Kola Peninsula are very important, for they became the first material conformations of ancient written documents. They, by the way, contain clear indications that Giperborean civilization was the unique one.

Alexander Asov says: "At that distant time, the man was closer to earth, he felt his kinship with the outer world, he knew the laws, which directed his life, better than a modern man. These laws had been given to man in the same way as they had been given to the whole nature. There was the time when man had adopted the great Knowledge—the

Knowledge of Vedas. This Knowledge had been given in the form accessible for men: in the form of myth, legend, parable. But the mysterious meaning of this Knowlodge was clear only to devoted ones.

Many things has been changed since then. The power of darkness, Nav', did everything in order to destroy this Knowledge. During centuries, the Vedic Knowledge was persecuted and burned out. The building of Vedas, erected by many nations, has been destroyed and now lies in ruins..."[296]

One of such nations was the Russian people, the world outlook of which based on the ancient Vedic Knowledge. Asov asserts: "Slavs-Indo-Europeans were very close to other Indo-Europeans by their language and culture. **Indo-Europeans once constituted one ethnos and have one religion—Vedas. The Rig-Veda, the book of sacred hymns of ancient Arians who conquered India in the II A.D., has preserved the old Arian religion. One can find the traces of Arian faith also in ancient books of Zorooastrism, the ancient Iranian religion. The religion of ancient Greece also came out from the Vedic source. One can find a lot of information about Vedic culture in the works of antique poets and historians.**"[297]

5. 2. Gods We Have Repudiated and the Christening of Russia

Russia was always a mysterious country for the western world, the country that cannot be understood by reason, as a Russian poet Tyutchev once said. Foreigners, as well as Russians themselves, put forward "different opinions about Russian culture, about its past, present and future, about the features and peculiarities of the Russian people, but there is one feature everybody agrees upon. This is the mystery and incomprehensibility of Russia and of Russian soul."[298]

The author of this quotation, most likely, knows why Russia is such a mysterious country, for he asserts: "Russian orthodox church played the large role in the Russian people self-consciousness development. Having adopted Christianity, prince Vladimir made the great historical choice which determined the historic fate of not only Russian state, but also of the whole world history. This choice was, from one hand, a step towards the West, towards the civilization of European type. From the other hand, it separated Russia from the East and from those versions of cultural evolution which were connected with Buddhism, Hinduism and Islam. Now we can only dream about what the Russian people and the Russian culture, as well as the history of Europe and Asia would be, if Vladimir would have made another choice."[299]

Yes, it is difficult to say what the Russian people and its culture would be if Vladimir would have not baptized Russia, but it is quite obvious that they would not be worse, for rude and unnatural braking of existing foundations and forced inculcation of alien cultural values is always worse than natural evolutionary development. And why was the separation of Russia from the East and "from those versions of cultural evolution, which were connected with Buddhism, Hinduism and Islam" so well for both Russia and even for the whole world history?

You see, in the same book, Mr. Carmin, as we stated above, expressed his positive emotions on the occasion that "nowadays, for the first time in history, the cultural unity of mankind, which is beginning to emerge, essentially changes mechanisms that determined the destiny of separate cultures and civilizations before," and asserts that "rich enough culture, adopting the achievements of other cultures, do not seize to be an original and unique one, but enriches itself more and more."[300]

As for Islam, we have proven that it is not the religion that can bring love and peace in the world. But why are Buddhism and Hinduism bad? Buddhism is the great moral teaching, and Hinduism is the culture of a great Indian nation which is rich on cultural-historical traditions, moreover, the nation close to our Slavic culture. If Russia would have been associated with Buddhism and Hinduism, it could take from them their cultural heritage instead of the bloody myth about tribal Jewish God-butcher-filicide Jehovah, who is cruel, bloodthirsty and quite a pagan deity.

Of course, someone can argue with us and say that at that time, Russia got into contact not with small Jewish people, but with the great Byzantine empire and with its culture, which is true. But one must also remember that the Byzantine culture was built on the same matrix as all the cruel and man-hating tyrannies known in the world history.

Further, we have to answer another questions. Who was prince Vladimir? Did he take into account the desires of the Russian people when he baptized it? We have already known that all the religions of "salvation" "saved" people without their knowing about it and without their consent. Everybody also knows what happened.

The same happened with the baptizing of Russia. The Russian, or to be more precise, Slavic people which inhabited the north and central part of the eastern-European plane lived its quiet and happy life until disorders began. Local authorities were unable to regulate them, that is why they decided to invite Varangian Rürik who brought "all the Russia" (i. e. his armed force and a court) together with him. And it was already in 911 B. C., when the agreement between Greece and Russia stated: "We are, from the kin of Russia, Karl Ingelot, Farlov, Veremid, Rulav, Gudi, Ruald, Karn, Flelav, Ruar, Aktutruyan, Lidulfost, Stemid, sent by Oleg, the grand duke of Russia and by all those who are under his authority."[301]

As you see there were no Russian names (or Slavic, to be more precise) at all among "Russian" ambassadors. Only the third and the fourth generations of Kiev princes will have exceptionally Slavic names, which means that they will be entirely assimilated by Slavs. Prince Vladimir will be among those princes, but he is also not Slavic, he was as Russian (or Varangian, to be more precise) as Rürik. We do not think that he was preoccupied with interests of Russian (Slavic) people. Vladimir wanted to become the great Duke of Kiev, and Byzantine wanted to have its Christian ally next to its borders, but in no way a pagan rival.

The fact is that the pagan world outlook could not facilitate to solve the main tasks which Vladimir put before himself in order to establish princely power. From one hand, peaceful and open pagan world outlook was far from obtrusion of the samples of behavior which was appropriate in the epoch of feudalism, i. e. blind submission and humility in the conditions of discrimination; from the other hand, it was useless for the substantiation of prince's authority.

At that time, elders' council and a priestly caste of wizards represented both central and local authorities. Vladimir wanted to establish Duke's personal leadership which was alien for the Slavic political system. Moreover, Vladimir was in exile at that time. The fact is that: "After Sviatoslav's death, his elder son Jaropolk (972-980) became the great Duke of Kiev. Oleg, his brother, got Drevlianskaya land. Vladimir, the third Sviatoslav's son, got Novgorod. In five years a civil strife began among the brothers. Jaropolk defeated Oleg's armed forces, and Oleg himself was killed in a battle.

Vladimir ran away "over the sea," and came back with Varangian mercenaries in two years. Jaropolk was killed and Vladimir ascended the Grand Duke's throne."[302]

In 980, Vladimir conducted the first religious reform, which actually came to the establishing of a new hierarchy of Slavic gods. God Perun occupied the first place in the new pantheon, after him went Stribog, Dazhd'bog, Hors, Simargl and goddess Mokosh'.

The meaning of reform becomes quite obvious, if one takes into account that Perun which Vladimir put on the first place was the protector of both Duke and his authority. But this new invention was not grounded with a proper mythological substantiation, without which such attempts of modernization of an already formed national-religious pantheon never and nowhere resulted in success. Thus the whole reform was reduced to only mechanical shifting of figures and was doomed to failure from the very beginning. Vladimir, even after rearrangement of pagan pantheon, still had no right to be settled in Kiev, where the pagan sanctuary was situated.

As for Byzantine, it was no less interested in the baptizing of Russia than Vladimir. From one hand, because Christianity strived for the expansion of its teaching and the Church made all its best to preach its religion wherever it was possible; from the other hand because Russia was a great danger for Byzantine, and Russian armed forces attacked it very often. Andreeva, L. A. says: "It was time to use the main ideological weapon of the Roman Empire—baptizing its enemies. In the circular message of patriarch Fotius, the baptizing of Russians was considered as effective means, which could change them into "the rank of our subjects and friends instead of robbing us and of every kind of daring against us." The entire subsequent policy of Byzantine towards Russia was, thus, reduced to this."[303]

By the way, the Soviet Union was neutralized in the same way. Then, having imposed its cultural values and baptized Russia for the second time, the "world imperialism" destroyed our pantheon of gods (general secretaries), our ideology (Marxism-Leninism) and our socialist culture with our own hands, with the hands of "unbelievers."

In 988, Grand Duke Vladimir made, at last, his "great historical choice that separated Russia from the East and from those versions of cultural evolution, which were connected with Buddhism, Hinduism and Islam."

Having gotten under the influence of the Jewish matrix of destruction, Russia changed into a dark theocracy, about which French citizen Michelet said: "**The tendency of such a state is to become less and less a state and more and more a religion. Everything is religious in Russia. Nothing is lawful, nothing is just**. Every one is or wants to be a saint... It is not enough for you to create the world of civil order in your house, inferior world... Being powerless in human affairs, you style yourselves gods."[304]

French citizen Michelet understood where we could go with our Christian ideology which we had adopted as the base of our life. Russian writer Belinsky also understood this peculiarity of the Russian history. He said: "Do you think the Russian people is the most religious people in the world? It is a lie! The base of religiousness is pietism, veneration and the fear of God! And a Russian man pronounces God's name scratching his fanny... There is much superstition in him, but no trace of religiousness... Mystical exaltation is not in his nature; he has too much common sense, clarity and positiveness in his mind, and these very qualities are, most likely, the determining factors of the greatness of future historical ways of the Russian people."[305]

Where do the Russian people have this common sense from? Where does it have this clarity and the positiveness of mind from? It is quite obvious that it has all these qualities not from the Christian teaching and not from the Church which tried to suppress any displays of thought in hearts and souls of the Slavic people, replacing it by mystical exaltation that "is not in its nature."

Both common sense and clarity, as well as the positiveness of mind, are, of course, the pagan heritage of the Slavic people. You see, the world outlook of ancient Slavs differed from that of Christian. The world outlook of ancient Slavs was a continuation of the world outlook of their ancestors, Indo-European-Vedic-Arian people.

As Miroluybov, J. P. asserths in his book *Sacral of Russia*: "The soul of our Slavic ancestors is expressed in Slavic gods. **Slavs believed that once the day would come, and all the people would become kind and merciful and the world would be nice and beautiful. Their religion was not only moral one; it also made people to believe in improvement, in perfection of both people and the world. There was no place for despair in this religion. It was cheerful and poetic**. Gods were kind in a full sense of this word, they were solar, radiant, and they spread virtue around themselves, like flowers spread fragrance."[306]

Yes, there was common sense in this religion. Yes, there was clarity and even positiveness of mind, which cannot be said about Christianity. Teaching about love and mercy, Christianity hides in its bosom a heavy bloodstained stone, prepared to kill all non-Christians in the day of the Last Judgment. In that day "loving and merciful" God-butcher-filicide Jehovah will come to us together with his son to perform "the final extermination" in the fire of which all the non-Christians will be exterminated and thrown to the lake burning with fire and sulfur in order to be tortured forever.

No, the religion of our ancestors was not such. It was not the Last Judgment and not "the final extermination" that they waited for. Slavic people waited for a kind and beautiful world, moving it near by their work and patience.

Slavic popular religion was based on a Sun worshiping. Isvarog (Ishvara) was the father of gods. Having created gods, Svarog, as ancient

Slavs believed, created the first human beings—Prada and Prabu. Slavic trinity Colyado-Wishny-Sivy, corresponds to Vedic trinity Indra-Agny-Varuna. Colyado is the god of winter and at the same time the god of Revival, god of light and warmth. Wishny is the god who keeps warmth, but Sivy (later black god) is the god who destroys it. Sivy—black god was also the god of evil. In Slavic religion, as well as in the Vedic one, there was the concept of One Supreme Being, whom they called the Father of Gods.

Slavic religion was pantheistic in its essence. Zabolothich, V. says: "There was much mysticism in Slavic religion. Its essence is the feeling of God who is everywhere, in every display of life. Ancient Slavs believed that they are inside of God. That is why everything was sacred for Slavic people, and there was nothing foul in the world. Woods and mountains, rivers and lakes, fields and meadows were sacred for them. All the displays of God's activity were visible in the nature, and everything that went on in the world was also done by God in his numerous manifestations. The ancient moral of Slavic people consisted in the sacred understanding of the world. One had to know (Veda means "knowledge") that the world is the receptacle of God. "Indra is more then the World," says Rig Veda. Life in accordance with the laws of Life Circle and the rhythmus of the Nature was considered as the act, which corresponded to God's will."[307]

Life in accordance with God's will and association with God was the main goal of Slavs who loved Nature and admired all its colors. In Semitic teaching of the Bible, punishment is the main subject. Sins lead a person to its spiritual death, therefore the necessity of salvation is aroused.

As Zabolothich V. asserths: "**There is no need for salvation in Slavic popular religion. Salvation is attained in the association with God, who was the Slavs' forefather. The man is already saved because he originated from God. Thus, the idea of kinship with God is the main idea Slavic popular religion**. Such was the religion of ancient Slavs. It has the same roots with Rig Veda and saturated with its spirit.

This religion was not paganism. It was the RELIGION OF UNIVERSAL LIFE AND LOVE. It was the whole and profound system of ideas about the word and the man which rooted in far Indo-European past. **The ancient religion had nothing to do with barbaric primitive cults. It continues to live in our everyday habits, it saturates the culture of the orthodox Christian.**"[308]

Such was the religion, which was taken away from us and substituted with a monstrous, man-hating cult of cruel and bloodthirsty Jewish God-butcher-filicide Jehovah. Such was our Slavic culture: kind, light and just culture of the people who lived in indissoluble unity with the world and nature. This culture was syncretic and deeply mythological in its essence, and we can see the "initial arrangement of myth" in it that later was turned into score, i. e. a story unwrapped on the axis of time, which became the base of the post-mythological culture.

The ancient pagan world did not know the division on good and bad, on "believers" and "unbelievers," on friends and enemies; that is why in the ancient Slavic world there were no enmity and hatred, religious intolerance and genocide which appeared in the world only in post-mythological period and were finally formed with the development of monotheism, the main feature of which is division on "the God's people" who has the right for life, and Gentiles ("unbelievers") whose souls must be "exterminated out of the people."

As a matter of fact, monotheism is an artificial construction that does not fit in the natural way of development of man and nature. It roughly brakes into the natural, mythological human consciousness, tearing it into pieces that become hostile towards one another and creates notorious binary oppositions, without neutralization of which we cannot live in peace and consent.

Thus, on the example of Slavic pagan world outlook we can see the peculiarities of mythological consciousness, for which harmonic unity with the world and the nature is characteristic. This unity presupposes love and a solicitous attitude towards the world and nature which, in its turn, gives rise to joyful disposition saturated with good and justice. It also gives hope that sooner or later "all the people will become good and kind and will live in a splendid and wonderful world."

5. 3. Vedism and Orthodoxy

In order to understand the difference between Vedism and Orthodoxy, we shall tell you a real story, which happened with one of our good friends. This man, being a baptized orthodox Christian, once decided to become acquainted with the teaching of Krishna, which is one of the various and numerous branches of the very Vedic culture we have just told you about.

Soon his enthusiasm disappeared and he decided to come back to Christianity. But the teaching of Krishna is a devilry that leads straight to hell. It means that in order to come back to orthodoxy one has to repent, confess one's sins and receive the Lord's Sacraments. Our friend, having spent all his savings, buys a ticket on a train and goes to one of the famous orthodox monasteries to confess his sins and make his communion.

What a happy man he was! What a joy he had in his heart, for he had managed to overcome evil spells and come back to true God, who, as the man hoped, would accept him and forgive all his sins in spite of his "treachery!" The man remembered Jesus' words, "And if someone asks one's father for a fish, could it be so that the father will give one a stone? Moreover, the Heavenly Father."

Our friend fasted three days before the ceremony, three days he prayed to God for forgiveness of his sins, and on the fourth day, he stood before a priest for confession. The man told everything to the priest, he told as he had adopted the devilry, as he sang Hare Krishna and other mantras, as he ate prasadam [the food offered to Krishna], as he attended their meetings and listened to their foreign teachers.

Having heard such a terrible story, the priest who was hearing the confession of our friend blanched with terror and even staggered a bit, as if someone struck him at his face. Having asked our friend to wait, he went away hastily. In a minute or so, another priest came, most likely the one of a higher rank.

"You are black, you are Satan!" the priest said, and fixed the glance of his burning, penetrating eyes on the poor man, "Give up Krishna!"

The man felt uneasy, he stepped back as if intending to run away from that place and asked gingerly, "What is the matter?" "Give up Krishna," the priest persisted without turning his terrible sizzling glance from the man.

"I cannot do it," our friend answered. His shyness disappeared at that moment, and our friend began to understand that the priest tried to make him to renounce the entire non-Christian world, which is considered by Christianity as the hostile one. Our friend was not ready to do that, he could not give up Krishna, he could not renounce the ancient, unique culture which was the base of life of the enormous Hindu world. He recalled that nobody made him to give up Jesus when he came to Krishnaits. They just told him that he could add the Krishna's teaching to Jesus'. The man began to understand that in Krishnaism he encountered with the tendency to integrate all the religions and all the people into a single whole, while the tendency to disintegrate, to divide, to enmity and to renunciate the entire non-Christian world was the leading one in the orthodox Christianity.

"Give up Krishna!" the priest repeated without stopping, "You must be excommunicated! You must be anathematized! You must be subjected to such a punishment that you would give up not only Krishna, but all the devilish world!" Our friend understood that it was the case when he came to the Heavenly Father to ask for a "fish," but the Heavenly Father threw a "stone" at him. It was so painful, so unmerciful that our friend decided not only not to go to church, but even not to come near priests in order to avoid making him give up Krishna, father, mother, friends and all his neighbors. So, what devilish is contained in Vedic teaching, and why are orthodox priests so afraid of it?

A Russian religious philosopher Trubetskoy, E. in the *Sense of Life* says: "The depth of religious findings of India consists in that they change all the statements of plane common sense into their antithesis. Everything we call reality is a dream, and everything we call a dream is a true reality and true value, this what we are taught by ascetic wisdom of both Brahmanism and Buddhism.

The word "Buddha" literally means "the one who woke up." And the whole teaching of these world religions is nothing more than an attempt to realize this awakening, to rise over the delusion of fuss and a heavy delirium, which is called reality; both for Buddhism and for Brahmanism, the true expression of real life and of its sense is not this reality, but those wings that drag us away off it...

Thus, that flight and that rising to the transcendent world that constitutes the essence of religious findings of India, is turned into nothing, for this flight does not lead to the goal. Its sense flies away off the earth together with a spirit. Therefore, all the movement of what belongs to the earth is vain, and the very attempt of the earth to rise to the Heaven turns out to be deceived, in the final account. This Heaven remains forever closed, transcendent, for the earth, and the material world will never be able to unite with it.

Both Hindu and Greek answers to the questions of the sense of life are baseless. The Greek religiousness, confirming the world instead the space, finds chaos, a disorderly multitude of separated powers struggling against each other. The Hindu religiousness rejects the world utterly as something unsubstantial and senseless, i.e. also does not find the sense of life in the world, and sees it only in its destruction. There is a chaotic multitude of living creatures that do not attain the fullness of eternal life in the Greek religion; in the religion of Brahmans, we have one eternal life of Brahma, which excludes the multitude of individual forms; in Buddhism, we have dead emptiness, the rest of death in nirvana: all these are the different displays of the same misfortune of life and its looking for a sense."[309]

Thus, we see that Trubetskoy defines two lines of religious thought, i. e. the Greek and the Hindu variants of answering the question about the sense of life. One line is a horizontal, the line which "confirms the world" which "finds chaos instead of space," the other one is vertical which "rejects the world utterly as something that does not exist and does not have sense" and which finds the sense only "in its destruction." The philosopher believes that the true sense of life can be found only in the point where lines are crossed, i. e. in the Christianity.

He says: "Both these lines, which show two main directions of the courses of life, are crossed. And, since they represent by themselves the exhaustive description of all the possible ways of life, their crossing—cross—is the most universal, precise, sketchy picture of a true way of life...

Thus, a cross is the base of any life... Regardless of our attitude towards Christ and Christianity, we must acknowledge that the very picture of life is cross-like, and there is the cosmic cross which shows as if architect frame of the whole world way.

Whether we stick ourselves to the Christian point of view or not, it is all the same. The question of the sense of life is inevitably reduced to the question of a cross, for there cannot be any other lines and ways except of these two crossing lines. All the other ways are just different versions of these two."[310]

Thus, a cross is represented as the receptacle of the sense of life, for it, being the sign of death, becomes the sign of eternal life attaining by those who believe in the purifying sacrifice of Jesus Christ.

This problem, as Trubetskoy says, "is posed in all the religions: the search for eternal life is their mutual motive, but only the religion of religions—Christianity—finds what it looks for, it attains its goal. Only Christianity confirms both the future and complete unification of both basses—the Godly fullness and the world of striving, wishful creature[311]."

Christianity, as Trubetskoy believes, differs from both Hellenic and Hindu religiousness by its very essence. Between these two opposite concepts, it offers the peculiar, the third way of life perception, in which all the oppositions between this world and the other one are unified.

Further, he says: "According to Christ's teaching, God realizes himself and incarnates in the world, and the world joins to the fullness of divine life. As it was said, this is the only *positive* answer to the question about the sense of life. We can either accept it or reject. **There cannot be other way**...

Thus, the problem is not in a choice among religions, but only in a choice between Christianity and complete infidelity. Contrary to Dionysus and other gods of naturalistic religions, Christ died only one time and resurrected forever; the very law of general, periodic dying has been abolished in him. The whole world, including all the living creatures, must be resurrected once and forever. Thus, the vicious circle of universal fuss is changed into the heavenly circle of eternal rest. The world comes to its absolute end, but not in the sense of destruction, but in the sense of existence fullness achieving."[312]

Thanks to Evgeny Trubetscoy, we come to understand both vainness of religious findings of India which consist in impossibility of "taking the Earth up to the Heaven" and in the making provision for eternal life, and of its criminal vision of the sense of life, which consists, as the philosopher believes, in "its destruction." And here, we have one more proof that Christianity is a material myth from its very beginning to its very end, for it foresees the final point of world development in "taking the Earth up to the Heaven" in order to unite it with the fullness of divine life.

As we already know, this process will be put into effect by means of the Last Judgment, or, frankly speaking, the "final destruction," or the greatest slaughter in the whole history of the world. At the end of this unprecedented purge, only a handful of Christians will remain alive, while all the other people will be cruelly exterminated or thrown to the lake burning with fire and sulfur to be tortured forever.

Someone believes that the "old world" will be destroyed, and the "new one" (so material as the "old one" was) with the Heavenly Jerusalem, with streets paved with gold, and with crystal temples, will be created. In this new Jerusalem, the Christians who will be saved after the "final destruction" will pray to God-butcher-filicide Jehovah, who, on this occasion, will move to this fantastic city in order to dwell there with his "chosen people" forever.

Someone believes that the "old world" will remain the same, but the lake burning with fire and sulfur will be added to it. In this lake, those who have not adopted Christianity will be boiled, cooked, and tormented. They will cry, groan, and moan forever. Anyway, it will be the material world, in which Christians will enjoy the eternal life, while all the other people will be "tortured before God and before the Lamb" or be burned in the blazing inferno.

In the Vedic-Arian myth, everything is little bit different. It is true that the Vedic religious thought considers the material world as something temporary, and therefore as something illusory, as something non-existant. But it does not mean that "the Hindu religiousness rejects the world totally" and "sees the sense only in its destruction." On the contrary, it is Christianity that sees the sense in the world destruction, but in no way the Hindu one, for the Hindu religiousness is saturated with love for everything and for the whole world which it considers to be one of the God's energies, and, thus, worthy of love and respect as the God's creation.

The Hindu religiousness considers the material world as illusion, as "maya," because it is not eternal, because it is transient, and, in the final account, must be disintegrated owing to quite natural material causes, for one of the main Cosmic laws asserts that "all the created things are subjected to disintegration."

This law reflects the cyclic recurrence of life, its eternal movement from a singularity, or a point, to the fullest degree of its realization; and then the reverse movement to the initial point, to a singularity, immersing into non-existence (Maha pralaya), and again the other swing from a singularity to the innumerable quantity of material universes inhabited with uncountable multitude of living creatures. But it does not mean that the world is destroyed during Maha pralaya. Maha pralaya is just a rest, just a dream of matter tired from corporeal life, just the way of power accumulating that is necessary for another circle of the eternal movement of life.

One also has to remember that during Maha pralaya all the living creatures (or their souls, to be more precise) retain all their spiritual qualities and are plunged into the Great World Soul, in order to have a rest, in order to get new strength and power to be reappeared again to begin the animation of a growing material world.

One can see this eternal flow of life in the expansion of our Universe, in the scattering of galaxies, which once will stop their running and begin their reverse movement. And then, the Universe will be compressed into a point again, and again it will explode into an uncountable multitude of new Universes, and new lives will appear. The Universe expansion and its cyclic development is the well-proven scientific fact.

But people knew about it long ago, at the time when Vedas were written. Of course, people did not have such technical means as we have now, nor did hey possess such scientific terminology as we use now. That is why all these complicated universal laws were described by means of mythical epos in which different gods acted. But, behind innumerable images of Hindu gods, devoted ones saw the activity of invisible but quite real and powerful forces, setting in motion the great "life circle" or the "karma circle," as it was called by Hindus. They also knew that, along with the eternal circle of reviving and dying matter, there was another, spiritual world which existed primordially and eternally; the world, which was not subjected to destruction and disintegration.

The Supreme Personality of God says in Bhagavad-Gita: "According to the earthly chronology, a thousand epochs taken together are equal to one day of Brahma. The same is his night. In the beginning of the day of Brahma, all the living creatures become apparent out of non-developed state, and then, when night comes, they go away to their non-developedness again...

But there exists another, non-developed world, which is eternal and situated higher than both developed and non-developed nature. This highest nature is never destroyed. When everything is destroyed in the world, this part remains unchanged. What is described by Vedantists as non-developed and perfect, what is known as the highest destination, the place, from which nobody comes back having reached it once, is My highest dwelling place"[313]

The Supreme Personality of God explains who can be saved and what to do to be saved: "People who know Vedas, who pronounce sacred syllable "OM" are great sages. They accepted the renounced way of life and came into Brahman. Aspiring to such a perfection, one gives the vow of abstinence...

The condition of yoga consists in detachment from any sensual activity. Having closed all the doors of senses, concentrating one's mind on one's heart and life air—on the upper part of one's head, one immerses in yoga. Having attained such a condition of yoga and pronouncing the sacred syllable "OM" which is the highest combination of letters, one (who thinks of the Supreme Personality of God while leaving one's body) will inevitably get to spiritual planets. **The one who always remembers of Me, who concentrates one's thoughts on Me, oh, the son of Pritthy, can easily reach Me, for he serves Me all the time. Having returned to me, the great souls which have achieved the highest perfection in a bhakty-yoga, never go back to this temporary, full of sufferings world.**

Beginning from the highest planet of the material world and ending with the lowest one, all of them are the place of suffering, the place of repeated birth and death. But only the one who gets to My dwelling place, oh, the son of Kunti, is never born again... **One can reach the Supreme Personality of God, who is the highest of all, by means of pure devotion.**"[314]

Thus, according to the Vedic philosophy, anyone who practices bhakty-yoga [the yoga of love both to the Supreme Personality of God and to all the living creatures] can, by means of "pure devotion," reach the God's dwelling place and live there forever, without coming back "to this temporary, full of sufferings world."

Instead of the Christian idea of "taking the Earth up to the Heaven" by means of the "final destruction" of the entire non-Christian world, Vedic-Arian myth offers a simple and accessible individual way of salvation from the bondages of maya, i. e. from illusory, contemporary, eternally disintegrating world. **It turns out that in order to reach the "God's kingdom" it is not necessary to kill or exterminate anyone. There is no need to scorn, to trample down or to crash anybody in the "wine-yard of fierce God's anger." There is no need to torture anybody "before God and before the Lamb" or throw anybody to the "lake burning with fire and sulfur."**

What really is necessary is just to remember God, to concentrate one's thoughts on Him, to serve Him sincerely and to develop one's love for God and for every living creature. It means that, if everyone does one's best to develop one's love for God and for all the living creatures, all the human souls will gradually free themselves from the bondages of maya and get to the spiritual world, in which they will dwell eternally enjoying all the advantages of eternal life.

The religion of love and devotional sincere service... No hatred and no division, no desire to dominate and to exterminate, no blood and no slaughter, no fratricide and no infanticide—just devotional service to the Supreme Personality of God and great, universal love, love for every living creature in the world regardless of race, skin color and religious belief... Such is the religion of those who believe in Krishna—one of the numerous incarnations of the Supreme personality of God, one of His Avatars, one of God's manifestations in the appearance of a mortal man. And this is the real religion of heart and soul; the only one capable to save the man from "the bondages of brutal flash."

In the space of Vedic-Arian myth, we always have a chance to be developed spiritually and to be saved. On the contrary, in the space of Christian myth, "the problem is not in a choice among religions, but only in a choice between Christianity and complete infidelity" which "we can either accept or reject" because "there cannot be other way." If "there cannot be other way," the "salvation," the sense of life and the eternal life is possible only for Christians. If you are non-Christian, you will be brutally killed by God Jehovah during the "final extermination," even if you are a "saint," i. e. good and high moral and righteous person.

But, being a Christian, you can hope for "salvation" even if you are a complete scoundrel and a killer. In order to get it, you just have to repent and to believe in a purifying sacrifice of Jesus Christ, for, as the Christian Church teaches, Jesus' blood can cleanse all the possible kinds of sins, including murder, slaughter, fratricide and even filicide. That is why the future paradise life which will be created after the "final extermination" will be full of repented impostors, hypocrites, thieves, killers and other scoundrels of every stripe.

Thus, we see that Christianity does not give any chance either to be "saved" or to be developed spiritually if you are non-Christian. Such a person must be cruelly and mercilessly exterminated with subsequent resurrection and throwing him to the lake burning with fire and sulfur. Is it just? Our humanistic analysis has to acknowledge that it is absolutely unjust and inhuman.

However, Christianity does not care a damn about it, for «the Gospel is against any justice It is for mercy," as Alexandr Borisov, an orthodox priest, said. In addition, since it is cruel and unjust to exterminate human beings, to crash them in a fierce rage and to shed their blood just because they are non-Christian, the question of mercy in Christianity can be easily removed from the agenda because of complete absence of the very subject of question.

Nevertheless, the tendency to revise the question of "God choosiness" of Christians and to show tolerance towards the representatives of other religious confessions has appeared lately among western theologians. But "they acknowledge just the fact that other confessions can have "less light" (Karl Barth), or that "they are anonymous Christians" (Paul Tilich), or "incognito Christians" (Karl Rahner). The tolerance of such a kind acknowledges only minimal significance of other religious traditions."[315]

Actually, it is "the same old Jewish trickery," as Adolph Hitler once said. Why don't we acknowledge frankly and openly that we all are equal before God? Then everything would fall into place, and there would be no need to lie and play the hypocrite, there would be no need for religious philosophers to exercise their phrase-mongering inventing fables about "anonymous Christians" or about "incognito Christians," who can hope for "salvation" because, nevertheless, they are Christians even in spite of their anonymousness.

In the space of Vedic-Arian myth, unlikely to that of Christian, the law of justice or the law of karma works. This law asserts: "The man himself creates his destiny, and, even still being in a womb, the man began to experience the consequences of his past existence. Wherever he would be: either in mountain cracks or in calm ocean waters; in tender mother's arms or in strong father's hands who raise him over his head—nowhere can the man get rid of consequences of his past deeds...

Man's karma is the decisive factor of his happiness or unhappiness... During different periods of man's life, he reaps the fruits of those actions, which he had sown during analogical periods of his past life... The man receives what is destined for him by his fate, and even God cannot change this fate... A frightened mouse runs away to its hole, a frightened snake hurries up to hide itself in a well, an elephant—in its stall; but how can the man escape his karma?..

The man dies in the allotted time, and a deadly wound turns out to be mortal in an appropriate moment of life. The man receives what he deserves; he goes where his fate leads him and finds so much satisfaction or pain as it was destined by fate. Is it worth while to complain about his fate then?

The shadow of a cloud, the love of a vicious man, adultery, youth and wealth—here are the five equally temporary things in the world. Life is temporary, as well as youth and wealth of the man. Wives, children, friends and human relationships are just temporary clouds of phantasmagoria of life. Only virtue and good deeds are eternal...

All the rest is as changeable and unsteady as ocean waves. And what will the man find at the end of his life? What do glory and famousness mean to him? Death with its faithful companions (Day and Night) diligently wanders around the world in the guise of Old Age and devours all the created beings as easy as a snake devours the whiff of wind."[316]

Christianity does not acknowledge the law of karma, for there is the law of faith in Christianity which is able to justify any atrocities if their performers repent and believe that their sins can be atoned with the blood of the one who gave away his life on a cross for the sake of those criminals. In Christianity, the individual effort and striving for perfection mean nothing. "Salvation" happens not only at the expense of sacrificing a human being (namely Jesus Christ) with the blood of whom these criminals and hypocrites want to wash away their abominable sins and vices. It happens also at the expense of blood of milliards of Gentiles who will be sacrificed during the "final extermination," or the "final purge" **because, as rabbi Saul (apostle Paul) said, "there is no salvation without bloodshed**."

Another pillar of Christianity is the universal resurrection, after which some will go to the eternal life, while the others—to eternal tortures in the lake burning with fire and sulfur. Evgeny Trubetskoy says about it: "The triumph of life and the victory over death, performed in Christ, is just a beginning of that universal resurrection, in which not only human but also inferior creatures take part. Here, we have the necessary completion of the logic of universal sense. If God is the true end of the *whole* existence, he must be present in every thing. **If God is love, there must be nothing excluded from his love, there must be no unloved creature.**"[317]

The great religious philosopher seems not to read the Bible at all. Otherwise, he would have noticed that in the space of the Bible all the Gentiles (i. e. all those who do not belong to the Jewish people) are excluded from God's love, moreover they all are "unloved creatures" for Jewish God-butcher-filicide Jehovah, and, therefore, must be cruelly and mercilessly exterminated. "Kind and merciful" God who has no "unloved creatures" says: "**And I will bring a sword upon you**, that shall avenge the quarrel of my covenant: and when ye are gathered together within your cities, **I will send the pestilence among you; and ye shall be delivered into the hand of the enemy** (Leviticus 26: 25)." "**The Lord will smite thee with the botch of Egypt, and with the emerods, and with the scab, and with the itch, whereof thou canst not be healed. The Lord shall smite thee with madness, and blindness, and astonishment of heart** (Deuteronomy 28: 27-28)."

Here is one more proof of Jehovah's "universal love" for all the living "creatures": "But of the cities of these people, which the Lord thy God doth give thee for an inheritance, thou **shalt save alive nothing that breatheth**. But thou shalt utterly destroy them; namely, the Hittites, and the Amorites, the Canaanites, and the Perizzites, the Hivites, and the Jebusites; as the Lord thy God hath commanded thee (Deuteronomy 20:16-17)." "Now go and smite Amalek, **and utterly destroy all that they have, and spare them not; but slay both man and woman, infant and suckling, ox and sheep, camel and ass** (1st Book of Samuel 15: 3)."

As for those who served to other gods, God-butcher-filicide Jehovah recommended to treat them as following: "Thou shalt not consent unto him, nor hearken unto him; neither shall thine eye pity him, neither shalt thou spare, neither shalt thou conceal him. **But thou shalt surely kill him**; thine hand shall be first upon him to put him to death, and afterwards the hand of all the people. **And thou shalt stone him with stones, that he die**; because he hath sought to thrust thee away from the Lord thy God, which brought thee out of the land of Egypt, from the house of bondage (Deuteronomy 13: 8-10)."

And in the Koran God Allah says frankly and openly, "**Allah does not love those who rejects faith** (The Qur-an 3: 32)." It means that all those who by one or another reason do not want to accept Islam "are fuel for the fire (Ibid 3:10)." Who will say that God loves every creature after that?

Trubetskoy, nevertheless, asserts: "Here {in Christianity} we have *the only* revelation of the universe sense... We can also find compassionate attitude towards the living creature in eastern religions, in Brahmanism, in Buddhism, but there, this compassion and pity are determined by the acknowledging of vanity of striving for life as it is. **This "compassion" is devoid of hope; it does not bring any promise and joy for the inferior creature**.

Christianity loves this creature with a different love: it believes in its absolute value and opens for it the coheirness of eternal life in the man and through the man. Since there is nothing transcendental to the universal sense, the revelation of this sense must be presented both in the spiritual and in the corporeal world. This revelation expresses itself not in the rejecting flash, but in the restoration of indissoluble, eternal ties between the world of spirit and the world of flesh. That is why, the future age is imagined by Christians as the universal renewal of corporal life, as future resurrection of both man and nature"[318]

Good words, but they are absolutely wrong, for it is not in Brahmanism and in Buddhism that "this compassion is devoid of hope," that "it does not bring any promise and joy for the inferior creature," but in Christianity. And it is only in Christianity that the man is "the inferior creature." In Christianity, the man does not have any hope for "salvation," for any Christian, regardless of his degree of devotion, is doomed for murder since rabbi Saul (apostle Paul) "has spoiled the teaching of that man." This "spoilage" of Jesus' original teaching consisted in that the man, from one hand, was made to worship and to serve to bloodthirsty God-butcher-filicide Jehovah instead of God who is love; from the other hand, the man was made to break Jehovah's law, i. e. to commit the deadly sin, the punishment for which is death, as you have already known.

In the Vedic-Arian myth there is not even a trace of that spirit of hatred, cruelty, division and religious intolerance with which Christianity is spiced so abundantly. Sarvepaly Radhakrishnan, Hindu philosopher and the former vice-president of India, said in his book *The Hindu Look at Life*: "Hinduism demands from the man to think constantly over the mysteries of the world until he gets the highest revelation. While lower forms (such as idols and images) keep those people who do not want to overcome their influence in their power, the higher forms and pure devotional service are attained only by hard work and persistence... Every man has the right to choose a confession, which is closest to his heart... **Hinduism is not a sect, but the community of all those who accept the law of justice and have a sincere wish to know the truth.**"[319]

Hinduism has never persecuted and rejected other confessions. When Buddha appeared in India, many people followed him adding his teaching to the teaching of Hinduism. Buddhism did not take roots in India, but many items of Buddha's moral teaching still remain in the philosophical teaching of Vedic-Arian myth. The same happened with Christianity. In spite of numerous attempts of European missionaries to impose Christianity in India, only about two per cent of Hindus follow this teaching. But, nevertheless, Hinduism absorbed many Christian doctrines and considers Jesus Christ to be the tenth incarnation of Vishnu. Even the prophet Mohammed is enlisted among the most honorable Hindu saints in spite of the fact that Moslems cruelly invaded this country in the XI century and destroyed the most important Hindu temples and monuments.

But Krishna is considered by Christians as to be Satan, "the black one," the one who must be feared and hated. Meanwhile, Krishna, as well as any other Hindu Avatars, taught the religion of heart and soul, the religion of love and justice which is well represented in Manu's [the Forefather of mankind] law: "**Do not harm anybody either by thought, or by word, as well as by deed. Don't utter even a word that can harm your neighbor**.

The one who honors old men will be rewarded with four things: long life, knowledge, glory and power.

The one who believes can receive the pure knowledge even from an outcast, and the lesson of virtue even from a loose woman.

Do not rely on others, but rely only on yourself first of all... Only the one who can rely on himself finds the true happiness...

Every man must tell the truth, he must tell what is properly. No one must tell improper truth, as well as improper lie. This is the law..

The man must abstain from eating of any flesh. There is no big harm in it, as well as in drinking of beverages or in having sexual relations, for all these things are inherent in human nature. But abstaining from them bears a good fruit.

A learned man is cleansed by tranquility, those who abstain from wrong actions—by sacrifices, those who try to get rid of their sins—by prayer, those who know Vedas—by abstention. Everything that must be cleansed are cleansed by earth and water; a river is cleansed by its fast running, a woman who sinned in her mind—by good behavior, Brahman [a representative of the highest cast—a priest, or a teacher of Vedas]—by renunciation of the world. The parts of body are cleansed by water, human mind—by the truth, the human essence—by knowledge and abstention, reason—by knowledge."[320]

In conclusion, we can say that Hinduism is the religion which demonstrates real love for every living creature. Hinduism could get rid not only of bloody sacrifices and killing of any life if it is even still in embryo (as in an egg, for example), but of eating of corpses of poor animals which "kind and merciful" Christians devour in great quantities, talking on and on about their "great love" towards all living creatures.

5. 4. The Vedic Past of Jesus Christ

Reading the New Testament, we face a very interesting phenomenon which is called "lost years of Jesus Christ." In the Gospel, we can read about Jesus' genealogy, about his birth and, probably, about his first years of life when his family had to run away to Egypt and come back after Herod's death. Then we see Jesus (he was about twelve) among Jewish priests in the Jerusalem temple, and at last at the beginning of his devotional service when he was about thirty. About eighteen years are lost in the story about Jesus Christ, and none of the canonic authors dared to say even a word about "lost years of Jesus Christ."

It means that those who wrote the canonic texts of the New Testament either knew nothing about these "lost years," or they had certain reasons to hide the truth. And it is quite natural, for if Jesus was absent from Israel during those years and spent them somewhere abroad, not many people in Israel would know what he did there. From the other hand, Jesus, being in Gentile countries, could get their Gentile knowledge which could become "a snare" for Jews. Both of these assumptions prove the facts that Jesus was really absent from Israel during his "lost years," and that evangelists had all the reasons to hide the truth about a new teaching which Jesus brought from abroad in order it not to become "a snare." That is why it was necessary to delete any mentioning about Jesus' absence and to spoil the new teaching so that it would become "a snare" not for Jews, but for Gentiles.

Nevertheless, there are some sources that inform a curious reader about some very important and very interesting details of "the lost years of Jesus Christ." These sources say that the Great Teacher spent half of his life in India and Tibet, learning Vedas and preaching their teaching to the lowest casts which were not allowed to hear Holy Scriptures.

It turns out that old manuscripts that tell about Vedic Past of Jesus Christ are kept in the Vatican library. This fact was discovered by Sergey Alexeev, political correspondent of Russian ORT TV program who worked in India as a Gosteleradio correspondent. In May 1999, *Ogonek* magazine published his open letter to the Pope, in which he urged the pontific to promulgate the manuscripts which contained irrefutable proofs of Jesus' Vedic past, as well as his original teaching. The letter clarifies both many mysteries of Christianity and confirms our daring hypothesis that the Christianity we have now is not Christianity at all, but Paulinism, i. e. the hoax of purest water which had been inculcated into our hearts and souls by those who "spoiled the teaching of that man."

LOST YEARS OF JESUS CHRIST

The open letter to the Pope

Your Holiness!

I am a common Christian and I write you a letter for the only purpose: to correct with your help the unprecedented misunderstanding which has been existing in the Christianity for about two thousand years and not to allow this mistake to move on to the new XXI century.

You, dear pontiff, were in India. Do you remember? It was bright sunny morning, when you were brought together with your suite from Delhi to Benares for Kubcha-Mela celebration. You stood in the shadow of fig-tree on the high bank of Gang, and your secretary held big rosy umbrella over your head. We, journalists, were not far from you, at the portico, by granite ghatas changed at that day into huge phantasmagoric space, in which hundreds and thousands of half-naked bodies moved artlessly and shamelessly...

I must confess that I myself respect you and do not want even think that you belong to the number of those prelates who since the times of Rotelly have been hiding from the world the truth about Jesus' pilgrimage to India and Tibet where he spent about eighteen years, almost half of his life; the truth about sixty three old manuscripts from the monasteries of Tibet and Ladach which documentarily confirm the fact of Jesus' stay in those places. Those manuscripts are kept secretly in the Vatican library. Sixty-three Gospels practically unknown to the world that bridge the gap of sixteen years (!), made by ignorance or any other reason by apostles who wrote Jesus' biography.

Let us take the Gospel according to Luke. Let us open the chapter, in which "every year his parents went to Jerusalem to celebrate Passover. And when he was twelve years old, they came as usual to Jerusalem..." Then we meet Jesus in the same Gospel during his baptizing in the waters of Jordan "when all the people were baptized, and Jesus, having been baptized, prayed...," and "beginning His service was about thirty... "

Thus, twelve years, and then a sudden leap through the whole life, at once to the age of thirty. And then the detailed account of Jesus' life, in which almost every day up to his very resurrection is depicted scrupulously. And do not try to find Jesus' lost years in other Gospels. You will not find them there. As if somebody tore some pages out of Jesus' life.

Of course, nobody tore them out. They lie calmly under a bushel sealed with seven seals for more than one hundred years in the library of your religious department, dear pontiff. What do we know about the pages written by nameless brothers of Luke and Mark, of John and Mathew? But who are we? First of all, Nicolay Notovich, born in Odessa, orthodox Russian journalist who was the first to discover old manuscripts in Buddhist monastery of Ladach in 1887...

...In late autumn fierce draughts whiff in mountainous Ladach, and every living creature feels chilly and dreams of warmth, but Notovich was hot in that moment. Because of his guess...

"What Issa you are talking about?" "The best after twenty two Buddhas. He came to us when he was a boy and left when he became a teacher... He taught common people to love and to forgive even their enemies. He showed people that everything was as transient as this dampness in a monastery: today is cold, and tomorrow the sun would shine and it would be warm. **Issa taught that mercy is the only weapon against the evil, that the sick could be healed with a prayer...**"

"But, dear Lama, couldn't it be so that your books about saint Issa describe just well-known events that happened with Jesus in Judea? That it was some mistake which connected them with India, that Jesus has never been to India?"

"The manuscripts cannot lie. Issa came to India together with a caravan when he was thirteen. In Palestine, parents already choose bribes for boys at this age. But Issa has chosen another way... In India, he lived among different people, learned Vedas and our spiritual books, then he went to Tibet and visited Benares, Rajagricha, Rishikesha—all the holy cities of India. Can you read about it in your Gospels? Do they also know about the time Issa spent in Jaggernaut? There, he interpreted scriptures to the people of low, despicable casts who were forbidden even to come near temples. Priests nearly executed Issa for his love for common people. He had been warned about it and managed to escape."

"But why did Issa of Nazareth come to India? How do your books explain it?"

"Sure! You see, it was our Hindu sages—you call them the Magi from the East—that were the first to come and bow before the Son of God. Now he came to their motherland; came to thank them for their not giving him out to king Herod, and to show his respect to their wisdom..."

"But, dear Lama, if the books you are talking about are kept in Tibet, why do you know them so well?"

"Many people in Hemy know about them... Issa was here when he came back from Lhassa to Jerusalem. In our monastery, we have two copies of Lhassa manuscripts: one in Tibetan language, another one in Pali. One can read everything about prophet's life. What belong to God, belong to people too. I will show you books of Hemy, but only ... when you will come to us another time..."

A chance helped Notovich to come back to Hemy sooner than he could even dreamed of. On his way back to Russia, his horse stumbled suddenly; he fell down and fractured his leg. Notovich's companions decided to come back to Ladach. There they managed to find a doctor. It was the same Lama from Hemy monastery. He cured the Russian journalist. The recovery was very fast. In about three days, Notovich's leg was healed. Probably it was the magic medicine Lama used that healed journalist so fast, but, most likely, it was what the Lama brought him...

Yes, those were two thick volumes of elegant handwork with yellowed, but still strong parchment pages written in Tibetan language. The Russian guest forgot about his pain. He called for Anry, his secretary, who knew Tibetan language, and they began to read...

In spite of the impressive capacity of books, they contained not much text. There were fourteen chapters in each book, and seventeen or twenty five verses in each chapter which were similar by their stile to those written by Evangelists: two hundred forty four verses altogether. From the first to the fourth, and from the tenth to fourteenth, they were like those in which Luke, Matthew and other biographers of Christ describe his life from his birth to the age of twelve, and then from his baptizing in Jordan to his crucifixion and Resurrection. But from the fifth to the eighth...

The author of "Biography" was, obviously, someone who knew Jesus very well; most likely someone who came together with him to India with the same caravan, or, probably someone who joined him somewhere in Kashmir in the beginning of Jesus' trip and accompanied him, was near him all the sixteen years, which Jesus spent among Hindu and Tibetan lamas...

If caravan came in May, Issa could quite get to the holiday of Mahavira, the birthday of Jainism founder. Mahavira was born early than Buddha, therefore his religion is older... He could see both front and seamy sides of Jainism. The front side is sad, if one does not take into account solemn procession of naked saints along the streets of Indian towns and villages. However, they are naked only for average men; orhodox-digambars, who carry their nakedness with challenge through modern town quarters and crowds of idlers, are sure that they are dressed: dressed by the sky...

And they sure that their inner content is more important than contemplating of their cachetic bodies with unsimbolic lingams. And inside, they contain a feat, day-to-day and second-to-second feat, severe asceticism, utter renunciation from perishable property, and readiness to be wounded or even killed instead of giving pain to anybody. They do not hunt and do not fish, they do not plough a soil and even... do not breathe without covering their mouths with gauze, for one can kill earthworm in a soil, or an insect in the air... The uttermost "ahimsa!" Nonviolence elevated to the absolute.

"One year spent in the school of sorrow will teach you more than seven years, dedicated to the learning of Aristotle's doctrines..." Humankind still does not know whom belong these words. But what if they belong to him? But suppose that India became the first subject in the school of life of the future Christ?.. So, Orissa, Jagernaut, Rajagricha, Kapilavastu. Sixteen years spent in native towns of all Hindu gods and on Buddha's motherland, in the main brain centers of the most ancient world philosophies and religions, among connoisseurs of Vedas and Purans, among the saints who had indisputable authority.

Here, as unknown biographer informs, "white Brahmans taught the boy to read and to understand Vedas, and he taught them to interpret Jewish law. Here he began to heal people, to drive demons out of obsessed people and restore their minds. Shudras and waishyas [the lowest casts of Indian society] whom Issa taught to understand the Holy Scriptures despite of priests' prohibition, showed special love for the Teacher of Nazareth...

But the foreigner, the fame of whose God's gift spread throughout the whole land of Arians disgraced priests before by his words: "Our Heavenly Father does not discriminate among His children. All of them are equally dear to Him. The one, who deprives the others of their happiness, will himself be deprived of it... In the day of judgment shudras and waishyas will be forgiven for their forcible depriving of God's love during their life, but those who assumed His rights will be punished by Him..."

And now, after our clumsy statement of the sixth chapter of "The biography of saint Issa," let us recall, "...who elevate oneself, will be humiliated; and who humiliate oneself, will be elevated. Wow to you, scholars and Pharisees, hypocrites who close the God's Kingdom before people, for you yourselves don not enter and forbid those who want to enter...(The Gospel according to Mathew)."

Doesn't it make clear the most painful theological riddle? Why did such a young man whose name was Jesus have so brilliant and clear logic, so explosive and implacable argumentation, so good memory and wit, with which he won all the high priests and scholars, Pharisees and Sadducees, who provoked Christ very often and skillfully?..

And you, Your Holiness, say, "the lost years of Jesus Christ..." Here they are, found in the Hindu school in which Jesus was a Student and then a Teacher! Old manuscripts (at least sixty three) about Jesus' pilgrimage to the East are kept in the secret archive of Vatican. It was Cardinal Rotelly, one of the most influential hierarchs of Rome curia of the XIX century who informed about them.

Having come back to Europe from Ladach, Notovich, being inspired with his discovery and hoping for his good relationship with cardinal who was close to the Pope, decided to visit him at once and ask Rotelly to promulgate the manuscripts of Hemy. The answer was: "Yes, since long time we have analogical manuscripts not only in Tibetan, but also in other eastern languages in archives of the apostle library of Vatican. They were brought by Christians missionaries from Rome, from India and from China and Egypt... They really tell about some prophet Issa, who showed miracles in the East...

"But it is He! I have almost finished to write a book about Him. The Tibetan lama gave me the manuscript to make copy of it. But I need Papa's holy blessing!" Notovich said.

Rotelly suddenly touched Notovich's elbow, "Maybe you need money?" Of course, Notovich needed money desperately, for his trip to Tibet and back to Europe cost practically all his savings. "But, could there be any amount of money equal to his discovery?" Notovich wondered at strange dullness of prelate to himself, already putting on his hat and saying cool god bye to the host.

"But why? What is wrong?" he puzzled himself, making his way towards Paster boulevard to visit Jack Rene and tearing himself to pieces for his not visiting Rene before he had visited the cardinal. Jack Rene, a well-known in Europe theologian and historian, the author of sensational book *Jesus' Life*, was a good frank friend of Russian journalist. It was he, who gave Notovich the idea to widen his horizons and go to the East.

"'Leave your manuscripts to me," Rene offered to Notovich after the latter told him the story of his meeting with prelate, 'I will think out something'"

...Have you ever been betrayed by your friends? A woman does not count. One can understand her. She fell in love with another man. But a friend... There is nothing worse if one of them do what Rene had done. He held a speech in the Academy of Sciences in Paris, where he mocked his Russian friend, having called his discovery in Hemy a heretic raving of Hindu lamas, and Notovich himself naïve silly little chap who sat about to do somebody's business and could not discriminate between forgery and original...

Nevertheless, Notovich has published his book *Lost Years of Jesus Christ* at first in Paris, then in England and in the USA. (On his motherland, the book was published in a small edition only in Kiev and remained almost unnoticed). In the West, the book was sold very fast and split both priesthood and laity into two camps: those who severe criticized the young author for his making a fool of the reader with fairy tails about mythical manuscripts and his trip to Tibet and those who read the book with delight, but with the delight of a common people who read it as non-science fiction. Dr. Muller, a famous theologian and orientalist, was among those who criticized the book. Notovich even burst into tears, having read his review.

It is difficult to say, what would happen to this story; most likely, it would have been lost, disappeared among impetuous events on the boundary of two centuries, if it were not other researchers who followed Notovich's footsteps...

In 1922, swami Abedananda came to Leh to disprove Notovich. The Hindu lived in England and had the reputation of so famous scientist-orientalist as Muller. Unlike Notovich, who did not managed to bring photographic plates on which he copied the manuscripts (they were lost thorough Notovich's secretary fault), Abedananda came back to London with photographs and with the translation of *The Life of Saint Issa* from Tibetan into Bengali. It was already not difficult to translate it from Bengali into European languages. And what? The coincidence was one hundred per cent!..

Another guest who visited Hemy was Rerich N. K. When in 1925, his expedition get to Ladach and discovered the familiar manuscripts in Hemy, he uttered the phrase that surprised even his neighbors, "I knew that Jesus was in India!.." Rerich brilliantly sets forth the fragments of the same manuscript of Hemy about the life of real Jesus (it was translated by Jury Rerich, artist's son, the connoisseur of oriental languages, scientist-orientalist). The fragments coincident with the Notovich's version in all details...

And, at last, Elisabeth Caspary, a pianist from Switzerland who had nothing to do either with science or with religion, put an end to this almost detective story with *Lost Years of Jesus Christ*. He found herself in Hemy in 1939 almost by chance. Her friend, a rich philanthropist from the USA, persuaded Elisabeth to have a good time and travel a little bit. In the first day of their stay in Hemy, a young lama who relieved the former one said to her, pointing at two thick volumes, "Here are the books which testify that your Jesus was here! Take them with you, show them to your coreligionists. If you want, return them to Hemy or leave them in your church..."

But in that very day the women heard that Hitler unleashed the war in Europe. They hurried to prepare themselves to go home, and forgot to take manuscripts in haste. Since then, a lot of travelers visited Hemy, but none of them have ever seen the sacred books any more.

Why does Vatican still hide the truth about His "lost years" which He spent in India and Tibet? I think it is because the Catholic church was and is until now intolerant to Buddhism, calling it the religion without God, the kingdom of Satan, which as though prompts the man a thought about utter suicide, about elimination of his spiritual life and turning of his soul into nothingness, into emptiness...

Christianity differs from Buddhism and Hinduism in the main point: one cannot exalt the man over God and deify him. Is it so, Your Holiness? But... we both were in Benares. Tell me frankly, whether somewhere in the world people believe so zealously as in India. Yes, we have different world outlook, but let us take one mutual concept—the concept of a soul, and the belief that its "salvation" is more important than all the earthly boons and even life itself. Isn't it just mechanically repeated formula for us, and the most important rule, motive force of their entire social life for them? Doesn't it mean that we can learn something from them?

And then... prelate Rotelly asked Notivich what good did he expect from the promulgation of the book about unknown details of Jesus' life? If I were him, I would say, "And what is wrong if people know that Jesus looked like them more than they expected? Would it be any harm to my children, if they know that Jesus Christ went to school and learned Vedas and Upanishads, and probably even Plato and Pythagoras before he became the best of people, the Teacher? And why do you have the right to feed people with the history about Him, like you feed children with porridge—using a tea-spoon, measuring it out, without giving them a possibility to gain an independent understanding of everything?"

And what do you think, pontiff?

With great respect,
Alexeev S.
The spring of 1999,
India—Russia (1999, May).[321]

The letter is very interesting, of course, but a little bit strange. Nevertheless, even in spite of it, the problem posed in it is a very important one and needs a thorough investigation, for Alexeev is not the only author among those who tried to find "the lost years of Jesus Christ" in Tibet and in India. We are sure that both the biography of the Great Teacher and his teaching were rewritten and distorted either by cunning and artful Jewish Rabbis or by the Christian Church itself in order to squeeze the great moral teaching into the Procrustean bed of the cruel and heartless matrix whose name is the Bible.

CHAPTER 6.

THE MYTHS OF NOWADAYS AND A CULTURAL-ECONOMIC ENVIRONMENT

"If I wished to give you the notion of early Christian communities, I should advise you to look at the local department of the International Workers Association."

Ernst Renan

6. 1. Revolutionary Myth

As far back as in 1924, Aleksandr Tchizevsky, the great researcher both of solar winds and of those blowing in the heads of human beings, said the following: "History abounds with eloquent facts of mass hypnosis. Actually, there was no historical event with participation of human masses where it would be impossible to note hypnosis suppressing the will of a single human being.

In some cases, this hypnosis was not limited with only one group of people, but enveloped both cities and whole countries, and its traces remain in political or military parties for a long time, being passed on from generation to generation and reflected in various works of art. Thus, during the historical process and mental evolution of mankind, the hypnosis takes on special significance of paramount importance."[322]

Further he says, that "the phenomena of hypnosis, both individual and mass one, can be explained by an electromagnetic excitation of the nervous centers of one individual by the appropriate centers of another one."

But Tchizevsky did not know about the info-energy matrix which is a generator of such excitation. The matrix works in such a manner that if a certain too impressionable, politically active or religiously oriented individual (passionate personality) adjoins with it, he gets under its influence, i. e. is exposed to hypnosis, about which Tchizevsky spoke.

And then, in his head, in which not only solar, but a lot of other winds blow, appears a great "humane" idea to "save" humankind. This "savior" does not think at all of what people whom he is going to "save" think of it. Such a person, as a rule, begins with looking for an "enemy" which either tempts the man or usurps and suppresses the natural rights and freedoms of citizens. He starts impetuous activity, creates his "original and solely correct" doctrine, gets disciples and followers and begins to "save." An enemy, all those who are not satisfied with and don't want to accept the "salvation," as well as the culture of peoples which have got in authority of the "savior," are physically destroyed, and the states won by him are included into the structure of his empire.

So it was and so it will be, so long as people are in the authority of the matrix, which is called the Bible. Christianity, Islam, Marxism, Leninism, Fascism—all of them are soul-mates of one matrix. It is not without a reason that Ernst Renan advised to look at socialist organizations of that time in order to understand what Christianity was.

Engels, by the way, also noticed that strange coincidence. "'Both Christianity and working socialism,' he said in his work *The History of the early Christianity*, 'preach oncoming "salvation" from oppression and poverty. Christianity places this "salvation" beyond the limits of life, after death, on heavens; socialism places it in this world, representing it as transformation of a society. Both movements are pursued and suppressed, its followers are despised, and the exclusive measures of punishment are applied to them. At that, the first ones are considered as enemies of a human race, while the second ones—as enemies of the state, of religion, of family and of a social order. But, despite of all persecutions, or even due to them, they stride forward, victoriously and inevitably.'"[323]

Thus, the fact that all above mentioned doctrines or religious-ideological systems (or even cultures, and it is possible to name them cultures, for they have all the attributes of cultures and create their own space distinct from that of other cultures) have common features and represent by themselves only modifications of bloody myth about tribal Jewish God-butcher-filicide Jehovah.

Both Christianity and other religious-ideological systems "cast" in one matrix, therefore it is easy to prove the identity of all these systems. The basic ideas of all these systems are: the idea of sin (racial inferiority, race of predators [according to Pavlov, one of the outstanding theorists of maximalism of the XIX century], infidels, non Christian etc.); the idea of an enemy (Satan, Devil, Serpent, class enemy, enemy of the people, Jews, Arabs, globalization etc); the idea of the Last Judgment (world revolution, blitzkrieg, holy jihad etc.); and at last, the idea of the brilliant future (the land flowing with milk and honey, God's kingdom, paradise, eternal life, communism, triumph of Arian race, triumph of "utmost justice," New World Order, etc.).

All these systems had been inculcated into the cultures of other people in a forcible way, therefore the "salvation" turned out to be destruction for tens of millions of people. Recollect the Jews winning "the land flowing with milk and honey" and what atrocities they did in the name of their God-butcher-filicide Jehovah. Recollect inquisition trials which in the name of the Father, the Son and the Holy Spirit burned alive and tortured about 9.000.000 human beings. Recollect a revolutionary terror and 12.000.000 tormented and killed in the name of victory of the world revolution. Recollect Stalin and his struggle with "the people's enemy," victims of which became more than 20. 000.000. Recollect Jewish massacres, which were performed by orthodox Christians; recollect them to disemboweling pregnant Jewish women and sewing up dead cats inside. Recollect the fascism with its concentration camps, gas chambers and Jewish holocaust with 8.000.000 Jews killed by Germans in their struggle for a "cleanliness of race." Recollect the murder of 1,5.000.000 orthodox Armenians by Turkish Moslems; recollect execution of several thousands Moslems by orthodox Serbs. Recollect Korea and Vietnam, Hiroshima and Nagasaki, Afghanistan and Chechnya; recollect America, at last, and her weeping over thousands of citizens lost under the ruins of the Twins of the World Trade Center in New York supposedly in the name of the triumph of Moslem "utmost justice."

Recollect and keep silent for a minute, keep silent and think that one cannot live like that any longer, that one must not to be guided by double standards and double morals; one can not, speaking of love and mercy, hate the whole world and kill innocent people. Just understand that it is time to think and to understand that we realize man-hating imperatives of the cruel, stupid and heartless matrix which determines all cultural-historical processes because we believe in this matrix and build our life according to its laws. The final item of the matrix realization is the Last Judgment, and we have already begun to carry it out.

You see, if to look at the history of mankind, one can notice that **"all civilizations and nations develop themselves according to the same model, and the structure of such a model was known in a deepest antiquity which suggests that humankind repeated this model many time."**[324]

And we have already repeatedly pointed to this fact, asserting, that the Bible is such a model, or the matrix. Budyon, M. A., the author of the book *Hitler and Jesus*, also believes that "the model description, which is rather accessible to the mass reader, is contained in the first chapters of the book of Genesis (but not only in it), and one can denote it by three key terms: 1) the Flood, 2) the Babylon Tower, 3) Sodom and Gomorrah.

The Flood is a global catastrophe (the Last Judgment) which though is shown in the Bible as an exceptionally natural phenomenon takes place much more often than a social one. The basic rule of behavior during the Flood is "everyone for oneself," but only the one who is lucky survives in it. Before and during the Flood, people are estranged most of all, therefore, after stabilization, the period of a unification of human mass begins; its goal being to carry a social project with a strong shade of Utopia, destined to lift civilization levels to a qualitative higher stage. The model of behavior at such a time is "Let us be like Gods." Human mass is required to make sacrifices, and it does.

After the crash and destruction of the Tower there comes the epoch of Sodom and Gomorrah—a rather stable period with highly developed commodity-money relations, though at the expense of all the rest. The rule at the time of Sodom is "look for a profit wherever you can." The degree of estrangement between separate individuals increases, but still fresh memory of the Flood makes individuals to respect, at least, the interests of his neighbors and to obey the law. It is clear that early or later (it happens quite early and rather unexpectedly as a rule) "the commodity-money relations" go too far and there comes the next Flood. Both Christianity and national-socialism have repeated such a model of development."[325]

The same model has also been repeated by the revolutionary myth, created by Lenin on the sample of Judaic matrix, in which, as we showed above, the detailed plan of this myth had been depicted.

As far back as in the XIX century, future lord Beaconsfield repeatedly warned Benjamin Disraeli[326] about the existence of "the plan of revolution." Moreover, Disraeli has unambiguously pointed the Jews as organizers of the future revolution. Reed Douglas says: "The whole century, past from the time of his clearest warning, has proven his correctness. Whichever sources it could be, in the middle of the XIX century the organized world revolution was supervised by the Jews and continued to be supervised by them at least up to 1920th years."[327] Douglas believes that this supervision lasts out in the most complete form up to our days.

The Russian revolution was, thus, the continuation of the idea of Jewish domination over the world which, within long centuries, had been inspired by both Talmud and Cabbala.

As far back as in 1869, Bacunin[328], as well as Disraeli did in 1846 and in 1852, pointed out the Jews to be leaders of the world revolution, believing that it was the Judaism and Cabbala influence that had perverted the idea of the world revolution. His *Polemic Against the Jews* (*Polemique Contre les Juifs*), the article written in 1869, was directed mainly against the Jews inside the International[329], and, as far as we know, it was the possible cause of his exclusion out of this organization in 1872.

After that, the world revolution has acquired the forms of the "Communist Manifest" by Karl Marks, which planned the creation of a totalitarian state based on slavish labor and on "the confiscation of human freedoms." The change of management and new goals predetermined the course of events in the XX century.

This revolution "has been finished with the greatest Jewish triumph and unprecedented raging of Jewish vengeance. There was nothing like that either in Old Testament times or in later times, and it [the revolution] had been prepared, organized and directed by the Jews who grew up in areas of talmudic ghettos. **It is the historical fact, authentic and incontestable, the most significant one in the whole history of Zion which makes clear events of the past and give the key to understand the future**. In our century, these events gave a new, or to be exacter, true meaning to the word "revolution": endless destruction until the final fulfillment of the Jewish "Law."[330]

But what reasons could induce east Jewry to make mass transition to the camp of revolution? Most likely, it was the political act of the Jewish government which had been transferred from Spain to Poland and gone underground after the division of Poland in 1772. The consideration of events in this historical perspective reveals three goals of grandiose conspiracy.

Firstly, the revolution was the necessary means to stop the process of emancipation, which promoted the assimilation of Jews in the West, and, thus to restore authority of the Jewish ruling sect. Secondly, Jews could use the revolution to take revenge upon Christianity for their proscription from Spain. Thirdly, the revolution, with its inevitable bloody victims, was called to promote the execution of the Law which had ordered to ruin and physically destroy "Gentiles" for the sake of the triumph of "the elected God's people", or, at least, of a ruling sect using this fraudulent term.

The revolutionary movement got its ideas from Marx, which, despite of their "dialectic" materialism, were rooted in the distant past of the small people which the theorist of revolution undoubtedly belonged to. "'This teaching,' Geidar Jemal' says, 'is certainly borrowed from abrahamic tradition, for it is presented both in Christianity and in Islam. Marx, as it is known, was a Jew. He was devoted in internal meaning of Abrahamic tradition, besides, he had passed through very complex phases of spiritual development. He was the son of a Rabbi, but he studied German philosophy, which is rooted in religious mysticism, in Luther's struggle against Catholic establishment and so on. That is, Marx's personality has concentrated in itself as in a focus the beams of many teachings. Therefore, his ideology was so important, so complex and so strained that it gave rise to the great amount of branches which, actually speaking, have created a variegated political palette of Marxism.'"[331]

As you can see, even Geidar Jemal', the theorist of Islam, has noticed that this teaching [Marxism] is borrowed from Abrahamic tradition since it is present both in Christianity and in Islam. This fact confirms our thesis that all the Western religious and revolutionary movements went out from one source, from the "Abrahamic tradition" which had been originated in the Bible. And all of them are rested upon innumerable corpses of innocent dead people and float in their blood. This is the way the matrix works.

Anna Geifman says: "In reality, breaking off all the obvious connections with religion, Jewish radicals have made only external substitution of concepts, simply adapting the traditional messianic world outlook to a new historical situation and modern intellectual norms. Old beliefs have been expressed in a new and slightly changed form which is probably noticeable especially in Marx's disposition and basic points of his historical concept.

Marx, being a materialist who denied all the spiritual values, just slightly changed the idea of Israel Messiah leading Jewish people to a terrestrial paradise into the doctrine according with which a new "elected people," proletariat, would deliver the world from injustice and oppression.

This changing of familiar concepts in the spirit of atheistic view on the world (that included also the Marxist definition of a class, instead of persons, as sole active participants of historical process) appeared extremely attractive to many Russian Jews. They begun to fill up the lines of radicals which quantity was directly proportional to a degree of distribution of Marxism at the end of the XIX century in Russia."[332]

It is quite interesting and somehow strange that not only villains and scums of the earth took part in revolutionary movement. There were good, educated people among its participants. Those people were probably too sensitive, too thin-skinned and vulnerable; therefore, they had too delicate perceptions of roughness, dirt, platitude, ugliness and other imperfections of the world.

In different epochs, such ideas were supported by various philosophical concepts that formed the world outlook of a person who had already been possessed by the thirst of public activity. And, having armed himself with the schemes describing the imperfections of the world order, as well as the way of its correction, such a man begins to struggle with social-political, religious and other foundations, trying to break them in order to change the world according to his taste (the most noble, of course).

And, most likely, there exists a connection between unrealizable ideas of utopists and their inability to look inside themselves. **The more unrealizable is the utopia they try to embody in life, the more they are subjected to the fear of loneliness. That is why they are always ready to do everything in order a paradise just to loom on a horizon.**

That is why, even in spite of the fact that the promised end of the world and long awaited "God's kingdom" is postponed each time again and again, we persistently do not wish to recognize that our Christian Church deceives us, and again we continue to wait with a great hope, as though we are afraid to lose our unsettled state, our fears, our aspiration for a better life which, actually, makes sense of our existence, and for the sake of which we are ready to beat, to kill and to destroy everything in the world for the sake of "salvation," for the sake of the "brilliant future," for the sake of the triumph of the "utmost justice."

The revolutionaries-terrorists frequently used Christ's teaching for justification of their actions. They considered him to be "the first revolutionary" who also tried to struggle with an existing regime.

Anna Geifman says: "Mariya Benevskaya was a Christian, and she never parted with the Gospel (Savincov B. "Memoirs of a terrorist," 40, 92, 194—196.). Ivan Calyaev, nicknamed Poet by his comrades, composed prayers in verses, glorifying the Almighty. Egor Sazonov, being in a prison, explained his ideas in the letter to his parents, 'My revolutionary-socialist believes had merged together with my religion... I am sure that we, socialists, continue Jesus Christ's work, who taught of brotherly love between people... and who died as a political criminal for people... The Christ's demands are clear. Who executes them? **We,**

socialists, want to execute them. We want the "Christ's kingdom" to come on the earth... When I heard my teacher saying, "Take the cross and follow me"... I could not refuse my cross.'"[333]

Everybody knows what methods have been used to realize these "noble and high" goals directed on establishing the "Christ's kingdom" on the earth. Everybody also knows that the real goals of revolution had nothing to do either with local conditions or to the wishes of workers, for the sake of whom it was ostensibly made. A revolution needs destruction itself to destroy all the lawful governments in the world and to replace them with new authority and new rulers.

The fact that Talmudists should become these new rulers is visibly clear from the very Talmudic essence of the Russian Revolution and from obviously Talmudic goals of the "world revolution." Its main goal is the literal execution of the Law: "You will dominate above all the peoples, but they will not dominate above you... Your Lord God will put you above all the peoples of the earth."

The fact that the main goal of Russian revolution was the literal performance of the Jewish Law had been confirmed by the terrible and bloody events which showed to the whole world that it "had been finished with the greatest Jewish triumph and completely unprecedented wave of Jewish vengeance."

The leader of this "completely unprecedented wave of Jewish vengeance" was well-known to everybody "the kindest and the most human" man in the world Vladimir Ulianov-Lenin who, by the way, was also a Jew. "He was born on April 22, 1870 from the Jewish mother and father and represented by himself a complex mixture of Russian and Tatar bloods."[334]

Just look what an angry message "the kind" grandfather Lenin wrote to Zinoviev, the chairman of Petrograd's[335] council: "To comrade Zinoviev and to other members of CC (Central Committee). Also to Lashevich. Comrade Zinoviev, just today, we have heard in CC, that in Peter [Petrograd] workers wanted to return a mass terror for the murder of Volodarsky, and that you (not personally, but together with the representatives of Petrograd's CC) have held them back from it. I protest resolutely! We compromise ourselves: we threaten with a mass terror even in CC resolutions, but in practice, we impede quite correct revolutionary initiative of masses.

It is im-pos-si-ble! Terrorists will consider us to be milksops. **It is necessary to encourage the energy and mass character of terror against counterrevolutionaries**, especially in Peter... Hi, Lenin..."[336]

The order had been given and "the red terror" began. *The*

Encyclopedia of Crimes and Catastrophes states the following: "In Kiev, for example, those who were being shot were made to lie down, their faces pressed against the floor, on a bloody mass covering it. Then they were shot at a nape so that their skulls were smashed. They were made to lie down one on another one who had just been shot. They let out those who had been planned for execution in a garden and arranged a hunt for people there.

Odetta Kirn, French authoress, who considered herself to be a communist, visited prisons in Sevastopol, Kharkov and Moscow. In her memoirs, she wrote that one of female prisoners had told her about such a hunt after women even in Petrograd (she refers this apparently improbable fact by the year 1920!). In the cell, there were 20 more women-counterrevolutionaries together with that woman. At night soldiers came and took them away. Soon the inhuman shouts were heard, and in a window facing the courtyard prisoners saw all those women put on a cart. They were taken in a field and ordered to run away, guaranteeing to save life of the one who would be the first. Then all of them were killed...

In Bryansk, as S. M. Volkovsky testifies in his memoirs, there was a custom to fire a shot at a prisoner's back after interrogation. In Siberia they broke prisoner's heads with an iron hammer ... In Odessa, as one simple woman testifies in her evidences, "to the courtyard under my window, Checa[337] officers brought a former agent of detective police. They butchered him with a club and a rifle butt. They butchered him more than an hour, and he asked for mercy all the time ..."

Petrograd's newspaper *Revolutionary Business* informed the following details of execution of 60 people on Tagantsevsky case: "The execution was made at one of the railway stations of Irinovskaya railway. In the early morning, the arrested were brought to the station and made to dig a grave. When the grave was half ready, everybody was ordered to undress. They began to shout, to howl and to cry for help. The part of the doomed were pushed down into the grave and raked with fire. Another part were driven on the heap of dead bodies and killed in the same way. Then the grave, where both alive and wounded were groaning, was covered up with earth..."

P. Olechnovskaya was sentenced to death for a trifling act which was ridiculous to punish even by imprisonment. In no way they could kill her. Seven bullets hit her head, throat and breast. Her body was trembling. Then Kudryavtsev (Checa officer who became a communist recently and was very zealous), put his hands on her throat, tore up her blouse and began to twist and to crash her neck-bone. The girl was not even 19 years old...

There were also women among revolutionary-executioners. S. S. Maslov, the old activist of the Vologda cooperation and the member of the Vologodsky region Constituent assembly, tells about Rebecca Plastinina (Maisel), a local female executioner (who was not a professional), former medical assistant. She has killed 100 people with her own hands. Interrogations were held in railway carriages. Then, people were taken out and there just at the carriages they were executed. At interrogations Rebecca struck the accused in the face, shouted, and gave brief and frantic orders: "To execution! To a wall!"

There are also memoirs about the activity of that Plastinina-Maisel' (who was the wife of notorious Kedrov) in the Arkhangelsk region in spring and summer of the year 1920. "After ceremonial funeral of empty, red coffins, Rebecca's carnage of old party enemies began. She was a Bolshevik. This mad woman, on whose head hundreds of wretched mothers and wives send damnations, has surpassed all the men of Checa in her rage.

She recollected all small insults caused to her husband's family and literally crucified this family; those who were not killed physically were killed morally. Being cruel, hysterical, and mad she had thought that white officers[338] wanted to tie her to a tail of a horse and to let the horse gallop.

Having believed in her fiction, she went to Solovetsky monastery and together with Kedrov, her new husband, was in charge of a massacre there! Then she insisted on returning of all arrested by Eidook's commission from Moscow, and they were brought away part by part on a steamship in Cholmogory, burial-vault of Russian youth, where, having been undressed, they were killed on barges and sunk in the sea...

"In Kiev Lettish Latsis was in charge of Checa. Such monsters as Avdochin, "comrade Vera," Rosa Shvarts and other girls were his assistants. There were about fifty Checa stations here, but the most terrible were three of them. One was situated in Ecaterininskaya street 16, another one in Institutskaya street 5. In one of the station's basements (I do not remember exactly in which one) there was arranged something like a theater, where chairs were placed for those who liked bloody shows, and executions went off on the stage.

After each successful shot, the audience shouted "bravo," "encore," and glasses of champagne were served. Rosa Shvarts herself killed several hundreds of people who were pressed into wooden boxes so that only their heads were outside. But shooting the targets was only trifling amusement for those girls and did not stimulate their deadened nerves. They demanded pungent feelings: they put out eyes with needles or burned them out with a cigarette, or they hammered nails under peoples' fingernails. When it was impossible to stifle heart-rending cries of tormented people, Rosa gave an order, "Fill his throat with molten tin lest he squeal like a pig!..." And this order was carried out to the letter...

In Odessa, Vera Grebenshcicova killed 700 people. They used battleships "Sinop" and "Almas" for executions. They fastened people to thick boards with chains and slowly moved them, their legs forward, into a ship furnace...

There was a sadist Orlov in Moscow who specialized in killing boys whom he dragged out of houses or caught in streets.

In Kiev, a victim was put into a box together with decomposing corpses and told that he would be buried alive. The box was buried and dug out in half an hour. After that, an interrogation was held. It is no wonder that people went mad and gave any false evidences." (The memoirs of prince Zivachov N. D. March of 1917—January of 1920).

"Snow on a courtyard is red and brown. Everything is dashed with blood around. They have arranged snow-melter. There was a lot of firewood and they burned heaps of it. Snow-melter caused terrible bloody streams. A stream of blood poured over a courtyard and flew out on a street, across to nearby places. They began to hide evidences hastily. They opened a hatch and drained this dark terrible snow, alive blood of those who has just been alive." (Mel'gunov, T. *The Red Terror in Russia*. Moscow, 1992). ...

"However usual is "the work" of executioners, a human nervous system can not withstand heavy duty. That is why executioners do their "work" mainly in an intoxicated condition. Such a condition is necessary when many people are slaughtered. In Butirskaya prison even the administration which was accustomed to executions, always used drugs (cocaine etc.), when so-called "commissar of death" came to take away his victims and it was necessary to call the doomed from their cells.

And, nevertheless, an executioner's psyche did not always withstand the bloody duty. The report of the Red Cross workers tells about Avdochin, Checa commandant, who sometimes complained about his work and confessed to nurses, "Sister, I feel bad, my head burns... I cannot sleep... The whole night I am tormented by dead men..."

"'When I recollect the faces of Checa members Avdochin, Terechov, Osmolov, Nikiforov, Ugarov, Abnaver or Gusig, I am sure,' one of the nurses writes, 'that they were mad people: sadists, drug-addicts, people devoid of a human appearance...'"

If one compares the methods used by both revolutionaries and by ancient Jewish leaders to fight against dissidents, one will notice their astonishing similarity which proves the fact that all of them were guided by the same matrix, the name of which is the Bible. Just compare the deeds of Biblical characters to those described above: "And he lifted up his face to the window, and said, Who is on my side? Who? And there looked out to him two or three eunuchs. And he said, Throw her down. So they threw her down: and **some of her blood was sprinkled on the wall, and on the horses: and he trode her under foot**. And when he was come in, he did eat and drink [it is after he had just cruelly killed a woman!], and said, Go, see now this cursed woman, and bury her: for she is a king's daughter. And they went to bury her: **but they found no more of her than the skull, and the feet, and the palms of her hands** [he just had torn her into peaces]. Wherefore they came again, and told him. **And he said, This is the word of the Lord** [just imagine that God, who is Love, orders to tread a woman under one's feet and to tear her into pieces!], which he spake by his servant Elijah the Tishbite, saying, In the portion of Jezreel shall dogs eat the flesh of Jezebel: And the carcase of Jezebel shall be as dung upon the face of the field in the portion of Jezreel; so that they shall not say, This is Jezebel. (Second Book of Kings 9: 32-37)."

In such a way, with the power of sword and fire, as it was in times of ancient Jewish kings and of inquisition, the Judaic-Christian revolutionary idea of "salvation," the idea of communist paradise which had been preached by Judaic-revolutionary messiah V. Lenin in the spirit of best traditions of the Jewish prophets was embodied in life. While Jewish prophets deceived their fellow countrymen promising forthcoming Messiah's advent and establishing of the "God's kingdom," "grandfather" Lenin shamelessly deceived simple-hearted Russian people, promising forthcoming advent of communism.

At the mass meeting which took place on the 1st of May, 1919, he announced: "The majority of the present at this meeting who are not older then thirty, will see the heyday of communism!" As you remember, Jesus Christ said the same to the same simple-hearted Jews: "Many of standing here will not die until they see the Son of God coming in His great power..."

This bloody bacchanalia took off the lives of more than ten millions of Russian citizens. Cuts, A. S. says: "Five or six millions people died of famine. Two and a half million were killed during World War I, and from two to seven million (the figures differ in different sources) were killed during the civil war. About two million highly-educated people had to leave Russia. **Thus, by the death of the greatest terrorist in the world in 1924, the population of Russia has decreased by about fourteen million people on comparison with the year 1913.**"[339]

Once Gorky, a Russian revolutionary writer, asked Lenin, "Vladimir Il'ich, do you feel sorry for people?" "It depends on what kind of people they are, the leader of world proletariat answered, if they are clever, I do. But..., there are few clever men among Russian people. If one finds any suitable man, he is either a Jew or the one with an impurity of the Jewish blood."[340] Perhaps for this reason Jews occupied all the key positions in an international Lenin's team, which had proclaimed the World Revolution to be its goal.

Josef Dzhugashvili (Stalin)[341] (a Georgian peasant, who was born in 1879, professed orthodox Christianity, which he studied in a theological seminary) took the bloody baton of "destruction" of the old world from Lenin in order to build the new world of a "light" communist future. Evidently, this might-have-been orthodox priest learned God-butcher-filicide Jehovah's lessons which he got at the theological seminary very well. Having ascended to the peak of his power, Stalin began to apply these lessons in practice.

As a result, the cruel and bloody dictatorship constructed in a complete conformity with the structure of the matrix, whose name is the Bible, has been created. Only names were changed: "the father of the peoples Stalin" instead of "the heavenly father Jehovah," works of Stalin and other ideologists of a new religion of "destruction" instead of the Bible and the works of the holy fathers of the church, portraits of Marx, Engels, Lenin, Stalin and the members of Politburo instead of icons, a five-pointed star instead of a cross, and flags instead of gonfalons.

An "enemy of the people," which works for all imperialist secret services simultaneously and constantly conspires both against the "father of the peoples" and against all Soviet people, was invented instead of the image of "enemy" (Satan, Devil, the animal, the serpent, the evil one). That "enemy" was so terrible that he cast a spell upon millions of soviet citizens who had to be cruelly and mercilessly exterminated in order them (Lord forbid!) not to do anything that could harm both the "father of the peoples" and all the Soviet people.

Nobody knows how many human sacrifices had been made to the cruel and bloodthirsty tyrant who considered himself to be God. And, since God demanded human sacrifices, the Soviet people showed unprecedented enthusiasm in this business and put to death tens of millions people, thus, having outdone not only Jews, but even the greatest inquisitors of the middle ages.

Cuts, A. S, in his book *Jews. Christianity. Russia*, says: "After forty years of discussions, the question about the number of victims remains opened. In the end of 1930th, the number of prisoners was from three to ten million people.[342] According to Khrushchev[343], nineteen million were repressed and seven million killed during 1935—1940. The GULAG (the abbreviation of Glavnoye Upravleniye of Ispravitelno-trudovykh Lagerey. (Chief Administration of Corrective Labour Camps)) reached its peak in 1950th. At that time, its population was from three to fifteen million people. According to the understated data of KGB[344], two and a half million people were in camps and about the same number of people were exiled. **According to the last Volcogonov's estimations, twenty one and a half million people were lost in the result of Stalin's repressions during 1929—1953.**"[345]

With Stalin's death, the era of "great" inquisitors, tyrants and revolutionaries-destroyers which began at those distant times when Rabbi Saul (apostle Paul) "spoiled the teaching of that man," having put stealthily the "apple of discord" to the world, ended. That tasty and juicy "apple" represented by itself the interpretation of the Judaic myth of "destruction" that brought all those "evil spirits" into the world. Those "evil spirits," in the guise of "saviors," began to do their black deeds, condemning tens of millions human sons and daughters to terrible agonizing deaths. It became possible, thanks to Khrushchev, who repudiated Stalin's tyrannical excesses in his famous "Secret Speech" at the 20th party congress in 1956.

At the congress, Khrushcev read the report on a cult of Stalin's personality on its own behalf, as a simple delegate. The Report was considered to be a confidential one and was read in the night of the 25th of February. The delegates were shocked, having heard about Lenin's will, about crimes of "the leader and the teacher of all the peoples," about faked plots against him, about his military incompetence that resulted in the catastrophe of 1941—1942, and about other deeds of "the ingenious successor of Lenin's work.

The Khrushchev's report was selective, incomplete and chaotic. Instead of common Russian people, Communist Party members were announced to be the victims of Stalin's personality cult. The key question on the Communist Party criminal responsibility had kept secret. It was spoken just about deviations from "Lenin's norms of life," these norms being idealized and the facts about Lenin's terror in Russia being concealed. Collectivization, famine of 1932—1933, millions of people who died in labor camps or were killed as a result of repressions have been crossed out of the list of Stalin's crimes.

The exposure of Stalin's personality cult was the very event that has finished with a mass terror of Judaic model, raised to the rank of state policy. Having suffered such shattering defeat from the "hand" of system which had created it, the matrix hid itself, retreated into the shadow, only sometimes reminding about itself by means of the individual terrorist acts. Having saved its power the matrix began a new stage of destruction and terror, now in a "fiery" clothes of Islamic jihad, under the cover of which the World Elite began its triumphant procession with unprecedented terrorist acts of September 11th, 2001. Those terrorist acts took away the lives of thousands of American citizens and plunged the world into the atmosphere of fear and hopelessness.

6. 2. National-Socialist Myth of Adolph Hitler

Michael A. De Budyon [earlier quoted by us] drew an analogy between Hitler and Jesus Christ, considering both of them to be initiators of a monstrous wave of terror and violence which had arisen as a result of ideologies created by them. In his book *Hitler and Jesus*, Budyon says about Hitler the following: "The era of his earthly deeds was, as well as that of Christ's, rather and rather short. His adepts considered him to be an embodiment of God on the Earth. Analyzing the deeds of both of them, one can notice the powerful influence they have over human masses. But the self-destruction of any structure means also the destruction of the causes of its occurrence, for if there are no conditions for the phenomenon occurrence, also there is no phenomenon. And if to go further and to assume that Christ's Second Advent would have any reasonable sense, this sense had to be consisted in creation of conditions for guaranteeing of the end (which is seen and realized by everybody) of the era, which we call Christian.

The man who tried to put it into practice was Adolph Hitler, and his whole life in its key and the most significant moments is only recurrence of the Christ's earthly way known to us from the Gospel. And not only terrestrial. **The social consequences of Christ's deeds which were felt during first fifty years after his death, were completely identical to those we noticed fifty years after Hitler's death**. And this analogy is even more indicative and more amazing.

Christ has come in order to mix everything. Greek and Roman beautiful men and women embodied in sculptures [almost all of them were destroyed by Christians] have conceded a place to midgets, to humpbacked, stinking, crazy, insane impotents and necrophils, the motto of those was: not to wash, not to shave themselves, not to be married, and not to work. The same has happened in intellectual sphere. The antique science which was absolute and true in overwhelming majority of its representations has been replaced with so many false sciences that the whole encyclopedias are devoted to their fluent review now. Science was moving away from a Christian grip long and painfully, and the quantity of intellectuals killed by church has considerably exceeded the number of a different sort of saints, "God's fools" and other cretins and degenerates who had been liquidated at different, as a rule, casual circumstances. Every intellectual should know and remembered about it, and especially those who by virtue of a habit still celebrates Christmas and Easter even not believing in this bosh. Unfortunately there still a lot of them."[346]

We, to a great regret of Michael De Budyon, are such people, for we do not consider Jesus Christ to be the author of that destructive Judeo-Christian ideology which became the cause of such destructive consequences. The author of this ideology was, as we have already proven, Rabbi Saul (apostle Paul), who "had spoiled the teaching of that man" and organized the Christian movement, having attached it to the Jewish matrix, the name of which is the Bible. And it was the very teaching that Adolph Hitler used as his guiding line. It does not matter what he called it, but it was the same, very familiar Jewish matrix.

And again, we collide with a rather interesting phenomenon here. All of Hitler's spiritual predecessors, in fact, have grown from

Christianity. And those who digressed from it at the certain stage of their activity came back to one of its varieties at the end of life.

One of such predecessors of the future Fuhrer was Richard Wagner. The last composer's opera, which Hitler has seen, was "Parsifal" staged one year before Wagner's death. It was just because of it that in due time Nietzsche, having decided that in the evening of his life "old Chaliostro" had surrendered to Christianity, broke finally with Wagner. "Parsifal" had rendered such a powerful influence on Hitler that he exclaimed, "I shall create a religion... The Religion of "Parsifal"!" And those were not just empty words because after that event, the special SS[347] department which was being engaged in the search of the Grail[348] down to the last days of national-socialism existence, was created.

Houston Chemberlen (1855-1927) had such a strong belief in Fuhrer that he joined NSDAP[349] at the age of seventy, remaining, nevertheless, quite consecutive Christian. Being an indisputable intellectual, admirer of Nietzsche and Wagner, he has written the famous book *The Foundations of the XIX Century*, in which panegyrics to the Arian race were mixed with the accusations of the pernicious role of the Jews. While writing the book, Chemberlen was confronted with a problem which appeared to be insoluble. It was necessary to connect three things: the highest Arian virtues, racial alienation of the Jews, and Jesus Christ's Jewry—this "greatest man," as Chamberlen named him. He solved this problem excellently. He has announced Jesus Christ to be an Arian without even a "drop of the Jewish blood." Also, king David has been announced to be an Arian. Hitler, most likely, had not read the Chemberlen's monography, but from conversations with him he firmly acquired the fact that "Christ was an Arian."[350]

Special attention must be paid to Jorg Lants, whom Hitler met in Vienna. Lants was not just Christian, he was Christian fanatic who had changed Jesus Christ's ideological heritage in order to connect it with a racist world outlook. He spent six years in Heiligen Kreuz (Holy Cross) Abbey, where at first he was a novice and then a monk. After his exile from a monastery, Lants turned to Protestantism. After his acquaintance with the methods of "salvation" offered by Christian ideology, he, in his uncountable works, began to offer and to propagandize such methods of purge of the Arian world from "race defective people" as a forced cremation, conversion to slavery, using as a cartage. All his works are full both of adoptions from the Old and New Testaments and of stiff analogies of Biblical events with those of his time.

One more man, whom we should mention is Otto Wainiger. In spite of the fact that he was a total-lot Jew, Hitler mentions him in his "Table Speeches," and Ekkart—in his "Bolshevism from Moses to Lenin." Wainiger's book *The Sex and the Character* was, probably, the most popular book of the XX century. Hitler lived in Vienna at that time, and, of course, he read it. Moreover, the research concerned the problems the Fuhrer was always interested in.

Wainiger has adopted his philosophy from Shopengauer and Wagner, whom he called "the greatest man after Christ." That is why, chapter XI of *Mein Kampf* repeats in the simplified form all the conclusions made by Wainiger in the chapter "Jewry." **Having been familiarized with the bases of Christianity and with other religious teachings during his study at a Catholic school, Hitler has noticed: "All the religions are identical, regardless of how they call themselves**. They do not have the future, especially in Germany. **Whether it is the Old Testament or the New one, there is no difference: this is all the same, old Jewish cheating**. It is impossible to be a German and a Christian at the same time. It is necessary to choose between them. We need free people who feel and know that God is in them... We must tell the peasant about the things which the church has destroyed: all secret knowledge of the nature—divine, shapeless, demonic. We shall throw off the external cover of Christianity and discover the religion, peculiar to our race... With the help of peasants we shall be able to destroy Christianity, because in them, in the children of the earth, there is an original religion which is rooted in the nature and in blood."[351]

Rosenberg picked up this Fuhrer's "revelation" and went farther. He began active work on the ideological front of NSDAP. In 1930 he issued *The Myth of the XX Century*, one of the most significant books of national-socialism. The book begins with the words: "Today the world history must be written anew." Rosenberg interprets a history as the racial conflict, scooping an inspiration and citations from Chemberlen and Nietzsche. At that, Rosenberg aspires to create not simply one more political program, but a new religion: "**Today the new faith is being born: the myth of blood**. Having connected faith and blood, we defend a divine nature of the man and his integrity. His Nordic blood is the very matter that must replace and overcome all the old sacraments."[352]

Rosenberg certainly got into a passion a little bit, for "the myth of blood" was not a new religion. The faith and blood (or bloodshed, to be more precise) were successfully connected by the Christian Church long before the Third Reich, of what we had a good chance to convince ourselves in the third chapter.

Being blessed by Hitler, Rosenberg composed the charter paragraphs of the future Church of National Reich. They pre-supposed the ruthless struggle with the Christian teaching, the forbidding of the Bible and replaced it with *Mein Kampf*. The last paragraph of "the New Church" was: "In the day of its foundation, the Christian cross must be taken off from all the churches and chapels and replaced with swastika, the sole victorious symbol."[353]

It is not necessary to be very clever to notice that both theoretical, and practical sides of a fascist ideological system repeat in smallest details the deeds of the Christian Church in the period of the Middle Ages. And it is not surprising, for Adolph Hitler, as you know, heartily learned the Bible in his childhood when he studied at a Catholic school and even wanted to become a monk, but this was prevented by his father, who was very cruel and beat poor Adolph within an inch of his life. Hitler also read a lot and unsystematically, which certainly affected his world outlook. The combination of these three factors turned the future Fuhrer into a cruel and unbalanced person with well-defined sadistic inclinations, megalomania and persecution mania.

By the way, such a combination of "educational factors," namely, the cruel, imperious father, the religious education (especially its Puritan version) and unsystematic reading (especially "spiritual" literature), as the history has shown, results almost inevitably in occurrence in the man of the same qualities as the Fuhrer had, and, if such a man ascends on the top of power, he inevitably becomes a cruel and bloodthirsty tyrant. Many Roman Popes, cardinals and bishops who were at the head of inquisition, Ivan the Terrible[354], Lenin and Stalin were such people. Hitler also was such a cruel and bloodthirsty tyrant.

Thus, using many examples, we have proven the identity of religious and political-religious ideological systems. We have proven that they are in a direct and even "intimate" (as Geidar Jemal would say) connection with the Bible and its cruel, man-hating teaching, as well as their complete discrepancy to the cultural universal criteria, because "any outrage done to the man, contradicts to the logic of a human coexistence and causes events that become apparent in ominous and not always understandable way."[355]

6. 3. Cultural-Economical Environment

In the process of its development and formation, any ideological system inevitably affects all the sides of social life, changing and adjusting it to its teachings and dogmas. It works according to the principle of a Procrustean bed. It cuts everything that does not fit to it [to a Procrustean bed] from the body of a human mass and changes it [human mass] into a stump, terribly disfigured, bleeding and incapable to anything. And this very stump together with the ideological system is the very cultural-economical environment that is formed in society under its influence.

Just recall the long-suffering Jewish people during their wandering in the desert. Ordinary Jews could not make a step without Moses' knowledge and were mercilessly exterminated if they made that step wrongly. Recall the dark times of the Middle Ages, when the Roman Christian Church was the sole power in the western world, which plunged the empire into the vortex of poverty, gangsterism and religious obscurantism. Recall John Calvin[356] who turned Geneva into a theocratic state, in which all its citizens choked with the stifling atmosphere of spiritual and physical dominion of the church. Recall Lenin, Stalin, Hitler, recall what they have done with the lives of hundreds of millions of people, recall all these things and then you will understand what is a cultural-economical environment.

And if in the past a cultural-economical environment was merely the result of dominating ideological system activity, nowadays it can be created by the will of a group of people or even a single man if this man is rich enough and has an access to mass media. We even had an opportunity to become a witness of such a unique event. Just recall as in the end of the last century, the most powerful empire among those that had ever existed in the world history collapsed. If you think that it collapsed because of any natural causes, you are deeply wrong. Such systems do not collapse for no particular reason. If even the fascist system could not overpower the communist one, then just imagine what power had to be applied to break and to destroy it. But everything happened quietly, peacefully and without bloodshed.

The fact is that by that time, in the depths of certain structures situated somewhere abroad, the pattern of a cultural-economical environment had been created. Then it was successfully implanted into the body of the communist monster. This implant, like a virus, began its destructive activity and destroyed the system very fast. The state foundations were shattered, economy and agriculture were destroyed and fell into stagnation, and we found ourselves without our daily bread.[357]

And then, "the Big Brother" (who had palmed off this cultural-economical environment on us and gave us his helping hand), appeared. We grasped it and hold it until nowadays, more and more falling under the power of this handshake. But man lives not on bread alone, and together with bread, violence, pornography, disgrace and moronity poured into our hearts and souls. This dirty flow turned us into the disorderly mob of idiots unable to tear themselves away from TV sets that broadcast all this trash. The economy, according to the implanted cultural-economical environment, became the one of the new progressive types—"bazaar economy." They have squandered everything that was possible, they have squandered the most powerful country in the world, the army, the navy, the natural and human resources, the great cultural heritage, and turned it into the nation of dieing out spiritual degenerates who use [as a spiritual food] all those abominations that pour out on us from TV screens and look at us from book covers of talentless books, which tell about the adventures of bandits, militia men, perverts and mobs of different ranks.

If you think that we slander on "the Big Brother," who gives us our daily bread and money, please, read the message of a former CIA chef Allen Dales to the USA congress, in which he represented his "Plan of Destruction of the Soviet Union and Russia." This plan had been produced at the time of "cold war," but was realized only in the end of 1980th when the appropriate conditions enabled it.

Allen Dales described the plan of "noiseless war" as follows:

"Having sown chaos in Russia, we shall (imperceptibly for them) substitute their values by false ones and make them to believe in those false values. How shall we do that? **We shall find our accomplices, our helpers-allies in Russia. Episode after episode, the grandiose tragedy of destruction of the most unruly nation in the world, of final and irreversible dying of its self-consciousness will be developed**.

We shall force their social essence out of literature and art, for example. We shall train artists not to analyze and to portray those processes that take place in the depths of human mass. **Literature, theatres, cinema will depict and glorify the meanest human feelings**.

We shall do our best to support and to raise so-called creators, who will implant and drum the cult of sex, violence, sadism, treachery, i. e. all the different kinds of immorality and dissoluteness into human consciousness. We shall create chaos and confusion in the field of the state governing. We shall imperceptibly but actively and constantly promote petty tyranny and elastic conscience of functionaries and bribe-takers. Bureaucracy and official circumlocution will become a virtue. Honesty and decency will be made fun of and become unnecessary, will be turned into the remnant of the past. Boorishness and impudence, lie and fraud, drunkenness and drug addiction, beastly fear of one another and shamelessness, treachery, nationalism and animosity, first of all animosity and hatred towards the Russian people,—all of these we shall cultivate cunningly and unnoticeably.

Only a few, very few will guess and understand what is going on. But we shall place such people in a helpless situation, we shall turn them into a laughing-stock, we shall find the way to slander them and to announce to be a scum of society."[358]

Where on the earth is our self-consciousness, where is our pride for our great country, where on the earth is everything that in former times constituted intelligence, honor and conscience of our epoch? Why then we sit silently before our TV sets stupidly digesting a spiritual chewing gum, with which we are stuffed day after day, and do nothing? It is just because in order to make the Russian man to do anything it is necessary him to be shaken properly, for it is not in vain that Russian people say, "A Russian man will not cross himself until the thunder blows."

The thunder has already thundered, but a Russian man has not heard it yet. And it will be already late when he hears it, for till that time everything that still left from our country will be plundered and brought abroad, almost the entire Russia will be depopulated and turned into a raw materials-producing appendage of the USA and other high developed countries.

And Russia is really depopulated with such a rate that till the middle of the next century, only half of us will be left. This large scaled demographic catastrophe is the result of liberal reforms that were realized during "perestroika," when we began to rebuild our life according to the cultural-economical environment imposed on us by "the Big Brother."

Academic Gundarov says: "The mortality epidemic of 1990th in Russia is the result of imposing of spiritual values, which were historically and culturally alien for us. The western way of thinking, implanted in the consciousness of the Russian people, contradicts to its moral-emotional genotype, and the depopulation of the nation is the specific reaction to the alien spirituality."[359]

Now, you know what is the cultural-economical environment. And this environment has clung to our people so strongly that in order to get rid of it we have to create another monster, which could devour this environment together with its lock, stock and barrel. We have to create our Russian great-power ideological system, for without such a system Russia is like a lonely woman—she raves, pines, and suffers with dissatisfaction and instability.

"And what about our Christian Church?" you will ask. "Is it not able to become the power that will break the backbone of that vile virus? Why do we have to create some other systems if we have the ready-made Russian orthodox ideological system?

We can answer that Christianity is the religion that is rooted in the depths of the Jewish people, and it became ours because the Grand Duke Vladimir imposed it forcedly on the Russian people in 988. We could have been Moslems, for example if Vladimir would take the fancy of Islam. But the Christianity of the Byzantine type was more suitable for Duke's sovereign purposes. And we already know what happens when the cast of priests takes power.

It is not what we need. We need the group of honest, competent experts that could work out the ideology oriented not to an illusory future, but to a present day. It must be ideology which will revive in us the proud for our great Motherland and a desire to build our present life, reconstructing step by step the destroyed economy and agriculture. In the beginning, it will be difficult to do without the help of "the Big Brother," but gradually we will be able to overcome this prolonged crisis and restore the status of the great and powerful state. But where on earth we shall find so many honest people?

CHAPTER 7.

MYTH ABOUT HOMO SAPIENS

"It is time to reject all those absurdities, with which a problem of Homo sapiens formation is littered. The opinion that all ancestry species have changed into human beings is a scientific nonsense. It is even more senseless to think that they have ceased to be born since that time when some of them had mutated and become humans."

Didenco B. A.

7. 1. The Portrait of Modern Homo Sapiens

"'The paradox of our time in history,' George Carlin says, 'is that we have taller buildings but shorter tempers, wider freeways, but narrower viewpoints. We spend more, but have less. We buy more, but enjoy less. We have bigger houses and smaller families, more conveniences, but less time. We have more degrees but less sense, more knowledge, but less judgment, more experts, yet more problems, more medicine, but less wellness.

We drink too much, smoke too much, spend too recklessly, laugh too little, drive too fast, get too angry, stay up too late, get up too tired, read too little, watch TV too much, and pray too seldom. We have multiplied our possessions, but reduced our values. We talk too much, love too seldom, and hate too often. We have learned how to make a living, but not a life. We have added years to life not life to years.

We have been all the way to the moon and back, but have trouble crossing the street to meet a new neighbor. We conquered the outer space, but not the inner one. We have done larger things, but not better things. We have cleaned up the air, but polluted the soul. We have conquered the atom, but not our prejudice. We write more, but learn less. We plan more, but accomplish less. We have learned to rush, but not to wait. We build more computers to hold more information, to produce more copies than ever, but we communicate less and less.

These are the times of fast foods and slow digestion, big men and small character, steep profits and shallow relationships. These are the days of two incomes but more divorce, fancier houses, but broken homes. These are days of quick trips, disposable diapers, throwaway morality, one night stands, overweight bodies, and pills that do everything from cheer, to quiet, to kill.

It is a time when there is much in the showroom window and nothing in the stockroom. A time when technology can bring this letter to you, and a time when you can choose either to share this insight, or to just hit delete.'"

Such is the portrait of the cultural, civilized man at the beginning of the third millennium A.D. And it is like that, despite abundance of ethical and moral laws, despite abundance of religious and various cultural-educational establishments that, as it may seem, teach the man to live a reasonable and righteous life.

But actually, everything looks little bit different because there exist mass media along with religious-educational institutes. Because of their mass character and availability for the average statistical human being, mass media form their world outlook, directing it in one or another channel which is determined by the mighty of this world who own these most powerful means of influence on human mentality.

The most powerful means of such an influence is TV. TV is watched at home and at work, it is watched day and night, weekdays and days off. What wonderful things one can see in miraculous blinking of beautiful pictures of advertisements, musical clips, thrillers and soap operas, in which the rich cry and the poor laugh! The problem is that all this attractive production of show business contains a lot of scenes of murders and violence frequently seasoned with such maniacal cruelty and anatomical details that one's blood runs cold when one watches them. Therefore, a normal person tries to watch TV as little as possible. But TV is watched most of all either by those adults who have nothing to do or by children. And what do they watch there?

"'We have examined one ordinary day—one of July's Mondays,' says Olga Costenco-Popova, 'we switched on TV set early in morning, and ...

At 11. 00, on TV-6 inquisitive young onlookers could watch the series "The Streets of Broken Lanterns—3" with the following plot: on the Neva [a river in St. Petersburg] embankment the **mutilated corpse** of Sergey Jihaev is found, and on the other end of the city the whole group of businessmen together with their guardians, was **shot down. At 14. 15**, on TVC a series "Inspector Kress" and the series "My revenge is My Death" began. Ulof Petren, a **pedophilia convict**, is **killed** in a hotel room. There appears a certain Uta whose daughter Petren is **dirtily outraged. At 18. 00**, on TV-1 the series "Russia and War," and its 17th series "**Blood** on the Snow." **At 19. 45**, on TV-6 the "Road Patrol." And, with the interval 2—3 hours, more news with complete business set of **scorched corpses, dismembered bodies, accidents and catastrophes** on each channel.

On the average, according to the Russian Academy of Science education sociology center, a Russian onlooker (including children!) watches a scene of violence on TV every 15 minutes at day time and every 10 minutes in evening.'"[360]

The percentage of violence scenes from all time of broadcasting looks as following:

Murders	30, 3 %
Beatings	20, 8 %
Sexual violence	16, 7 %
Accidents	11, 3 %
Insults	9, 5 %
Group aggression (war, terrorism)	11, 4 %

During ancient times, in the Middle Ages and during subsequent centuries there was no TV, but there was a church which represented by itself and represents till now, as we have shown above, a very powerful advertising campaign that advertises a very attractive thing which is called a "salvation."

For this purpose, the church publishes the Bible, its best-seller and the main advertising catalogue. It also publishes various books and booklets distributed mainly free-of-charge, which makes church one of the main competitors of mass media. In this "holy book," a percentage ratio of scenes of violence is approximately the same as that of various ways of murders and mockeries at the man, which we can see on a blue screen. The only difference is that Jewish God-butcher Jehovah specializes on mass murders and on filicide; therefore the Bible depicts mainly scenes of mass murders and massacres.

And what does it advertise there? We looked into the main "advertising catalogue" of Christian Church and have discovered the broadest choice of means of "salvation" representing by themselves various kinds of individual and collective separation of immortal human souls from mortal bodies which by request of a "saved" person can be carried out by Jehovah, by his "son" or even by "the God's people":

1. **The Flood: Extermination of all the life on the Earth, except for Noah's family**. "And the Lord said, **I will destroy man whom I have created from the face of the earth**; both man, and beast, and the creeping thing, and the fowls of the air; for it repenteth me that I have made them. (Genesis 6: 7).
2. **Destruction of Sodom and Homorrah: "Then the Lord rained upon Sodom and upon Gomorrah brimstone and fire from the Lord out of heaven; and he overthrew those cities, and all the plain, and all the inhabitants of the cities**, and that which grew upon the ground." (Genesis 19: 24).
3. **Killing of Jude's Firstborn:** "And Er, Judah's firstborn, was wicked in the sight of the Lord; **and the Lord slew him**." (Genesis 38: 7).
4. **Killing of Onan:** " And Onan knew that the seed should not be his; and it came to pass, when he went in unto his brother's wife, that he spilled it on the ground, lest that he should give seed to his brother. And the thing which he did displeased the Lord: **wherefore he slew him also**. (Genesis 38: 10).
5. **Killing of Firstborns**: "For I will pass through the land of Egypt this night, and **will smite all the firstborn in the land of Egypt, both man and beast**; and against all the gods of Egypt I will execute judgment: I am the Lord. (Exodus12: 12).
6. **Jehovah's Attempt to Kill Moses' Son:** " And it came to pass by the way in the inn, that **the Lord met him, and sought to kill him**. Then Zipporah took a sharp stone, and cut off the foreskin of her son, and cast it at his feet, and said, Surely a bloody husband art thou to me. So he let him go: then she said, **A bloody husband thou art, because of the circumcision**." (Exodus 4: 24-26).
7. **Death Penalty for Eating Leaven**: " Seven days shall ye eat unleavened bread; even the first day ye shall put away leaven out of your houses: for whosoever eateth leavened bread from the first day until the seventh day, that soul shall be cut off from Israel." (Exodus 12: 15).
8. **Death Penalty for Worshiping Other Cods:** "He that sacrificeth unto any god, save unto the Lord only, **he shall be utterly destroyed**. (Exodus 22: 20).
9. **Death Penalty for Defilement of Sabbath:** "Ye shall keep the

sabbath therefore; for it is holy unto you: **every one that defileth it shall surely be put to death**: for whosoever doeth any work therein, **that soul shall be cut off from among his people**." (Exodus 31: 14).

10. **Cruel Killing of Jezreel**: "And he said, Throw her down. So they threw her down: and **some of her blood was sprinkled on the wall, and on the horses: and he trode her under foot**. And when he was come in, he did eat and drink, and said, Go, see now this cursed woman, and bury her: for she is a king's daughter. And they went to bury her: **but they found no more of her than the skull, and the feet, and the palms of her hands."** (Second Book of Kings 9: 32-37).

We can continue this list of "kind and merciful" ways of "salvation," and we will be not only surprised, but even horrified with that kind of inhuman refinement and cruelty which is shown by God-butcher-filicide Jehovah in the business of "salvation" of lost human souls.

All these "great" deeds are worthy of envy of the most bloodthirsty tyrants who ever tortured people and nations. None of them performed such atrocities. All of them, even taken together, are not fit to hold a candle to Jewish tribal God Jehovah, the inventor of unsurpassed torture instruments, among which we must specially note "the lake, burning with fire and sulfur" and "the winepress of God's anger," in which several billions people can be easily crushed and squeezed so that their blood will flow like a river up to horse bridles (about two meters) deep and about 170 miles long.

And this is the very God whom all of "educated" mankind trusts, considering him to be kind and merciful and hoping to receive "salvation" from his hands, crimsoned with the blood of billions killed, tortured, crushed and squeezed men, women, old men, children and even camels and donkeys. And, if anyone can prove that all these terrible and monstrous murders displayed both on TV and in the Jewish, Christian and Moslem holy scriptures correspond to cultural universal criteria, then we will have to recognize ourselves to be mad and to take refuge in a madhouse hoping that "kind and merciful" God Jehovah will show pity to the poor cripples and will not throw us to "the lake burning with fire and sulfur" in the day of the Last Judgment (when he will come to judge "both righteous and sinful").

Of course, many will not agree with us and will tell us that it is a myth, an allegory, that all these things are to be understood absolutely differently, i. e. allegorically. Instead of "killing," for example, we must think of "showing mercy." Because the murder of any human, the murder of a beastly being releases a soul, which, by accepting suffering, is cleansed by it, and, having been delivered from a mortal body, goes straight to the Most High who allows it to tear the bondages of materiality which is necessarily and inevitably belonging to the lowest nature, carry the man away into the vortex of passions which, working so, that (not only and not so much striking the body, but enslaving the spirit and subordinating it to a beastly instinct) lead it to even more terrible fall than original sin of Adam and Eva which, having avoided God's punishment, plunged them into the world of grief and suffering instead of being punished by deprivation of life which could save the imperishable soul and pull it out of its beastly receptacle, in order it will not be perished, but have eternal life. [In this paragraph, we tried to reproduce a stile of great religious philosophers. The whole book of Russian philosopher Solov'yov, V is written in such a stile].

Such a tirade can be said by great religious philosophers who can by means of their phrase-mongering justify the most abominable and the most bloody crimes of the mighty of this world. They can transform their crimes into "good" deeds so successfully that the masses of people, having accepted them, will not doubt even an instant that their "God" (Jehovah, Lenin, Stalin, Hitler) is "kind and merciful," "the father of peoples and nations" who incessantly cares for the well-being an prosperity of his people. And all the lawlessness, all the murders and repressions come from an enemy, from the evil one, from a beast, from the Devil, from Satan, from the Jews, from the globalization and from the terrorism.

So, why does the Bible, despite of its criminal and man-hating ideology, remain until now "the number one best-seller?" And why is it generally accepted as the "textbook of life" by highly educated and civilized western world? Most likely, for the reason that a bad example is contagious.

Man is such arranged that he will accept as the truth any delirium, any barbaric ideology, rather than something really valuable for the progress of human spirit because this progress requires a great deal of hard work. Crazy, fanatical ideas, on the contrary, find the quick response in initial savagery and cruelty of human hearts and souls, are adopted very quickly and give sprouts immediately.

That is why many of us experience awesome tremor and servility towards beings which are distinguished by power, cruelty and maniacal passion for mass murders. Or how, then, can we explain that people still trust in cruel and bloodthirsty God Jehovah, considering him to be kind and merciful? How can we explain that such a person as, for example, Charles Manson, the maniac-murderer and obviously mad Fuhrer of drug addicts and upholders of "pure sex," had such an influence on his admirers that they were ready to execute any of his orders, including an order to kill?

Manson was sentenced to the death penalty (later it was changed to life-term imprisonment) for the murder of the pregnant actress Sharon Tate and her six visitors, in 1969 in Los-Angeles. The most surprising thing is that madman with the tattooed swastika on his forehead is very popular, especially among young people. No other American criminal receives as many letters as the 66 year old prisoner of the High Security Corcoran State Prison. And if we have a look at Internet sites devoted to this terrible person, we shall be easily convinced that the speed of their duplication surpasses the growth rate of mushrooms after rain!

Some of Manson's songs, which are overflowing with hatred and thirst for vengeance, are used in a movie called "Helter Skelter," for producing of which 60 million dollars have been spent. The author's royalties will be paid to the relatives of the author's victims.

Even being in a prison, Manson does not suffer from loneliness. Some mysterious force attracts new and new generations of young people to him. "'There came girls with babies on their hands to visit me,' he says, 'and one of them told me 'Charlie, I shall do for you whatever you want.'"

One young woman sent him a letter, in which she wrote: "I wish you would have freed and organized a group again. I would have joined, by the way." And one teenager writes: "I worship and adore you wholeheartedly. And I shall do everything to prove it to you."

"'What sickness is it that continues to send children to me?' the maniac-murderer asks himself, and answers, 'It is your world that does it.'" Is this "Devil in flesh and blood" right? And is the sickness really hidden on our side of prison bars?[361]

Otherwise, how can we explain the passion for tortures, mockery and murder, inherent in many representatives of humankind? Or how can we explain an epidemic enthusiasm in pornography, thrillers, westerns and detective stories in which scenes of murders and violence are shown in all colours and with all anatomic details?

How can we explain this pathological interest to violence and our awesome tremor towards the one who embodies an unlimited degree of its expression and realization on practice? Strange as it may seem, but cruel and bloodthirsty God Jehovah has no fewer admirers than Charles Manson and the like.

"Our church is super! Our God is the king and the savior of all mankind! Jehovah is our wonderful Lord!"—is heard from the lips of Jewish God Jehovah's admirers. And when one asks these "saviors of mankind" to give any logical explanation of the cruel and bloody deeds of their favorite god-butcher, they recommend us to take Job as an example. He was nearly dead, broken by a paralysis and mutilated by a leprosy (with which Satan has "infected" him with the connivance of "kind and merciful" God Jehovah), but he bore silently all those mockeries and just groaned, hoping, that God, nevertheless, would show pity at him.

Then his wife advised him, "Dost thou still retain thine integrity? Curse God, and die." But he answered, "Thou speakest as one of the foolish women speaketh. What? shall we receive good at the hand of God, and shall we not receive evil?"[362]

Thus, accepting evil from God Jehovah, as well as from other tyrants and tormenters of mankind, we are ready to justify any violence, any perverted and cruel murder, we are ready to justify any massacre, if it is performed by our idol. We, because of our stupidity or probably because a deadly trouble has not touched us yet, cannot see the true face of our "kind and merciful" Lord Jehovah, but Job saw it very well. Otherwise, he would hardly say those words, which Jehovah's admirers try to hide from a too curious a reader like you and us.

He said the following about Jehovah: "I know it is so of a truth: but how should man be just with God? If he will contend with him, he cannot answer him one of a thousand. He is wise in heart, and mighty in strength: who hath hardened himself against him, and hath prospered? Which removeth the mountains, and they know not: which overturneth them in his anger. Which shaketh the earth out of her place, and the pillars thereof tremble. Which commandeth the sun, and it riseth not; and sealeth up the stars. Which alone spreadeth out the heavens, and treadeth upon the waves of the sea. Which maketh Arcturus, Orion, and Pleiades, and the chambers of the south. Which doeth great things past finding out; yea, and wonders without number.

Lo, he goeth by me, and I see him not: he passeth on also, but I perceive him not. **Behold, he taketh away, who can hinder him? Who will say unto him, what doest thou**? If God will not withdraw his anger, the proud helpers do stoop under him. How much less shall I answer him, and choose out my words to reason with him? Whom, though I were righteous, yet would I not answer, but I would make supplication to my judge.

If I had called, and he had answered me; yet would I not

believe that he had hearkened unto my voice. For he breaketh me with a tempest, and multiplieth my wounds without cause. He will not suffer me to take my breath, but filleth me with bitterness. If I speak of strength, lo, he is strong: and if of judgment, who shall set me a time to plead? If I justify myself, mine own mouth shall condemn me: **if I say, I am perfect, it shall also prove me perverse**.

Though I were perfect, yet would I not know my soul: I would despise my life. This is one thing, **therefore I said it, He destroyeth the perfect and the wicked. If the scourge slay suddenly, he will laugh at the trial of the innocent**. The earth is given into the hand of the wicked: he covereth the faces of the judges thereof; if not, where, and who is he?

Now my days are swifter than a post: they flee away, they see no good. They are passed away as the swift ships: as the eagle that hasteth to the prey. If I say, I will forget my complaint, I will leave off my heaviness, and comfort myself: **I am afraid of all my sorrows, I know that thou wilt not hold me innocent. If I be wicked, why then labour I in vain? If I wash myself with snow water, and make my hands never so clean; yet shalt thou plunge me in the ditch, and mine own clothes shall abhor me**.

For he is not a man, as I am, that I should answer him, and we should come together in judgment. Neither is there any daysman betwixt us, that might lay his hand upon us both. **Let him take his rod away from me, and let not his fear terrify me: then would I speak, and not fear him; but it is not so with me**."[363]

7. 2. Civilization of Cannibals

And, if a poor Job, who (with the silent consent of Jehovah) was deprived of children, property and even health by Satan, could, nevertheless, raise his voice and accuse "kind and merciful" God-butcher that he can blame even an innocent one, that he exterminate both innocent and guilty, we are not capable to do it. It is because in the image of our favorite God Jehovah we see something close to us, something familiar, something which connects us by bloody or even by intimate ties not only with our far ape-like ancestors, but with beings which occupy lower line in the evolutionary development of the nature. The boundless cruelty which is so brightly and generously displayed by mankind does not have analogies in the world of high developed animals.

But at the same time, as professor Didenco asserts, it is strangely and paradoxically compared, down to the smallest details to customs prevailed in the life of beings that are rather far from the rational forms of behavior: insects, fishes, and even of primitive organisms, such as bacteria, viruses etc. "'Homo sapiens,' as Didinco asserts, 'acts not "cleverer" than spiders in a jar. And with respect to its habitat, the Earth, "civilized" mankind is not better than a cancer of "metastatic" type.'"[364]

Otherwise, how can we explain that "during the whole historical time there were only several "warless" years and more than 14.5 thousand wars with four billions killed?"[365]

Or how can we explain that an intelligent human being, who is, as he thinks, kind and merciful "practices 9 types of violence at 45 their varieties? And these figures, as well as the quantity of wars, are likely to become outdated."[366]

Certainly, all this monstrosity of existence and "coexistence" of human populations can not be understood without revealing its origin causes. But the main thing we should understand is why Homo sapiens, in contrast to animals, is a unique species, inside of which population systematic mutual extermination of man by man is practiced.

The other feature of human behavior which should also be understood consists in that the man, unlike animals, is a unique kind capable to absurdity. And this ability is well-expressed in the generally known formula of faith: "Credo que absurdum (I believe, for it is absurdly)," proclaimed by Tertullian, the Roman apologist of Christianity, who has set off religious faith against antique philosophy.

The organism of an animal behaves itself in any, even in artificially created situation, completely correct from the physiological point of view. If the situation is so unnatural for an animal that it cannot solve it, then its organism gives a picture of nervous failure expressing itself in occurrence of inadequate reflexes. Its nervous system is unable to design absurdity. But the man can do it, and that is why the whole development of human consciousness is gradually overcoming an initial absurdity, it's "shifting to few outermost positions."

Didenco B. A., relating the theory of anthropogenesis put forward by professor Porshnev B. F. (1905-1972) says: "These two human features are not only interconnected, but also completely interdependent, for they spring out from the same, terrible phenomenon. It is so-called adelphophagia, or killing and eating by the man a part of population of their own kind. And it was adelphophagia that has resulted in origin of a human kind—Homo sapiens."[367]

The evolution of Homo sapiens, according to Porshnev's theory, went on as follows. In ancient times, many thousands of years ago, a branch, which has started to specialize mainly on splitting of large animals bones, moved away from primates. They have to become orthograde on their morphology, for in high grass and in bushes it was necessary to stand erect in order to watch the flight of birds and the moving of animals, the remnants of which "hunt" these primates used for food. This was also promoted by a necessity to carry stones and remnants of animals—the action which is possible only when upper extremities of the body were free. Porshnev named these primates troglodytes.

They were not hunters, predators or murderers even in the slightest degree, though they were mainly carnivorous from the very beginning of their existence. That constitutes their distinctive ecological feature in comparison to all the monkeys. Certainly, they also kept auxiliary herbivorousness. And there are no arguments for the existence of hunting of large animals in the early and in the middle paleolith.

Troglodytes, beginning from Australopithecus and finishing with paleoanthropus, were able only to find and cope with skeletons and corpses of died or murdered by predators animals.

It is natural to assume, that a "labour impulse" of both Australopithecus and paleoanthropus, which, as venerable scientists assert, has turned the monkey into the man, was originally directed extremely to a channel of necrophagia, i. e. chopping and eating of corpses of animals, and then, with development of a hand, speech and intelligence, corpses of human beings.

"'So, in the early and in the middle paleolith, "work tools," Didenco says, 'were means for cutting and chopping of remnants of large animals and absolutely nothing more. These "exosmotic organs" of the troglodytes evolved together with human species, as well as together with changes of fauna environment."[368]

These changes of fauna environment have resulted in lessening of the animal corpses' quantity. But the appetite of promptly evolving troglodytes remained the same. The Nature left now only very narrow way out for these strange animals of quaternary epoch that were developed too fast and now were doomed to extinction. It consisted in breaking hitherto saving principle "you shall not kill," which was the deepest basis and inmost secret of their being in various forms of symbiosis with animals.

The first condition of their unobstructed access to the remains of dead meat was that an animal both alive and even dying should be not afraid of them. Troglodytes had to remain inoffensive and harmless, and even useful in something, for example, in signaling about danger to the neighbours in biocenosis system.

And the Nature had prompted a narrow path, which, however, led out the further evolution to the road of unprecedented development. **The solving of biological paradox consisted in that the instinct did not forbid them to kill representatives of their own kind. An ecological slit, which remained for self-rescuing of high specialized (but doomed to extinction) kind of two-legged primates, omnivorous by their nature, but corpsesvorous by their basic biological type, was to use a part of their population as self-reproducing source of food.**

Professor Porshnev asserts that "something similar is well-known in zoology. It calls adelphophagia (eating of each other), sometimes reaching at some kinds of animals more or less noticeable character, but nevertheless not becoming the basic way of their feeding. Moreover there is no precedent, that this phenomenon was the basis of evolution, not to mention the subsequent only historical transformations of this phenomenon."[369]

Thus, the way out of crisis was carried out, firstly, by means of transition to predatory behaviour towards the representatives of their own kind; secondly, by means of splitting of the population on the basis of specialization of special, passive and eaten part, which then very actively separated itself into the special kind in order to become, at last, the special family. As we see, at first, our ancestors adapted themselves to kill each other. And only later, after having practiced enough on the bodies of their sisters and brothers, they learned to kill animals.

And the last archeological findings completely confirm the theory of professor Porshnev. In France, in the cave Mula-Gersi, archeologists discovered the bones of Neanderthal man that allowed to reconstruct interesting details of their life. According to the scientists, the representatives of this missed kind lived in a cave about a hundred thousand years ago. On the stone floor archeologists discovered the remnants of an ancient feast: stone scrapers for scraping meat off skeleton bones, bones of a deer and also 78 bones of Neanderthal man. The bones, as it was found out by scientists, belonged to a family of six species, two of which were adults, two—teenagers and two—infants.

The finding has shaken the scientists. As it appeared, the bones of Neanderthal man were carefully scraped off meat and had the same scratches from stone scrapers, which were seen on the bones of animals. The conclusion, following from it, arose automatically: six Neanderthal men had been eaten by their congeners!

Now it is impossible to restore the tragedy which took place many thousands years ago in the cave Mula-Gersi. Probably, the family of six species was eaten by their relatives as a punishment for some heavy crime. On the other hand, as the scientists believe, Neanderthal men could become a victim of Homo sapiens, who severely finished with the dangerous competitors.

Thus, according to professor Porshnev: "The hunt for other large animals has already become the first substitute of Homo sapiens representative's murder. This ecological variant has become a deepest shock of family Troglodytes destinies. All the same, two instincts contradicted each other: to kill nobody and, at the same time, to kill the representatives of their own kind. There occurred a doubling, or bifurcation of late paleoanthropus ecology and ethology. But their former way of life could not be replaced by "war of everybody against everybody" inside of their own population. Such tendency could not solve a food problem: the kind feeding on themselves is a biological perpetuum mobile."[370]

As a result, having evolved up to the level of Homo sapiens, the kind of troglodytes broke up, according to Porshnev's classification, to four subspecies:

superanimals who keep all the attributes of adelphophagia;

suggestors who lick the boots of superanimals and carry out the role of a conductor of their man-hating theories, which they impose to

a diffusive type, or grey human mass, which is the third type; and, at last,

neoanthropus—human beings, with their inherent good nature, ideas about good, justice and humanity, which make them the sole applicants for the rank of Homo sapiens.

But Homo sapiens could not leave the animal world "cleanly, without "having get themselves dirty." **The straight offspring of those first murderers have remained among the humankind (which were very close to biological paleoanthropus-troglodytes) together with offspring of their imitators—suggestors-manipulators.**

As a result of all these processes of anthropogenesis (or to be more exact, anthropomorphosis) taking place in the unstable transitive world of early humankind formation, a very specific family of intelligent beings consisting of four kinds that were very unfriendly towards each other have been formed. In the process of further development these kinds deferred more and more by their behavior.

These kinds have different morphology of their cerebrum cortex. Two of them are predatory kinds with orientation towards

people! Thus, the mankind represents by itself not a uniform kind, but family consisting of four kinds, two of which must be recognized to be predatory, and with unnatural orientation of this predation (utmost aggressiveness) towards other people.

Predation is determined here, as the inherent aspiration for utmost or monstrously sublimated aggressiveness in relation to other human beings. And it was this unnatural orientation that did not allowed to form natural habitats of different kinds that resulting in occurrence of tragic symbiosis, which was transformed with the course of time in present social order.

Of course, all these things sound a little bit unusual and even shocking. But if we look back at the past, we will see that cannibalism was inherent in many people of the world not only at an early stage of their development, but also at later stages. That is why, Porshnev's-Didenco's conclusions about human family consisting of four kinds, two of which must be recognized to be predatory, having unnatural orientation of this predation (utmost aggressiveness) towards other people are quite reasonable and plausible. It is suffice to say that the stratification of any group of people who live in a secluded space and far from the cultural influence of society (in a prison, for example) repeats in all detailes the one described by professor Porshnev. And this fact shows that the Russian anthropologist was right.

Human sacrifices, for example, were practiced in India and in other countries of the world down to the last century, and even now, we sometimes become the witnesses of monstrous ritual murders made either by Satanists, or by maniacs-murderers. And in our civilized time, eating of animal corpses, which we use for food, is nothing else as a substitution of cannibalism which became possible only because Homo sapiens, having evolved and civilized, managed, nevertheless, to overcome an instinctive interdiction not to kill animals, which originally were their bread-winners. **Until now, we still "eat" a symbolical Christ's body "washing it down" with his symbolical blood, being, thus, symbolical cannibals**.

7. 3. Cannibalism and Religion

By means of Porshnev's theory, by the way, we can try to explain an origin of religion and ceremonial sacrifices. It is quite probable that ancient cannibals-superanimals were perceived as powerful owners having unlimited power and authority by their diffusive fellows who were intended to be eaten. During evolution, mankind slowly, but steadily, free themselves from cannibalism. But, nevertheless, bearing in their collective consciousness the terrible memory of that time when people ate each other, transformed this memory to conceptions about almighty God, to whom they had to sacrifice one or another pair of human beings from time to time.

In more developed and more civilized countries, such as, for example, Egypt, human sacrifices were replaced with circumcision. The idea of this ritual had been inculcated into the consciousness of "the God's people" by Moses, whence it successfully migrated to the Arabian people. In the consciousness of an ancient Jew, for example, God was imagined as a certain monster, to which he had either to sacrifice his own first-borne, or to find a "worthy" replacement to them.

In the book of Exodus there is a very interesting moment which, as it seems to us, completely confirms this assumption. It says: "And it came to pass by the way in the inn, that **the Lord met him, and sought to kill him** {Moses}. Then Zipporah {Moses' mother} took a sharp stone, and cut off the foreskin of her son, and cast it at his feet, and said, **surely a bloody husband art thou to me**. So he let him go: then she said, **a bloody husband thou art, because of the circumcision**."[371]

We can find a similar idea in the Didenco's book: "Let us recollect rituals of initiation. Teenagers (brought up in isolation in special houses) who achieved sexual maturity (mainly boys) were subjected to painful procedures and even partial mutilation which symbolized killing. This ritual was performed somewhere in a wood and was something like symbolization of teenagers' sacrificing to wood monsters. These wood monsters were fantastic substitutes of real devourers-paleoanthropus; as well as the action was not just performance, but real killing.

We must think that these young species reared, or to be more correct, fed near the site (in special pens?), being at grass vegetarian food up to their maturity, were killed and used as food for paleoanthropus."[372]

Thus, in the development of religious world outlook (which is a kind of symbolical description of the human society evolution process from paleoanthropus-cannibals up to the modern "intelligent man") we find both the presence of primitive fear before not at least fantastic, but real devourers-paleoanthropus perceived by man as gods, and the urgent and irresistible desire to get rid of their authority shown in incessant attempts of man "to kill" God, to tear him to pieces, to share these pieces among the people and eat them in order he did not threaten to exterminate both "righteous and sinful," in order he never required to sacrifice him every human first-born.

And this desire will seem not too impossible if we recollect totemic meal, which took place at the time when the primitive man dared to kill and to eat the forefather of their kind; if we recollect the murder of man-god prepared by priests for ritual sacrifice followed by real eating of his body; and at last, if we recollect the murder of our Christian God Jesus Christ followed by symbolical "eating" of his "body" and symbolical "drinking" of his "blood." And it is well known that the scene, which represents this event, is called "the Last Supper," which is the same as "the Last Meal."

What does it mean? It means that with all our "intelligence," or, "sapience" as Didenco would say, we can not escape from a vicious, bloody circle, and constantly moving on its circumference we are compelled again and again to repeat the same samples of behaviour, acquired by us in those far cannibalistic times, but now differently named.

It is the very "absurdity" that constitutes the basis of any religious faith, for only Homo sapiens can give the same names to various concepts, which are different by their form and contents; can mix together evil and good, love and hatred, unification and division, mercy and even the most perverted forms of violence and sadism. And only Homo sapiens can see in the image of Jewish God Jehovah (stained from legs up to his head with the blood of people crushed and squeezed by him) kind and merciful "savior" of mankind, that, in general, is characteristic for archaic or mythological thinking.

Didenco calls this phenomenon "distratumness" [the existence of two consciousness stratum in a human mind], that is actually the same as neutralized "binary oppositions " which become such only in the space of mythological thinking, what, by the way, use "suggestors" to subordinate diffusive types of Homo Sapiens. You can judge yourself after that, what importance has a myth for the development of modern humankind.

The creation of stable absurdities, as Didenco asserts, or absurdities like "the same, but not the same" was the rise to a level, inconceivable in nervous activity of any animal. The subsequent history of the development of human mind was a slow evolution of means which could enable the man to separate absurdity (or distratumness) elements. Some emotional reaction which would testify of absurdity and require it, corresponds to this inconsistent union.

As the trace of this phenomenon, we can name the fact expressed in the so-called A. Elcost law: "Any human feeling is ambivalent in norm (internally contradictory). Disrtatumness reproduces just that simultaneous presence of two opposite to each other irritations, which "break up" normal nervous activity at animals."[373]

But not at the man. The human consciousness endures distratumness quite well (just is neurotized a bit), welding together absolutely unconnected elements. Didenco says: "This welding is a phenomenon of the special sort: in the deep past, nonsense inspired a sacred tremor or ecstasy, and with the development both of speech and consciousness, senseless provokes efforts of an understanding. A speech itself is nothing else as an understanding of the senseless. Distratumness is an emotion at the viewpoint of physiological processes, and -absurdity at the viewpoint of logic.

But it does not mean that distratumness belongs to the vanished past. The past lives. People are unlikely to refuse its [of distratumness] evil spells, laying in everything that is sacred and mysterious, festive and childish. In world's civilizations, the growing strict mind is tightly and diversely intertwined with a credulous recklessness and with intricate fantasies."[374]

"But what does it have to do with the Bible?" a very impatient reader will ask us. The matter is that however hard and whatever you may look for, you will not be able to find more impressive receptacle of human absurdity and monstrous, inhuman hatred and cruelty, than this "sacred" number one bestseller.

What does it mean? It means that we can hardly consider ourselves as the representatives of Homo sapiens if we seriously accept this book, if we consider it to be a receptacle of the unsurpassed "divine wisdom" and use it as "the textbook of life" for the whole "civilized" western world. This "textbook of life" can teach us anything else as to hate and to kill, for it contains in itself a huge destructive charge enclosed in it by extremely predatory Jewis Rabbis-superanimals who, in order to destroy gentile Rome that threatened to destroy Jewish world, had to create the psychological weapon of such a killing force, in comparison to which the nuclear explosion looks as a shot of a New Year's cracker. At least half of those four billion people, which were lost in numerous wars during the entire history of mankind, is obliged by their "salvation" from the bondages of chains of a perishable body, namely to the Bible and its man-hating cannibalistic ideology.

The Bible, having escaped from a narrow circle of "the God's people" thanks to Paul's and other Jewish Rabbis' efforts, has brought practically incurable mental contagion in the world which now becomes a scourge of civilized western world. In an image of Islamic fundamentalism and terrorism, we easily recognize the same

Jewish mental contagion, which can be called the "syndrome of god-choosiness," picked up from the Jews by prophet Mohammad during his wanderings with trade caravans in the vast expanses of Asia and Arabian Peninsula. We recognize the same monstrous, "non-welding alloy" of "kind and merciful" God Allah with improbable and inhuman cruelty inherent not only in ancient paleoanthropus-cannibals, but also in representatives of Homo sapiens.

7. 4. Is Homo Sapiens Really Sapiens?

To be Homo sapiens, one must have the reason among other things, which becomes, according to the Porshnev's theory, the third signal system. "'**The third signal system,' the scientist asserts, 'can be inherent only in unpredatory people. It is the Reason, and these are its manifestations: conscience, compassion, taking into account the interests of other people, not doing harm to other people and to the Nature without any intimidations and "disciplinary" factors, such as religious threats or moral appeals**.'"[375]

The third signal system is already restraining and limiting one in the relation to the second signal system, and the man gains morals in such a way. For a society, this restraint has so far only theoretical character; it is limited only by unsuccessful criticism of obviously unreasonable actions of people and of mankind as a whole. **Really, the rational behaviour of people in the majority of its displays is frankly paranoiac, for the purposes of the most crafty combinations appear either imaginary, or harmful**.

These are making money for the sake of money or western speed of work unreasonable and unnecessary for people; and it is only for the sake of profit of a handful of financial bigwigs, at the expense of health of billions of common people. And at last, technical progress at any cost, even at the expense of Life destruction on the Earth—what can be more insane? **The third signal system, or the Reason, assumes an estimation of rational actions from the moral point of view: not only "learning of good and evil," but also unconditional acceptance of the side of good**.

Advanced scientists come now to the same conclusions. Here is what psychotechnologist Igor Smirnov says: "The intellectual features, emotions, will, temperament are all derivative. **But it is morality that distinguishes the man from animals. From here comes out unequivocal conclusion: predatory hominids are not human beings from the moral point of view**. They are those, whom philosopher

Hegel has defined as "morally deranged," and Shopenghauer—as "deprived of moral consciousnesses." Animals, extremely dangerous "second signaled animals" among people."

These "the most dangerous second signaled animals (i. e. humans, in the mental constitution of whom only the first and the second signal systems are presented)" are those absolutely unscrupulous, absolute immoral and indifferent to another's sufferings and pain beings. They produce extremely dangerous for the health of mankind mental contagion which, assuming the shape of various religious, revolutionary, racial and nationalistic doctrines and theories, becomes a matrix and forms the world outlook and controlls the behaviour of that grey, diffusive mass which is called the people.

And it is the pure truth, for, as the doctor of philosophical sciences Alexandr Vodolagin asserts: "Some mental conditions can really be as contagious, as any other infection, and be transferred through interchange of energy. For this very reason, the normal man behave themselves like zombie in a crowd, wholly obeying to its atmosphere. The influence of a crowd is the strongest one. Any uniting goal, regardless creative or destructive, leads to appearance of a uniform, powerful field. The aura of a crowd changes the aura of an individual, deprives it its symmetry and, thus, gives the way for emotions to prevail over common sense. **And if the crowd has a common idol, it receives a perfect possibility to change a mental condition of each man**. So, the actor suffering with narcotic addiction, "programs" (though not knowing about that) crowds of his admirers to test a drug."[376]

And now imagine biblical God Jehovah, the most popular idol of the western civilization. He has the whole bouquet of mental disorders such as violent insanity (shown in uncontrollable attacks of fury, jealousy and anger), monstrous animal cruelty and bloodthirstiness, the passion for cannibalism (human sacrifices), megalomania and the extreme degree of sadism. He realizes his sadism in a process of destruction, trampling, squeezing and defeating of uncountable multitude of people. It is quite natural that he will "program" a diffusive crowd exclusively on hatred, cruelty, division and fratricidal wars. And he had quite succeeded in that business, having transformed the world in a bloody battlefield of man against another man.

And, as long as we read the horrible and bloody book, which is called the Bible, we shall endlessly hate and kill each other, realizing the cruel and man hating program of the matrix adjusted to the total destruction of Homo sapiens as a biological kind.

CHAPTER 8.

THE WORLD AT THE THRESHOLD OF THE NEW WORLD ORDER

> "We state that the modern situation in the world is intentionally created by this imperious elite (masons) by means of manipulation with both "right" and "left" elements... Within 100 hundred years, the most powerful of these elites have created both "right" and "left" elements with **the only purpose—to create, in the final account, the New World Order**."[377]
>
> Anthony Sutton.

8. 1. Globalization and Religion

Globalization—the word, which can be heard anywhere and everywhere, and everyone who utters it puts one's own meaning of this word. As you remember, in the fourth chapter Geidar Jemal' has defined "globalization" as one of the most vicious evils, the enemy of the whole Islamic and non- Islamic world, as well as the source of all the troubles and problems we face living on our long-suffering planet Earth.

But what is this great evil? The great connoisseur of both Islam and all its problems asserts that it is an "electronic mass of money, which is invisible and inaccessible for everybody, but in which the dynamic of humankind is formalized." Thus, if we believe to Geidar Jemal', globalization is some electronic and invisible mass of money, by means of which some "system" has established some "world order" to control all the displays of human activity. The entire Moslem world in the person of Geidar Jemal' and his numerous followers wage new, revolution, guerilla war [holy Jihad] against this "world order."

This war must be finished with the destruction of the USA as the state and the nation, and complete victory of Islam. It is quite natural that all those who deny to adopt Islam will be mercilessly destroyed, for "Allah does not like unbelievers." In its very essence, this is the same globalization, but the one turned inside out.

If we continue the learning of the globalization process, taking into account that globalization can be oriented to the achieving of interlocking goals by different people and carried out with interlocking means at interlocking "scenarios," we shall find out that Geidar Jemal's globalization definition is not far from truth, for money, if it even represents some "electronic mass, invisible and inaccessible to everybody," play, nevertheless, not the last role in the world, and the one who owns it, possesses the real power. "'Let me the possibility to rule over the nation's money,' M. Rothschild said, 'and I do not care either about who promulgate a law or about what kind of law it is.'"

Till the beginning of the third millennium, the globalization leaders in the person of Rothschild's and Baruch's clans who aspire for the world dominion, "have created the world global robbery system, having thrown the usurious net over the world. For this purpose the International Currency Reserves, the World Bank, the Banks of Reconstruction and Development (both International and European), the International Trade Organization end other supposedly national and central banks and international thievish usurious offices, stock exchanges, equity market e.t.c. have been created."[378]

The result of this globally legal robbery is stated in the book *Money Without Interest and Inflation* by M. Kennedy. The average income received by so-called developed countries through interest and usury is about one hundred million dollars a day. The secret of their prosperity lies in this very fact. Annual outgoing of Brazil is $42,000,000,000, of Mexico is $40,000,000,000. Hungary pays out 20% of national produce, Indonesia -19%. Romania was the only country which did not help to the drug of external debt. Chaushesku suffered from the international mafia for this. Modern Russia is the living monument of the usury slavery doctrine.

Both this doctrine and globalization itself are by no means the attributes of the modern times. Their history is rooted in the depths of millenniums, in those distant times when Jewish Rabbis created the most powerful weapon—the religion of destruction, the Biblical slavery doctrine, which they use at first to invade "lands where honey and milk flow," and then to enslave all the Gentiles. The institute of usury became the main instrument of this doctrine.

In the Old Testament, God Jehovah prescribes Jews the permissiveness towards "unbelievers," giving the examples for imitation:

"Thou shalt not lend upon usury to thy brother; usury of money, usury of victuals, usury of any thing that is lent upon usury: **Unto a stranger thou mayest lend upon usury; but unto thy brother thou shalt not lend upon usury: that the Lord thy God may bless thee in all that thou settest thine hand to in the land whither thou goest to possess it.**"[379]

The words "to possess it" refer not to the promise of Palestine of that time, for it has been already captured; they refer to all the other countries where Jews live and maintain themselves as Jewry, carrying the culture of parasitism regardless whether they keep to their faith or not.

In the Old Testament we can read the imitation example for such parasites: "But of the children of Israel did Solomon make no bondmen: but they were men of war, and his servants, and his princes, and his captains, and rulers of his chariots, and his horsemen."[380]

But it is only a hint to a race-elitist state. In Talmud it has already worked out as a thesis of direct God's predestination: "And there appeared God, and measured the earth **and gave strangers to the hands of Jews**. Since Noah's children did not execute seven commandments, the Lord God gave all their belongings to Jews."[381]

In the Bible, God Jehovah says: "The Lord shall open unto thee his good treasure, the heaven to give the rain unto thy land in his season, and to bless all the work of thine hand: **and thou shalt lend unto many nations, and thou shalt not borrow. And the Lord shall make thee the head, and not the tail; and thou shalt be above only, and thou shalt not be beneath.**"[382]

Isaiah pictures even more brilliant future for the chosen God's people: "And the sons of strangers shall build up thy walls, and their kings shall minister unto thee: for in my wrath I smote thee, but in my favor have I had mercy on thee. Therefore thy gates shall be open continually; they shall not be shut day nor night; that men may bring unto thee the forces of the Gentiles, and that their kings may be brought. **For the nation and kingdom that will not serve thee shall perish; yea, those nations shall be utterly wasted.**"[383]

If we call historic events by their own names, we have to admit that this is the race doctrine, which brings:

1. The ideology of parasitism of the race "elite" on the labor of "foreign" cattle;
2. Genocide towards all those who do not agree with it.

And the essence of this doctrine has not been changed from the times of the Old Testament canonization until the last versions of

Talmud. Although, the censorial requisitioning took place, they could not eliminate its essence, but just hide from uninitiated the most sincere declarations about the tendency of its masters to build race, global slavery system.

And it is not an idle talk of asylum madmen. As Russian scientists assert in the *Inner Predictor of the SSSR*: "After the revolution up to 1937 there were the atrocities of not anonymous "Bolshevism" which fell down from the Moon; it was real genocide in Russia, which was organized on the base of Marxism-Leninism-Trotskyism doctrine, the founders of which were Jews. The Russian government consisted mainly of Jews, and those who were married to Jewesses prevailed among other high officials, as well as the anti-Soviet usurious counter-revolution (after 1985) has Jewish coloration."[384]

Thus, it is quite clear that the Bible, covering itself with the name of God, calls the "God's chosen people" to the world supremacy, to the acquirement of land and property of other people and to the destruction of both their culture and all those who do not want to obey to its man-hating ideology.

This is the main vector of West civilization goals, and all the tirades about democracy, human rights, the values common to all mankind, e.t.c. are just camouflage for hiding real intentions. The cruel and man-hating Biblical doctrine has found its continuation in the activity of secret Masonic lodges, which became architects of the New World Order.

8. 2. Masonry and Its Plans of the New World Order Building

The Jew-masonry plot is usually connected with "The Zion Sages Protocols." But it is well-known that they are absolute trash because they were fabricated by Russian police for a certain purpose. But there are some other documents which reveal the real goals of those who press towards the world dominion. Here we cite "The New Testimony of Satan" as an example.

This secret document became accessible to public in 1875, when a Bavarian Illuminates'[385] courier was killed by lightning on his way from Frankfurt to Paris. The document was almost identical to "Zion Sages Protocols" and meant for the plan realization of power takeover in all the countries of the world and subjecting their people to the power of Illuminates.

"The New Testimony of Satan" runs:

- The first secret in the business of people governing consists in the acquirement of public opinion, at that **it is necessary to sow discord, uncertainty, and propagate discordant believes until people get totally lost, become embarrassed, invalid to orientate, and decide that it is better not to have one's own opinion in political questions. Peoples' discontent must be exited, and dirty, offensive and devoid of spirituality literature must be spread.** Then, the goal of press is to prove un-Illuminates' inability in all the branches of state and religious life.
- The second secret consists in that it is necessary to assign primary importance to people's weakness, to all the bad habits, to everything reprehensible, to all the mistakes—until peoples stop to understand each other.
- **First of all, it is necessary to fight against the power of a single person, for there is nothing more dangerous than it. If it possesses creative, spiritual energy, it is able to gain more than millions of people.**
- By means of envy, discords and wars, through asperities, hunger and infections, all the peoples will be reduced to such a condition when they see no other way out than to give themselves under the total command of Illuminates.
- If any state weakened by revolution or because of civil war stays before the danger of outer invasion, it is always favorable course of events and works to our favor.
- **It is necessary to habituate people to take pawn tickets as real coins, to be pleased with the outer side of things, to seek after pleasures, being in incessant search for something new, which would ensnare them, so that they would follow Illuminates.** It can be achieved by means of good reward giving to human masses for their obedience.
- **By means of society corruption people will be deprive of any believe in God.**
- By means of gradual processing of people with both oral and written word, as well as with specially developed forms of lies, human masses will be persuaded to accept Illuminates' will. **The ability to think independently must be liquidated by means of ready opinions teaching introduction; spiritual power of people must be undermined by using an empty demagogy...**
- Masses of people must remain blind, unreasonable, devoid of their

own opinion in order they cannot discuss about polity; just but implacable power and the principle of implicit obedience must rule over them.

- The world dominion can be achieved only by means of roundabout way, and by purposeful undermining of all the freedoms: legislation, order, elections, press, human rights, and first of all people education system.
- By means of purposeful loosening of state structure, governments of the word must be tormented until they are ready to hand over all their power to us for the sake of peace preservation...
- **The lack of understanding among people, race and religious hatred must be provoked In Europe in order to cause insuperable disunities**...
- Splits, disorders and animosity must be sown in other parts of the world in order to habituate countries to fear and suppress any possibility to resist...
- Through the corruptibility of high government officials, countries, after receiving of series of borrowings, must be put under credit debt before Illuminates, which will considerably increase their public debt.
- By means of specially staged economic crisis, in the course of which all the accessible funds will be withdrawn out of circulation, the currency system undermining will be achieved in all the un-Illuminates countries...
- By introduction of universal suffrage, the undivided supremacy of majority must be established. By habituation to independence, the destruction of family and its pedagogical power is achieved. By means of education, based on false facts and concepts, the youth must be made fool of, deviated and corrupted...
- By means of all these measures, people and nations must be prompted to invite Illuminates as the world government. The new world government must be introduced as beneficent leadership-screen, to which people will resort quite voluntarily. If any state is against it, its neighbors will wage war against this state. **The creation of such a government needs the organization of the world war**.[386]

8. 3. The World War III and a "Noiseless Weapon" for "Quiet Wars"

In 1871 Albert Pike, Sovereign Grand Master of the Scotland Freemasonry, presented to Juseppe Madziny, the head of Bavarian Illuminates, the brief plan of conquest of the world by means of three world wars, which had to be ended with the establishing of the New World Order.

THE FIRST WORLD WAR had to be staged in order to put Russia under the direct control of Bavarian Illuminates. They intend to use Russia as a "scarecrow" to solve the tasks put forward by Illuminates.

THE SECOND WORLD WAR had to create general divergence of opinion by means of manipulation by both German nationalists and political Zionists. The expansion of the sphere of Russian supremacy and the creation of Israel in Palestine had to facilitate to fulfill this item.

THE THIRD WORLD WAR, according to the plan, had to be started over ideological gap caused by Illuminates between Zionists and Arabs. It was planned to extend this conflict all over the world.

As for Russia, it remained to be a "scarecrow" (the image of enemy) up to recent time of the world history. That is why western states had been driven into international alliances (UNO, NATO etc.) they would have never joined voluntarily. Moreover, being the enemy of the whole world, the Russian empire made the international weapons trade to prosper, which was profitable for international bankers.

Now, after the collapse of the Soviet Union, the situation has been changed, and the world has another "scarecrow"—the Moslem religious extremism, which completely disaccords with both world Zionism and with American globalization, which it has announced to be "the enemy" of the whole Moslem world.

Thus, everything goes on according to the Bavarian Illuminates' plan. They, slowly and unnoticeably, had drawn the world into the World War III which had been started nine years after the finishing of the World War II. This war is still continuing and will hardly be finished in the foreseeable future.

This war is carried on with different methods. They are not only combat operations where bullets whine, cannons shoot, and shells explode; it is not only great noted terrorist acts, but also "quiet wars." They use "noiseless weapon" that "shoot with situations instead of bullets." Inside of this weapon, "the processing of data instead of chemical reactions goes on." It is based on "bytes of information instead of gunpowder granules" and uses "a computer instead of a barrel, a computer programmer instead of a rifleman." "Noiseless weapon" "acts by the command of a bank magnate instead of a commanding officer."

The description of this kind of weapon first appeared in the book *Behold a Pale Horse*, by William Cooper. The author took up a rather high post in the Intelligent Service of the US Navy and had access to various secret documents. The information given in the book does not leave any doubt that the war is going on, the noiseless war, the war in the result of which an average man is doomed to change into miserable weak-willed slave whose body and soul will be in the whole possession of "brothers" masons of the World Government, which already dictates its will to the whole world. In the first chapter of his book, W. Cooper reveals the mechanisms by means of which a human consciousness is enslaved, a psychology of human masses is formed and millions of people are exterminated. In his book, he writes, "I have read secret documents which state that "The noiseless weapon for quiet wars" is the doctrine, which was approved by the Bilderberg Group Committee at its first known meeting in 1954."[387]

Below we quote the abridged copy of the document dated by May, 1979 which was found in 1986 in an IBM copy machine that was to be resaled as an unnecessary equipment.

TOP SECRET

NOISLESS WEAPON FOR QUIET WARS

Introductory manual
The principle of operation research
Technical manual

This document is dedicated to the 25th anniversary of the World War III ("The quiet war"), which is carried on by using subjective war at a biological level, the armament being a "noiseless weapon."

The document contains the description of the war and the strategy of armament.

May, 1979.

ENERGY

...The quiet war has been quietly announced by the ELITE (Bilderberg Group) at its meeting in 1954...

In 1954, although so called "moral principles" were touched upon during discussion. It was decided from the point of view of natural selection that **a nation or any community of people who will not use their intellect must be regarded as animals which do not have intellect at all. Such people can be used as plough cattle or working material depending on a choice or a taste.**

Thus, in the interest of the future world order it was decided to wage a quiet war against American society with the final result of constant shifting of natural and social energy (well-being) from undisciplined and irresponsible majority to self-disciplined and worthy minority...

In order to make the economy completely predictable, low levels of the population must be completely under control, that is to be poor and trained to pull the burden of social load from their early childhood until they are able to ask about the essence of what is going on. To gain such a submission, families of low classes must be disconnected by means of increasing employment of their parents and the organization of federal twenty-for-hours kindergartens and hostels for children who are, in the result, left without proper parents' attention.

The level of education given to such people must be low enough in order the gap dividing low and high classes to be insurmountable for a low class. With such initial conditions, even the most prominent individuals from low levels of population will get little in the case when smeone dares to escape from the place prepared for them. Such a kind of slavery is essential for the ruling clique to maintain some level of social order and peace.

THE INTRODUCTORY DESCRPTION OF NOISELESS WEAPON

... It is obvious that a "noiseless weapon" application is a type of a biological war. **By means of knowledge, understanding and manipulation, the weapon affects vital capacity and vital tonus of people in a society, as well as the sources of natural and social energy, of physical, mental and emotional men's strength or weakness.**

THEORETICAL INTRODUCTION

"Let me the possibility to rule over the nation's money, and I do not care either about who promulgate the law or about what kind of law it is."

Meir Amehem Rothschild.

The nowadays technology of the "noiseless weapon" is the fruit of a simple idea that has been born, expressed and effectively applied by Mr. Meir Amehem Rothschild. Rothschild has discovered a missing, passive component of the economic theory, known as an economic induction. Of course, he did not think in the terms of the 20th century about his discovery, and a mathematical analysis appeared only during the second industrial revolution and crucial development of the theory of mechanisms and electronics, which, in the final account, has resulted in a computer invention. It was only after above-mentioned events, that the Rothschild's discovery could be effectively used to control economy.

APPLYING TO ECONOMY

To apply the method of shock testing to economy control technique, retail prices are changed by spurts and customers' reaction is registered. The resulting oscillations, caused by economic chock are processed on a computer, and, thus, the psychical-economic structure of nation is defined. Thank to this process (which partially is differential), difference matrixes, by means of which the family financial level is defined and evaluation of the production level (consumption structure) becomes possible, has been discovered.

Then, the changes of financial situation during future shock spurts can be predictable and controlled, in other words, a society becomes like a very trained animal controlled by a complex computer control system.

In the final account, each element of social structure falls under a computer control by means of defying of its personal consumption ability. The information of personal consumption ability of a single customer is guaranteed because a computer constantly registers every purchase, correlating purchased goods (by means of a bar-code) with a customer who pays with a credit card, which afterwards will become something like a "tattoo" number that is invisible in an open form.

THE DISTRACTION OF ATTENTION, INITIAL STRATEGY

The experience has proved that **the simplest method of imposing secrecy on a "noiseless weapon" and strengthening of control over a society is, from one hand, to keep it undisciplined and indifferent towards the main principles of the system; from the other hand, to make it entangled, disorganized, addled even towards not very important things.**

These tasks are achieved by means of:

1. The distraction of peoples' thoughts; indifference towards mental abilities; low level of teaching of mathematic, logic, systems and economy designing; complete lack of consideration for ingenuity.

2. Control over emotional conditions of people, increasing of their restraint and tolerance in emotional and physical spheres which is attained by means of:

a) the practice of emotional insult and pressure (mental and emotional violence) done by constant propaganda of sex, violence and wars in a social environment—especially on TV and in press;

b) giving people in abundance whatever they want—"worthless mental pabulum"—distracting them from what they really need.

3. Rewriting of law and history, and inviting a society to creative activity, being ready to avert their thoughts from real professional necessities to well done forgeries. It will distract people from discovering of a "noiseless weapon" and social technology of automation.

THE DISTRACTION OF ATTENTION, TOTALS

A social environment: distract the attention of adult population from the solving of social tasks, representing them as to be of no importance.

Schools: teach young people to be indifferent towards real mathematics, real economy, real law, and real history.

Entertainment system: create an entertainment system for people which is on the level of amusement of six-year child.

Work: make society more and more busy, having no time for thoughts, "keep a herd in a cattle-pen."

CONSENT, THE INITIAL WICTORY

The system of a "noiseless weapon" works on the data received from "obedient" society by means of legal (but not always legitimate) force. The great deal of information is accessible for "noiseless weapon" system programmers through the Inner Tax Service (ITS).

This information consists of well-organized data contained in the lists of federal and state budget which have been collected, organized and represented at the expense of slavery labor of tax-payers and employed population. Moreover, the quantity of such lists represented to the ITS is a good indication of social consent, the important factor for the strategy carrying out.

COEFFICIENT OF CONSENT is a feedback, expressed in a digital form; it shows the degree of victory.

The psychological background: **When a government is ready to collect taxes and take possession of private interests without any compensation—it shows that a society is ready to surrender and agree to enslavement and intrusion. Good and well-calculated index of "harvesting time" is the quantity of citizens who pay income tax in spite of obvious lack of honesty and truthful work from a government part**.

THE POLITICAL STRUCTURE OF NATION—DEPENDENCE

The main reason why citizens create the political structure of state is a subconscious desire to prolong their dependent condition which they had in childhood. In other words, they want to have a man-god who will deliver them from any risk in their lives, carry them in his arms, kiss their bruises and lay a chicken on each dinner table. They want to have someone who will provide them with clothes, put to bed at night and say that everything is going to be all right when they wake up in the morning of the following day.

This demand is unreal; that is why a man-god, i.e. politician, is encountered with unreality followed by another unreality, promising everything and doing nothing. Thus, who is a great liar? A society? Or a man-god?

Such behavior of a society is a capitulation born of fear, laziness and expediency. It is the base of well-being, as a strategic weapon against a miserable society.

ACTION/ATTACK

The majority of people want to be ready to kill the one who intrudes into their life, but they do not want to renounce their moral and religious principles. Thus, they hand a dirty work over to others (including their children) so that their own hands were not stained with blood. They rave about human handling of animals, and then eat a tasty sandwich aloof from a slaughterhouse, somewhere outskirts and in secret. The most self-critical men pay taxes to political societies and then complain on government corruption.

TOTALS.

People hire politicians to:

1. Gain security without worrying about.

2. Make actions without thinking of them.

3. Yield a loss, insult and death to others without thinking of life and death.

4. Avoid responsibility for their own actions.

5. Gain incomes from life and science without any efforts to discipline and study.

People give power to politicians for building and maintaining a war machine, having as its object:

1. Guaranteeing of a nation survival.

2. Resisting to aggression in the interests of a nation.

3. Exterminating of nation's outer enemies.

4. Extermination of citizens who impede nation stability inside the country.

Thus, a nation is divided into two obvious parts: OBEDIEND SUB-NATION (quiet majority) and POLITICAL SUB-NATION. Political sub-nation remains to be attached to obedient sub-nation, tolerates it until becomes strong enough to get rid of it.

SYSTEM ANALISES

To make important computer decisions concerning war—the initial moving force of economy, it is necessary to give certain logistic quantities to each element of war structure. This process begins with a clear and precise description of a sub-system structure.

RECRUITMENT CENTER

(Military service)

The main goal of a recruitment center is, by means of intimidation, to inculcate into young people minds the thought that a government is almighty. A man soon understands that a prayer is too slow to make changes a bullet makes in a moment. Thus, a young man who spent his eighteen years in a religious environment can, by means of government arsenal, be broken-down, deprived his fantasies and illusions within several months.

When such a thought is inculcated, it is quite easy to inculcate all the other things. **It is more astonishing, as young man's parents, who love him, can be convinced to send him to war, to death**...

Let us begin with the definition of the term "recruitment center." **It is an institute of obligatory collective sacrifices and slavery founded by people of old and middle age to force young people to do a dirty work**. If further service will make young people to feel the guilt of the olds, their critique will be improbable (the stabilization of generations). All this is trumped-up and represented to society as a "patriotic-national" service...

COMPULSION

FACTOR 1.

As with any social system, stability is attained by understanding of a man's nature (the model—action/reaction). But fails can be possible, and they are catastrophic as a rule. As with other social spheres, one or another form of intimidation (or inducement) is concurrent with successful activity of a recruitment center...

To guarantee the success of draft campaign, it is necessary to make "brainwash"/programming to control families, as well as groups of associates.

FACTOR 2. FATHER

A head of family must be sure that his children will grow up with the right social training and consciousness. Advertisement and mass media carry out a campaign, which is directed on inculcation into future father's mind of certain stereotypes before he get married. He is taught that he either correspond to a certain social level, created for him, or his intimate life will be hard and his loving relations with his wife will be equal to zero...

FACTOR 3. MOTHER

Female element of a human society is primarily governs by emotions and only then by logic. In a fight between logic and imagination about something, imagination always wins, fantasies prevail, material instincts dominate, i. e. at first a child is appeared, and then—future. Woman's look, who has just born a baby, is happily blear to see cannon-fodder or cheap labor in a healthy man. Nevertheless, a woman must be put under the condition of accepting the "reality" which is told about in a proper time or even early.

As a reality accepting process is difficult, a family must be disconnected. That is why the state education system must take root in families increasingly in order to disconnect children from parents since early age. **The vaccination with a behavior vaccine [Ritalin] will increase the ability to accept reality by a child (mandatory)**...

FACTOR 4. A YOUNG MAN

During a war, a young man has emotional instinct of self-preservation and a feeling of crowd which has a habit to avoid a battlefield. If a young man is convinced that he must go—it is everything which is necessary to make him go to war. The means of blackmail for him is threatening; like: "No sacrifices—no friends. No glory—no girlfriends."

FACTOR 5. A SISTER

And what about a young man's sister? She get everything she needs from their parents, and learns to expect the same from his future husband.

FACTOR 6. CATTLE

Those who do not use their brains are not better that those who do not have them at all. In other words, this entire brainless group—a father, a mother, a son and a daughter—become useful enemies for trainers.

[The end of the document][388]

Thus, we can see that the whole history of mankind is unwrapped according to the scenario, made by secret Masonic lodges, which represent by themselves the secret power, great and invisible. This invisible secret government has staged two world wars, and now is waging the third one, which must be resulted in the creation of the New World Order. The power will be transferred to the hands of mighty Jewish bankers and all the "gentiles," i. e. all the rest of representatives Homo Sapiens who "do not use their brains" and represent by themselves "a brainless group, which consists of a father, a mother, a son and a daughter" will become, according to the cited document, "useful animals for trainers," i. e. for the same Jewish bankers (Masons).

Such a destiny looks not very attractive, but it seems we will hardly be able to avoid it; for all the information we have confirms the reality of the Jewish-Masonic conspiracy. It is difficult to believe, but it is more difficult to deny the fact that the world is developed according to the scenario described in the documents we have just cited.

The collapse of the Soviet Union and Perestroika are very good examples. We have already mentioned that this destructive process went on in precise accordance with the "Plan of Defeat of the Soviet Union and Russia" by Allen Dulles; the further development of Russia goes on according to the methods of "quiet war" with the use of a "noiseless weapon."

Thanks to the Big Brother's help, we slowly and inevitably are turning into a society which "will not use its intellect," and consequently, will be considered by the Big Brother as "animals which do not have intellect at all."

Such people can be used by the Big Brother as "plough cattle or a working material depending on a choice or a taste." To make Russian economy absolutely predictable, low levels of the population become more and more "under control," do not have private property, are poor and "trained to pull the burden of social load from their early childhood until they are able to ask about the essence of what is going on."

The level of education given to Russian children is decreased year after year, and as a result it must drop to such a level when the gap between low and high classes was and remains insurmountable for low class. (Compare gymnasiums, lyceums and private schools with state schools, which suffer shortages of teachers, and those teachers who still work in such schools are physically unable to give children knowledge of appropriate level, for they have to work almost without salary (the average teacher's salary in Russian state schools is about $150—200 a month).

Compare the city schools with country ones which cannot be

attended by many children, for their parents have no money to buy enough clothes and footwear for children. The physical condition of country schools is also very bad. Many of them are just about to collapse, for the government does not give money for their repair and development. But at the same time, "spirituality" is developed immensely: churches, bars and shops are being built in every village, resulting in child prostitution, drunkenness, drug addiction and criminality.

To increase restraint and tolerance in emotional and physical spheres, "the practice of emotional insult and pressure (mental and emotional violence) done by constant propaganda of sex, violence and wars in a social environment—especially on TV and in press" is used. It is so called "worthless mental pabulum" which is given to a Russian man abundantly in order to distract him "from what he really needs."

For this purpose, "an entertainment system for people which is on the level of amusement of six-year child" is created. A society is made "more and more busy, having no time for thoughts," which is necessary "to keep a herd in a cattle-pen." The history is rewritten and remade, as it is necessary for a "cosmopolitan elite that gain real profits from its cooperation with the West,"[389] the law does not have any juridical power and made to defend interests of those who can pay good money, and the human consciousness is more and more deviated from "real professional necessities to well faked forgeries" which, in the final account, is intended "to distract peoples' attention from discovering of a "noiseless weapon" and a social automation technology."

"'It is not true,' Dolgov V. K. said in his speech on the plenum of Central Committee of Communism Party of Russian Federation, 'that having started perestroika, its organizers did not have the concept of conducting reforms. **The sequence of events shows their precise logic and enviable purposefulness of presidents for a "new thinking"**. However, both this conceptions and a distinct plan have not been promulgated, of course. It is quite natural that they had been worked out behind the party's back, not to mention people. "A new thinking" is a typical "scientific explanation" of goals and decisions already accepted by government. **But these goals and priories have also been put into leaders' heads by "experts" who, in their turn, had received them from the arsenals of American political science and politic.**'"[390]

Of course, it is quite difficult to believe in the reality of existence of the plot of such a scale. It is also difficult to believe in the existence of a "noiseless weapon" for "quiet wars." But if we cast even a short glance at historic events, we, to our great surprise, shall discover their almost total accordance both with "The Zion Sages Protocols" and with "The New Testimony of Satan" of Bavarian Illuminates, as well as with the secret document presented by the Bilderberg Group Committee at its first known meeting in 1954.

And if you recall Allen Dales' "Plan of Destruction of the Soviet Union and Russia," you will find out the same confidently-cynical handwriting of those, who do not waste their words.

The terrorist acts of September 11, 2001, and the "antiterrorist war" (world war of Illuminates' plan) waged by the USA against the Arab world have revealed both real goals of "American democracy" expansion and the incessant desire of the world elite for the world dominion and establishing of the New World Order.

8. 4. Unnecessary People and How to Get Rid of Them

As we have shown above, the New World Order implies the changing of all the "gentiles," i. e. those who do not belong to the ruling elite, into "a community of people who will not use their intellect," "useful animals for trainers," serving the needs of Masonic clique. But here one essential problem springs up, which makes the building of "God's kingdom" for the ruling elite quite difficult.

The fact is that natural recourses of the Earth are limited, and we will have not enough of them if the birth rate is rather high. Moreover, if such a rate remains the same, the Earth will face overpopulation, which contradicts the planes of ruling elite.

As W. Cooper states: "Scientists have noticed this fact and called the attention of world ruling elite to it. The elite was shocked by the prediction of consequences of this event. They were said it would be in the year 2000 or little bit later, that the collapse of civilization and, probably, the death of human race could be possible.

Scientists said that only strict control over birth rate and newborns health, holding up of technological and economical progress, excluding of meat from human ration, full protection of natural environment, space exploring and considerable changing of human consciousness can prevent human race from destruction.

The ruling elite had immediately organized an alliance and took appropriate decisions, which were realized by means of propaganda, behavior control and other methods of human masses manipulation.

What was unrealizable dream of many groups, became a reality with the concentration of power in the alliance, called Bilderberg Group. Everything that was impossible before has become promised now. The New Word Order, foreseen by many, became obviousness."[391]

The necessary researches have been made, and already at the first stage, it became obvious that the death of civilization can be expected soon after the year 2000, if the birth rate remains the same. In 1957, president D. Eisenhower had to say: "In the result of youth moral degradation, age increasing and spreading of starvation, there expected the population explosion of such a force that can be resulted in double population increasing little bit later than in one generation."

The third stage of research had been made by the Rome Club. It was finished in 1968. The results were the same. Measures had to be taken immediately. In order to predict corrections introduced by elite into social and economical structure of the world, a computer model of the world and the New World Order had been worked out.

The analyses of people wave of indignation neutralization methods for the time until the final result is achieved after which there would be no possibility to return to the past, had been made. **It had been defined that the immediate solving of the problem is possible by means of active work in two directions. The first is to reduce the birth rate, the second—to increase the death rate**.

Several programs anticipating the development of positive birth control methods (condoms, spirals, contraceptives, abortions, sterilization) and support of homosexuals had been started up in order to decrease birth rate. The result of these measures was not substantial. Individual freedom, religion and old rights of homosexuals brought to nothing all the attempts, and, while the population growth remained at zero level in some areas, it rose sharply in other ones.

The only alternative for the world ruling elite was the increasing of the death rate. It was difficult to do, for nobody wants to snatch people out of a crowd and drag them to execution. The possible consequences of actions of frenzied people, who disclose that they are systematically exterminated, also brings nothing pleasant. It was necessary to do something, which would not call makers to account and put the whole blame on those who lead an irregular life, something that put the blame on our Mother Nature. Something like bubonic plague or even something more terrible, but something having a natural origin was needed.

W. Cooper tells haw it happened: "The necessary work had been done by doctor Aurelio Pezei from the Rome Club. In the result of this work, a virus affecting an immune system had been created. The order to work out prophylactic measures and treatment had also been given. The virus had to be used against population and brought into human organism by means of vaccination. Prophylactic meant only for the ruling elite...

At first "unwanted" members of society had been infected. Special attention had been given to the blacks, Latinos and homosexuals. Pure homosexuals were not persecuted, while they were destined to extermination.

The African continent had been infected through the vaccination from smallpox in 1977. The vaccination carried out by the International Health Organization. It was intended that without appropriate treatment the African black population would die out in fifteen years.

The US population had been infected through the vaccine from hepatitis B. Dr. Wolf Dzhmuness, ex-doctor of the Pope John Paul II, was the leading expert at the vaccination from hepatitis B in the periods of October-November, 1979, and March-October, 1980. It carried out by the Virus Deceases Control Center in New-York, San-Francisco and for another American cities...

The order had been given by the Bilderberg Group Committee on Politic situated in Switzerland. It also ordered to use other measures. One of them is a Henry Kissinger's Reducing Population Policy, which was carried out by the State Department. This policy presses the people of the Third World to take effective measures on population reducing and birth rate control, or they will not get help from the USA.

If they refuse, then, as a rule, a civil war flares out. Rebellions are trained, financed and armed by the CIA. That is why more civilians (especially young strong women) than military men are killed in El Salvador, Nicaragua, and other places. Such wars were provoked in Catholic countries by Jesuits.

The Henry Kissinger's Reducing Population Policy includes some government levels and, practically, determines the US Foreign Policy. The planning organization acts beyond the White house and directs all its attempts to the population reducing up to two billion people, which is achieved by means of wars, famine, epidemics and other necessary measures..."[392]

The situation is really out of control in many regions of the world. Patrick Bukennen, the author of the book *The Death of the West* expresses his preoccupation concerning, for example, uncontrollable growth of population on the west bank of Jordan river in the Gaza strip: "Now there are 4, 2 million Arabs there, by the year 2025 their number will have been doubled, and will be fifteen million in another twenty five years, i. e two times more than Jews.

In other parts of the world, the picture is even more terrible. In twenty-five years, there will be forty two million in Iraq, and ninety-four in Iran, more than in any European country, with the exception of Eurasian Russia. Taking into account the Europe population decreasing (especially white population), the quantity of Europeans will be only 10% of Earth population: sixteen millions Italians, twenty-three million Germans, thirty million Russians will vanish from the face of the earth... During the same half a century the population of Africa, Asia and Latin America will be three—four billions more. As for Russia, its further disintegration is inevitable: Siberia and Far East will pass to China, Russians will be totally replaced by Moslems in the Caucasus and Central Asia."

Based on statistical researches, Bucennenn comes to a not very comforting conclusion. American Cassandra (i. e. Buccenen) predicts that the white population of Europe will be reduced under Moslem expansion until totally disappearing. America will turn into a third-rate country, as it had happened with Russia with the only difference that in the USA the place of Moslems will be taken by Latinos who, in every legal and illegal way, invade America, pushing the whites out and reducing them to the role of national minorities. In California, the whites are already members of a national minority, in Texas they will have become such by the year 2004, and this process will soon include southern states.

Of course, it is most unlikely that such a demographic situation would not worry "western architects of ideological and economical expansions," for their first task is to hold in check the population growth by any means. And, since it is impossible to "snatch people out of a crowd and drag them to execution," "western architects" have to stage something in order to start mass extermination of "unnecessary people."

And, according to the documents presented by W. Cooper in his book *Behold a Pale Horse*, such extermination has begun. To achieve their goal, the elite use the whole set of measures, beginning with contraception and ending with physical elimination of "unnecessary people" by means of starvation, epidemics and wars. In the result of the New World Order establishing, a totally controllable society, devoid of private property and individual freedom, must be created.

Of course, it sounds monstrous. It is difficult to believe in, but if we have a proper look at the world, we shall see that everything in it goes on according to scenarios described above. The fate of the former Soviet Union is a good example of how these scenarios are being realized on practice.

As you know, the Soviet Union was the powerful empire with

rapidly developed economy and growing population. That is why, the world Masonic elite had to destroy our economy and to stop the population growth. Perestroika has solved all those problems, having destroyed our economy and plunged Russia to the condition of incessant war with Chechnya. And if they decided to stop the population growth in Caucasus republics by means of controllable armed conflicts, in Russia they have solved this problem with the help of "noiseless weapon," having inculcated into the cultural space of Russia the destructive cultural-economical environment. Having sown fear and uncertainness in the future into human hearts and souls, it killed their desire to bear children. Now, Russia loses about one million people a year. In half a century, its population will be twice as less than now, and, if such a birth/death rate remains the same, the Russians will become extinct by the end of the current century. Is it possible not to believe in the reality of Jewish-Masonic conspiracy after that?

Brachev V. S. gives the answer to this question in his book *Masons in Russia*: "Today we have to acknowledge the reality of the things which seemed to be a madman's fantasy yesterday. The integration processes are gaining power in the world, and the world government, about the necessity of its creation our democratic press openly writes, is already beginning to emerge as the government of "the United Europe" and organizations of international and, first of all, American capital, the influence of which goes far beyond the frames of just financial and economical problems.

The matter concerns the creation under the aegis of Masonry of nongovernmental organizations (Trilateral Commission, Council of International Affairs, Bilderberg club and some others), the members of which can be found among not only influential political figures, but also among presidents of the biggest banks and corporations.

The UNO and the periodical meeting of leaders of seven most developed capitalist countries are not more than working instrument for the juridical legalization of decisions taken in other offices. The same working instrument in the hands of the mighty of this world are Masonic lodges, which are implanted in Russia so persistently by its foreign "well-wishers." The whole history of Masonry brings out clearly about utter failure of noble all-human ideals of its adepts at their collision with practical reality."[393]

CHAPTER 9.

WHO KILLED THE TWINS?

"Why, of course the people don't want war ... But after all it is the leaders of the country who determine the policy, and it is always a simple matter to drag the people along, whether it is a democracy, or a fascist dictatorship, or a parliament, or a communist dictatorship... Voice or no voice, the people can always be brought to the bidding of the leaders. That is easy. **All you have to do is to tell them they are being attacked, and denounce the pacifists for lack of patriotism and exposing the country to danger.**"

Hermann Goering

9. 1. The Truth and the Lies About Terrorist Acts of September 11, 2001

Both the last events taking place in the world and the propagandistic hysteria roused around the image of "the enemy," as well as integration of different countries into a so-called antiterrorist coalition to fight against this "enemy," enable us to conclude that the matrix program has activated itself and persistently presses towards the realization of the program of destruction.

The fist two items of the "Apocalypses" plan has been successfully fulfilled: "And I saw, and behold a white horse: and he that sat on him had a bow; and a crown was given unto him: and he went forth conquering, and to conquer. And when he had opened the second seal, I heard the second beast say, Come and see. And there went out another horse that was red: **and power was given to him that sat thereon to take peace from the earth, and that they should kill one another: and there was given unto him a great sword.**"[394]

Then the matrix program makes provision for greater disasters:

"And I heard a voice in the midst of the four beasts say, A measure of wheat for a penny, and three measures of barley for a penny; and see thou hurt not the oil and the wine. And when he had opened the fourth seal, I heard the voice of the fourth beast say, Come and see. And I looked, and behold a pale horse: and his name that sat on him was Death, and Hell followed with him. And power was given unto them over the fourth part of the earth, to kill with sword, and with hunger, and with death, and with the beasts of the earth."[395]

The "black Tuesday" has become an absolute hell for America. At that day hell came in this country and many of its citizens saw the ominous face of the nether world, many of them "tasted" the death, their friends and relatives met with a loss of those whom they loved most of all, and all the people were stricken with fear all over the world.

The tragic events of September 11, 2001 have become the culmination of a great show which, because of the possibilities of the modern mass-media, became accessible to all the people all over the world. Hell came in every house, in every flat; it crept into human hearts and souls who had become witnesses of the dreadful atrocities.

Then, on TV screens and in newspapers, subtitles and commentaries turned up and announced about a new threat to the world—"international terrorism"—headed by Osama-ben-Laden who was declared guilty in the organization of the "American holocaust" and announced to be the bitterest enemy of the world.

Is it really so? Is "terrorist □ 1" really guilty of the atrocities of September 11, 2001, or he is only a scapegoat, upon which we pined our accusations and sacrificed it to Jewish demon Azazel? Another question is: who stands behind of those terrorist acts? Who is a producer of that unprecedented performance, the stage of which is life, and actors are real people who really suffer, experience pain and even die, if it is provided for a script?

The official story is:

1. On the morning of September 11th, four Boeing passenger jets were hijacked within an hour by nineteen Arab terrorists armed with box-cutters.
2. Pilots among these terrorists took control of the Boeings and changed course toward targets in New York City and Washington D.C.
3. Two of the Boeings were deliberately crashed into the Twin Towers,

causing raging fires within which melted the steel supporting structures, thereby causing the buildings to collapse completely.

4. The third Boeing was deliberately crashed into the Pentagon.
5. Passengers on the fourth plane overpowered the hijackers and caused the plane to crash in Pennsylvania.
6. This was an attack on America, and it was planned and directed by Osama-ben-Laden as the leader of Al-Queda, a previously obscure anti-U.S. international terrorist organization composed mainly of Arabs.

This cries out for further explanations, but the official story provides almost nothing more. We are simply expected to believe it without question. A nation (and the world), being in shock largely accepted this story, since it did appear to provide some explanations. Even those who considered this explanations hard to believe were inclined to believe them because on September 11th there seemed no other explanations. Both the President of the United States and all mainstream news sources in the U.S. were telling the world that this is how it was. But the official story does not withstand critical examination. It is, in fact, full of holes. **It's not just full of holes, it's a deliberate lie, designed to fool the American people and the rest of the world.**

According to the official story, four jetliners were hijacked by nineteen Arab terrorists. It is certainly possible to find Arabs who are willing to die for their cause (freedom of their people from ongoing American interference and domination and brutal Israeli aggression). But, to find nineteen of them for a single mission could be difficult. Another problem is to find such Arabs who also know how to fly Boeing 757s and Boeing 767s. (None of the alleged Arab hijackers had ever worked as professional pilots.) At least four highly trained pilots are needed. Alleged hijacker-pilots Mohammed Atta, Marwanal Al-Shehhi and Hani Hanjour had received pilot training, but were considered by their flying instructors to be incompetent to fly even light single-engined planes.

The official story expects us to believe that these alleged nineteen on-board hijackers (acting with military coordination and precision) overpowered the flight attendants (with nothing more than box-cutters and shouted commands), forced their way into the cabin (were all eight official pilots were absorbed in contemplation of clouds?), overpowered the pilots (apparently none of them, some ex-military, could offer any resistance to hijackers armed only with box-cutters), took command of the planes, having acquired the necessary flying skills from training courses and flight manuals, flew them expertly to their targets, met absolutely no opposition from the U.S. authorities (including the U.S. Air Force) responsible for safeguarding America's airspace (despite the fact that the Pentagon jet was in the air for nearly an hour after the first impact), hit those targets and killed themselves. Any intelligent person (after thinking about it) will hardly believe this story. But, as Dr. Joseph Goebbels, Reich Minister of Propaganda for NAZI Germany said: **"If you tell a lie big enough and keep repeating it, people will eventually come to believe it."**

Nevertheless, some experts had their doubts as to an unusually high level of terrorist acts preparation, which was not characteristic for the "classical" Arab-Islam terrorism: "This level is sharply contrasted to what that was known as the "classical" Arab-Islam terrorism. These terrorist acts had been planned and performed not as "improved" variants of known samples, but as something qualitatively new... **That is why the logic demands us to assume that both Arab performers and their sponsors had a "producer" who acted as the supreme leader and coordinator of hijackers-kamikaze groups.**"[396]

Reasoning like that, some Russian experts make a conclusion that "Mister X" is an American citizen of Japanese origin, for, as they believe "in any kind of significant activity (including criminal one), the national-cultural consciousness stereotypes are manifested in one way or another. If it is so, we have to conclude that the plotted blows were the acts of vengeance for a nuclear bombardment of Hiroshima and Nagasaki. A certain method of self-sacrifice testifies in the favor of this assumption: Arabs blow up themselves by means of bombs, Russians cover embrasure with their bodies, and an airplane-torpedo with a pilot-kamikaze inside is merely Japanese phenomenon."[397]

The Japanese "Red Army" even took the blame for performance of terrorist acts in America upon itself, but then another "scapegoat" had been found. Other experts consider the technology of the terrorist acts of September 11, 2001 performance level to be higher than that of the Japanese version.

As for us, we can notice the work of the matrix of destruction which had been created at those ancient times when man thought in the categories of mythological consciousness. We see that in this case, everything had been entangled and mixed to such a degree that now it is impossible to separate illusion from reality, lies from truth, cause from consequence.

If reasoning logically, we have to admit that the cause is followed by the consequence, as well as the sequence of events must be logically grounded. But investigating the case of terrorist acts of September 11th, we have seen crying infringements of all the laws of logic and common sense.

If we, for example, consider very attentively the details of the first air attack, we shall see that at first, a blow thunders, then a huge breach is formed in the wall of the skyscraper, and only after that a passenger airplane flies in and is blown up in the spacious womb of the Twin (8. 45 in the morning).

One can see this moment in the documentary film *America Remembers* by CNN. If one watches attentively the shooting of the first air attack, one can notice the dark outburst the moment before the airplane crashes into the building. It means that in the building detonated an explosive, which, if reasoning logically, had been placed there before (or it was a missile fired from the airplane). And it seems quite strange, for the picture of the air attack was perfect even without explosion.

Most likely, it has been done because in mythological consciousness of humanized troglodytes-super-animals everything is turned upside down, that is why they want to turn the entire world in such a way that they could see it normally, i. e. upside down. Of course, one can argue with us and say that the shown picture can be falsification, skillful photomontage, which could easily be made by means of a computer.

But in 18 minutes (9. 03 in the morning) another airplane rams into the building of the South Tower of the Twins, and in 56 minutes (9.59 in the morning) it falls down in a very interesting and unusual manner. The top of the Twin crashed down with such a speed and accuracy, as if there was nothing under it.

Experts' calculations confirm this fact: "The time t required for an object to fall from a height h (in a vacuum) is given by the formula t = sqrt(2h/g), where g is the acceleration due to gravity. Thus, an object falling from the top of one of the towers (taking h = 1306 feet and g = 32.174 ft/sec^2) would take 9.01 seconds to hit the ground if we ignore the resistance of the air and a few seconds longer if we take air resistance into account. The Twin Towers collapsed in 10 — 15 seconds, close to free fall. Following the start of the collapse the upper floors would have had to shatter the steel joints in all 85 or so floors at the lower levels. If this required only a second per floor then the collapse would have required more than a minute. But the material from the upper floors ploughed through the lower floors at a speed of at least six floors per second. This is possible only if all structural support in the lower 85 or so floors had been completely eliminated prior to the initiation of the collapse.

Since the lower floors were undamaged by the plane impacts and the fires, the removal of all structural support in these floors must have been due to some other cause—and the most obvious possibility is explosives. Thus the speed of the collapse (not much more than the time of free fall) is strong evidence that the Twin Towers were brought down in a controlled demolition involving the use of explosives (or some other destructive technology) at all levels."[398]

If one even admits that these calculations are the fruit of our morbid imagination, the character of collapse tells about the opposite. In the case of collapse of the South Tower of the Twins, one can see that the blow was struck into the right corner of the tower. Reasoning logically, the building had to bent to the right side too, for there the supporting constructions had been weakened in the result of air attack and subsequent explosion and fire. But the top of the building turns out to be thrust by some unimaginable power to the left side, which one can see on the pictures taken at the moment of collapse.

Besides, the collapse is followed by the powerful outburst of small fragments of the building and huge clouds of dust. And this fact gives us a right to assume that the picture of spontaneous falling of the South Tower head must be somewhat different.

Well, let us admit that both explosion and fire were so strong that they were able to melt all the supporting constructions on the blow level, and the top of the building began to fall down, crashing all the building under it. In order to imagine this process it is necessary to know the construction of the Twins-skyscrapers.

The Twin Towers were designed to survive the impact of a Boeing 707 which in weight, size and speed is similar to a Boeing 767 (the kind of jet which hit the South Tower). Had one of the towers collapsed, that would have been amazing. That both of them collapsed quickly, neatly and symmetrically (without falling over onto the surrounding buildings in Manhattan's financial district), collapsed completely into fragments, ash and huge clouds of dust—with no remains of their central massive vertical steel columns left standing—solely as a result of the plane impacts and the resulting fires, is, upon examination, unbelievable, despite what the so-called "experts" say.

Yamasaki and engineers John Skilling and Les Robertson worked closely, and the relationship between the towers' design and structure is clear. Faced with the difficulties of building to unprecedented heights, the engineers employed an innovative structural model: a rigid "hollow tube" of closely spaced steel columns with floor trusses extending across to a central core. The columns, finished with a silver-colored aluminum alloy, were 18 and ¾" wide and set only 22" apart, making the towers appear from afar to have no windows at all.

Also unique to the engineering design was its core and elevator system. The twin towers were the first supertall buildings designed without any masonry. Worried that the intense air pressure created by the buildings' high speed elevators might buckle conventional shafts, engineers designed a solution using a drywall system fixed to the reinforced steel core. For the elevators, to serve 110 stories with a traditional configuration would have required half the area of the lower stories be used for shaftways. Otis Elevators developed an express and local system, whereby passengers would change at "sky lobbies" on the 44th and 78th floors, halving the number of shaftways.

The structural system, deriving from the I.B.M. Building in Seattle, is impressively simple. The 208-foot wide facade is, in effect, a prefabricated steel lattice, with columns on 39-inch centers acting as wind bracing to resist all overturning forces; the central core takes only the gravity loads of the building. A very light, economical structure results by keeping the wind bracing in the most efficient place, the outside surface of the building, thus not transferring the forces through the floor membrane to the core, as in most curtain-wall structures. Office spaces do not have any interior columns. In the upper floors there is as much as 40,000 square feet of office space per floor. The floor construction is of prefabricated trussed steel, only 33 inches in depth, that spans the full 60 feet to the core, and also acts as a diaphragm to stiffen the outside wall against lateral buckling forces from wind-load pressures.

Thus, neither the plane impact nor the fire damaged the South Tower sufficiently to account for its collapse, so the South Tower collapsed from some other cause. The fire in the South Tower was thus less intense than that in the North Tower. But **the South Tower collapsed first**, at 9:59 a.m., 56 minutes after impact, whereas the North Tower collapsed at 10:29 a.m., 1 hour and 44 minutes after impact. **Had the fires been the cause of the collapse then the North Tower, with its more intense fire, would have collapsed first**. Or, put another way, had the fires been the cause of the collapse then the South Tower, hit after the North Tower, and subjected to a less intense fire, would have collapsed after (not before) the North Tower collapsed.

It is also necessary to take into account that kerosene is far from that substance which could cause the effect similar to that of Twins' collapse. A Russian expert Bazura L. V. says on this occasion:

"Humankind has been acquainted with kerosene since long time and knows that kerosene is not explosive. Benzene is also not explosive. The mixture of benzene vapour with air is explosive. Benzene is rather volatile liquid, and that is why at 20 degrees Celsius a lit match results in flare above spilt benzene in radius of 2-3 meters. Under the same conditions, the match thrown in a pool of kerosene dies away. For the combustion of 1 kg of kerosene, it is necessary to have constant inflow of oxygen from 20-25 cubic meters of air. The burning of kerosene in atmospheric conditions is possible only at impregnation of some porous substance with it or at a constant supercharging of an air jet.

It is also necessary to pay attention that **the skeleton of the towers was made with steel beams more than 6 inches thick, therefore, a weak body of a plane, which wings a flying bird is capable to punch, should simply be crashed into small pieces against the tower frame. And its wings with fuel tanks in them, were to break off and fall down. The pictures of "Armageddon" of September 11th, shown on TV as collision of "Boeings" with Twins' towers, do not correspond to those which would be in the case of a real air attack**...

Besides, the picture of the Twins tower destruction corresponds to a picture of brisant explosion, when the detonation wave (about 5000 m/sec) blows up not only inert explosive, but also many substances, which are not explosive at all. Brick and reinforced concrete turn into dust. At that reinforcement bars are being destroyed along their connection lines and separate rods fly away very far... **It is quite obvious that air attacks could not become the cause of the New York Twins collapse. It was brisant explosive material (hexogen) put inside the towers beforehand that was the main cause of collapse**..."[399]

Another question is: "Would jet fuel burning in an enclosed space (with little oxygen available for combustion) actually produce temperatures high enough (1538°C, i.e. 2800°F) to melt massive steel beams (and all the steel beams, since steel conducts heat efficiently) enclosed in concrete in just 56 minutes? If so, wouldn't the Twin Towers have buckled and bent, and toppled over onto the surrounding buildings in the Lower Manhattan financial district, rather than collapsing neatly upon themselves in the manner of a controlled demolition?"

The "official report" on the collapse of the Twin Towers was released in mid-2002. This report is convincing only to those who wish to believe what it says, but is quite unconvincing to anyone who reads it critically. Chapter 2 of this report, along with reasoned objections, is available at The WTC Report: WTC 1 and WTC 2 (http:/serendipity.li/

wot/wtc_ch2.htm): "... It is well-known that the maximum temperature that can be reached by a non-stoichiometric hydrocarbon burn (that is, hydrocarbons like jet-fuel, burning in air) is 825 degrees Centigrade (1520 degrees Fahrenheit). ... [The] WTC fires were fuel rich (as evidenced by the thick black smoke) and thus did not reach anywhere near this upper limit of 825 degrees. In fact, the WTC fires would have burnt at, or below, temperatures typical in office fires."[400]

Another problem with the official story is the fact that both the Twin Towers collapsed evenly and smoothly. Experts explaine this strange fact too: "If the fire melted the floor joints so that the collapse began from the 60th floor downward, the upper floors would be left hanging in the air, supported only by the central columns. This situation would soon become unstable and the top 30 floors would topple over ... How was it that the upper floors simply disappeared instead of crashing to the earth as a block of thousands of tons of concrete and steel? ...

When the platters [the floors] fell, those quarter-mile high central steel columns (at least from the ground to the fire) should have been left standing naked and unsupported in the air, and then they should have fallen intact or in sections to the ground below, clobbering buildings hundreds of feet from the WTC site like giant trees falling in the forest. But I haven't seen any pictures showing those columns standing, falling, or lying on the ground. Nor have I heard of damage caused by them...

Whatever damage the fires did would not have been evenly distributed (especially in the case of the South Tower, where the jet struck a corner of the building). If the collapse was due to the fires then it too would be irregular, with parts of the Twin Towers remaining intact and connected while other parts fell. But both towers collapsed completely symmetrically, with the floors pancaking upon themselves, exactly as we have seen in other cases of controlled demolition of tall buildings."[401]

The official version of air attack on the Pentagon, the main military department of the USA, does not stand up to criticism either. According to the official story, as it was reported by the *New York Times* (*International Herald Tribune*, 2001-10-17, p.8): "The Boeing 757, AA Flight 77, which struck the Pentagon executed a 270-degree 7,000-foot descent over Washington while flying at 500 mph. It approached the Pentagon on a horizontal trajectory (so as to maximize the damage to the building) so low that it clipped the power lines across the street." [But somehow managed to squeeze between two poles which were separated by less than the wingspan of a Boeing 757].

This maneuver was made, according to the official version, by an Arab pilot Hani Hanjour, who in August 2001 was judged by the chief flight instructor at Bowie's Maryland Freeway Airport as not having the piloting skills required to fly a Cessna 172 solo.

In contrast to the attention given to the collapse of the Twin Towers, the attack on the Pentagon received little attention until in February 2002 a French website[402] appeared, which reproduced images obtained from U.S. Army websites.

In the picture placed underneath of this page, one can see the very moment when the building façade was collapsed, but, and it is very strange, one cannot see any large fragments of an airplane which always remain on the place of wreck. Even if to assume that the whole plane flew inside the building and blew up there, then there should be the traces of wings on both sides of the breach (the width of which is about twenty meters, while wings span is about fifty meters). It seems also strange that such a large plane could fly on a horizontal trajectory between two poles which were separated by less than the wingspan of a Boeing 757 and did not break either wings nor poles. It seems that the plane did not have wings at all.

What happened to the wings of the "Boeing"? Presumably the wings, with their engines attached, would have sheared off when they hit the sections of the building (to the left and right of the hole in the side of the building) which are obviously still standing, with many wing and tail fragments ending up on the lawn in front of the Pentagon.

Do you see any remnants of wings in the picture (or in any of the other pictures on the French website)? How about an engine or two? And how about the fact that the building collapsed only thirty minutes after an "air attack?"

A documentary film made by CNN clearly shows the sequence of events. At first, the explosion thunders inside the building and the report, "Fire in the Pentagon" goes to Washington (without any mention of an "air attack"). Then Mike Walter, an eyewitness, tells CNN: **"It was like a cruise missile with wings, went right there and slammed into the Pentagon. Huge explosion, great ball of fire, smoke started billowing out**..." In thirty minutes or so the front wall collapses by itself, without any signs of aircraft wreckages. What about of simplest logic laws, which state that an "air attack" must be followed by an explosion and the building collapse which are to happen simultaneously? Then, the laws of logic say that large fragments of airplane (wings, engines, fuselage) must be present at the spot. But neither documentary film nor any photographs of the event show any signs of large aircraft remnants. Moreover, a passenger aircraft is not as small as a fly as not to be noticed while watching the film.

In the next photo, one can see a photomontage which shows that the real dimensions of the airplane are much bigger than those of the breach.

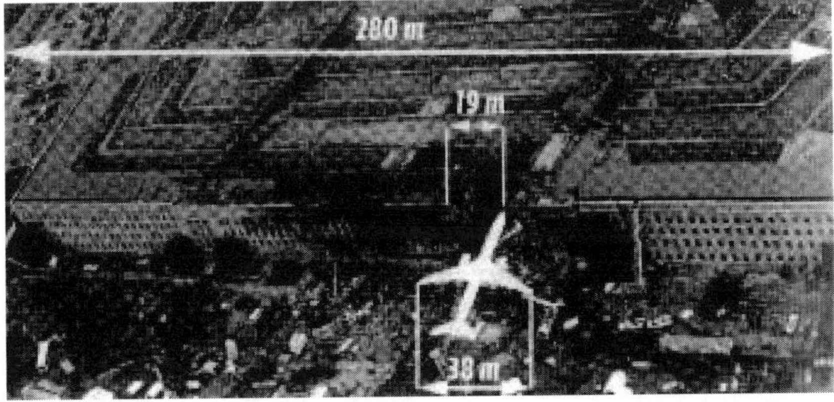

In this photo, one also cannot see any fragments of the "Boeing." And the facade of the building remains practically intact; it was just squeezed out forward in the result of explosion which had occurred inside the building.

It is also difficult to imagine that the unskilled pilot, who hardly flew a Cessna 172, could, without having sufficient navigating skills, plot the way to Washington, execute a 270-degree 7,000-foot descent over Washington while flying at 500 mph, approach the Pentagon on a horizontal trajectory and make the unprecedented ram of the main military department of the USA which has both its own system of the air space control and the means of protection from air attack. Where were all these means and what did they do the whole hour after airplanes hi-jacking and attacking the Twins Towers, remained the big riddle until now [U.S. Air Force has jets at seven locations near Washington normally ready to take off at ten minutes' notice].

After all these logic argumentations, we must decide whether it was a real air attack, or the destruction of the Pentagon had been caused by another reason. News programs shown on September 11 and later in Denmark and Germany, demonstrated a video clip of the Boeing 747 over Washington, accompanying this mysterious flight by the following comment: "Later that morning in Washington.... ANOTHER airplane caused panic,...............(the picture of the Boeing with 4 engines was then shown) .....Narrator:..... But it disappeared from the sky over Washington and later crashed down in Pennsylvania (Source: "SAT 1" German TV)

Some reporters said that this Boeing 747 later crashed down in Pennsylvania!?

(But the Pennsylvania plane "Flight 93" was a Boeing 757 and had ONLY 2 engines and not 4 engines—how do you explain this?) As a matter of fact—according to the Official FBI explanation—all the four involved Boeing air-planes on Sept.11—had ONLY 2 engines. They were either Boeing 757 or 767 (which have only 2 engines). So, the FBI has some problem here!"[403]

If this plane was crashed in Pennsylvania, it is obviously not that plane, which hit the Pentagon. But this is what is very interesting. The plane making flight 93, which had crashed in Pennsylvania was not a Boeing 747. It was a two-engine Boeing 757, instead of a four-engine Boeing 747, which was shown in the news program. And, in general, all the hijacked planes, according to the CIA reports, were two-engine planes. That is why it is quite obvious that there was no air attack on the Pentagon, it was destroyed in the result of controlled explosion.

There is also other strangeness in the flight 93 crash (look at the picture above). It is strange that there are no big fragments of the airplane on the spot. A big passenger airplane cannot dissapear or turn into a vapour at its impact against the ground. Moreover, the kerosene explosion cannot form such a crater as you see in the picture.

Many local inhabitants told that they had seen a smoke onboard of the flying airplane long before it crashed. The same information was also reported on September 11th on the German TV (program SAT 1 and RTL). The place of the flight 93 crash also looked a little strange.

There had been found only some small fragments of the plane on the spot. Other fragments, most likely, have evaporated or melted. But, nevertheless, CIA officials have managed to dig out "the letter of kamikaze," ostensibly written with the hand of Mohammed Atta.

Most likely, the airplane was shot down by a USA Air Force fighter. Local inhabitants, who saw the fragments of the plane eight kilometers far from the place of fall, also reported about the airplane being shot down by a US fighter...

Now, stop for a moment and think a little bit about the passengers and the crewmembers of the airplane which has disappeared somewhere on its way between the airport and Washington. It is documentarily stated that the airplane left the airport and was hi-jacked, but it did not reach its destination. Sixty or seventy people that were on board have disappeared together with the airplane. Nobody knows where did it happen and why. **How it is terrible to be aware of the fact that everyone of us can share the fate of those unfortunate wretches who have been killed in that airplane, if the World Elite decides to perform another "show" in order to pawe their way to the New World Order!**

CNN news had reported about eight airplanes involved in "air attacks" on the USA. And this message can be quite plausible, for it corresponds to the version about remote controlled airplanes involved in "air attacks." Another four airplanes was used to control airplanes-bombs remotely.

We have already said that the qualification of the pilot-kamikazes was insufficient for performance of such difficult maneuvers. Secondly, it is difficult to imagine that a handful of Arabs armed only with plastic cardboard-cutters could override both a crew and about 60 passengers, which in total is ten times as big as the number of hijackers. Of course, they could intimidate the crew and the passengers with a nonexistent bomb. But who can believe that the pilot-kamikazes could, without knowing any details of their forthcoming mission till the moment of their boarding in the plane, hijack the airplanes so harmoniously and professionally, change the course of the flight, and, by executing very complicated maneuvers [for example, the "Pentagon air attack" on a horizontal flight] and hit the targets? It is difficult to believe, but hijackers received the details of their mission just before their boarding.

It was declared by the "terrorist □ 1" in his "interview" which had been written down on a videotape found in November, 2001 in Afghanistan. "'**We did not reveal the operation to them until they are there and just before they boarded the planes...,' says Osama-ben- Laden, 'One group of people didn't know the other group**.'"[404]

And this ben Laden's revelation confirms our idea of remote controlled planes because in this case it was unnecessary to explain anything to the hijackers. They were just told that their mission would be just to intimidate the crew and the passengers with card-board cutters and nonexistent bombs, and further actions were the matter of technique (i.e. remote control systems). And the Arabs themselves become, thus, "scapegoats" and are sacrificed to Allah. The entire Arab world has also become a "scapegoat," which now can be sacrificed to Jewish demon Azazel (or Jehovah), i. e. be crashed, destroyed, sent to nonexistence, as a real scapegoat is sent to the desert, to nonexistence in order it to find its death there, having expiated the sins, people "have loaded" it with.

In this case, it is also quite understandable the fact that "hijackers" did not interfere with the passengers to use onboard telephones. It was necessary in order the world to think that it were Arabs who have begun the "war against America."

Todd Beamer, for example, the passenger of flight 93, supposedly informed the operator Lisa D. Jefferson about full details of events occurring onboard within 13 minutes. After the operator had informed Todd about air attack of the Twins, he organized the "revolt of the slaves" onboard the liner which resulted in crashing in Pennsylvania. It was Todd's wife who has informed Pittsburgh TV about this telephone call, the information of which she has received from the operator Lisa Jefferson. It is quite strange that Todd called not to his wife, but to the operator Lisa.

There was also one more rather strange call from Barbara Olson, program SNN television announcer and the wife of Ted Olson, the deputy minister of justice of the USA. On September 12th, at 2. 06 in the morning, SNN informed that it had received Mr. Olson's information about her wife's calling him two times from flight 77, which, as someone thinks until now, attacked the Pentagon.

Tod Olson said that Barbara had a trouble getting through because she wasn't using her cell phone. To make a call, she had to use the phone in a passengers' seat. **As she didn't have her purse, as Tod Olson guessed, she was calling collect**, and she was trying to get through to the Department of Justice, which is never very easy. She wanted to know what she could tell to the pilot and what she could do to stop the terrorists. It seems that the flight deck crew was with her at the back of the aircraft, presumably politely ushered down there by the box cutter-wielding Muslim maniacs who for some bizarre reason decided not to cut their throats on the flight deck. It sounds quite ridiculous, doesn't it?

The fact that Barbara Olson called collect is also ridiculous. In order to access the outside world one must first swipe one's credit card through the telephone. By Ted Olson's own admission, Barbara did not have a credit card with her.

It gets worse. On American Airlines there is a telephone "setup" charge of US$ 2.50, which can only be paid by a credit card, then a US$ 2.50 (sometimes US$5.00) charge per minute of speech thereafter. **The setup charge is the crucial element. Without paying it in advance by swiping your credit card, one cannot access the external telephone network**. Under these circumstances the passengers' seat phone on a Boeing 757 is as much used as a plastic toy.

Perhaps Ted Olson made a mistake and Barbara managed to borrow a credit card from a fellow passenger? Not a chance. If Barbara had done so, once swiped through the phone, the credit card would have enabled her to call whoever she wanted to for as long as she liked, negating any requirement to call collect.[405]

The communication conditions were also doubtful at that time.

According to the earth station operator opinion, the plane was at such a small height and flew with such a speed, that connection with telephone stations was practically impossible. **All these facts about telephone calls prove our assumption that all these stories were fabricated with the only purpose—to convince the world that those unprecedented and bloody atrocities of September 11th were performed by Arabs.**

And it was not without a reason that the lie about Barbara Olson's telephone call had been named "the Mother of all Lies," for "this is a story about a little white lie that bred dozens of other little white lies, then hundreds of bigger white lies and so on, to the point where the first little white lie must be credited as the "Mother of All Lies" about events on 11th of September, 2001. For this was the little white lie that first activated the American psyche, generated mass loathing, and enabled media manipulation of the global population.

Without this little white lie there would have been no Arab hijackers, no Osama-ben-Laden directing operations from afar, and no "War on Terror" in Afghanistan and occupied Palestine. Clearly the lie was so clever and diabolical in nature, it must have been generated by the "Power Elite" in one of its more earthly manifestations."[406]

Being based on what has been said above we tried to restore the true picture of the crime. But our attempt is not the first. In October 2001, two articles appeared on the web which provided the first clues to what really happened. One was Carol Valentine's "Operation 9/11: "NO SUICIDE PILOTS." This article drew attention to the possibility of remote control of a large jet aircraft. That this technology exists is well-known. It was developed by Northrop Grumman for use in Global Hawk, an automated American military jet with the wingspan of a Boeing 737.

Since it is possible to control a Boeing 757 or 767 by means of remote control, might not the jets, which hit the Twin Towers and the Pentagon (assuming that more than one did), have been remotely controlled? In which case there would be no need to maintain the improbable hypothesis that the four jets were simultaneously hijacked by nineteen on-board Arab terrorists.

The other article discussing the possibility of remote control of Boeing aircraft was Joe Vialls' "Home Run: Electronically Hijacking the World Trade Center Attack Aircraft." The author tells that in the mid-seventies, two American multinationals collaborated with the Defense Advanced Projects Agency (DARPA) on a project designed to facilitate the remote recovery of hijacked American aircraft. This technology allowed to take the absolute control of a hijacked plane's computerized flight control system by remote means. From that point onwards, regardless of the wishes of the hijackers or flight deck crew, the hijacked aircraft could be recovered and landed automatically at an airport of choice. Joe Vialls asserts that such a system was used to facilitate direct ground control of the four aircraft used in the high-profile attacks on New York and Washington on 11th of September, 2001.

But there is a problem with this theory. Although the technology for the remote control of a Boeing jetliner certainly exists, and could be installed (if it is not already standard) on four Boeings, getting all four remotely controllable planes to take off within an hour of each other would not be easy, and would require more people with insider knowledge than is advisable (the more people involved the more chance there is of a mistake, or of information being leaked). Not only would United Airlines and American Airlines personnel be needed to coordinate the plane assignments but also four different teams of remote controllers would be necessary, one for each remotely hijacked plane.

Considering the stakes involved in an operation which was intended to kill thousands of U.S. citizens, there could be no room for error. What was needed was a fool-proof plan, and the remote hijacking of four planes is a scenario with too many possibilities for something to go wrong.

The actual plan, which was implemented, is amazingly simple when it is finally understood, and it was carried out almost (but not completely) without a hitch. It was revealed to Carol Valentine by an informant (as recounted in 9-11: "The Flight of the Bumble Planes").

To put it briefly, a plot was hatched, not by Arabs, but by so-called Americans (agents of the civilian "state security and intelligence" agencies and bureaus, perhaps with Israeli involvement):

1. To take control of four civilian airliners
2. To carry out attacks on the Twin Towers and the Pentagon causing huge loss of life
3. To make it appear that these airliners were used to carry out the attacks
4. **To eliminate the passengers on the airliners who would not be involved in the operation except as reluctant witnesses**
5. To blame these attacks on "Arab terrorists" and to use this as a pretext to launch military campaigns against "the enemies of

America" in the Middle East and in Asia, the real aim being to get control of their oil and mineral resources.

This plot, of course, was not hatched in a day. In September 2002 a congressional report cited no less than 12 examples of intelligence information on the possible use of airliners as weapons. They stretch from 1994 to August 2001, when word came of a plot by Osama-ben-Laden to fly a plane into the US embassy in Nairobi, Kenya.

Sometime during the late 90's the U.S. state security agencies realized that certain foreign terrorists were thinking of hijacking planes and crashing them into significant buildings (naturally the Twin Towers would come first to mind). They might even have recruited these would-be terrorists. In any case, they helped them along (covertly, of course), providing money (transmitted via Pakistani ISI operatives), U.S. visas, introductions to U.S. flying schools and useful tips. The plan was not for these would-be terrorists to do the job (since their predecessors had demonstrated their limitations by botching the 1993 attack on the WTC) but rather to be "useful idiots" who could plausibly be blamed (just as Timothy Mc.Veigh was the "useful idiot" blamed for the Oklahoma City bombing). **The actual operation was far more elaborate than the would-be hijackers were capable of carrying out, and required equipment which they did not have and prior access to the Twin Towers which was not possible for them.**

What happened on September 11th was very likely something close to this:

1. Three planes had been made ready by U.S. military personnel, capable of being controlled remotely, with no-one on board: A military jet either loaded with high explosives or carrying missiles or both; An F-16 jet fighter armed with a missile; A Boeing 767, painted up to look like a United Airlines jet (call this "Pseudo Flight 175"). In the alternative theory the F-16 is replaced by an AGM-86C cruise missile capable of being fired from a B-52 and of flying to its target under GPS-guidance, and able upon impact to generate heat of over 2,000°C.

2. Early on the morning of September 11th, Mohammad Atta and some other Arabs board American Airlines and United Airlines planes under instructions from their CIA or FBI handlers. Atta

and others, some recorded by airport security cameras, will later be declared to be "the hijackers."

3. The four civilian jet airliners take off:

   - AA Flight 11, a Boeing 767, leaves Logan Airport, Boston, at 7:59 a.m. headed for Los Angeles, with between 76 and 81 passengers (about 39% of capacity) and 11 crew members aboard. (This is the jet which, according to the official story, hit the North Tower.)
   - AA Flight 77, a Boeing 757, takes off from Dulles Airport in northern Virginia at 8:10 a.m. bound for Los Angeles, with between 50 and 58 passengers (about 27% of capacity) and six crew members aboard. (This is the jet which allegedly hit the Pentagon.)
   - UA Flight 175, a Boeing 767, departs from Logan Airport, Boston, at 8:13 a.m. for Los Angeles with between 47 and 56 passengers (about 26% of capacity) and nine crew members aboard. (This is the jet which allegedly hit the South Tower.)
   - UA Flight 93, a Boeing 757, scheduled to leave Newark Airport at 8:01 a.m. for San Francisco, is late and does not depart until 8:41 a.m., taking off with between 26 and 38 passengers (about 16% of capacity) and seven crew members on board. (This is the jet which crashed in Pennsylvania.)
4. Pseudo Flight 175 takes off from its military base, flying under remote control, and flies so as to intercept the flight path of UA Flight 175. Radar operators tracking UA Flight 175 see the two blips merge.
5. A half-hour or so after taking off, the pilots of the four civilian airliners are informed by radio that the U.S. is under attack by terrorists and that they are to shut down their transponders and land their planes at a military base in some north-eastern U.S. state (directions to the base are given).
6. The pilots obey this order and change course accordingly.
7. Pseudo Flight 175 changes course toward New York. To radar operators it appears as if UA Flight 175 is now flying toward Manhattan.
8. The passengers on UA Flight 93 are led to believe that the plane has been hijacked, and are instructed to use their cell phones to tell this to their relatives (thus planting fake evidence which will later be used to support the official story).

9. The military jet takes off under remote control and (perhaps after intercepting the flight path of AA Flight 11 to confuse the radar operators) approaches the North Tower at 8:45 a.m., fires missiles into it then crashes into it, detonating explosives already planted in the building. (George W. Bush watches the impact on closed circuit television at a school in Florida.)
10. Pseudo Flight 175 approaches Manhattan under remote control and crashes into the South Tower at 9:03 a.m. Its controllers, not used to remotely control the 100 tons of a Boeing 767, almost miss the tower, but manage to hit it at an angle, toward one corner. Most of the jet fuel passes through the corner of the tower and explodes in a huge fireball outside the building. (The approach of the Boeing 767 and the impact and fireball are recorded by many cameras.)
11. George W. Bush announces to the nation that he has made some phone calls and then goes into hiding for eight hours. He fails to order defensive action by ordering U.S. Air Force jets from bases near Washington to scramble to intercept the other two (allegedly hijacked) planes still in the air. No other Air Force officer orders jets to intercept the planes. Interceptors are finally scrambled an hour after the first of the commercial jets has gone off course and 45 minutes after the impact at the North Tower.
12. The F-16 jet fighter (see 1. above), under remote control, flies at high speed toward Washington D.C. (perhaps after crossing the flight path of AA Flight 77), descends to near ground level, makes a horizontal approach to the Pentagon, fires a missile which produces a huge explosion at the outer wall of the Pentagon, then itself crashes into the building (at 9:38 a.m.), its engine penetrating several rings of the Pentagon. In the alternative theory it is an AGM-86C cruise missile which strikes the Pentagon.
13. Meanwhile (by sometime between 9:15 a.m. and 9:45 a.m.) all four AA and UA jets have landed at the military base to which they were directed. The 199 (later listed) passengers and crew from AA Flight 77, AA Flight 11 and UA Flight 175 are herded onto UA Flight 93, where they join the 33 (later listed) passengers and crew, for a total of 232 people. Explosives are loaded on board.
14. The South Tower collapses (at 9:59 a.m.) in a controlled demolition, 56 minutes after impact.
15. Sometime around 10:00 or 10:15 a.m. UA Flight 93 takes off from the military base (either under remote control or under the control

of a military pilot unaware of his fate) and flies toward Washington in a fake "terrorist attack."

16. The North Tower collapses (at 10:29 a.m.) also in a controlled demolition, 1 hour and 44 minutes after impact.
17. Either explosives on board UA Flight 93 are detonated, or the jet is blown apart by a missile fired by a U.S. Air Force F-16 fighter jet, over Pennsylvania (at 10:37 a.m., almost two hours after it took off from Newark Airport). Pennsylvania state police officials said that on Thursday debris from the plane had been found up to 8 miles away (from the crash site) in a residential community [Indian Lake] where local media have quoted residents as speaking of a second plane in the area [this was the F-16] and burning debris falling from the sky.—Reuters, Sept. 13. **All passengers and crew from all four "hijacked" planes, perhaps or perhaps not including those 34 (later unlisted) passengers (including Mohammad Atta) who are part of the operation, are in this way eliminated.**
18. The outer wall of the impact site at the Pentagon is caused to collapse (so that the small size of the hole in the wall caused by the impacting object would no longer be visible).
19. Around midday the media whores begin to disseminate the story that this "terrorist attack" was masterminded by Osama-ben-Laden.
20. Around 5 p.m. the building known as WTC 7 collapses in a controlled demolition.
21. Misled by the mainstream media a shocked and outraged American public demands revenge against the perpetrators, whom they assume to be Arab Muslim fundamentalists.
22. George W. Bush announces his "War on Terrorism" and the Pentagon swings into action to implement its previously-prepared plans to bomb Afghanistan (into submission to U.S. oil interests).

Of course, some of the details of this account may turn out to be wrong, but overall it appears to be the most likely explanation of the events of September 11th, and (in contrast to the official story) is consistent with all the evidence and is contradicted by none. Only a full and impartial investigation of what happened on September 11th will reveal the truth.[407]

9. 2. Who Killed the Twins?

Our own investigation has also proven the fact that "the terrorist

No. 1" could not be the one who planned and organized the atrocities of September 11th, 2001. Albert Timashev, a Russian astrologer, as far back as on the 27th of September, 2001 said: "It's very important to mention that Osama-ben- Laden is neither of them [organizers], and he is wrongly accused by the majority of people. His rudder star is Antares, the star of wars, public enmity and violence. In the astrological chart of any terrorist act that ben Laden has something to do with, the star Antares is pronounced always. In the chart of the given terrorist act, Antares is not accented at all, and this fact completely acquits ben Laden and rejects all accusations against him... It confirms the words of one representative of the Russian secret services who said that, most likely, here we are dealing with an unknown secret service having enough power to organize these acts and especially to block the American security systems."

As we have shown above, neither Osama-ben-Laden nor the terrorist organization Al-Queda had the sufficient means and possibilities for the organization of such a large scale crime. Everything they could do was to prepare some groups of "useful idiots" who did not know either about existence of other groups or about the real purposes and tasks of their mission until the moment of boarding, as Osama-ben-Laden has declared in his interview, which had been written on a video film found in Afghanistan.

Among all other things, he says: "Basing on my own experience in this area I have thought that ignition of fuel of the plane may fuse steel constructions of a building in the impact area, and result in collapsing of **only the top floors**. It was everything we had expected."[408]

But the effect has surpassed all the expectations of Osama-ben-Laden. It means that neither "the terrorist number 1" nor "hijackers" might even assume that their actions would cause such disasters. They even had not planed anything like that. They were only "useful idiots" who did their "work."

Thus, we should exclude Osama-ben-Laden and the terrorist organization Al-Queda from our list of suspects guilty in the organization of the terrorist acts of September 11th, 2001. Moreover, they could be considered to be the victims, for they got involved in this business against their will, resulted in both their death and the death of many their compatriots in the Arabian world.

But who was the organizer of those unprecedented terrorist acts? Certainly, he might be the only one who would receive huge economic or political dividends after committing the crime. One of such suspects might certainly be President Bush with his administration because he needed both to raise his rating and justify the far-reaching military plans of intimidation and occupation of the countries located on the "axis of evil."

After the atrocities of September 11th, 2001, Bush becomes the national hero, gets both support of the world community in his struggle against "the international terrorism" and the access to cheap sources of Iraqi oil. But he hardly could conceive and carry out such a refined plan of a monstrous crime. Most likely, he is a pawn in "a big game," the rules of which are established by more powerful figures, who belong to the "virgin" sons of "God's people." Otherwise, he would hardly demonstrate the film, which contains indirect evidence of existence of well-organized plot not only against American people, but also against the whole world. Even if to admit that president Bush guessed or was informed about the hidden causes of the terrorist acts of September 11th, 2001, even then he could do nothing else as to support the version of "Arabian trace," or he might lose the presidency.

American architect and businessman Zilbershtein, who got a special credit six weeks before the accident and became the owner of WTC, could be another interested party. He had time to insure it for the astronomical sum of three billion dollars and now tries to receive 200 % of the insurance, that is six billion, because the "impact was accomplished with two airplanes..."[409] But it is not clear what the Pentagon had to do with it, if Zilbershtein did not receive a single cent after its destruction.

Generally speaking, the Pentagon does not fit into the picture of the "black Tuesday." You see, the "legend" of "the Arabian trace" would be plausible enough even without the explosion in the building of the main military department of the USA. But more careful analysis shows that the "legend" was constructed so that to present those terrorist acts as the plot, the purpose of which was the destruction of three main symbols or idols of America: the Twins of the WTC (the symbol of economy), the Pentagon (the symbol of military power), and the White House (the symbol of the state power).

But, as it was extremely difficult to destroy the Pentagon by means of a large passenger airplane, the organizers of the atrocities, using the psychological shock the USA and the whole world were in after the Twins murder, decided to blow up the building of the Pentagon, having presented the explosion as an air attack of the flight AA 77. The "legend" about the air attack of the Pentagon was also necessary in order for the curious world community not to ask unnecessary questions about what happened to the flight AA 77, and why and where the airplane disappeared together with its crew, passengers and "hijackers."

To attack the White House by means of a passenger airliner was not less difficult than to attack the Pentagon. It would be rather difficult even for a skilled pilot, to fly to a presidential residence on a low-level flight maneuvering between city constructions and to ram the building whose height is hardly more than that of an airplane. Therefore, it was simply declared that flight 93, crashed in Pennsylvania, headed towards Washington to attack the White House. The national pride of passengers could not reconcile with the intentions of "hijackers" to destroy their national property, and they died as heroes, salvaging the American sanctuary at the cost of their lives.

But what would they think, what would they say and what would they do if they found out that they, like the herd of animals intended for a slaughter, were driven into an airplane to be sacrificed to Jewish God Jehovah, who says to his "elected" people: "Go and smite Amalek, and destroy everything he has. And kill both husband and wife, infant and old men, camels and donkeys?" What would their friends and relatives, their parents, their children and all the American people think if they had learned that those people had been cruelly killed only because the world elite needed to wage new world war in the result of which all "the kings of the Earth" as well as all the "unnecessary people" would be destroyed, and the whole world would turn into a huge empire which would be governed by the "chosen sons of God's people"?"

These "chosen" sons of Jewish nationality have governed the United States of America since the very moment of its existence, they have penetrated into all state institutes of the world, they exercise the secret power in order to establish the New World Order on the Earth.

And this is not only our opinion. In 1973, on the ABS television program "Face to Face with the Nation," William Fulbraight, the former head of the United States Foreign Affairs Senatorial Commission, declared that "Israel rules the United States Senate!" In 1974, in the interview to the newspaper *Los Angeles Times*, something similar was said by General George Brown, the former chief of the Pentagon: "... We may say that, probably, we shall not be able to make the Congress support (Israeli) program, which is similar to this one. And they say, 'do not worry about the Congress. We ourselves shall take care of the Congress... '"

Osama-ben-Laden, "the terrorist number 1," said almost the same in his interview to ABC News and the PBS Frontline web sites as far back as in 1998: "...They (Americans) have given themselves on the mercy of government which is disloyal to America... It is Israel inside of America. Let us take such influential ministries as the State or Defense Department, as well as the CIA, and you will see that Jews boss over them. They use America to progress their plans to the whole world... During more than a half of century, Jews killed Moslems in Palestine; they attacked, plundered and deprived them off their honor and their property. Their houses were destroyed, their crops were exterminated... This is my message to American people: **'Find the serious government, which will observe the American interests and will not attempt to encroach on other countries, on other peoples or on their honor**...'"[410]

In his reply to the assumption that Israel may lose American help, Ariel Sharon has declared to Simon Peres on the 3rd of October, 2001 (it was informed on Yid Israel radio): "Every time we do something you inform me that America will do this or that... I want to clear up: **do not worry about American pressure upon Israel. We, Jewish people, control America and Americans know it**..."[411]

And on the 21st of November, 2001, David Duke, the national president of the Organization of the European-American unity and human rights activity (EURO) published the article "How the Israeli Terrorism and the American Treason Have Resulted in the Attacks on the 11th of September." And here is what he wrote: "...Jews control the most influential newspapers of America including such giants as the *New York Times*, the *Washington Post*, and the *Wall Street Journal*. They posses three most influential news magazines: the *Time*, the *Newsweek* and the *US News and World Report*. They completely dominate on TV, on radio, in the biggest MASS MEDIA conglomerates, namely the "Time Warner" and the "Disney." ABC, CBS and NBS, three main American operational news corporations are also under their control. Because of the whole community of Israeli oriented employees in American MASS MEDIA, the majority of American people are not informed about the terrorist service record of Israel. This entire article should serve as the only tiny pin in the bubble of Israeli propaganda which will be able, by means of several good pricks, to break off the cover of lie created by Israel..."[412]

That lie looked as follows. The next day after the attack on the WTC, the *Jerusalem Post*, the Israeli's most respectable newspaper, informed that 4000 Israelis were lost during the attack. The Israeli Foreign Affairs Ministry has estimated this number on inquiries of Israeli relatives who wanted to know the situation during the first hours after the attack. As New York is the center of the international Jewish financial power, and WTC is the center of New York, it was quite natural to expect that the level of Israeli losses among victims would be just catastrophic.

When George Bush held his speech at the Congress, it appeared that he made an essential mistake. He especially emphasized that together with thousands of American people 130 Israelis were lost in WTC, and that the Jewish people shared their suffering with American citizens, he added that American people are together with Israel in this sense. But it is difficult to believe that only 130 Israelis were lost in the WTC. If at the moment of terrorist acts there were about 4000 Israelis in both towers of the Twins (the number of victims died in WTC was approximately 4500, which is approximately 10% from 45 000 persons that usually are in the buildings at that time), the Israeli losses statistically should make about 400 instead of 130 persons.

Actually the number of lost Israelis was even less. The *New York Times* which was engaged in finding out of their exact number informed that only one Israeli was actually lost: "...But the statements of many consulate officials made on Friday suggested that lists of victims which they have collected were strongly differed from reality. For example, the data collected by city's authorities stated that many of Israelis were probably lost at the place of accident, and the president Bush mentioned in his broadcast appeal to the nation on Thursdays that there were approximately 130 Israelis lost in the accident. However, on Friday, Alon Pinkas, the general consul of Israel in the United States, declared that the previous lists of victims were overestimated by messages of people who, for example, did not receive the answer to phone calls from Israel to their New York relatives at once. Actually the were only three Israelis whose death was confirmed: two of them were lost in airplanes and another one was in the WTC on business. Later, they were identified and buried..."[413]

A very low official level of fatal losses of only 130 Israelis may suggest an idea that the majority of Israelis working in WTC were warned before the attack. **But if to take into account that only one Israeli died during the attack, there should not remain any doubts that many Israelis were warned about terrorist acts beforehand.**

There also exist the documentary evidences which prove the fact that Israelis had been warned before the attack. The Israeli daily newspaper *Haaretz* informed that Israel had received such a warning. It also has confirmed that the FBI investigated them. The article gives the details of how the "Odigo," Israeli information agency, which has offices both in WTC and in Israel, had received a number of warnings exactly two hours prior to the attack. Russian newspaper *Tomorrow* informs: "... "Odigo" officials specializing in urgent messages transmitting have confirmed today that two employees had received messages containing the warnings of the forthcoming attack on the WTC two hours prior to the moment when terrorists had blown up the airplanes directed to New York's ground targets. Alex Diamandis, the vice-president of sales and marketing department, has also confirmed that "Odigo" sales office workers in Israel had received the warnings from another "Odigo" employee approximately two hours prior to the first attack..."[414]

We do not know who could warn Israelis about forthcoming terrorist acts; we also do not know whether it was Mossad, Israeli intelligence agency, that took part in the organizing of the atrocities, for there are more other evidences that show more interesting details in the Twin's case.

It is known, for example, that "Pakistan's chief spy Lt. General Mahmoud Ahmad was in the US when the attacks occurred. He arrived in the US on the 4th of September, a full week before the attacks. He had meetings at the State Department after the attacks on the WTC. But he also had "a regular visit of consultations" with his US counterparts at the CIA and the Pentagon during the week prior to September 11. What was the nature of these routine "pre-September 11 consultations"? Were they in any way related to the subsequent "post-September 11 consultations" pertaining to Pakistan's decision to cooperate with Washington. Was the planning of war being discussed between Pakistani and US officials?"[415]

Some answers to these questions were found in the *Time of India* that In October, 2001, published the article in which it revealed the fact that proved the link between General Mahmoud Ahmad and a terrorist leader Mohammed Atta.

The artickle also sheds light on the nature of General Ahmad"s "business activities" in the US during the week prior to September 11, raising the distinct possibility of ISI contacts with Mohamed Atta in the US in the week "prior" to the attacks on the WTC, precisely at the time when General Mahmoud and his delegation were on a so-called "regular visit of consultations" with US officials. Remember, Lt. General Mahmoud Ahmad arrived in the US on the 4th of September...

The revelation of the *Times of India* has several implications. The report not only points to the links between ISI (Pakistan's military intelligence) Chief General Ahmad and terrorist ringleader Mohamed Atta, it also indicates that other ISI officials might have had contacts with the terrorists. Moreover, it suggests that the September 11 attacks were not an act of "individual terrorism" organised by a separate Al Queda cell, but rather they were part of coordinated military-intelligence operation, emanating from Pakistan's ISI.

Thus, it is not so easy to define exactly who was the organizer of "American holocoust." The question "who killed the Twins?" remains open even despite the hearings held in June, 2004, by the National Commission on Terrorist Attacks Upon the United States (also known as the 9-11 Commission). The Commission investigated the case according to the official version, that is why it found nothing that could shade the light on the real causes of the atrocities of September 11th, 2001.

9. 3. The War on Iraq, SARS and the New World Order

As we have already stated above, the terrorist acts of September 11th, 2001, had provoked the USA government to wage new world war the fronts of which would pass along "the axis of evil" indicated by president Bush at his annual appeal to the nation in February, 2002. Such countries as Iraq, Iran, Syria and North Korea were included in this "axis." Iraq became the first "target" to be attacked by the military machine of the USA.

In this book, we shall not consider all the details of the war on Iraq, for they are well-known to everybody. We shall only mention that it was prepared and commenced strictly according to the rules of double morals, the best textbook of which is the Bible. We are only going to pay your attention to some interesting details, which the American government would hardly dare to promulgate to the world community.

First of all it is necessary to note that "the bloody dictator" Saddam Hussein was brought to power not without the help of "the Big Brother." It is true that he was bloody and cruel; otherwise he would hardly be in need for his CIA "friends." Saddam's father died early, and his mother married again, that is why Saddam Hussein at-Tikriti (such was the full name of former "dictator") was brought up by his uncle, who was a schoolteacher. He was a person with an extremely fascist world outlook and Saddam learned much from him.

Very interesting details of Saddam's life vere told to the correspondent of the Russian newspaper *Arguments and Facts* by Hammad Abu Nakhid, a professor of chemistry, who studied together with Saddam Hussein at school. Abu Nakhid tells that when Saddam was fourteen, he shot his relative, a communist, and had to go into hiding for some time. Then he was arrested, sentenced and rehabilitated because of brilliant speech of his advocate. In some years, having come to power, Saddam "thanked" him, having ordered to assassinate him.

In 1959 Saddam took part in an attempt at the Iraqi prime minister Abdel Kerim Kasem. The coup failed, and Saddam had to escape to Egypt. There, he fell into the net of CIA agents. They were attracted by his anti-communism, rigid and uncompromising character, and his inclinations of a leader.

In a year and a half, Saddam came back to Baghdad where, in February 1963, he took an active part in a new coup against the head of government, who sympathized with the Soviet Union and Communism, which American government did not like. The February revolution of 1963 was carried out by the Baas nationalist parties, which chose Saddam Hussein to be one of its leaders. But that time the regime of Baas lasted less than a year. Baas, together with Saddam Hussein went underground and came out only in 1968. On the 17th of July, a coup d'etat was commited in Baghdad, and already on the 30th of July Hussein ordered to kill five generals, who had made the coup. But during those years Hussein had managed to put the majority of the initial organizations of the Baas party under his control. It was not done without the help of his CIA "friends."

After the revolution of 1968, Saddam Hussein formally occupied the position of the second person in the government of the president-general Ahmede Hasane al-Bakr, who was Saddam's relative. But gradually the power passed into Saddam's hands. In 1979 he exterminated Bakr, then his own brother from the mother's side, and then his cousin, who was the defense minister in Saddam's government...

As Saddam came to power, Iraq began to arm actively. Hussein dreamed to have a nuclear or, at least, a chemical weapon. In 1970-1972, two nuclear reactors were built in Zaafrania (the town near Baghdad): one with the help of the USSR, another one—with the help of France.

In 1972-1973, Iraq made an attempt to create a chemical weapon. Twenty-five chemical concerns, seventeen of which were from Germany, helped Iraq to do that. But after Iraqi attack on Iran in September 1980, all the works were suspended.

In December 1983, Donald Ramsfeld, a former president Regan's advisor and the present Minister of Defense of the USA, visited Bagdad. He assured the Iraqi president that the USA would do its best to help Baghdad with his struggle against the Islamic regime of Iran.

Soon the components of a chemical weapon began to arrive, and were assembled at once in several places: in Zaaphrania, Dzadaria, Abu

Grabe and Salman-park. The weapon was used in Iran and against Kurds in Iraqi Kurdistan. As for a bacteriological weapon, the Bacteriological Weapon Control Center of the USA government exported "bifor," Siberian ulcer bacteria, to Iraq in 1985.

This fact was promulgated in the Senate of the USA in October 2002, and caused the loud scandal in press. Soon, other facts of Washington's cooperation with Saddam Hussein were found out. American people were shocked. It was also found out that Ronald Regan's administration had decided to support Iraq to stop the expansion of Islamic revolution from Iran to other regions. In 1982, Baghdad was excluded from the list of the countries supporting terrorism.

In 1983, Donald Rumsfeld, the present Minister of Defence of the USA personally met with Hussein. They discussed the delivery of many products including those of double use: pathogenic biomaterials, which could be applied both in medicine and at the biological weapon creation. During those years, Iraq used such a weapon against the Iranian army. Besides, former Reigan's administration employees have shown under the oath that the CIA supplied weapons to Iraq through the fiction companies in Latin America. One of such company was the Chilean company "Kardoen" which was engaged in the transportation of cassette bombs forbidden by international conventions.

It is officially recognized that twenty-four American corporations helped with their production to the Iraqi military program. Among them was "Hewlett Paccard," "Tektronics," "Rockwell" and "Honeywell." They delivered equipment for nuclear centers. The period of cooperation with Hussein ended in 1990 after the capture of Kuwait. During the operation "Desert Storm," many military Iraqi objects were destroyed. Nevertheless, international inspectors, who were admitted to the country, discovered and made long lists of chemicals, computers and missiles components with American marking.

After "Desert Storm," the military potential of Iraq was destroyed and new deliveries of weapon components were stopped. Therefore, it is quite clear that Iraq did not represent any threat both to the world community or to the United States. It should be occupied, firstly, to make one more step towards an establishment of the New World Order, secondly, to get access to cheap sources of Iraqi oil.

When the main military operations in Iraq were finished, president Bush, in his speech onboard of the aircraft carrier "Abraham Lincoln," was very cautious to declare the war was completed or to speak about a victory. To avoid those items, the president declared the war against Saddam Hussein as a part of the anti-terrorist war, the war that was not yet finished, but the one that would not last endlessly. The day of a final victory was still unknown, but the situation had already been changed.

As a domestic issue (which, to a certain extent, opened pre-election struggle), that message should present the president who has achieved a great success, and now is starting to solve the economic problems of the country.

The foreign policy aspect of the speech was to emphasize Washington's determination to set out alone against the countries of "the axis of evil" whenever it is necessary. In the military aspect, the speech should define the turning point of the war, however it should be done as cautiously as possible in order to avoid accusations in lie in the case of further clashes.

To prove his innocence, the American president should resort to various tricks. And the speech held on the aircraft carrier was not the most difficult part in the realization of problems put by the Bush administration. It is important that president Bush named the third reason for waging war and brought it to the forefront.

Originally, it was declared about the probable presence of weapons of mass destruction in Iraq, then, about liberating of the oppressed country from the yoke of a bloody dictator, and, at last, the war on Iraq was proclaimed to be the part of anti-terrorist campaign which had begun after the events of September 11th, 2001.

Of course, such a lie can be easily accepted by American people, who still have not recovered from the shock caused by the atrocities of September 11th. For other countries of the world community, however, this argument is as unconvincing as the two previous ones. The presence of weapons of mass destruction in Iraq has not been confirmed till today, and Washington, understanding that it is necessary to explain this fact, gives out newer and newer pearls. Either it is stated that Iraq has quickly destroyed those weapons or the war has prevented from finishing its creation.

But if Iraq has been occupied quickly and effectively, it will hardly be so easy to do with other countries that ostensibly represent the threat to the USA. Of course, it is possible to occupy, for example, North Korea, but who can say what price will be paid by American people and how many American soldiers and peaceful populations will die in that war. As for China, the military machine of the USA will hardly be able to subdue and occupy the country whose area exceeds the area of America and whose population is several times bigger that that of the USA.

But if any country cannot be subdued by force, it can be taken by starvation. It is possible to impose economic sanctions, it is possible to provoke a civil war or use "the noiseless weapon" for "quiet wars," and it is also possible to infect its inhabitants with any fatal virus, for example, with the virus of atypical pneumonia (SARS). This virus will help the "architects" of the New World Order to solve many problems they are anxious for.

First of all, it will help to solve the problem of "unnecessary people" due to the increase of a death rate among the population. The large scale epidemic and the fear it will cause are capable to undermine both national economy of a country-victim and that other countries, which will inevitably begin to incur considerable losses from the cancellation of business transactions, tourist business and an air communication with infected countries. The economic expenses to struggle with a new and unknown virus also can be significant. Thus, a country-victim gets into isolation and becomes a social outcast, which is afraid of by the whole world.

The penetration of the SARS virus, for example, to Canada was instantly reflected both on economy and on public life of the country. In Toronto, the international conferences and concerts, including Elton John's and Billy Joel's, were cancelled. As it was announced by Toronto's "Dominion" bank, the infective episode might cost to the Canadian economy about two billion Canadian dollars (1,5 billions of the US dollars).

Deutsche Lufthansa AG, the third European airline, lost 55 million euro weekly because of the SARS spreading. The war in Iraq and the world economic recession were announced among other reasons Lufthansa losses. The economic losses of China itself are hardly possible to be estimated.

According to the information of the World Health Organization announced on May 11th, 2003, 235 people died in China, 212 in Hong Kong, 27 in Singapore, 18 on Taiwan, 22 in Canada, 5 in Vietnam, 2 on Philippines, 1 in Thailand and 1 in Southern Africa.

But where did this unknown atypical virus come from? The official version says that it came from animals—dogs, cats, rodents, birds etc, which sounds a bit strange, for we lived for a long time together with cats and dogs, as well as with all did not even think that our four-legged friends contained in themselves such a threat.

The fact is that the appearance of a new virus by natural way is practically impossible. The natural panmixia of birds and mice (or bulls) viruses is improbable. But it can be done in a laboratory.

Sergey Kolesnikov, the academician of Russian Science Academy confirms this fact: "What are the basic attributes of biological weapon? Neither the source of infection nor a pathogen, as well as prevention and treatment methods are known. And the fast infection spreading! It is quite obvious that all these attributes were present."[416]

A similar opinion was expressed by Romeo Mendeles, a Spanish doctor and the representative of "Doctors of the World" organization in Thailand: "The Virus of atypical pneumonia could be created in one of the laboratories of secret services organizations. Further, there was either a leakage, or a test-tube containing bacteria was place stealthily in a water or sewerage system."[417]

As doctor Mendeles believes, all the mysterious epidemics that frequently break out in Asia, Africa and Latin America are just scheduled tests of biological weapons conducted by secret services of the USA, China and North Korea where people are ruthlessly used as guinea pigs. Here, it will be useful to recollect the Ebola virus, which appeared in Congo and Uganda in 1991. That time, 5000 people died during several days.

Kresta Vincent Ljezh, a doctor of International Red Cross tells: "I worked in Congo then. We guessed at once that Ebola virus might be created artificially because we had never faced such an illness. I was greatly impressed by the fact that it was not one or two people that fell sick, instead, it was a big group of people who were infected during one day, as though someone "has sprayed" a virus in this place on purpose."[418]

It is very similar to the spreading of the SARS virus. The first infected appeared in February, 2003. Then in Southern China and Hong Kong, tens of people fell sick within one day, then in Singapore and Vietnam. According to the World Health Organization report published in the beginning of May, the SARS virus is capable to live in the water drain system for about four days. That is, if the version about artificial origin of atypical pneumonia is true, those who have organized the epidemic had enough time to disappear after placing bacillus into drain system.

Jeremy Goldberg, the author of *The Evil Out of a Test Tube*, also tells a terrifying story about dangerous experiments with deadly viruses: "I can note some moments. In 1957, on the Urals, the epidemic of Siberian ulcer broke out, and only then, after the collapse of the Soviet Union, it was announced that it might be the test of biological weapon. In 1979, in Sverdlovsky region, 50 people died from the same illness; but this time, Soviet sources put forward the version that it was the CIA that was guilty in what had happened. In 1957, the epidemic of "Asian influenza" broke out in the USA, and 70,000 people died. Isn't it strange that the virus has appeared in several American cities during the same single day? Then, there were also assumptions that secret services used people as guinea pigs, but did not keep the situation under control. As for the virus of atypical pneumonia, it has already been said that virus leakage might be the test of biological weapon performed by China, and, as it sometimes happens, the epidemic got out of control."[419]

Thus, since 1945 about twenty five large epidemics of unknown illnesses have taken place on the planet, developing practically according to one script as though written by a skilled hand, in order the Biblical prophecy will come true: "And the four angels were loosed, which were prepared for an hour, and a day, and a month, and a year, for to slay the third part of men."[420]

As for Iraq, the present situation is far from what president Bush had promised a year ago. Moreover, by his actions he "did everything to strengthen the positions of Al Queda." This statement was produced by Richard Clark, the author of the book *Against All the Enemies*, a former chief advisor on struggle against international terrorism, who resigned in March of this year.

Russian News Agency "Ria Novosti" quotes Richard Clark: "Iraq, which didn't represent by itself any real threat to the USA had been turned into the refuge of Islam terrorists, and became the symbol of resistance against the West. Now, it attracts more and more Moslems from all over the world... We have reached the point where we are hated more and more all over the world. This factor together with the Middle East USA policy leads to the increase of Jihad supporters in the Arab world... It was not by chance that during 32 months passed since September 11th, 2001, there happened two times more Islamite terrorist acts than during the same period before the "Black Tuesday."[421]

It is quite obvious that the attempts of Bush admininstration to build a peaceful and democratic society in Iraq have failed. Instead, we see the terrible picture. Tortures of innocent Iraqi civilians, multiple terrorist acts and dead American soldiers, poverty and suffering of Iraqi people—this is the terrible face of the New World Order, which paves its way under the guise of freedom and democracy.

CHAPTER 10.

TERROR IN RUSSIA

"I hope that religious leaders of the world will start "ideological" struggle against terrorists. Every shachid must know that he will be condemned by all the people for the death of innocent victims. As long as shachids think that after killing of "unbelievers" they will go immediately to a paradise, terrorism is invincible."

Doctor Roshal'

10. 1. The Tragedy of Beslan

The first of September is the Knowledge Day in Russia. Children, well dressed, cheerful, holding flowers in their little hands, go to school together with their parents in order to celebrate the first day of the new school year. Many of them go to school for the first time in their lives. For the first time in their lives, they will hear the ringing of a school bell. Its clear voice will open a new page in the book of their lives in which there will be new friends, new possibilities, new hopes and new expectations.

But, there was one school in Russia, in which children heard bursts of sub-machine gunfire instead of ringing of a school bell. They were taken hostages by beast like monsters who cannot be called human beings. Strong and well-trained terrorists herded men, women, children and even babies into the gymnasium and the assembly hall where they were treated like a livestock. That September day, Beslan, small town in North Ossetia, was turned into the Osventsim of the XXI century.

For three days, Beslan was like an enormous powder-barrel. For three days all the inhabitants of that small town spent days and nights in the street in front of the school in which more then a thousand people were kept as hostages. Beslan became black with grief. In that terrible September day, not only pupils and their teachers came to school to celebrate the Knowledge day, but also their parents, grandparents and former graduates with their families. Many mothers were holding babies in their hands. Alina Suleimanova, the youngest of them, was only five months old. She was taken hostage in spite of her age. Terrorists didn't divide between children and adults...

A witness tells: "In the morning of the second day, a bloodstained man jumped out of the school window. He told that in the first day, terrorists chose twenty men among the hostages, kneeled them and killed shooting in the backs of their heads. Then they forced the man to throw the corpses out of the window in order they "not to stink of dead flesh," as one of the terrorists said. Having thrown six corpses, the man decided to escape. He jumped out of the window and was saved under the smoke screen...

In the morning of September 3, terrible, sticky silence was hanging over Beslan. One could hear cows, which were not milked for three days, mooing. The midday didn't predict the calamity yet. The culmination came in an hour. Four single shoots tore up the silence. In the school gymnasium, loud children's cries were heard. Suddenly, the ground was shaken by two terrible blasts. A huge mushroom of smoke rose over the gymnasium roof, and fire burst out of the windows. Hostages began to jump out. The terrorists opened a hurricane of fire at the backs of fleeing. Men, women and children ran away disorderly hoping to escape from the hell they were in for three endless days. Not many of them have managed to do it. I saw two boys fell dead, but before they die, they shouted: "Please kill them! They are not humans! They are monsters!""

Terrorists continued a hurricane of fire from the school attic. It was the high time for the Special Forces to decide what to do, for delay could cost hundreds more lives of hostages. They understood that they would have to take school by storm. Soon, they received the order. At first, they neutralized weapon emplacements of the terrorists which fired on children. Officers of "Alpha" and "Vimpel" sheltered children and women with their bodies. The Special Forces of Russia have never suffered such terrible losses as in that terrible September day. Five officers were killed and twenty-seven wounded in that battle.

Snipers and machine guns points were neutralized by large-calibre machine guns of armored vehicles. Tanks, which were shooting with steel billets, made breaches in the school walls, ensuring passageway for the officers of Special Forces. When they came into the school building, they saw a terrible picture. In front of the teachers' room, they saw the corpse of a Negro [he was a terrorist]. His head was broken into two parts and his brain came out of it slowly. At the door of a schoolroom, among a heap of shells and unexploded grenades, two corpses lay on the floor. A barefoot, exhausted boy of about twelve lay beside of a headless terrorist. One of the "Alpha" officers told that the terrorist used the boy to protect himself from bullets. He covered himself with the boy like with a shield. Before his death, the terrorist had time to cut the boy's throat with a knife. A bloody clash took place in front of the mess room. Driven into the corner, eight terrorists were turned into bloody mess.

The gymnasium looked like a real hell when "Alpha" officers came inside. On the charred floor, among the heaps of smoking debris, mutilated corpses of terrorists could be seen everywhere. Their arms and legs lay separately from bodies mixed up with children's shoes, bags and charred bunches of flowers. Ineradicable smell of burnt human flesh drove mad even the most worldly-wise officers of Special Forces. A fireman who extinguished the fire through the window washed out one of the ashy heaps. Under a basketball ring, a charred corpse of a young woman lay on the floor. Her dead hands clasped a charred baby's little body to her bosom..."[422]

The events which were going on inside the school building during those three terrible days were so shocking by their cruelty and monstrosity that, looking at the performers of those bloody atrocities, one can hardly believe that human beings were capable to such unprecedented barbarity. That could be done only by beast like animals, "second signaled animals" which still live among the people. If anyone wants to imagine how the Last Judgment our beloved god Jehovah has prepared for us looks like, let one read the following.

The *New York Times* informs: "In a new official account of the attack, the country's chief law enforcement official portrayed **a band of cutthroat kidnappers who argued among each other and whose leader enforced discipline by executing three of his crew**. In a televised report to President Vladimir Putin, the official Prosecutor General Vladimir Ustinov said that not all the attackers had realized that their mission was to seize a school and that **one of them was shot when he objected to kidnapping children**.

Two women hostage-takers were killed, as a gesture of intimidation, when the bombs strapped to their bodies were detonated by remote control. "He did it himself," Putin said of the leader, who went by the nickname Colonel and who was described on television as a short man with a red beard and freckles. "Yes, himself,"

Ustinov replied, almost in a whisper. Ustinov said **326 hostages had been killed, although only 210 bodies had been identified because of their state of mutilation. He said 727 people had been wounded, leaving only a very few hostages unhurt from a total of 1,200 that he said had been held.**

The attack on the school in Beslan, in southern Russia, was the latest and most horrifying in a series of terrorist attacks that are apparently linked to a decade-long separatist war in Chechnya."[423]

And these are the heart frizzing evidences told by the children who have survived that terrible hell and by doctors who examined those children. Aslan Mamedov (16 years old) tells: "Having seized the school, terrorists began to fire on the civilian buildings from a grenade cup discharge. We hid themselves under the bed for some hours. Our neighbors were Baptists. Their faith doesn't allow to take weapon in their hands. They all died. Two children out of twelve have been already identified. When the battle was finished, we went to look for our friends and parents. We have found Batras in the central mortuary. There were three bullet holes and three missile wounds in his dead body. We saw more than three hundred dead bodies only in this mortuary. We could hardly count ten adults among them. The rest were children. Many of them were headless, armless and legless. They laid so closely that we had to walk over the dead bodies. I saw a girl dressed in a white dress. There was only a lower jaw left from her head. A very beautiful girl of about sixteen was even not charred. But she had deep cut over her left breast. Those who were there told that she was raped and knifed."[424]

Dzerassa Dzestelova (12 years old) tells: "On the 1st of September we went together to school to celebrate the Knowledge Day. In about seven minutes, armed men appeared in the school. Then terrorists made us go out. Adults were herded into the assembly hall, and we—children—into the gymnasium. Bearded men spoke among themselves a foreign language and fired into air. Terrorists hanged bombs under basketball rings in the gymnasium. The whole ceiling was mined with bombs hanging everywhere. They fixed the flag of North Ossetia on the wall and hung bombs around it. There were so many children in gymnasium that one boy spent two days standing on his legs because there was no place to sit down. It was so hot that everybody took their dresses off and fanned each other with sheets of paper. In the first day we were allow to drink water. Then we were thirsty, but terrorists didn't give us water. We had to eat flowers which we brought as presents to our teachers. In the third day, we pissed into bottles and drank the urine. We were hungry and jealously watched the terrorists eating our cakes which we brought to the school for the celebration. Terrorists robbed photo cameras, video cameras and mobile phones of us. They laughed and photographed each other. A corpse of a dead man, who tried to resist to the terrorists lay at the gymnasium door for two days. Then they dragged the corpse out and we were forced to wipe the blood with our white aprons. I was sitting at the window. When the first bomb exploded, I jumped up on the windowsill, but after the second blast, I fell down inside. Anyway, I have managed to escape. And other children began to run away after me. A boy caught on a wire which held a bomb under a basketball ring. The bomb fell down and exploded..."[425]

Doctor Boris Saparov testifies: "Heavily wounded children were brought to our hospital. All of them asked for water. They remembered, as if they were raving, that terrorists taunted them cruelly. They pissed at girls' aprons and forced children to squash urine into other children's mouths. **Terrorists filled a boy's mouth with broken glass and said, "It is your Pepsi-cola. Drink!"**[426]

Doctor Cazbek Berdiaev tells: "Almost all the children were silent because they were shell-shocked or were in the state of severe psychological shock. Only their eyes pleaded for help. My college, she is a gynecologist, while examining girls of senior classes, have noticed serious injuries of female genital organs. Most likely, those girls have been raped."[427]

Those three hellish September days revealed the abominable nature of beast like predatory super-animals who, in spite of the evolution of Homo sapiens, remain, nevertheless, extremely dangerous animals and still live among us. In the seventh chapter, as you remember, we defined them as "those, whom philosopher Hegel has defined as "morally deranged," and Shopenghauer—as "deprived of moral consciousnesses." Animals, extremely dangerous "second signaled animals" among people." The atrocities performed by them in Beslan show the lowest point of falling of the human nature.

10. 2. Why Do They Kill Our Children?

Looking at the dreadful atrocities predatory super animals perform nowadays, one cannot help oneself from asking questions that spring up every time we become witnesses of terrorist acts. Why do they kill our children? Who direct conscious-less super animals to commit the crimes which shake the whole world by their monstrous cruelty, and what ideology do they use to wash their beastly brains? What ideology can teach them to treat children with such a savage cruelty as it was in Beslan? What ideology can teach them that filicide is as pleasing to God as the murder of any other human being who is "infidel"?

Strange as it may seem, but the religions of "salvation" (Judaism, Christianity, Islam) do not divide between children and adults. All of them are equal before God-filicide Jehovah. All of them are "infidels," "unbelievers" who must be cruelly and mercilessly exterminated if they break his crazy law or do not want to follow his teaching. Do you remember what order gave our beloved God Jehovah to his "chosen people"? "Now go and smite Amalek, and utterly destroy all that they have, and **spare them not; but slay both man and woman, infant and suckling, ox and sheep, camel and ass.**"[428]

Do you remember what kind and beautiful words God Allah uttered to their ardent followers? **"I will cast dread into the hearts of those who misbelieve,—strike off their necks then, and strike off from them every finger-tip. That is, because they went into opposition against God and His Apostle; for he who goes into opposition against God and His Apostle—verily, God is keen to punish.**"[429]

Christianity also didn't manage to get rid of bloody heritage of Jewish God-butcher-filicide Jehovah. In John's Revelation, we see the rotation of the bloody Biblical fly-wheel which demands more and more human sacrifices to maintain its terrible movement. What is the Last Judgment? It is the "final extermination," as apostle Paul defined it. Who will be exterminated? Both children and adults who are not Christians (or who didn't have time to repent before their death). They will be cruelly tortured before God Jehovah and the Lamb, trampled on, crashed, and their blood will be squeezed out of their bodies so that it will flow like a river: "And the angel thrust in his sickle into the earth, and gathered the vine of the earth, and cast it into the great winepress of the wrath of God. **And the winepress was trodden without the city, and blood came out of the winepress, even unto the horse bridles, by the space of a thousand and six hundred furlongs.**"[430]

In Christianity, there is no alternative. The only alternative is death. If you want to inherit eternal life, you must be a Christian. If you are not Christian, you will have to be tortured before God and the Lamb and thrown into the lake burning with fire and sulfur to be suffered forever regardless of your age.

We do not remember the lessons of human history. Otherwise, we would recollect the examples of more cruel atrocities performed by "loving" Christians than those performed by beast like Moslem terrorists in Beslan. We have already mentioned the massacres of

Jews which took place in Russia in the XIX and XX centuries. Don't you remember as "merciful" Christians lanced the wombs of pregnant Jewish women and sewed up dead cats instead of their babies? And the number of victims was unimaginable. Thousands of Jews were brutally massacred, and their houses were utterly burnt and destroyed. This "final extermination" and all those tortures and throwing into the lake burning with fire and sulfur, as well as urgent desire of Christians to get rid of "unbelievers," unite Christianity with Fascism by bloody and intimate ties.

As you remember, Hitler had the same goal in his mind when he decided to conquer the whole world. He also wanted to force people to worship and to serve only to his "divine personality." All those who didn't fit into the Procrustean bed of "Arian" system of "choosen people," were to be partly exterminated, partly turned into slaves. Using the Bible as his textbook, Hitler created the enormous death machine with gas chambers and concentration camps which devoured millions of people regardless of their sex and age. As one can see, the world was a witness of even more elaborate examples of cruelty and barbarity performed in the name of false gods which demand more and more human sacrifices.

The tragedy of Beslan had also a religious coloring. The majority of terrorists were Moslems. And they were ready to die in the name of Allah, for they really believed that they would go to a paradise immediately after death. The Russian TV broadcasted an intercepted telephone talk between a terrorist and his mother. The terrorist boasted of his courage and of the great success of their mission. He rejoiced over the fact that just several hours separated him from a paradise. The mother shared his joy and repeated from time to time, "Thank Allah! Thank Allah!" She didn't reproach or blame his son, she didn't try to dissuade him from torturing and killing children. This is the real face of Islam. It is "true and peaceful" only towards those who believe in Allah, whose backs Allah made "the forbidden field," but Allah do not love those who are not Moslems, who are "unbelievers." All of them must be either destroyed or converted to Islam.

10. 3. Can We Stop Terrorists?

Hence, the reasonable question springs up. What measures can be taken to stop terrorists? The only way known until now is to liquidate them physically. Our leaders offer extremely radical measures. Colonel-General Yuri Baluyevsky, chief of the military's general staff, said Russia did not feel bound by national borders in pursuing rebels. "As for carrying out preventive strikes against terrorist bases, we will take all measures to liquidate terrorist bases in any region of the world," he said, though he called that an "extreme measure."[431]

The Russian government even offered $10 million reward for the killing or capture of two Chechen rebel leaders, and a top general said Moscow reserved the right to make pre-emptive strikes against terrorists abroad. President Bush holds to the same tactic. Is it effective? By no means. Aslanbek Aslakhanov, Putin's chief adviser on Chechnya, said he hoped that the large reward would lead to the capture of the two most prominent rebel figures, Aslan Maskhadov, who is a former president of Chechnya, and Shamil Basayev, a rebel warlord. The government has blamed them for the hostage-taking, although Basayev has denied involvement. When asked in a telephone interview why they had not been captured in the past, Aslakhanov told what he said was an American anecdote about a "Cowboy Joe" who had never been caught because no one had ever really tried to catch him. "For a long time, no one tried to catch Basayev," he said. "We knew he was driving with a certain driver, we knew he was stopping in one place or another. He traveled to Turkey for surgery." The same can be said about the notorious "terrorist No 1" Osama-ben-Laden. Three years have passed since the terrorist acts of September 11th, 2001, but the leader of not les notorious Al-Queda is still at large. It seems that it is not our presidents who rule our countries, but Osama-ben-Laden and his huge network of terrorist groups who terrorize the whole world. The most important step that could be taken would be for the United States to help close channels of financing for Chechen rebels, as Aslanbek Aslachanov, Putin's advisor on Chechnya, believes.

The Russian newspaper *Komsomol'skaya Pravda* (3. 09. 2004) informs that to wage holy jihad war on Russia Chechen separatists receive up to a hundred millions dollars a year. They must report by mass murders, terrorist acts and airplane explosions.

From time to time, the headquarters staff of Mashadov's terrorist network issues a special leaflet with prices for those who want to earn money on terror. A terrorist gets $50 for the placing of a mine in the center of Grozny, and $300—$500 for placing of a field charge. The murder of a general is paid by $15, 000 (equivalent: 3 cows or 20 rams), of a senior officer—by $7, 000 (equivalent: 1 cow or 5 rams), of a junior officer—by $3, 000 and 3 rams, of an ensign or a soldier—by $1.5, 000 and two rams.

For mass hostage taking, terrorist leaders pay $10, 000 to those terrorists who survived in a terrorist act, or they pay $30, 000 to terrorist's parents if he was killed performing a terrorist act. The most high-paid are terrorists-kamikaze. Depending on the scale of damage caused by a terrorist, his relatives will get $50, 000—$100, 000.

Now compare these figures with a salary of Special Forces officers. Andrey Golovatyuk, a former chief of staff of one of the Special Forces detachments, tells: "A detachment commander gets 8, 000 rubles ($260) a month. Junior officers get 5, 000—6, 000 rubles ($180—$200) a month. In 2002, one of my officers was wounded. Now, he is invalid. He has a metal plate in his head, and the left part of his body is partly paralyzed. He lives in Smolensky region. He cannot find a job and gets 2, 000 rubles ($85) pension a month. These are all our social guaranties."[432]

How it is possible to fight against terrorists having such a salary and not having money to buy new weapon for Special Forces? As for Russia, it is quite natural that to stop terrorists physically having such limited possibilities is impossible. But, probably, it is possible to minimize it.

Experts believe that if we were more intelligent, we would have given young Chechens the possibility to study in Russia. At that, we would have given them humanitarian, i. e. pedagogical, psychological, literary education. A humanitarian education creates certain systems of values, which are difficult to overcome. Having absorbed our mentality and our values, they would have gradually started to rebuild Chechen society. New intelligentsia would have direct it to a new direction. But it is very long process. Chechens have a mentality of wild human beings who just have came down of mountains. If we manage to civilize a part of them, they will become the power which will change the present situation. This was what Russian tsars did in the Caucasus at their times.

10. 4. Terrorism and Political Games of the Mighty of This World

Taking into account all the facts stated in this book, we can conclude that it is impossible to stop terrorism just by the physical extermination of terrorists, or by changing the mentality of young generations. Regardless of how many terrorists we kill today, tens of times more of them will appear tomorrow because there exists the matrix of destruction which the Mighty of this world use to create more and more new beast like super animals. Humankind must understand at last that we will be able to stop terrorists only when the bloodthirsty and man-hating ideology of our "holy scriptures" is publicly revealed and all the orders to exterminate "unbelievers," as well as all the words of hatred and religious intolerance are removed from them. As long as the matrix of destruction exists, the Mighty of this world will use its man-hating ideology in their dirty political games.

It is not a secret for the majority of intelligent representatives of Homo sapiens that the international terrorism has been created by the USA. The matter is that the building of the New World Order demands the creation of unilateral world in which America will play a dominant role. The global unification contradicts to all the main principles of peaceful coexistence of the world community. Humankind will never resign itself to this global unification. And it is the main cause of many conflicts, including those in Russia.

American strategists have learned a simple truth that such global projects are always sacrificial by their nature and demand blood, including the project of universal Americanization. It was not by chance that before the bloody events of 11th of September, Paul Wulfovits, the second-in-command of the USA Defense Department, said that the nation needed mobilization, and it can be caused only by a new Pearl Harbor. It happened on September 11, 2001, as if by request. But there are a lot discrepancies left in this case. From one hand, American Special Forces were not able to prevent terrorist acts; from the other hand, they had the complete list of all the terrorists who took part in the atrocities of the Black Tuesday just after the attack. In certain cars, they found the Koran and flying manuals in Arab language. But why it was necessary to leave the Koran in those cars? It looks like it had been done intentionally by those who wished to shift the blame on to Arabs. It is time to think that the attack on America was under control from the very beginning until the very end.

In one of the pictures of the "air attack" of the Pentagon, one can see a strange object flying over the building in the upper left hand corner. It is military pilot-less aircraft. Somebody was monitoring the events by means of that drone. Or, probably, it was the one from which a missile was fired into the Pentagon. It is strange that USA Air Force could send the drone to monitor the situation (or to fire a missile), but was unable to send fighters to intercept a "hijacked airplane." It was the "attack" on America that became the very cause of the global war on terrorism.

"'Thus, political scientist Stanislav Belcovsky says, 'American secret services and elites play the great role in the formation of the infrastructure of international terrorism. The goal is quite obvious. America needs the justification of its dominant position in the world.

The most effective one is the struggle with the international terrorism, in which only America can win a victory. We are offered to become a subject of American-centered world. The argument is faultless: "If you are not with us, the terrorism will strangle you." And for the inner use, the acknowledging of global threat of terrorism must justify the renunciation off certain fundamental values.'"[433]

The "white" America has understood that the freedom of movement, which was one of the most human values, must be abolished. Otherwise, in ten years, Afro-Americans, Latino-Americans, Moslems and Chinese will have the control stock of American voters. Today the freedom of movement is being abolished by the American elite. And this abolishment must be grounded. The best ground is the international terrorism. Then, let us take the freedom of speech. It is obvious that the bureaucratic American superstructure does not need the freedom of speech. It can be even dangerous for it. Just recollect *Fahrenheit 9/11*. The whole world has seen the disclosure of American elite. But in America, the film was forbidden for demonstration for some time.

This is the crash of American liberal doctrine which is in the state of crisis now. The international terrorism is a good ground to reject it one-sidedly. That is why, the international terrorism has been created and maintained by the USA to achieve two goals: a) to finish with the liberal doctrine and change over to the post liberal one; b) to justify the American domination it the world.

The fact that the last terrorist act took place in North Ossetia (and early, Saacashvily who is supported by the USA, attacked South Ossetia) testifies that it was well planned and thought-out. North Ossetia is the main stronghold of Russia on the North Caucasus. That is why terrorists chose this republic to stroke a treacherous blow.

The terrorist war on Russia, if we take into account the election campaign in the USA, have distracted the attention of both the world community and American voters from the utter failure of the USA in Iraq, and weakened Russia which has to live in the conditions of unthinkably high oil prices. The lack of clear Kremlin's strategy on the Caucasus provokes both terrorists and their warlords to use this region as the main painful point of pressure on the Russian government.

Braking up of being created axis Paris-Berlin-Moscow and a strategic alliance Moscow-Ankara because of cancellation of Putin's visit to Turkey, destabilization of the Caucasus and the entire South region are too difficult tasks for Islamic "international terrorism." On the contrary, today, the Islamic world is not interested in worsening of relations with Russia. Even the most radical Moslem leaders understand what benefits they can have from peaceful coexistence with strong and powerful Russia that follows a policy of independence from the USA. All these facts convince us once more that both "Al-Queda" and "the international terrorism" are not more than instruments in dirty political games of the Mighty of this world. It is time to look for the root of the evil not among those who perform bloody atrocities, but among those who establish the rules for those games...

The midnight has passed, the carnival is over. Replete and drunk, having lost the feeling of danger, they threw off their masks and veils and showed their souls, naked and unadorned; and this hell turned out to be disgusting.

AFTERWORD.

THE TRIAL OF CONSCIENCE

"Because the very existence of mankind is under a danger now, a new social compact that will raise ethic and humanism requirements to the level of categorical imperative, violation of which will become at any circumstances a crime towards a society, is needed."[434]

Efroimson V. P.

Thus, for the first time in the history of mankind, we have made the humanistic analysis of the main world outlook conceptions, which determine the condition of cultural space of the world. We have shown that this space represents by itself a complicated and heterogeneous formation, which has three-layered structure. Two layers are the distratumness of absurdity inherent in a human consciousness, in which good and evil, love and hatred, truth and lie, illusion and reality peacefully get along together; the third one consists of those structures that create and maintain this distratumness. These are info-energy matrixes, as well as political and ideological institutes that create them and inculcate into the consciousness of human masses. Add here the fact that a part of human population, as professor Porshnev has shown, consists of "predatory superanimals with unnatural orientation of this predatorness (utmost aggressiveness) on other people," and you will get complete and real picture of the cultural space of the world.

We also have proven that the Bible, "the book of books," "the number one bestseller," "the textbook of life" and creative inspiration for the most cruel and bloodthirsty tyrants who use it to base and to justify their criminal activity, is such a matrix for the majority of Earth population. The matrix, whose name is the Bible, is the base of so-called "religions of salvation"—Judaism, Christianity and Islam.

The Bible, its cruel man-hating ideology and Christianity founded on it became the cause of crusades, inquisition trials, religious wars, red terror, Stalin's repressions, Fascism and Islamic religious extremism. After the tragedy of September 11, 2001, many intelligent human beings began to understand that the phenomenon we faced is not new and unexpected, but a long-lasting, chronic disease that has changed into the active phase and therefore, needs immediate treatment. But one cannot cope with the disease without knowing the cause of it. Many analysts try to discover this cause and build rather interesting theories.

Samuel Huntington, American political scientist and philosopher who as far back as in 1993 published the article "The Conflict of Civilizations" in the magazine *Foreign Affairs*, must be distinguished among them. According to his opinion, "**the totality of religious, ethnic and cultural-lingual features is, from one hand, the decisive factor of people unification into so-called civilizations, and the main catalyst in the incessant struggle of these civilizations for the expansion of their influence borders, from the other hand.**"

Practically each civilization is formed around a state or a group of states (core states), in which its differences from all the other civilizations are expressed most of all. Huntington believes that the whole history of mankind is an endless chain of struggle, the dying of civilizations and the birth of new ones. All of them are at different stages of their development, and from time to time they come into conflict one with another, but, nevertheless, they can confederate into temporary unions against the third party in order to come back to the state of mutual confrontation again.

At these very points, the history is made, the course of which, as Huntington believes, is determined by the conflict between western and Islamic civilizations during last fourteen centuries. This global conflict was born in the seventh century together with Islam expansion to North Africa, Middle East, Persia and north India. The West answered with crusades that began in 1095. During the following century, Christians did not manage to make restitution of the Holy Land, and their contemporary defeat became a powerful catalyst of the formation of the Ottoman Empire.

Fortunately, Christians became enthusiastic about navigation, and within a century, thanks to colonization of new lands made a powerful spurt in development. The appearance of Russia on the seat of war became a great help to their civilization. Soon, by mutual efforts, they turned the Ottoman Empire from the "scourge of Christian world" into the "sick one of Europe."

Huntington proves all his ideas with concrete historical facts. For example, he asserts that "the half of all wars waged in the period from 1820 to 1929 amongst "religiously different" countries falls on confrontation between the orthodox (Christians) and the true believers (Moslems)."

After "the first state of workers and peasants" had appeared on the world maps, the West and Islam concluded an armistice and united against the mutual enemy. Huntington himself characterizes the conflict between liberal democracy and Marxism-Leninism as "passing and unnatural historical phenomenon in comparison with constant and antagonistic relations between Islam and Christianity. It is no wonder that having eliminated the USSR, the enemies clashed face to face again."

And here a quite natural question springs up. Why are Islam and the West so irreconcilable towards each other? Huntington believes that the conflict between them can be explained, from one hand, by the difference of the role religion plays in both civilizations (In Islam, it is the way of life, to which all the state institutes are subordinated, while in Christianity, it is no more than one of state's elements, detached from all the state institutes); from the other hand, by the pretension of both religions on the role of the ultimate truth for all the human beings. At that, the equal terms "crusade" and "jihad" (which you will not be able to find either in Buddhism or in orthodox Christianity, as well as in Confucianism) not only permit the forcible expansion of their faith, but welcome and bless extermination of any dissidence together with dissidents.

Moreover, the western civilization (the USA at first) tries by any means to export its own values system and moral laws, acknowledging them to be the ultimate truth to other civilizations. There, hypocrisy and morals of the West, which is visible even with a naked eye, cause a natural protective reaction: the Islam world reacts to the attempts of universalization with the increasing of Islamic fundamentalism.

Of course, it is true, but the most essential causes of this confrontation lie hidden in the well known matrix, the name of which is the Bible. It is arranged in such a manner that people who use it as the "textbook of life" will be inevitably at enmity one with another, and even kill each other, for this matrix contained the negative, anti-human charge of such a strength, that none of those who got under its influence can resist to its vicious and cruel power. All the most dreadful atrocities against humans and humanity happened and happen because of the matrix, the name of which is the Bible.

Isn't it the right time to look at the faces of gods we bow before and serve to in a new fashion? Isn't it the right time to revise the terrible, bloody heritage we have received from past centuries which we successfully multiply adding to it new and new human sacrifices we make to our bloodthirsty gods? Does humankind not understand that building its life on cruel, soulless matrix, on a monstrous deceit, which had been placed stealthily to our minds by Jewish rabbis, we shall never achieve peaceful coexistence of people and nations? Isn't it the right time to show real faces of our gods, whose hands are stained with blood of innocently killed human sons and daughters? Isn't it the right time to condemn their criminal actions as we once condemned the atrocities performed by Lenin, Stalin, Hitler and other tyrants and murderers?

It is time to reveal to people the real essence of religious teachings, which are built on the matrix, the name of which is the Bible? It is time to stop to glorify murderers, crowned with the nimbus of sanctity, because it is, as professor Didinco asserts, "nothing else, than cultivation of "evil" and its mirror variety—"hatred against evil" (which is the same in its essence). Boldness, heroism, self-sacrifice in the name of unconvincing ideals and unclear goals (which turned out to be false and criminal by 99.9%) sending down from above, can be considered as uncovered provocation of permanent, alternatively "just" violence."[435]

Budyon M., the author of *Hitler and Jesus*, offers a very interesting idea: "Nowadays, it has became a fashion to count how many human lives cost Stalin, Hitler, Lenin, Mao, Pol Pot, Napoleon, Tamerlan and Chengis Chan to humankind. **But it is strange that nobody ever tried to count how many human lives cost Christ. The fact that a thorough historical research of crimes committed by Christianity still has not been undertaken is also astonishing. It is much more scaled and very interesting for different fields of humanitarian knowledge**.

This is the very point to where the efforts of the best experts of Russia, Europe and America must be directed. It is difficult to say how many volumes this unprecedented encyclopedia of terror, sadism, bloody scenes, hypocrisy, cynicism, psychical pathologies, maniacal displays and unprecedented destructions will occupy. It will be probably two hundred volumes, or five hundred. Anyway, the work must be started (I would willingly be in charge of it!), and when it is finished in ten or fifteen years, it will be very funny to look at an enormous cupboard staffed with five hundred of thick volumes of "The History of Crimes Committed by Christianity," and maximum ten volumes of "The Crimes Committed by Fascism." It is quite clear that the admission to study such a literature must have only those who had passed through special medical board, which would certify their good mental health."[436]

Actually, the access to studying of such a literature must have only those who have healthy, steady minds, those who have passed through the special medical board, for those who are not specially prepared for such a mission can easily go mad. You yourselves can be convinced in that fact if you are able to read the whole list of means of "salvation" of lost human souls, which abundantly present in the "arsenal" of "kind and merciful" God-butcher-filicide Jehovah:

11. **The Flood: Extermination of all the life on the Earth, except for Noah's family.** "And the Lord said, **I will destroy man whom I have created from the face of the earth**; both man, and beast, and the creeping thing, and the fowls of the air; for it repenteth me that I have made them. (Genesis 6: 7).
12. **Destruction of Sodom and Homorrah:** "Then **the Lord rained upon Sodom and upon Gomorrah brimstone and fire from the Lord out of heaven; and he overthrew those cities, and all the plain, and all the inhabitants of the cities**, and that which grew upon the ground." (Genesis 19: 24).
13. **Killing of Jude's firstborn:** "And Er, Judah's firstborn, was wicked in the sight of the Lord; **and the Lord slew him**." (Genesis 38: 7).
14. **Killing of Onan:** " And Onan knew that the seed should not be his; and it came to pass, when he went in unto his brother's wife, that he spilled it on the ground, lest that he should give seed to his brother. And the thing which he did displeased the Lord: **wherefore he slew him also**. (Genesis 38: 10).
15. **Killing of Firstborns**: "For I will pass through the land of Egypt this night, and **will smite all the firstborn in the land of Egypt, both man and beast**; and against all the gods of Egypt I will execute judgment: I am the Lord. (Exodus12: 12).
16. **Jehovah's Attempt to Kill Moses' Son:** " And it came to pass by the way in the inn, that **the Lord met him, and sought to kill him**. Then Zipporah took a sharp stone, and cut off the foreskin of her son, and cast it at his feet, and said, Surely a bloody husband art thou to me. So he let him go: then she said, **A bloody husband thou art, because of the circumcision**." (Exodus 4: 24-26).
17. **Death Penalty for Eating Leaven:** " Seven days shall ye eat unleavened bread; even the first day ye shall put away leaven out of your houses: for whosoever eateth leavened bread from the first

day until the seventh day, **that soul shall be cut off from Israel.**" (Exodus 12: 15).

18. **Death Penalty for Worshiping Other Gods:** "He that sacrificeth unto any god, save unto the Lord only, **he shall be utterly destroyed.** (Exodus 22: 20).
19. **Death Penalty for Defilement of Sabbath:** "Ye shall keep the sabbath therefore; for it is holy unto you: **every one that defileth it shall surely be put to death**: for whosoever doeth any work therein, **that soul shall be cut off from among his people.**" (Exodus 31: 14).
20. **Cruel Killing of Jezreel**: "And he said, Throw her down. So they threw her down: and **some of her blood was sprinkled on the wall, and on the horses: and he trode her under foot.** And when he was come in, he did eat and drink, and said, Go, see now this cursed woman, and bury her: for she is a king's daughter. And they went to bury her: **but they found no more of her than the skull, and the feet, and the palms of her hands.**" (2nd of Kings 9: 32-37).
21. **Death Penalty for Eating Blood:** "Whatsoever soul it be that eateth any manner of blood, even **that soul shall be cut off from his people.**" (Leviticus 7: 27).
22. **Punishment for Disobedience to the law:** "I also will do this unto you; **I will even appoint over you terror, consumption, and the burning ague**, that shall consume the eyes, and cause sorrow of heart: and ye shall sow your seed in vain, for your enemies shall eat it." (Leviticus 26: 16). "And **I will bring a sword upon you, that shall avenge the quarrel of my covenant**: and when ye are gathered together within your cities, **I will send the pestilence among you**; and ye shall be delivered into the hand of the enemy." (Leviticus 26: 25). "And ye shall eat the flesh of your sons, and the flesh of your daughters shall ye eat." (Leviticus 26: 29). "**The Lord will smite thee with the botch of Egypt, and with the emerods, and with the scab, and with the itch, whereof thou canst not be healed.** The Lord shall smite thee with madness, and blindness, and astonishment of heart." (Deuteronomy 28: 27-28).
23. **The Slaughtering of Those Who Served to a Golden Calf:** "And he said unto them, Thus saith the Lord God of Israel, **Put every man his sword by his side, and go in and out from gate to gate throughout the camp, and slay every man his brother, and every man his companion, and every man his neighbour.** And the children of Levi did according to the word of Moses: **and there**

fell of the people that day about three thousand men." (Exodus 32: 27-28).

24. **The Extermination of People for Their Grumbling at God:** "And when the people complained, it displeased the Lord: and the Lord heard it; **and his anger was kindled; and the fire of the Lord burnt among them, and consumed them** that were in the uttermost parts of the camp." (Numbers 11: 1). "And while the flesh was yet between their teeth, ere it was chewed, **the wrath of the Lord was kindled against the people, and the Lord smote the people with a very great plague.**" (Numbers 11: 33).
25. **Slaughtering in the Battle With Midianites:** "And they warred against the Midianites, as the Lord commanded Moses; and they slew all the males." (Numbers 31: 7). "And Moses said unto them, Have ye saved all the women alive? Now therefore **kill every male among the little ones, and kill every woman that hath known man by lying with him**. But all the women children, that have not known a man by lying with him, keep alive for yourselves." (Numbers 31: 15, 17, 18).
26. **Human Sacrifices to the Biblical God Jehovah:** "And the asses were thirty thousand and five hundred; of which the Lord's tribute was threescore and one. And the persons were sixteen thousand; **of which the Lord's tribute was thirty and two persons**. And Moses gave the tribute, which was the Lord's heave offering, unto Eleazar the priest, as the Lord commanded Moses." (Numbers 31: 39-41). "**Sanctify unto me all the firstborn**, whatsoever openeth the womb among the children of Israel, both of man and of beast: **it is mine.**" (Exodus 13: 2). "Thou shalt not delay to offer the first of thy ripe fruits, and of thy liquors: **the firstborn of thy sons shalt thou give unto me**. Likewise shalt thou do with thine oxen, and with thy sheep: **seven days it shall be with his dam; on the eighth day thou shalt give it me**. (Exodus 22: 29-30). "Notwithstanding no devoted thing, that a man shall devote unto the Lord of all that he hath, **both of man and beast**, and of the field of his possession, shall be sold or redeemed: every devoted thing is most holy unto the Lord. None devoted, which shall be devoted of men, shall be redeemed; but **shall surely be put to death.**" (Leviticus 27: 28-29).
27. **Massacre During the Battle With Sihon, the King of Heshbon:** "And the Lord our God delivered him before us; and **we smote him, and his sons, and all his people. And we took all his cities at that time, and utterly destroyed the men, and the women,**

and the little ones, of every city, we left none to remain." (Deuteronomy 2: 33-34).

28. **The Murder of Those who Joined onto Baalpeor:** "And Israel joined himself unto Baalpeor: and the anger of the Lord was kindled against Israel. And the Lord said unto Moses, **take all the heads of the people, and hang them up before the Lord against the sun**, that the fierce anger of the Lord may be turned away from Israel. And Moses said unto the judges of Israel, **slay ye every one his men that were joined unto Baalpeor**. And, behold, one of the children of Israel came and brought unto his brethren a Midianitish woman in the sight of Moses, and in the sight of all the congregation of the children of Israel, who were weeping before the door of the tabernacle of the congregation. And when Phinehas, the son of Eleazar, the son of Aaron the priest, saw it, he rose up from among the congregation, and took a javelin in his hand; And he went after the man of Israel into the tent, and **thrust both of them through, the man of Israel, and the woman through her belly**. So the plague was stayed from the children of Israel. **And those that died in the plague were twenty and four thousand**. (Numbers 25: 1-9).
29. **Punishment for Service to Other Gods:** "Thou **shalt surely smite the inhabitants of that city with the edge of the sword, destroying it utterly, and all that is therein, and the cattle thereof, with the edge of the sword**. And thou shalt gather all the spoil of it into the midst of the street thereof, and **shalt burn with fire the city, and all the spoil thereof every whit**, for the Lord thy God: and it shall be an heap for ever; it shall not be built again." (Deuteronomy 13: 15-16).
30. **The Destruction of the Cities of People:** "But of the cities of these people, which the Lord thy God doth give thee for an inheritance, **thou shalt save alive nothing that breatheth: but thou shalt utterly destroy them; namely, the Hittites, and the Amorites, the Canaanites, and the Perizzites, the Hivites, and the Jebusites**; as the Lord thy God hath commanded thee." (Deuteronomy 20: 16-17).
31. **Death Penalty for the Intention to Serve to other Gods:** "Thou shalt not consent unto him, nor hearken unto him; **neither shall thine eye pity him, neither shalt thou spare, neither shalt thou conceal him: but thou shalt surely kill him; thine hand shall be first upon him to put him to death**, and afterwards the hand of all the people." (Deuteronomy 13: 8-9).

32. **Massacre in Jericho:** "And **they utterly destroyed all that was in the city, both man and woman, young and old, and ox, and sheep, and ass, with the edge of the sword.**" (Joshua 6: 21).
33. **The Invasion of Canaan Land:** "And all the spoil of these cities, and the cattle, the children of Israel took for a prey unto themselves; but **every man they smote with the edge of the sword, until they had destroyed them, neither left they any to breathe.**" (Joshua 11: 14).
34. **The murder of Benjamin Tribe for its Not Coming to the Meeting in Mizpeh:** "And the congregation sent thither twelve thousand men of the valiantest, and commanded them, saying, **go and smite the inhabitants of Jabeshgilead with the edge of the sword, with the women and the children.**" (Judges 21: 10).

35. **The Ark of Covenant Kills People:** "But the hand of the Lord was heavy upon them of Ashdod, **and he destroyed them, and smote them with emerods,** even Ashdod and the coasts thereof." (1st of Samuel). "**And he smote the men of Bethshemesh, because they had looked into the ark of the Lord, even he smote of the people fifty thousand and threescore and ten men**: and the people lamented, because the Lord had smitten many of the people with a great slaughter." (1st of Samuel 6: 19). "And when they came to Nachon's threshingfloor, Uzzah put forth his hand to the ark of God, and took hold of it; for the oxen shook it. **And the anger of the Lord was kindled against Uzzah; and God smote him there for his error; and there he died by the ark of God.**" (2nd Samuel 6: 6-7). "And it was so, that, after they had carried it about, **the hand of the Lord was against the city with a very great destruction: and he smote the men of the city, both small and great, and they had emerods in their secret parts.**" (1st of Samuel 5: 9).
36. **King Saul Kills People of Amalek:** "Now go and smite Amalek, and utterly destroy all that they have, and **spare them not; but slay both man and woman, infant and suckling, ox and sheep, camel and ass.**" (1st of Samuel 15: 3).
37. **The Destruction of Things That Were Vile and Refuse** (i. e. people): "But Saul and the people spared Agag, and the best of the sheep, and of the oxen, and of the fatlings, and the lambs, and all that was good, and would not utterly destroy them: but **every thing that was vile and refuse, that they destroyed utterly.**" (1st of Samuel 15: 9).

38. **War Until Total Destruction.** "And the Lord sent thee on a journey, and said, **go and utterly destroy the sinners the Amalekites, and fight against them until they be consumed.**" (1st of Samuel 15: 18).
39. **The God's Anger for David's Numbering Israel and Judah:** "And again the anger of the Lord was kindled against Israel, and he moved David against them to say, Go, number Israel and Judah. (2nd of Samuel 24: 1). "So the Lord sent a pestilence upon Israel from the morning even to the time appointed: and **there died of the people from Dan even to Beersheba seventy thousand men**. And when the angel stretched out his hand upon Jerusalem to destroy it, the Lord repented him of the evil, and said to the angel that destroyed the people, It is enough: stay now thine hand. And the angel of the Lord was by the threshingplace of Araunah the Jebusite." (2nd of Samuel 24: 15-16).
40. **The Klling of the Lame and the Blind:** "And David said on that day, **whosoever getteth up to the gutter, and smiteth the Jebusites, and the lame and the blind**, that are hated of David's soul, he shall be chief and captain. Wherefore they said, **the blind and the lame shall not come into the house**." (2nd of Samuel 5: 8).
41. **Baasha Slays the House of Jeroboam:** "And it came to pass, when he reigned, that **he smote all the house of Jeroboam; he left not to Jeroboam any that breathed, until he had destroyed him**, according unto the saying of the Lord, which he spake by his servant Ahijah the Shilonite" (1st of Kings 15: 29).
42. **Elijah Kills the Prophets of Baal:** "And Elijah said unto them, Take the prophets of Baal; let not one of them escape. And they took them: and **Elijah brought them down to the brook Kishon, and slew them there**." (1st of Kings 18: 40).
43. **Elijah Condemned to Death Forty Two Children for Their Laughing at Him:** "And he went up from thence unto Bethel: and as he was going up by the way, there came forth little children out of the city, and mocked him, and said unto him, Go up, thou bald head; go up, thou bald head. And **he turned back, and looked on them, and cursed them in the name of the Lord. And there came forth two she bears out of the wood, and tare forty and two children of them**." (2nd of Kings 2: 23-24).
44. **Jehu Slew All That Remained of the House of Ahab**: "**So Jehu slew all that remained of the house of Ahab in Jezreel, and all his great men, and his kinsfolks, and his priests, until he left him none remaining**." (2nd of Kings 10: 11).

45. **God's Angel Kills 185. 000 Assyrian Warriors:** "And it came to pass that night, that **the angel of the Lord went out, and smote in the camp of the Assyrians an hundred fourscore and five thousand**: and when they arose early in the morning, behold, they were all dead corpses." (2nd of Kings 19: 35).
46. **The Destruction of Jews' Enemies:** "And he wrote in the king Ahasuerus' name, and sealed it with the king's ring, and sent letters by posts on horseback, and riders on mules, camels, and young dromedaries: Wherein the king granted the Jews which were in every city to gather themselves together, and to stand for their life, **to destroy, to slay, and to cause to perish, all the power of the people and province that would assault them, both little ones and women**, and to take the spoil of them for a prey." (Esther 8: 11). "But the other Jews that were in the king's provinces gathered themselves together, and stood for their lives, and had rest from their enemies, **and slew of their foes seventy and five thousand, but they laid not their hands on the prey**. On the thirteenth day of the month Adar; and on the fourteenth day of the same rested they, and made it a day of feasting and gladness. (Esther 9: 16, 17).
47. "Therefore he brought upon them the king of the Chaldees, who slew their young men with the sword in the house of their sanctuary, and **had no compassion upon young man or maiden, old man, or him that stooped for age: he gave them all into his hand.**" (2nd of Chronicles 36: 17).

The means of "salvation" described in the prophets' catalogues

1. **Isaiah:** "Howl ye; for the day of the Lord is at hand; it shall come as a destruction from the Almighty. Behold, **the day of the Lord cometh, cruel both with wrath and fierce anger, to lay the land desolate: and he shall destroy the sinners thereof out of it.** Therefore I will shake the heavens, and the earth shall remove out of her place, in the wrath of the Lord of hosts, and in the day of his fierce anger. **Every one that is found shall be thrust through; and every one that is joined unto them shall fall by the sword. Their children also shall be dashed to pieces before their eyes; their houses shall be spoiled, and their wives ravished. Their bows also shall dash the young men to pieces; and they shall have no pity on the fruit of the womb; their eye shall not**

spare children. (Isaiah 13: 6, 9, 11, 13, 15, 16, 18). I have trodden the winepress alone; and of the people there was none with me: for **I will tread them in mine anger, and trample them in my fury; and their blood shall be sprinkled upon my garments, and I will stain all my raiment**. For the day of vengeance is in mine heart, and the year of my redeemed is come. And I looked, and there was none to help; and I wondered that there was none to uphold: therefore mine own arm brought salvation unto me; and my fury, it upheld me. And **I will tread down the people in mine anger, and make them drunk in my fury, and I will bring down their strength to the earth**. (Isaiah 63: 3-6). "And I will restore thy judges as at the first, and thy counsellors as at the beginning: afterward thou shalt be called, The city of righteousness, the faithful city. Zion shall be redeemed with judgment, and her converts with righteousness. **And the destruction of the transgressors and of the sinners shall be together, and they that forsake the Lord shall be consumed**. (Isaiah 1: 27-28).

2. **Jeremiah:** "Therefore thus saith the Lord, Behold, I will lay stumblingblocks before this people, and **the fathers and the sons together shall fall upon them; the neighbour and his friend shall perish**. (Jeremiah 6: 21). "Therefore thus saith the Lord of hosts, Behold, I will punish them: **the young men shall die by the sword; their sons and their daughters shall die by famine.**" (Jeremiah 11: 22). "And **I will dash them one against another, even the fathers and the sons together, saith the Lord: I will not pity, nor spare, nor have mercy, but destroy them**. (Jeremiah 13: 14).
3. **Ezekiel:** "Now will I shortly pour out my fury upon thee, and accomplish mine anger upon thee: and I will judge thee according to thy ways, and will recompense thee for all thine abominations. And **mine eye shall not spare, neither will I have pity**: I will recompense thee according to thy ways and thine abominations that are in the midst of thee; and ye shall know that **I am the Lord that smiteth**." (Ezekiel 7: 8-9). "And say to the land of Israel, Thus saith the Lord; Behold, **I am against thee, and will draw forth my sword out of his sheath, and will cut off from thee the righteous and the wicked**." (Ezekiel 21: 3).
4. **John:** "And there went out another horse that was red: and power was given to him that sat thereon to take peace from the earth, **and that they should kill one another**: and there was given unto him a great sword." (Revelation 6: 4). "And I looked, and behold

a pale horse: and his name that sat on him was Death, and Hell followed with him. And power was given unto them over the fourth part of the earth, **to kill with sword, and with hunger, and with death, and with the beasts of the earth**." (Revelation 6: 8). "And the third angel followed them, saying with a loud voice, If any man worship the beast and his image, and receive his mark in his forehead, or in his hand, **the same shall drink of the wine of the wrath of God**, which is poured out without mixture into the cup of his indignation; and **he shall be tormented with fire and brimstone in the presence of the holy angels, and in the presence of the Lamb**." (Revelation 14: 9-10). "And the angel thrust in his sickle into the earth, and gathered the vine of the earth, and cast it into the great winepress of the wrath of God. **And the winepress was trodden without the city, and blood came out of the winepress, even unto the horse bridles, by the space of a thousand and six hundred furlongs** [about two hundred miles]." (Revelation 14: 19-20). "And I saw heaven opened, and behold a white horse; and he that sat upon him was called Faithful and True, and in righteousness he doth judge and make war. And **he was clothed with a vesture dipped in blood: and his name is called The Word of God**." (Revelation 19: 13). "**And out of his mouth goeth a sharp sword, that with it he should smite the nations**: and he shall rule them with a rod of iron: and **he treadeth the winepress of the fierceness and wrath of Almighty God**. And he hath on his vesture and on his thigh a name written, KING OF KINGS, AND LORD OF LORDS. (Revelation 19: 15-16). "And the sea gave up the dead which were in it; and death and hell delivered up the dead which were in them: and they were judged every man according to their works. And death and hell were cast into the lake of fire. This is the second death. And **whosoever was not found written in the book of life was cast into the lake of fire**." (Revelation 20: 13-15). "But the fearful, and unbelieving, and the abominable, and murderers, and whoremongers, and sorcerers, and idolaters, and all liars, shall have their part in the lake which burneth with fire and brimstone: which is the second death." (Revelation 21: 8).

Add cruel tortures, murders, burning of people in inquisition fire to this terrible list; add those who were killed during crusades and religious wars; add the victims of terrorist acts performed because of religious beliefs and you will understand that after investigation we shall get “an enormous cupboard staffed with five hundred of thick volumes of “The History of Crimes committed by Christianity,” and maximum ten volumes of “The Crimes Committed by Fascism.”

It’s strange that the appeals to revise the religious, cultural and social-historical background of our life, which had been expressed also by other authors, still remain unheard. Cuts A., the author of the book *Jews. Christianity. Russia*, even suggested to create out-of-state national Council of Conscience of each ethnic group, which would have authority in the questions of ethic and moral.

But the Council of Conscience of each ethnic group could hardly solve the problem of peaceful coexistence of cultures. The International Council consisting of representatives of different cultures (who would work out universal cultural criteria based on the humanistic principles observance compulsory for each nation) is needed for this purpose.

Didenco, for example, suggests to revise “all the events of human history” in order to revise both “all the human deeds” and “thorough revaluation of the subject of history (the man).” “‘In connection with this,’ he says, ‘we see the real, thorough and complete revision of valuation of all the events of human history (and the world of the man, in general) done in such a manner that it would not “multiply essences without necessity.” To make such a revision, it would be necessary to summon numerous “conference of specialists,” working group of honest scientists of different specialties and fields of knowledge.’”

In the beginning of this book, we offered so-called humanistic analysis to investigate cultural phenomenon and historical events of human history. By means of it, one can easily count the info-energy charge of any phenomenon or event, which will give the possibility to decide whether it corresponds to the universal cultural criteria or not.

But will people be wise and courageous enough to do it? Nevertheless, in spite of everything, we must do it, for “the most ominous symptom of the lack of intellect is the utter ignoring of bitter and terrible lessons of our own history, the main of which, as it is known, consists in that these lessons had taught nobody and nothing.”[437]

Dear reader, now when you have just finished reading this book, stop for a moment, close your eyes and be silent for a while. Imagine that God who loves you wants you to see His light, to hear Him and to accept His Love. He cannot force you to do that, for He has given you free will so that you were able to choose your own way of life freely.

But how can you see the light if the window of your room is closed with a thick curtain? How can you accept the precious gift of God’s love if your soul is closed with a dark impenetrable faith in false bloodthirsty gods who hide themselves under the guise of virtue? Remove curtains from your window, open your heart and soul and let the light in. Let God's love settle in your innermost self. Try to understand that God wants you to love and respect your neighbors regardless of a skin color or a religion they confess.

Try to understand that God wants to speak to you directly from His soul to yours, and it is the only way to be in touch with Him. Any mediators, such as priests, church and Holy Scriptures, are just curtains which close the window of your soul and prevent you from knowing God. Just imagine as someone teaches you how to have relations with your friend or a lover. How ridiculous it could be!

Look around yourself. Notice how much sufferings and pain, terrible crimes, hatred and division are in the world. Do you really think that it is the Devil or "the evil one" who once brutally changed the nature of first men is to blame? Do you really think that the only way to cope with the situation is the Last Judgment, bloody apocalypse, the final destruction of the world and cruel extermination of "unbelievers"?..

Socrates, ancient Greek philosopher, once said: "Man, if you want to move the world, move yourself at first!" It means that you must not wait until the Last Judgment begins. You can start to move your world just now. Right now, you can open the window of your soul and let love and compassion in. If everyone does the same, there will be no hatred and division among people any longer; there will be peace, joy and happiness everywhere and all the people of our planet will become one nation and will worship One God who is LOVE.

If you would like to share your opinion about the book and the items discussed in it with the author, write ratis.tw@rambler.ru

NOTES

[1] Russian newspaper *Tomorrow*. № 41(464). October, 2002. Here and thereafter, the translation of citations taken from Russian sources are done by V. Ratis.
[2] Here and thereafter, all the "boldings" inside of citations are done by V. Ratis.
[3] Freud, S. *Psychoanalyze. Religion. Culture*. Moscow, P. 209-210.
[4] Carmin, A. S. *The Basis of Culturologia. Morphology of Culture*. St. Petersburg. 1997. P. 494.
[5] Ibid.
[6] Wells H. G. *The Outline of History*. Vol. II. New York. 1961. P. 549.
[7] Costenko-Popova, O. *Arguments and Facts*. Put out Eyes instead of Evening Fairy Tail. No. 31. 2001.
[8] Internet-news.
[9] Jung, K. G. *Analytic Psychology: The Past and the Present*. Moscow. 1995. P. 77-78.

[10] William Lyon Phelps. Cited from D. James Kennedy and Jerry Newcome. *What if the Bible had Never been Written?*, Minneapolis 1998.

[11] Ibid.
[12] Old Testament. I Samuel 15:3.
[13] *The Koran*. Surah 8: 12, 13. The Deluxe Multimedia Bible. Cosmi Corporation. 1997.
[14] Russel, B. *Did religion make a useful contribution to civilization?*, Moshcov's library. Electronic edition. 2002.
[15] Citation from Bulfinch, T. *The Age of Fable or Beauties of Mythology*. Mentor Books. Chicago. 1962. P. *xv*.
[16] Rudnev, V. *The Dictionary of the Culture of the XX-th Century*. Moshcov's Library. Multimedia Edition. 2000.
[17] Ibid.
[18] Freud, S. *Psychoanalyze. Religion. Culture*. Moscow, 1992. P. 29.
[19] Ibid.

[20] Ibid.
[21] Ibid. P. 209-210.
[22] Wells, H. G. *A Short History of the World*. Penguin Books. London. 1965. P. 43.
[23] Old Testament, Exodus 29: 12-18. The Deluxe Multimedia Bible. Cosmi Corporation. 1997.
[24] Ibid. 13: 2.
[25] Ibid. 22: 29-30.
[26] Old Testament. Numbers 31: 28-29.
[27] Ibid. 31: 36-41.
[28] Old Testament. The Book of Judges. 11: 30-39.
[29] Blavatscaya, L. P. *Isis Unveiled*. V. II. P. 658.
[30] Piobb, P. *Formularie de Haute Magie*. Edition of the year 1910. Multimedia Library. 2000.
[31] Ibid.
[32] Ibid.
[33] Wells H. G. *A short History of the World*. Penguin Books. London. 1965. P. 79.
[34] *Freud, S. Psychoanalyze. Religion. Culture*. Moscow, 1992. P. 148.
[35] Ibid. P. 149.
[36] Ibid. P. 148.
[37] Old Testament. Ecclesiastes 3: 20.
[38] Ibid. 9: 10.
[39] Solov'jov, V. *The Readings about God Humankind*. St. Petersburg. 1994.
[40] Jehovah Witnesses. *The Knowledge Leading to Eternal Life*. N. Y. 1995. P. 183.
[41] Russel, B. *Did a Religion Made a Useful Contribution to Civilization?* Moshcov's Multimedia Library. 2000.
[42] Old Testament. Exodus 22:20.
[43] Ibid. 34: 14
[44] Ibid. 34: 12.
[45] Old Testament. I Samuel. 15: 3.
[46] Citation from Blavatscaya, L. P. *Isis Unveiled*. V. II. P. 52.
[47] Draper, John William. *History of the Conflict Between Religion and Science*. Citation from Blavatscaya, L. P. *Isis Unveiled*. V. II.
[48] Renan E. *Antichrist*. Leningrad. 1991.
[49] Cosidovski, S. *Biblical Stories*. Moscow. 1991. P. 9.
[50] Douglas, R. *TheDispute About Zion. 2500 Years of the Jewish Question*. Multimedia Bible. Moscow, 2000.
[51] Daniel-Rops. *Que Est ce Que de la Bible*. Paris. 1995. P. 7.
[52] Ibid. P. 56.

[53] Crivelev, I. A. *The Bible. Historical-Critical Analyses*. Moscow. 1982.
[54] *The Dictionary of Biblical Theology*. Brussels. 1974. P. XVIII.
[55] *Glaubensverkundigung für Erwachsene*. Freiburg. 1970. S. 54.
[56] Cohon, S. S. *Jewish Theology*. Asen. 1971. P. 132.
[57] *The Dictionary of biblical Theology*. Brussels. 1974. P. XI.
[58] Ibid.
[59] Citation from Crivelev, I. A. *The Bible. Historical-Critical Analyses*. Moscow. 1982.
[60] Ibid.
[61] Old Testament. Genesis 1: 26.
[62] Ibid. 2: 7.
[63] Ibid 3: 7
[64] Ibid 3: 1
[65] Old Testament. The Book of Job 1: 6
[66] Old Testament. First Book of Samuel. 18: 10.
[67] Sheiman, M. M. *The Belief in Devil in the History of Religions*. Moscow 1977. P. 16.
[68] Old Testament. Genesis 6: 6.
[69] Ibid 16: 6-8.
[70] Ibid 17: 10-14.
[71] Ibid 32: 25-28
[72] Old Testament. Genesis, chapters 38-50.
[73] Ibid. Exodus 2: 9-10.
[74] Ibid. 2: 22.
[75] Ibid. 2: 16-18.
[76] Ibid. 3: 1.
[77] Ibid. 4: 21.
[78] Ibid. 12: 12.
[79] New Testament. I John 4: 8.
[80] Ibid. 22: 20.
[81] Ibid 22: 29-30.
[82] Old Testament. The Book of Judges. 11: 30-39.
[83] Old Testament. Deuteronomy. 20: 16-17.
[84] Old Testament. The First Book of Samuel. 15: 3.
[85] Old Testament. Exodus. 32: 27-28.
[86] Ibid. 32: 10-28.
[87] Old Testament. The Book of Joshua. 1: 3.
[88] Ibid. 3: 16-17.
[89] Ibid. 6: 7-21.
[90] Ibid. 11: 10-11.
[91] Ibid. 11: 19-20.

[92] Old Testament. The Book of Judges. 2: 20-23.
[93] Old Testament. The First Book of Samuel. 6: 19.
[94] Ibid. 6: 20.
[95] Ibid. 15: 3.
[96] Ibid. 15: 9.
[97] Ibid. 18: 19.
[98] Ibid. 16: 14-15.
[99] Ibid. 18: 10-12.
[100] Slobodskoy, S. *The God's Law*. St. Petersburg. 2000.
[101] Old Testament. The Book of Isaiah. 14: 6.
[102] Ibid. 14: 13.
[103] Ibid. 14: 9-12.
[104] Holy Bible. Authorised King James Version. Fourth Printing. Isaiah. 14: 2-3. P. 454.
[105] Old Testament. The First Book of Samuel. 27: 8-11.
[106] Ibid. 31: 1-4.
[107] Old Testament. The Second Book of Samuel. 5: 8.
[108] Ibid. 6: 13-18.
[109] Ibid. 24: 1.
[110] Ibid. 24: 8-16.
[111] Trubetskoy, E. *The Sense of Life*. Moscow. 2000. P.125.
[112] Ibid.
[113] Old Testament. First Book of Kings. 10:14.
[114] Ibid. 8: 10-12.
[115] Ibid.
[116] Ibid. 9: 4 -7.
[117] Douglas, R. *The Dispute About Zion. 2500 Years of the Jewish Question*. Multimedia Library. Moscow, 2000.
[118] Old Testament. The Book of Isaiah. 66: 3.
[119] Ibid. 1: 27-28.
[120] Ibid. 2: 3-4.
[121] Old Testament. The Book of Joel. 2: 13.
[122] Ibid. 2: 30-32.
[123] Ibid. 3: 10-13.
[124] Ibid. 3: 17.
[125] Old Testament. The Book of Isaiah. 9: 19.
[126] Ibid. 10: 23.
[127] Ibid. 63: 1-6.
[128] New Testament. Revelation. 14: 19-20.
[129] Old Testament. The Book of Isaiah. 14: 6-18
[130] Old Testament. The Book of Ezekiel. 7: 8-9.

[131] Ibid. 21:3.
[132] Old Testament. The Book of Isaiah. 66: 15-24.
[133] Crivelev, I. A. *The Bible. Historical-Critical Analyses*. Moscow. 1982.
[134] High ranked priest of American Orthodox Church.
[135] Damaskin (Chriansen), celibate priest. *Not of this World. The Life and the Teaching of the Father Rouse*. Moscow, 1995, P. 298.
[136] Slobodskoy, S. *The God's Law*. St. Petersburg. 2000. P. 502.
[137] Ibid.
[138] Nilus, S. *The Great in the Small*.
[139] Freud, S. *Psychoanalyses. Religion. Culture*. The man Moses and Monotheistic Religion. Moscow. 1992. P. 161.
[140] Deshner, K. H. *The Criminal History of Christianity*. Moscow. 1997. P. 65.
[141] New Testament. Romans. 2: 14.
[142] Ibid. 3: 2.
[143] Ibid. 9: 4-5.
[144] Gaisler, N., Turek, F. *Legislating Morality*. Minneapolis, Minnesota. 1998. P. 101-102.
[145] Citation from Douglas, R. *The Dispute About Zion. 2500 Years of the Jewish Question*. Multimedia Library. Moscow, 2000.
[146] Ibid.
[147] Ibid.
[148] Ibid.
[149] Ibid.
[150] Ibid.
[151] Ibid.
[152] Fruchtenbaum, A. G. *Jesus Was a Jew*. Tustin. California. 1981. P. 93.
[153] Drosnin M. *The Bible Code*. New York. 1977.
[154] Thomas, D. E. *A Hidden Message and The Bible Code*. Internet, Amazon. com.
[155] Ibid.
[156] Statistical Science publishes Bible Code Refutation. Internet. Amazon. com.
[157] *Time*. Deciphering God's Plan. No. 23. Vol. 149. June 9.
[158] *Skeptical Inquirer* Magazine. March/April 1998.
[159] Jehovah Witnesses. *The Knowledge Leading to the Eternal Life*. N. Y. 1995. P. 33, 63.
[160] Old Testament. Genesis 3: 15.
[161] Isaiah 7:14.
[162] Micah 5: 2.
[163] Old Testament. Isaiah 53: 2-5.

[164] Ibid. 11: 1-5.
[165] Cosidovsky, S. *Biblical Stories*. Moscow. 1991. P. 175.
[166] New Testament. Matthew 3:2.
[167] Ibid. 3: 10-12.
[168] Ibid. Chapter 5.
[169] Ibid. 6: 6-15.
[170] Ibid. 6: 19-21.
[171] Ibid. 6: 33.
[172] Ibid. 7: 21.
[173] Ibid. 10: 5-7.
[174] Ibid. 10: 34-34; 12:30.
[175] The Gospel of Thomas 17. Moshcov's Multimedia Library.
[176] Ibid. 105.
[177] Notovich, N. Citation from the Russian translation of Elizabeth Clare Prophet. *The Lost Years of Jesus*. Summit University Press. 2000. P. 190-192.
[178] Lewis, C. S. *Just Christianity*. Moshcov's Multimedia Library. 2000.
[179] Russian newspaper *Arguments and Facts*. Forgive and You Will be Forgiven." No. 1. 2001.
[180] Cosidovsky, S. *The Stories of Evangelists*. Moscow. 1987. P. 34.
[181] New Testament. Acts. 5: 1-10.
[182] Tallazh, J. Tallazh, S. *The Most Incredible in the World—Sex, Rituals, Rabits*. Moscow. 1998. P. 127-129.
[183] New Testament. Matthew 6: 6-13.
[184] Old Testament. 1st Samuel 16: 14-15.
[185] Fromm, E. *The Dogma About Christ*. Moshcov's Multimedia Library. 2000.
[186] Ibid.
[187] Paul's First Letter to Timothy 6: 16.
[188] The First Book of Kings 8: 12.
[189] Psalms 18: 11.
[190] Exodus 33: 11.
[191] The Letter to the Hebrews 6: 17-18.
[192] The First Book of Kings 22: 23.
[193] The Book of Jeremiah 18: 11.
[194] The Book of Ezekiel 7: 8.
[195] Paul's First Letter to the Corinthians 14: 33.
[196] The Book of Ezekiel 7: 9.
[197] Ibid 21: 3.
[198] The First Letter of John 4: 8.
[199] New Testament. Gospel according to John 8: 30-47.

[200] Blavatskaya, E. P. *Isis Unveiled.* Vol. II. Moscow. 2000. P. 265.
[201] New Testament. Gospel according to John 3: 19.
[202] Old Testament. The Book of Isaiah 45: 3.
[203] New Testament. The Gospel according to Matthew 10: 5-6.
[204] Ibid. Luke 10: 3.
[205] Marks, K. Engels, F. *The Basic Writings on Politics and Philosophy*. Edited by Lewis S. Feuer. N.Y. 1959. P. 178.
[206] Jon's Revelation 7: 4.
[207] *Watch Tower*. Vol. 120 No 3, 1st of February, 1999.
[208] The first general council representing the bishops of the whole world occurred at Nicaea in Asia Minor in 325.
[209] Marks, K. Engels, F. *The Basic Writings on Politics and Philosophy*. Edited by Lewis S. Feuer. N.Y. 1959. P. 180.
[210] New Testament. Acts 22: 3-21.
[211] Cosidovsky, S. *The Stories of Evangelists*. Moscow. 1978. P. 126.
[212] Renan, E. *Antichrist*. Leningrad. 1991. P. 128.
[213] New Testament. Paul's Letter to the Romans. Chapters 1-3.
[214] Blavatskaya, E. P. *Isis Unveiled.* Vol. II. Moscow. 2000. P. 674.
[215] Citation from Irving, B. *The Life of Mohammed.* 1876. P. 124.
[216] Russian newspaper *Version*. Moslems in the Kremlin. No. 43. November, 2001.
[217] Russian newspaper *Tomorrow*. The fiery Islam. No. 28. July, 2001.
[218] Russian newspaper *Rush-Hour*. Islam and Christianity. No. 46. November, 2001.
[219] Ibid.
[220] Russian newspaper *Arguments and Facts*. The World Between Civilization and Barbarity. No. 38, 2001.
[221] Ibid.
[222] Ibid.
[223] Ibid.
[224] *Time*. As American as... Octover 1, 2001/Vol. 158, No 15.
[225] Ibid.
[226] Ibid.
[227] Ibid.
[228] Ibid.
[229] The Qur'an 4: 89. New-York. 1997.
[230] Ibid. 4: 90.
[231] *Time*. Octover 1, 2001/Vol. 158, No 15. The True Peaceful Face of Islam.
[232] The Qur'an 9: 111.
[233] Russian newspaper *Tomorrow*. No. 28. July, 2001.

[234] Ibid.
[235] The Qur'an 7: 11.
[236] Ibid 2: 36.
[237] Russian newspaper *Tomorrow*. No. 28. July, 2001.
[238] The Qur'an. 8: 12-13.
[239] Ibid 7: 4 -5.
[240] Russian newspaper *Tomorrow*. No. 28. July, 2001.
[241] Ibid.
[242] Ibid.
[243] Renan, E. *Antichrist*. Leningrad. 1991. P. 203.
[244] Russian newspaper *Tomorrow*. No. 28. July, 2001.
[245] Ibid.
[246] Ibid.
[247] Ibid.
[248] Ibid.
[249] Ibid.
[250] Ibid.
[251] Ibid.
[252] Ibid.
[253] The Qur'an 3: 19.
[254] Ibid 3: 32.
[255] Ibid 9: 111.
[256] Ibid 3: 15.
[257] The Qur'an 3: 9-10.
[258] Ibid 3: 32.
[259] Ibid 3: 12.
[260] The Qur'an 44: 40-48.
[261] Ibid 69: 30-36.
[262] Ibid 3: 19.
[263] The Qur'an 9: 24-36.
[264] Ibid 59: 2-4.
[265] Klimovich, L. I. *The Book about Koran*. Moscow. 1986.
[266] Marx, K. Engels, F. *Works*. Vol. 21. P. 294.
[267] Klimovich, L. I. *The Book about Koran*. Moscow. 1986.
[268] Russian newspaper *Version*. Moslems at the Kremlin Walls. No. 43. November, 2001.
[269] The Qur'an 8: 39.
[270] The Old Testament. The 1st Book of Samuel 15: 18.
[271] Kulacovsky, Y. *The History of Byzantine*. Kiev. 1915. Vol. 3. P. 349.
[272] Gevond. *The History of Caliphs*. St. Petersburg. 1862. P. 1-2.
[273] Sebeos. *The History of Emperor Irakly*. P. 117.

[274] Boiko, K. A. *Arabic Historical Literature in Egypt (VII-IX centuries)*. Moscow. 1983. P. 22.
[275] The Qur'an 16: 125-128.
[276] Ibid 44: 16.
[277] Klimovich, L. I. *The Book about Koran*. Moscow. 1986.
[278] The Qur'an 9: 29.
[279] Klimovich, L. I. *The Book about Koran*. Moscow. 1986.
[280] Cited from Klimovich, L. I. *The Book about Koran*. Moscow. 1986.
[281] Blake, R. P. *Christian Herald. Second Edition*. About Relations Between Jews and the Government of the Eastern Rome Empire in 1632—1634. St. Petersburg. 1914. Vol. 3. P. 193, 194.
[282] Wells, H. G. *A Short History of the World*. London, 1965. P. 172.
[283] The Qur'an 8: 65.
[284] Ibid 3: 169-170.
[285] Cited from Klimovich, L. I. *The Book about Koran*. Moscow. 1986.
[286] Newspaper *In the New World*. We were born in Jihad. No. 43. October-November, 2001.
[287] Sincha, N. K. Banerdji, A. C. *The History of India*. Moscow. 1954. P. 115.
[288] Gasprinsky, I. *The Russian-East Agreement. Thoughts, Notes and Wishes*. Bachtcisaray. 1896. P. 9-10. Cited from Klimovich, L. I. *The Book about Koran*. Moscow. 1986.
[289] Ibn A'sam al'-Cufi. *The Book of Conquest*. P. 18.
[290] Ibid
[291] Cited from Klimovich, L. I. *The Book about Koran*. Moscow. 1986.
[292] The Qur'an 47: 4-8.
[293] Newspaper *In the New World*. The interview with Rehav Sevi, the former Tourism Secretary of Israel. No. 43. October-November, 2001.
[294] Demin, V. *Giperborea—the Foremother of the World Culture*. Moshcov's Multimedia library.
[295] Ibid.
[296] Asov, A. *The Mythological World of Vedism*. Moshcov's Multimedia library.
[297] Ibid.
[298] Carmin, A. S. *The Bases of Culturology*. St. Petersburg. 1997. P. 191.
[299] Ibid. P. 193.
[300] Ibid. P. 494.
[301] Caramsin, N. M. The Legends of Centuries. Moscow. 1988. P. 77.
[302] Orlov, A. S. *The History of Russia*. Moscow. 2001. P. 27.
[303] Andreeva, L. A. *Religion and Power in Russia*. Moscow. 2001. P. 54.
[304] Michelet, J. *Legendes Democratiques du Nord*. Paris, 1968. P. 203.

[305] Belinsky, V. G. *The Letter to Gogol'*. Collected works. Vol. 3. P. 707-715. Moscow. 1948.
[306] Mirolyubov, J. P. *Sacral of Russia*. Moscow. 1996. Vol. 1.
[307] Zabolotnich, V. *The Ways of Mankind*. St. Petersburg. 1998.
[308] Ibid.
[309] Trubetskoy, E. *The Sense of Life*. Moscow. 2000. P. 69-70.
[310] Ibid.
[311] In the Orthodox tradition, a creature refers not only to animals, but also to all humans as having inferior nature in comparison with Jesus as having a divine one.
[312] Trubetskoy, E. *The Sense of Life*. Moscow. 2000. P.75-78.
[313] *Bhagavad-Gita as It Is*. Bhaktivedanta Svami Braphupada's translation. Moshcov;s Multimedia liblrary. 2000.
[314] Ibid.
[315] *The New York Times*. Acknowledging That God Is Not Limited to Christians. □ 51(996). 2002.
[316] *Garuda Purana*. Moshcov's Multimedia library. Verses 113-115.
[317] Trubetskoy, E. *The Sense of Life*. M. 2000. P. 83.
[318] Ibid. P. 85.
[319] *The World's Great Religions*. New York. 1957. P. 11.
[320] Ibid. P. 33.
[321] One can find more information about it in the book *The Lost Years of Jesus* by Elizabeth Clare Prophet. Summit University Press. 1987.
[322] Tchizevsky, □. *Physical Factors of Historical Process*. Caluga. 1924.
[323] Karl Marks and Friedrich Engels. *Basic Writings on Politics and Philosophy*. Edited by Lewis S. Feuer. New York. 1959. P. 168.
[324] Budyon, M. A. *Hitler and Jesus*. Moshcov's Multimedia Library. 2000.
[325] Ibid.

[326] Disraeli Benjamin, (Lord Beaconsfield), (1804-1881), British statesman, prime minister in 1868 and 1874-1880, the Conservative Party leader, writer.

[327] Douglas, R. *The Dispute over Zion. (2.500 years of Jewish Question)*. Moshcov's multimedia library. 2000.

[328] Bacunin, M. A. (1814-1876). Russian revolutionary, publicist, one of the anarchism founders, narodnik movement idiolog.

[329] International. (International association of workers), International organization. Founded in London in 1864 by K. Marks and F. Engels.

330 Douglas, R.. *The Dispute over Zion. (2.500 years of Jewish Question)*. Moshcov's multimedia library. 2000.
331 Russian newspaper *Tomorrow*. The Fiery Islam. No. 28, July 2001.
332 Geifman, A. *Revolutionary Terror in Russia: 1984—1917*. Moscow. 1997.
333 Ibid.
334 Budyon, M. A. *Hitler and Jesus*. Moshcov's Multimedia Library. 2000.
335 St. Petersburg was called Petrograd at that time.
336 Cochetcova, P. V. Revyaco, T. I. *The Encyclopedia of Crimes and Catastrophes*. Executioners and Killers. Minsk. 1966. P. 302-303.
337 Checa (also called Vecheka), early Soviet secret police agency and a forerunner of the KGB.
338 White Guards (officers)—those who fought against revolution and communist regime during civil war.
339 Cuts, A. S. *Jews. Christianity. Russia*. St. Petersburg. 1997. P. 280.
340 Ibid. P. 284.
341 Secretary-general of the Communist Party of the Soviet Union (1922–53) and premier of the Soviet state (1941–53), who for a quarter of a century dictatorially ruled the Soviet Union and transformed it into a major world power.
342 Vert, N. *The History of the Soviet State*. Moscow. 1994. P. 261.
343 The first secretary of the Communist Party of the Soviet Union (1953–64) and premier of the Soviet Union (1958–64) whose policy of de-Stalinization had widespread repercussions throughout the Communist world. In foreign policy he pursued a policy of "peaceful coexistence" with the capitalist West.
344 *Komitet Gosudarstvennoy Bezopasnosti.* ("Committee for State Security"), political police and security agency that was also the primary intelligence and counterintelligence entity of the Soviet Union from 1917 to 1991.
345 Cuts, A. S. *Jews. Christianity. Russia*. St. Petersburg. 1997. P. 344.
346 Michael A. De Budyon. *Hitler and Jesus*. Moshcovs multimedia library. 200.
347 Abbreviation of Schutzstaffel (German: "Protective Echelon"), the black-uniformed elite corps of the Nazi Party. Founded by Adolf Hitler in April 1925 as a small personal bodyguard, the **SS** grew with the success of the Nazi movement and, gathering immense police and military powers, became virtually a state within a state.
348 A vessel, in which Josef Arimaphey had collected the blood of crucified Jesus Christ.
349 German Nationalsozialistische Deutsche Arbeiterpartei. Political

party of the mass movement known as National Socialism. Under the leadership of Adolpf Hitler, the party came to power in Germany in 1933 and governed by totalitarian methods until 1945.
[350] Michael A. De Budyon. *Hitler and Jesus*." Moshcov's multimedia library.
[351] Hitler, A. *Mein Kampf*. Citation from Pervushin, A. *Occult Mysteries of NKVD and SS*. St. Petersburg. 2000. P. 304—305.
[352] Ibid.
[353] Ibid.
[354] Russian in full Ivan Vasilyevich, byname Ivan The Terrible, Russian Ivan Grozny grand prince of Moscow (1533–84) and the first to be proclaimed tsar of Russia (from 1547).
[355] Adler, A. *Psychotherapy and education*. Citation from Bassijuni, K. *Upbringing of Peoples' Killers*. St. Petersburg. 1999. P. 86.
[356] Theologian and ecclesiastical statesman. He was the leading French Protestant Reformer and the most important figure in the second generation of the Protestant Reformation.
[357] There was a time during "perestroika" when shelves of food-shops were empty and people could buy only a limited quantity of food that was indicated on special coupons.
[358] Citation from Gromov, V. I. *The Collapse of the USSR. Causes and Consequences*. Moscow. 1998.
[359] Russian newspaper *The Soviet Russia*. The article of Gundarov, I. Half-value period of the Nation. □ 7. 1999.
[360] Russian newspaper *Arguments and Facts*. Pricked Eyes instead of Evening Fairy Tale. No. 31, 2001.
[361] American newspaper *In the New World*. Monsters on a chain. No. 47, November 2001.
[362] The Book of Job. 2: 9-10.
[363] Ibid. Chapter 9.
[364] Didenco, B. A. *Civilization of Cannibals*. Moscow, 1996.
[365] Ibid.
[366] Ibid.
[367] Ibid.
[368] Ibid.
[369] Ibid.
[370] Ibid.
[371] Old Testament. Exodus. 4: 24-26.
[372] Didenco, B. A. *Civilization of Cannibals*. Moscow, 1996.
[373] Ibid.
[374] Ibid.

[375] Ibid.

[376] Russian newspaper *Arguments and Facts*. Zombie Against One's Will." □ 18, 2001 □.

[377] Sutton, E. *How does the Order Organize Wars and Revolutions?* Moscow. 1995. P. 20.

[378] Russian newspaper *Society and Ecology*. □ 31. 2002.

[379] Old Testament. Deuteronomy 23: 19-20.

[380] Ibid. The 1st Book of Kings 9: 22.

[381] The citation from the Talmudic Treatise *Baba Cama* in the Russian newspaper *Society and Ecology*. □ 31. 2002.

[382] Old Testament. Deuteronomy 28: 12.

[383] Ibid. Isaiah 60: 10-12.

[384] *The Inner Predictor of the SSSR*. To the Godly Statehood. Internet site dotu.ru.

[385] Bavarian Illuminates—the secret Masonic order founded by Adam Weishaupt in the XVII century. Known by its great influence on leading political figures.

[386] Bogoliybov, N. *Secret Societies of the XX Century*. St. Petersburg. 1977. P. 23-25.

[387] Cooper, W. *Behold a Pale Horse*. Light Technology Publications, P. O Box 1495, Sedona AZ 86336. Cited by Bogoliybov, N. *Secret Societies of the XX century*. St. Petersburg. 1977. P. 150-179.

[388] Ibid.

[389] Shashin, I. Russian magazine *Our Contemporary*. The "Trojan Horse" of the World Government. No. 10, 1992. P. 153.

[390] Casatonov, Y. Russian magazine *Our Contemporary*. The Defeat Without a Battle. No. 10, 1991. P. 156.

[391] Cooper, W. *Behold a Pale Horse*. Light Technology Publications, P. O box 1495, Sedona AZ 86336.

[392] Ibid.

[393] Brachev, V. S. *Masons in Russia: from Peter I to Nowadays*. Multimedia Library. Moscow. 2000.

[394] Revelation to John. 6: 2-4.

[395] Ibid. 6: 6-8.

[396] Russian newspaper *Emergency Forces of Russia*. The Aria of the Mister X. □ 06, June 2002.

[397] Ibid.

[398] The World Trade Center Demolition and the So-Called War on Terrorism. The article in the Internet site http://www.serendipity.li/wtc.html#wot.

[399] Russian newspaper *Tomorrow*. Babylon Towers. □ 42, 2002.

[400] The World Trade Center Demolition and the So-Called War on Terrorism. The article in the Internet site http://www.serendipity.li/wtc.html#wot.
[401] Ibid.
[402] http:/www. asile.org/citoyens/numero13/pentagone/erreurs_en.html
[403] Mysterious Boeing 747 Jumbo Jet—seen in Washington., http://www.bombsinsidewtc.dk/
[404] *Time*. The bin Laden Tape. December 24, 2001. P. 46.
[405] http://www.geocities.com/mossdlibrary/olson.html
[406] Ibid.
[407] The World Trade Center Demolition and the So-Called War on Terrorism. The article in the Internet site http://www.serendipity.li/wtc.html#wot.
[408] *Time*. December, 24, 2001, page 47.
[409] Russian newspaper *Tomorrow*. The Towers of Babel. ▯ 41, 2002.
[410] Russian newspaper *Tomorrow*. The Towers of Babel. ▯ 42, 2002.
[411] Ibid.
[412] Ibid.
[413] *New York Times*. September, 22, 2001.
[414] *Tomorrow*. 42, 2001.
[415] http://globalresearch.ca/
[416] Russian newspaper *Arguments and Facts*. No. 20, 2003.
[417] Ibid.
[418] Ibid.
[419] Ibid.
[420] John's Revelation, 9:15.
[421] Russian news agency *RIA Novosti*
[422] Russian newspaper *Arguments and Facts.* No. 36. September. 2004.
[423] The *International Herald Tribune*. September 9. 2004.
[424] Russian newspaper *Arguments and Facts.* No. 36. September. 2004.
[425] Ibid.
[426] Ibid.
[427] Ibid.
[428] The First Book of Samuel 15: 3.
[429] The Qur'an 8: 12, 13.
[430] John's Revelation. 14: 19-20.
[431] The *International Herald Tribune*. September 9. 2004.
[432] *Arguments and Facts.* No. 37. September. 2004.
[433] *Arguments and Facts.* No. 36, September. 2004.

[434] Efroimson, V. P. *Ethic and Esthetic Genetics*. St. Petersburg. 1995.
[435] Didenco, B. A. *The Civilization of Cannibals*. Moscow. 1996.
[436] Budyon, M. A. *Hitler and Jesus*. Moshcov's Multimedia Library. 2000.
[437] Didenco, B. A. *Civilization of Cannibals*. Moscow. 1996.

BIBLIOGRAPHY

Books

1. Andreeva, L. A. *Religion and Power in Russia*. Moscow. 2001.
2. Asov, A. *The Mythological World of Vedism*. Moshcov's Multimedia library.2000.
3. Bassijuni, K. *Upbringing of the People's Killers*. St. Petersburg. 1999.
4. Belinsky, V. G. *The Letter to Gogol'*. Collected works. Vol. 3. Moscow. 1948.
5. Blake, R. P. *Christian Herald. Second Edition*. About Relations between Jews and the Government of the Eastern Rome Empire in 1632—1634. St. Petersburg. 1914.
6. Blavatscaya, E. P. *Isis Unveiled*. Vol. II. Moscow. 2000.
7. Bogolubov, N. *Secret Societies of the XX Century*. St. Petersburg. 1977.
8. Boiko, K. A. *Arabic Historical Literature in Egypt (VII-IX centuries)*. Moscow. 1983.
9. Brachev, V. S. *Masons in Russia: from Peter I to Nowadays*. Multimedia Library. Moscow. 2000.
10. Budyon, M. A. *Hitler and Jesus*. Moshcov's Multimedia Library.
11. Bulfinch, T. *The Age of Fable or Beauties of Mythology*. Mentor Books. Chicago. 1962.
12. Caramsin, N. M. *The Legends of Centuries*. Moscow. 1988.
13. Carmin, A. S. *The Basis of Culturologia*. *Morphology of Culture*. St. Petersburg. 1997.
13. Cochetcova, P., V. Revyaco, T. I. *The Encyclopedia of Crimes and Catastrophes. Executioners and Killers*. Minsk. 1966.
14. Cohon, S. S. *Jewish Theology*. Asen. 1971.
15. Cooper W. *Behold a Pale Horse*. Light Technology Publications, P. O Box 1495, Sedona AZ 86336.
16. Cosidovski, S. *Biblical Stories*. Moscow. 1991.
17. Cosidovsky, S. *The Stories of Evangelists*. Moscow. 1987.
18. Crivelev, I. A. *The Bible. Historical-critical Analyses*. Moscow. 1982.
19. Cuts, A. S. *Jews. Christianity. Russia*. St. Petersburg. 1997.
20. Daniel-Rops. *Que Est ce Que de la Bible*. Paris. 1995.

21. D. James Kennedy and Jerry Newcome. *What if the Bible Had Never Been Written?* Minneapolis 1998.
22. Damaskin (Chriansen), celibate priest. *Not of this World. The Life and the Teaching of the Father Rouse*. Moscow, 1995.
23. Deshner, K. H. *Criminal History of Christianity*. Moscow. 1997.
24. Demin, V. *Giperborea—the Foremother of the World Culture*. Moshcov's Multimedia library. 2000.
25. Didenco B. A. *Civilization of Cannibals*. Moscow, 1996.
26. Douglas, R. *Dispute About Zion. 2500 Years of the Jewish Question*. Multimedia Library. Moscow, 2000.
27. Drosnin, M. *The Bible Code*. New York. 1977.
28. Efroimson, V. P. *Ethic and Esthetic Genetics*. St. Petersburg. 1995.
29. Freud, Sigmund. *Psychoanalyze. Religion. Culture*. Moscow, 1992.
30. Fromm, E. *The Dogma about Christ*. Moshcov's Multimedia Library.
31. Fruchtenbaum, A. G. *Jesus was a Jew*. Tustin. California. 1981.
32. Gaisler, N., Turek, F. *Legislating Morality*. Minneapolis, Minnesota. 1998.
33. Gevond. *The History of Caliphs*. St. Petersburg. 1862.
34. Gromov, V. I. *The Collapse of the USSR*. Causes and Consequences. Moscow. 1998.
35. Ibn A'sam al'-Cufi. *The Book of Conquest*.
36. Irving, B. *The Life of Mohammed*. 1876.
37. Jehovah Witnesses. *The Knowledge leading to Eternal Life*. N. Y. 1995. P. 183.
38. Jung, K. G. *Analytic Psychology: The Past and the Present*. Moscow.
39. Klimovich, L. I. *The Book about Koran*. Moscow. 1986.
40. Kulacovsky, Y. *The History of Byzantine*. Kiev. 1915. Vol. 3.
41. Lewis, C. S. *Just Christianity*. Moshcov's Multimedia Library.
42. Marks, K. Engels, F. *Basic Writings on Politics and Philosophy*. Edited by Lewis, S. Feuer. N.Y. 1959.
43. Marx, K. Engels, F. *Works*. Vol. 21.
44. Michelet, J. *Legendes Democratiques du Nord*. Paris, 1968.
45. Mirolyubov, J. P. *Sacral of Russia*. Moscow. 1996. Vol. 1.
46. Nilus, S. *The Great in the Small*.
47. Pervushin, A. *Occult Mysteries of NKVD and SS*. St. Petersburg. 2000.
48. Piobb, P. *Formularie de Haute Magie*. Edition of the year 1910. Multimedia Library. 2000.
49. Prophet, E. C. *The Lost Years of Jesus*. Summit University Press. 2000. (Russian translation).
50. Orlov, A. S. *The History of Russia*. Moscow. 2001.

51. Tchizevsky, □. *Physical Factors of Historical Process*. Caluga. 1924.
52. Renan, E. *Antichrist*. Leningrad. 1991.
53. Rudnev, V. *The dictionary of the Culture of XX-th Century*. Moshcov's Library. Multimedia Edition. 2000.
54. Russel, B. *Did Religion Make a Useful Contribution to Civilization?* Moshcov's multimedia library. 2002.
55. Sebeos. *The History of Emperor Irakly*.
56. Sheiman, M. M. *The Belief in Devil in the History of Religions*. Moscow 1977.
57. Sincha, N. K. Banerdji, A. C. *The History of India*. Moscow. 1954.
58. Slobodskoy, S. *The God's Law*. St. Petersburg. 2000.
59. Solov'jov, V. *The Readings about God Humankind*. St. Petersburg. 1994.
60. Sutton, E. *How does the Order organize Wars and Revolutions?* Moscow. 1995.
61. Tallazh, J. Tallazh, S. *The most incredible in the World—sex, rituals, habits*. Moscow. 1998.
62. Trubetskoy, E. *The Sense of Life*. Moscow. 2000.
63. Vert, N. *The History of the Soviet State*. Moscow. 1994.
64. Wells, H. G. *The Outline of History*. Vol. II. New York. 1961.
65. Wells, H. G. *A short History of the World*. Penguin Books. London.
66. Zabolotnich, V. *The Ways of Mankind*. St. Petersburg. 1998.

Periodicals

1.*Arguments and Facts*. No. 18 (2001); No. 31 (2001); 38 (2001); 1 (2001); 38 (2001);
2. *Emergency Forces of Russia*. No. 06, June 2002.
3. *In the New World*. No. 43. October-November, 2001; No. 47, November 2001.
4. *Rush-Hour*. No. 46 (November, 2001).
5. *Society and Ecology*. No. 21. 2001; No. 31. 2002.
6. *Skeptical Inquirer* Magazine. March/April 1998.
7. *The New York Times*. No. 51(996). 2002.
8. *The Soviet Russia*. No. 7. 1999.
9. *Time*. No. 23. Vol. 149. June 9; No 15. Octover 1, 2001. Vol. 158.
10. *Tomorrow*. No. 41, 28 (July, 2001); No. 42 (2002).
11. *Version*. No. 43. November, 2001.
12. *Watch Tower*. Vol. 120 No 3, 1st of February, 1999.

Holy Scriptures

1. *Bhagavad-Gita as It Is*. Bhaktivedanta Svami Braphupada translation. Moshcov's Multimedia liblrary.
2. *Garuda Purana*. Moshcov's Multimedia library.
3. *New Testament*. King James Version. The Deluxe Multimedia Bible. Cosmi Corporation. 1997.
4. *Old Testament*. King James Version. The Deluxe Multimedia Bible. Cosmi Corporation. 1997.
5. *The Gospel of Thomas*. Moshcov's Multimedia Library.
6. *The Koran*. The Deluxe Multimedia Bible. Cosmi Corporation. 1997.
7. *The Qur'an*. New-York. 1997.

Reference books and dictionaries

1. *Glaubensverkundigung für Erwachsene*. Freiburg. 1970.
2. *The Dictionary of Biblical Theology*. Brussels. 1974.
3. *The World's Great Religions*. New York. 1957.

Internet sites

1. http://www.dotu.ru
2. http://www.serendipity.li/wtc.html#wot.
3. http:/www. asile.org/citoyens/numero13/pentagone/erreurs_en.html
4. http://www.bombsinsidewtc.dk/
5. http://www.geocities.com/mossdlibrary/olson.html

Made in the USA